Framework for the Evaluation of Data Models (cont.)

	HIERARCHICAL	NETWORK	RELATIONAL
Performance	High—with well-defined access paths Low—with unstructured access paths	High—with well-defined access paths Low—with unstructured access paths	High—with unstructured access paths Low—in comparison to hierarchical and network models that have well-defined access paths
Additional pointers available to improve peformance	Yes—retrieval	Yes—retrieval	Yes—but SQL may choose not to use them
Security	Defined in subschema	Defined in subschema	Defined in subschema—but may be modified at any time including during on-line execution
Security officer	DBA or equivalent	DBA or equivalent	DBA or equivalent—may be delegated
Responsibility for adding data to the data base	Data base management system—governed by INSERT, REPLACE, DELETE rules	Data base management system or application program—governed by insertion status	Data base management system
Modification of the data structure	Redefine structure, reload new structure	Redefine structure, reload new structure	Restructure at any time, including during operation in an on-line environment

UNDERSTANDING DATA BASE MANAGEMENT SYSTEMS

Students:

A project workbook has been specially designed to help you master the concepts presented in this textbook. Purchase or order at your bookstore.

Wadsworth Series in Computer Information Systems

Senn, Information Systems in Management, II

Clarke and Prinz, Contemporary Systems Analysis and Design

Vasta, Understanding Data Base Management Systems

Ageloff and Mojena, Applied Structured BASIC

Rob, Big Blue BASIC: Programming the IBM PC and Compatibles

Athappilly, Programming and Problem Solving in VAX-11 BASIC

Rob, Introduction to Microcomputer Programming

Amsbury, Data Structures: From Arrays to Priority Queues

Brown, From Pascal to C: An Introduction to the C Programming Language

UNDERSTANDING DATA BASE MANAGEMENT SYSTEMS

JOSEPH A. VASTA

Bethlehem Steel Corporation
Essex Community College

Wadsworth Publishing Company
Belmont, California
A Division of Wadsworth, Inc.

Data Processing Editor: Frank Ruggirello
Production Editor: Harold Humphrey
Cover Designer: Paula Shuhert
Text Designer: Cheryl Carrington
Print Buyer: Karen Hunt
Cover Photo: Mason Morfit

All chapter photos ©Image Bank West:

Chapter 1: Hans Wendler; *Chapters 2, 3, 4, 7:* Lilyan Schwartz;
Chapter 5: Ken Cooper; *Chapter 6:* Gary Glastone;
Chapter 8: P. Turner; *Chapter 9:* Ken Cooper;
Chapter 10: Mel Di Giacomo;
Chapter 11: Ken Cooper

Printed in the United States of America
1 2 3 4 5 6 7 8 9 10——89 88 87 86 85

ISBN 0-534-04029-2

Library of Congress Cataloging in Publication Data

Vasta, Joseph A.
Understanding data base management systems.

(Wadsworth series in computer information systems)
Bibliography: p.
Includes index.
1. Data base management. I. Title. II. Series.
QA76.9.D3V37 1985 001.64 84-19532
ISBN 0-534-04029-2

To Josephine and Michele

PREFACE

While chairman of a text selection committee for an introductory data processing course, I attempted to kill two birds with one stone by also trying to find a satisfactory book to use in my course on data base management systems.

Previously, I had spent considerable time developing examples with which my DBMS students could identify, developing practical applications of theory, researching current trends in the use of data bases, and developing a comparison of data models—all to supplement the texts which I have used. I had done this because my students complained that the texts were dry, and they had difficulty understanding the examples.

As I chaired the DP selection committee, the texts I reviewed had pieces of what I desired for my DBMS course, but I would have to buy several books to satisfy my objectives. Thus, when a Wadsworth Publishing Company representative suggested I write my own text, I saw the opportunity to satisfy my own needs as well as the needs of other instructors having the same problems as me.

While trying to find my writing style, I experimented, trying to capture my attitude toward education. I feel students learn more when they enjoy what they are doing, and I believe true education does not mean rote memorization. Instead, I believe the key to education is an understanding of cause and effect, or at least of relationships. For example, one of my sources of relaxation is being a "shade tree mechanic," and I find that shop manuals provide a high degree of education by decomposing complex systems into simple structures that are easily understood. In a similar manner, I have tried to decompose data base management systems into simple structures that are easily understood.

This book evolved from my notes, collected over many years, used to teach a course in data base management systems. The course itself is based on my experiences working with data base management systems since the early 1970s. My students range from those who have a purely educational background and are trying to grasp the fundamentals of data base management systems, to systems programmers and data base administrators who wish to put the work they perform into perspective. The book was class tested by this diverse audience, and it was then modified to aid students in the learning process. Due to the class-testing process, the text is more like a second edition than a first. It can be used by everyone from the college student to the seasoned data processing veteran and provide insight into the past, present, and future of data base management systems.

PEDAGOGY This book takes a "shop manual approach" to data base management systems in its solutions to students' and instructors' problems, its unique features, and its pedagogy.

At the beginning and end of each chapter, and periodically in other places, the book lets students know where they are and where they are going:

The *objectives* listed at the beginning of each chapter let students know what they are expected to achieve by reading the chapter.

The *new words and phrases* listed at the beginning of each chapter notify students of new terminology which will be encountered.

The *chapter introduction* orients students regarding the direction of the chapter.

The several *comparison charts* in chapters permit students to compare the features of the various data models and access methods, to reinforce understanding of their similarities and differences. (See, for example, Figure 7.21 on p. 220.)

The *summary* at the end of each chapter identifies important points which have been presented.

Review questions at the end of each chapter allow students to test their understanding of important concepts. (Answers to even-numbered questions are provided in the back of the book.)

The *glossary/index* at the end of the book gives concise definitions of important words or phrases.

A *bibliography* at the end of the book gives students places to turn to for in-depth reading if more information is desired.

The *examples* in this book are ones with which students can easily identify and which they can enjoy—for example, a radio station, a college, a medical clinic, and a gizmo manufacturer. To facilitate an understanding of similarities and differences in DBMS methods and applications, several continuing examples appear from chapter to chapter. Each example is given a prefix letter to identify which continuing example it is part of; each instance of a continuing example is identified by a number. In all, there are 54 example sections.

UNIQUE FEATURES The unique features of this text include balanced coverage of all three data models, with separate discussions of logical and physical data structures, data base design, on-line systems, and current directions. The important features of each model are compared to those of the other models. All this is written by an author with practical experience, and it is all under one cover.

Balanced coverage Chapter 4 prepares the student for analysis of the data models by introducing the three major data models, the basic terminology, and a list of items which will be compared in succeeding chapters. Chapter 4 also lays the groundwork for the separation of logical and physical structures. Chapters 5, 6, and 7 present the logical structures of the hierarchical, network, and relational models, respectively.

Chapter 2 presents the basic foundation for physical structures, and Modules A and B show the mapping of logical structures onto physical structures. This not only permits the reader to distinguish between logical and physical structures and discern their interaction, but also permits skipping the discussion of physical structures, if one has no interest in the area, without disrupting the flow of the book.

Data base design In the past, many used the design techniques of conventional file structures for data base management systems. This approach caused many problems with data integration. Chapter 8 describes multiple levels of data base design starting with top management and ending with physical data base design considerations. Along the way, it describes anomalies which occur with certain data groupings and presents considerations for the use of distributed data bases. While normalization of data is usually presented along with the relational model, anomalies, caused by unnormalized data, can be encountered with any data model. Therefore, I believe they are more properly presented, as here, under the topic of data base design.

Direct comparison of important features Remembering the many differences and similarities of each data model is sometimes difficult. While many illustrations are used throughout the book, special emphasis has been placed in chapters 4 through 7 on illustrating similarities and differences of each data model, ending with a direct comparison of all three models in chapter 7.

On-line systems While batch data base management systems have their place in the world, most installations use them as a training ground to acquire the skills to master the on-line operation. Chapter 9 identifies the potential problems in an uncontrolled on-line system and presents the techniques that can be implemented to prevent the problems. It also includes a detailed description of several types of failures and the recovery mechanisms necessary to ensure data integrity. Chapter 9 also demonstrates the importance of short response times and a means to extend the data dictionary for use in trouble-shooting problems encountered during on-line operation.

Current directions Too often, students learn theoretical concepts without understanding how they are applied or how they are relevant to today's technology. Chapter 11 describes the need for information at all levels of the enterprise and how the need is being satisfied through the use of the Information Center and decision support systems which have their foundation in data bases.

Practical experience In their lectures, most instructors must supplement textbook theory with some words about practical experience, to show the difference between the text and the real world. I have used my 13 years of experience working with data base management systems—as well as the experience of others—and included practical experience as an integral part of this book in "Data Base in the Workplace" sections at the ends of seven chapters. Although fictitious names have been used in these articles, and in some cases, experiences from two or more installations have been combined into one article, all of the situations occurred at real installations.

ACKNOWLEDGEMENTS I thank Elaine F. Laube for pushing me to take the first step of a thousand-mile journey and Tom Kane for his guidance when the journey began. I thank John C. McFadden, Jim Smith, Kay Wayne, and all others who provided input for the "Data Base in the Workplace" articles.

I am grateful to C. Gardner Mallonee for giving me the opportunity to create and implement a course in data base management systems at Essex Community College in Baltimore, Maryland. I am grateful to my students, who provided me additional insight into their learning process and gave me their feedback during the class test of the manuscript. I thank Nick Palmere and his associates for their efforts in obtaining research materials.

I thank Frank Chisolm and Rich Wieskoff of Cullinet for providing me information on IDMS. Thanks go to Edda Rosskopf for aiding and coordinating my search for IBM materials and to Geoff Abbott for providing me research materials. I would also like to acknowledge the constructive criticism offered by the following reviewers of drafts of the manuscript:

Robert A. Barrett, Indiana–Purdue University; Norman D. Brammer, Colorado State University; George W. Dailey, Stephen F. Austin University; F.

Paul Fuhs, Virginia Commonwealth University; John Gillespie, University of San Francisco; John Grant, Towson State University; Robin K. Hill, Metro State College; William Jones, Modesto College; Bill Lockhart, IBM Corporation and West Valley College; Satya P. Saraswat, San Diego State University; Daniel Stubbs, California Polytechnic State University, San Luis Obispo; and Suzanne Tuthill, Delaware Technical Community College.

A special thanks goes to Mary and Joe Joseph, who have helped me more than they will ever know. I owe a great debt of thanks to my wife, Michele, for her continued support and her editorial assistance in developing the first draft of the manuscript. Last, but not least, thanks Mom!

CONTENTS

UNDERSTANDING DATA BASE MANAGEMENT SYSTEMS

1

INTRODUCTION TO DATA BASE MANAGEMENT SYSTEMS

CHAPTER OBJECTIVES

Upon completion of this chapter, you should be able to:

1. List five problems with storing data using conventional access methods
2. List five advantages gained by using a data base management system
3. List five disadvantages of using data base management systems to store and retrieve data
4. Define *data security* and explain why it is important
5. Define *data integrity* and explain why it is important
6. Define *incompatible data*
7. Present the need for privacy of data
8. List the groups of people in the data base environment and describe the function of each

NEW WORDS AND PHRASES

data integrity
data consistency
data security
access method
data independence
redundant data

1.1 CHAPTER INTRODUCTION

The world of business data processing began with the installation of the UNIVAC I in 1954 at General Electric Appliance Park in Louisville, Kentucky. Since then, changes in the ways in which data is processed have been dramatic. However, these changes also have been gradual—evolutionary rather than revolutionary.

For example, file organization methods were first developed to store data that was not currently being manipulated in the primary storage area (memory) of the computer. They evolved over time to address specific requirements for access to data. While they served their purposes, each file organization method had several problems inherent in its design, such as the duplication of data in more than one file or the lack of a means to secure the data from unauthorized access. Then data base management systems evolved, solving many of the problems that existed in conventional data storage techniques.

But data base management systems also have problems. Indeed, as you enter the world of data processing, you will discover that there is no one best way to accomplish a task. The world of data processing is a world of compromise.

To understand the compromises that have occurred and the reasons they were made, it helps to look back at the problems that previously existed and to examine the techniques that have evolved over the years. That is what we shall do in this first chapter.

The problems of conventional file processing will be presented first, because an understanding of those problems provides a foundation for understanding the advantages of a data base management system. However, it is also important to know the disadvantages of a data base management system, and so we shall also discuss those. Many individuals who study data base management systems intend to work with them in the future. Therefore, we also shall examine the general responsibilities of the people who use the systems.

1.2 CONVENTIONAL FILE PROCESSING

In the early years of data processing, the United States concentrated on using the computer to perform clerical tasks, such as payroll and order entry processing. Data processing thus reduced the costs associated with manual labor and the errors that can occur whenever a human performs any clerical task. Example A1 provides a foundation for this chapter because it represents a collection of problems that exist when storing data in conventional files. Although it is improbable that all of these problems would exist in a single system, it is not impossible.

Example A1 Conventional File Problems at Acme Widgets

Jane Doe works for Acme Widgets, one of the companies with the foresight to install an automated payroll system when data processing was in its infancy. The automated payroll system provided Acme Widgets with several advantages over the manual system. First, it was programmed to calculate Jane's and the other employees' gross pay at the end of the week, when the number of hours worked was entered into the system. It also calculated the amount of federal and state tax that Jane must pay and withheld that amount from her gross pay. Similarly, it calculated her FICA contribution. After deducting all of the withholding from her wages, the system printed a pay-a Payroll Record

123-45-6789 (zoned decimal)	JANE DOE	111 FIRST STREET	$1000 PER WEEK	303-193
Social Security Number	Name	Address	Pay Rate	Employee Number

b Personnel Record

JANE DOE	123-45-6789 (packed decimal)	111 FIRST STREET	P.S. 101	HARVARD	ASSISTANT DIRECTOR OF PERSONNEL
Name	Social Security Number	Address	Education		Job Title

Figure 1.1 Acme Widgets conventional files: Records for Jane Doe in the payroll and personnel files.

check in the amount of her net pay. And at the end of the year, the system provided W-2 forms for Jane, which were promptly mailed to her residence after the first of the year. This is not unlike many systems developed in the infancy of data processing.

Since Acme Widgets has many employees, it also has a Personnel Department. The Personnel Department places individuals in vacant positions based on their qualifications, maintains an education history of each employee, and keeps a history of the positions each of the workers holds during his or her career with Acme Widgets. To boost employee morale, a company newsletter is mailed to employees on the fifteenth of each month.

After a lengthy study, the personnel director found that the labor costs for his department were high, due to the vast amount of data being maintained on $3\frac{1}{2}'' \times 5''$ cards for each employee. He decided that these costs could be reduced if the entire system were automated like the payroll system. After much persuasion, he convinced management that an automated system would provide a satisfactory return on investment. The Data Processing Department produced the desired automation based upon the record layouts shown in Figure 1.1b. This was a separate file, different from the payroll record (Figure 1.1a).

Record Length and File Sequence

Before we proceed with this example, let's examine the factors that led to this design. The decision made by the systems analyst to create separate files for the Payroll and the Personnel Departments may have been influenced by the following:

1. The data in the two files is not alike. The only data common to both files is name, address, and social security number.
2. If the personnel data was added to the end of the payroll record, every program that processed the payroll file would have to be modified to account for the increased record length.
3. The sequence of each file is different. The payroll file is in sequence by employee number, but the personnel file is in sequence by social security number.

In light of these facts, it appears that the decision of the systems analyst to use two different files was correct.

Example A1 is typical of the decisions that had to be made when additional systems were added to existing systems in the early days of data processing: where to place the new data. Programs that process data stored using conventional file organizations are dependent upon data. And with conventional file organizations, if the length of a record changes when new systems are added, every program that accesses that record must be changed to allow for the increased record length. Changing all of the programs in an existing system is a simple task, but it can significantly add to the cost of installing a new system.

Data Integrity

Now back to Jane Doe and Acme Widgets. Jane met and married Tom Smith. She changed her name to Smith and went on a honeymoon with Tom. When they returned, they moved to 222 Second Street. The first day Jane returned to her job at Acme Widgets, she went to the Payroll Department and completed the necessary paperwork to change her name and address. The Payroll Department used this source document to update the payroll file and sent the source document to the Personnel Department so they could update their records. They did this, of course, because *when data is stored twice, it must be updated in both locations whenever it changes*. This causes additional processing overhead. The result of this process at Acme Widgets is shown in Figure 1.2.

Notice that the address in the personnel record is different from the one in the payroll record. It is easy to argue that stricter control procedures could prevent this occurrence. However, in any area of data processing, errors occur regardless of control procedures. The important point is that two fields in two separate files which purport to describe the same thing are different. In this example, once the error is detected, it is easy to correct by tracing the procedures that were followed from the completion of the source document until the time the address field was updated in the personnel record.

But let's examine an error using a different field, one involving a quantity of some important item. Suppose the number of 10-millimeter widgets in inventory was maintained in two separate files, and the quantity-on-hand field in the order analysis file shows 490,000 but the quantity-on-hand field a Payroll Record

123-45-6789	JANE SMITH	222 SECOND STREET	$1000 PER WEEK	303-193
Social Security Number	Name	Address	Pay Rate	Employee Number

b Personnel Record

JANE SMITH	123-45-6789	111 SECOND STREET	P.S. 101	HARVARD	ASSISTANT DIRECTOR OF PERSONNEL
Name	Social Security Number	Address	Education		Job Title

Figure 1.2 Acme Widgets conventional files: Updated records for Jane Doe in the payroll and personnel files.

in the inventory status file shows 500,000. What procedures must be followed to resolve the difference between these two fields? In all likelihood, unfortunately, a physical inventory which requires every item to be counted will be necessary to resolve this error.

Data Consistency

Another problem with conventional files occurs when data from two different files is necessary to satisfy a request.

Assume that the president of Acme Widgets asked a programmer to provide a list of all directors who earn more than $50,000 a year. The data for salary is in the payroll file, which is in sequence by employee number. But the data for job positions is only in the personnel file, which is in sequence by social security number. With a field such as social security number, one would expect a nine-digit field in secondary storage. This is the way it is stored in the payroll file. But in the personnel file, it has been stored in packed decimal format. Thus the methods used to store data in the two files are inconsistent. Additional data manipulation by the programmer is required to make them consistent when they are being manipulated. To provide the president with the list he wants, one of the files must be sorted into the same sequence as the other, and then the files must be matched to find salary and position. A moderate amount of data manipulation is required for just two files, but if the data requested to satisfy a question was contained in five or ten files, the task would be even greater.

Thus we see that when data is stored in two different files, two consistency problems may occur:

Combined Payroll and Personnel Record

123-45-6789	JANE SMITH	222 SECOND STREET	$1000 PER WEEK	303-193	P.S. 101	HARVARD	ASSISTANT DIRECTOR OF PERSONNEL
Social Security Number	Name	Address	Pay Rate	Employee Number	Education		Job Title

Figure 1.3
Acme Widgets conventional files: Combined payroll and personnel record for Jane Doe.

1. Data may be stored in two different formats.
2. A programmer will have to manipulate one or more files when data from two different files must be matched to provide an answer to a query.

Data Security

The problem of data being stored in two separate files can be overcome by agreeing upon a standard format for common data and combining the fields from both files into one. If the two files are to be combined into one as shown in Figure 1.3, the data will be stored only once, and thus it cannot be in conflict. However, this requires all programs that access the personnel and payroll files to be recompiled to account for the changes in the length of the record. And when the combined file is updated, it must of course be sorted into a different sequence before the update can occur. Does this solve all of the problems presented? Does it create any new problems? Before you answer, consider the following:

1. Jane works in the Personnel Department.
2. Jane routinely updates the personnel file with data about employees' previous job experience.
3. Assume you are an auditor for Acme Widgets. As part of your responsibility, you must ensure that no one in the company has access to more data than is necessary to do his or her job.

This places a different light on the consolidation of the two files. Using the consolidated file, Jane has access to far more data than is required for her to do her job. This is also true for all of the employees who update the payroll file. Is this a problem? If you believe everyone will flawlessly perform the exact operations for which they are responsible—nothing more, nothing less—the answer is no. But if employees do something that exceeds the scope of their responsibility, or if employees, while performing their responsibility, make an error, it could be disastrous to the enterprise. Critical data might be obtained and given to competitors, or an incorrect field might be updated accidently. Whether this occurs accidently or on purpose, the result may be just as devastating to the business.

Conventional File Processing Summary

Thus we see that Acme Widgets has incurred a number of problems using conventional files for its systems:

1. Each file is processed in a different sequence. Acme Widgets can either sort the files into the appropriate sequence as each file is updated, or create two separate files. Neither choice is the optimal solution.
2. If the record length is changed to satisfy the needs of one program in a system, all programs that access the file containing the changed record must be changed to account for the increased record length.
3. When using two files, data is duplicated. Therefore, the process of updating the data must occur multiple times. Conventional files do not ensure the data is correctly updated.
4. The data may not be consistent in each location in which it is stored.
5. Conventional files do not have a built-in security system to prevent unauthorized access of data.

1.3 ADVANTAGES OF DATA BASE MANAGEMENT SYSTEMS

We will now contrast data base management systems to the conventional file processing just described. The details of data base management systems are explored in the succeeding chapters. For now, let's say they are *a collection of programs which interface with application programs and manage data on the application programs' behalf.*

To conceptualize how a data base management system is used, examine Figure 1.4. Using a conventional file access method (one of the three which will be described in Chapter 2), an application program can access data in secondary storage through a program called an **access method.*** Access methods are programs that store and retrieve data on various secondary storage media, based upon the parameters specified by the application program. Access methods allow programs to access data from multiple types of devices with no change in the application program.

Data base management systems add a layer of software between the application program and the access method. With conventional file processing, the application program interfaces directly with the access method. In a data base management system, the application program requests data from the data base management system. The data base management system determines what data is needed, whether the user is authorized to view the data, and where in secondary storage the data is located; it then issues a request to the access method to retrieve the data from secondary storage. The data is then presented to the application program (see Figure 1.4b).

*Terms set in **boldface** type are defined in the Glossary at the end of the book.

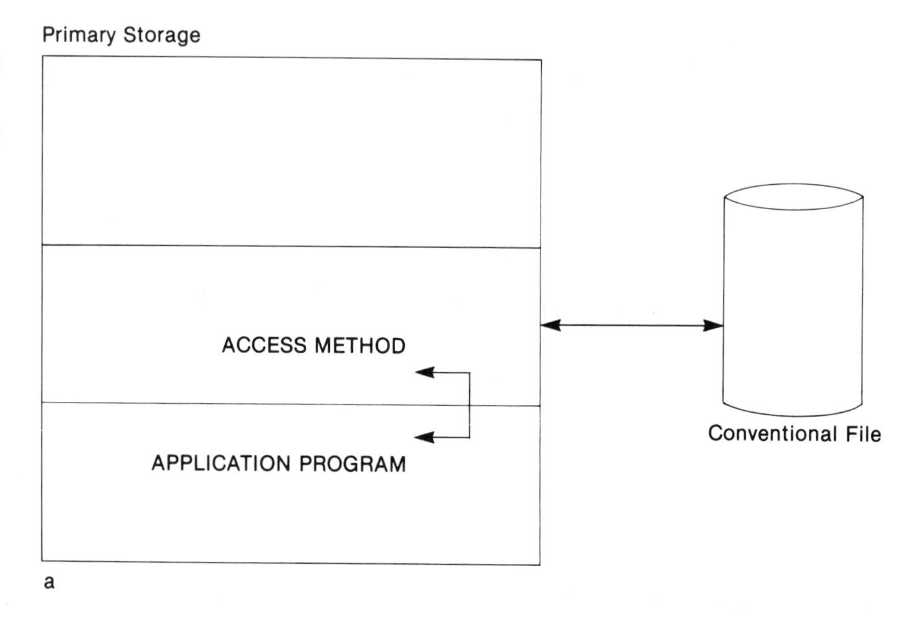

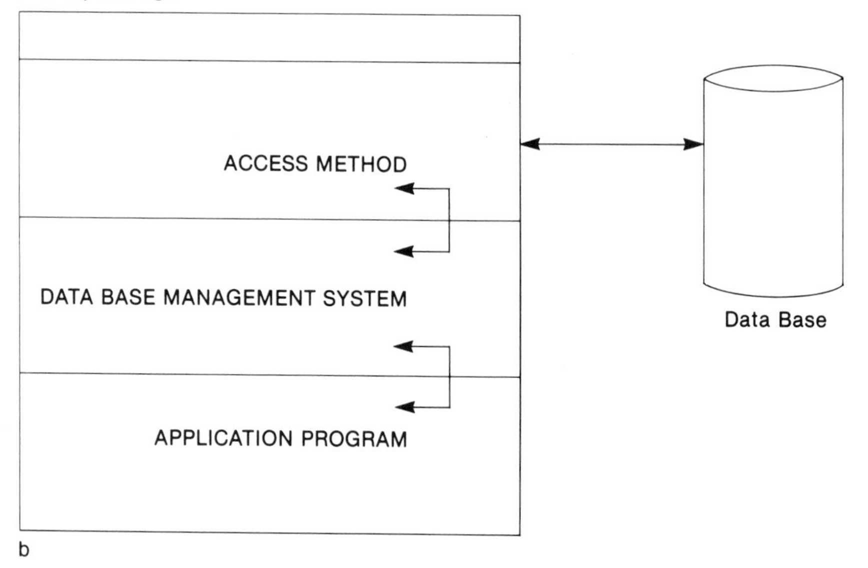

Figure 1.4
(a) Application program accessing data from a conventional file.
(b) Application program accessing data through a data base management system.

Data Independence

New applications may be desired that require access to the data. The data base management system stores the data in such a fashion that additional programs may be added to process the data (possibly with additional data requirements) as new systems are developed. This is done without rewriting existing programs.

The data base management system can be tailored to continue to present data in the same format to existing programs and also present data in a new format to the new programs being installed. This facility is called **data independence**. Thus, using a data base management system, only the programs that have a need for the additional data need be changed (as long as certain rules are followed).

If the system for Acme Widgets had been installed using a data base management system, the considerations that caused the analyst to develop two separate conventional files would not have existed. Remember, two of the reasons for Acme Widgets to use a second file were the modification of all programs which used the file and the different sequence of the files. But since the programs that execute within a data base management system have data independence, the programs are independent of both the sequence of the data and the length of the stored records.

Redundant Data

A data base management system can store a data element one time and allow multiple programs to access it. When a program references a field by name, that field has a defined length.

In Figure 1.2, the data was stored in two separate files. It is possible the Acme payroll file used 25 characters to store the NAME field and the personnel file reserved 30 characters to store the same data. When data is stored once by a data base management system, many of the incompatibility problems cease to exist. If two different fields that are to be compared are stored using different formats, the data base management system makes the appropriate conversions before manipulating data.

In Example A1, the NAME and ADDRESS fields from the personnel and payroll files could have been stored in the same data base. Since they will only be stored one time, there would never be a question concerning the length of the field. It is consistent.

This process is known as providing *nonredundant data* (no unplanned duplicate data items). Since the data is only stored once, the update process is executed once to change the data common to both systems. This eliminates the execution of a second set of programs required for the second update, which in turn saves time in program development, program maintenance, and program execution, and also saves additional space on a secondary storage device. Nonredundant data also eliminates the type of error that occurred in the ADDRESS field for Jane Doe.

Data Security

On Halloween, I might wonder if I have been visited by 500 different children or visited 500 times by the same child who has 500 different masks. Since you cannot see behind the mask, it is difficult to prove which situation exists.

A data base management system functions similarly. The system can be instructed to place a software "mask" over the data stored in the data base.

The data base management system examines each request from an application program to ensure that the program has the authority to manipulate the data it has requested. This allows any given user to manipulate only the data that falls within his or her authorization. Even though the data base contains additional data, an individual program will only be able to see that for which it has been authorized.

If a data base management system had been used to store the payroll and personnel data for Acme Widgets, the Payroll Department could have viewed the payroll data and the Personnel Department could have viewed the personnel data, but neither department would be able to view data that belonged to the other department or even be aware it exists.

This concept is called **data security**: Data is secure from unauthorized access. People who do not have a legitimate need for specific data are not allowed access to that data. And of the data that can be accessed, only specific operations are authorized against the data. For example, one program may be allowed to retrieve data but not update it. A second program may be allowed to delete records but not add records. A third program may be allowed to update records but not add or delete them.

Thus the security features built into a data base management system are an aid to the privacy and protection of data that has been mandated in today's society.

Data Integrity

The data base management system also provides **data integrity**: that is, the data represents what it purports to. This means that a field provides the correct data to the viewer at all times. This is not a guarantee that faulty programs will not generate incorrect data, but it is a warranty on the design and construction of the data base management system itself. The data base management system will provide the proper update of all related data within the data base, if it has been requested to do so, without the need for the user to request the data to be updated more than once.

Economy of Scale

Using a data base management system allows what is called *economy of scale*. Since the applications are concentrated in one location, larger and more powerful computers and secondary storage devices can be purchased. This has the same effect as buying the extra large giant economy size of Real Natural Pure Artificial Lemon Juice at the grocery store. The price for one large container is generally cheaper than the price of an equivalent volume stored in many smaller containers. In addition, the facilities for the people who support the data base management system, as well as the hardware and software, are concentrated, providing a reduction in cost over several smaller facilities.

Another benefit related to economy of scale is concentration of technical expertise. In the typical configuration, one data base management system exists within a host computer. The data base management system services all applications that have data stored in the data base. In an on-line environment, requests for data base services sometimes back up like long check-out lines in supermarkets. Supermarkets have tried various techniques to get more customers through the lines faster, such as the 10-items-or-less express line. In a data processing organization, there are people who are performance specialists, whose responsibility is to move requests through the data base management system as fast as possible. When a performance problem exists, one of these specialists determines the cause. The problem may be in the software that supports the data base management system, in the data base management system itself, or in an application program. The problem is determined and the appropriate corrective action is taken. When a new technique speeds the flow of traffic through the lines, all applications that use the data base management system benefit.

1.4 DISADVANTAGES OF A DATA BASE MANAGEMENT SYSTEM

As we stated in the introduction to this chapter, data base management systems are not without disadvantages. The principal ones are listed below.

Size

Many of the disadvantages of a data base management system stem from the sheer size of the program required to support it. The previous examples have only scratched the surface of the facilities offered with a data base management system, but think about the programming necessary to provide even the facilities presented thus far. The programming is very complex and requires many instructions. Some data base management systems require over 2 million bytes of storage!

Complexity

The size and number of services—such as data independence, compatible and nonredundant data, data security, and data integrity—that a data base management system provides lead to the next disadvantage: Data base management systems are complex. This creates two problems.

First, personnel must understand the inner workings of the system to a degree that will provide the best service to the business enterprise. People who possess these skills are in short supply, and a high price must be paid to obtain them.

Second, data base management systems offer many choices in the way data is stored, retrieved, and protected. Without adequate training, individuals may not understand the implications of a specific choice, and they will encounter unexpected side effects. The selection of an incorrect option can cause poor performance not only for one application, but also for all other applications that interface with the data base management system, because each application must wait in line for service from the system.

Cost

The size of the data base management system contributes to its relatively high cost. There is a correspondence between the number of instructions in a program and the length of time and cost required to write the program. Labor costs for qualified data processing personnel are high. Also, the vendors who develop data base management systems must recoup their development costs and make a profit. Some vendors sell their data base management systems for over $100,000. Others make a practice of renting their software rather than selling it. Some of those who rent charge over $2000 a month.

Hardware Requirements

The size of a data base management system contributes to another problem. The execution of millions of instructions to support a data base management system consumes a significant number of computer cycles, as well as a significant amount of primary and secondary storage. To execute the instructions to provide the services of the data base management system, the instructions must reside in real storage. Virtual storage made available by the current generation of computers increases the capacity to store instructions, but it does not cause instructions to be executed faster. Therefore, the new user of a data base management system must increase the "horsepower" of his or her current computer. This translates into additional dollars that the enterprise must spend to have the computer resources required to support a data base management system.

Higher Impact of a Failure

To achieve economy of scale and provide data base management system services, all of the data processing resources are concentrated in one location. The data base management system thus is only as strong as the weakest link in its chain. If for any reason there is a failure in either the host computer, the operating system, the secondary storage media, or the data base management system itself, it may prevent hundreds of people from performing the business of the enterprise. The length of time required to correct the problem can range from minutes to days.

1.5 THE PLAYERS

The first cry you hear when you enter a ballpark is, "Get your scorecard! You don't know the players without a scorecard!" In a data base environment, there are four major groups of players: systems engineers, data base administration staff, application programmers, and end users of the data.

Systems Engineers

Systems engineers are the highly trained specialists who install the data base management system. Data base management systems are written by a vendor to execute with a wide variety of operating systems, application programs, and terminals. Systems engineers then customize the software to meet the requirements of a specific installation.

Data base management systems are composed of a series of programs. Just as with any other program, they contain latent errors (or "bugs") that periodically surface. One function of systems engineers is to report errors in the software to the vendors, so that the vendors can provide corrections.

Like other programs, data base management systems are often enhanced to provide additional facilities. The vendor supplies enhancements to the software, and they are installed by the systems engineers.

Systems engineers also perform some of the tuning of the data base management system to provide better performance. In all, the systems engineer's work on a data base management system is not significantly different from his or her work with other software.

Data Base Administration

The data base administration staff establishes the procedures for interfacing with the data base management system. The data base administrator must have the foresight to anticipate the future needs of the enterprise. She or he either designs data bases to be installed or provides data base design assistance to application programmers or analysts who are installing new systems.

A data base management system is made up of two major ingredients: the software that makes it perform, and an underlying philosophy about the way in which data is incorporated in new systems. The philosophy is that all data bases should be designed and planned independent of the data base management system software. Individual systems are merely placed in their proper positions when it becomes time to implement them. When a new system is installed, there should be little, if any, impact on existing systems. The ability of the data base administrator to plan for future systems is a key to minimizing disruptions to existing applications when new applications are installed.

Even with data base management systems, an application such as the one described at Acme Widgets (Example A1), where the data for the payroll system is placed in one data base and the data for the personnel system is placed in another, does occur. The key to reduce the problems is the planning done by the data base administrator, who must be aware of the systems needed for the successful operation of the business. The administrator must envision the data required to support these systems and know in which data base the data will be stored. Without proper planning, success cannot be guaranteed.

Programs written within the data processing organization are like merchandise: The quality of the product is extremely important to both the manufacturer and the end user. The data base administrator is a quality control checkpoint for systems being installed. When the administrator performs installation chores, he or she can make checks to ensure that the program meets specifications.

The data base administrator must also describe the data to be stored in terms consistent with the rules of the data base management system. This description allows the data base management system to manipulate the data.

The theory presented in all subsequent chapters of this book is a base of knowledge for a data base administrator. The data base administration function is investigated in detail in Chapter 10.

Application Programmers

Application programmers are charged with the navigation of the data bases for the users. After the design and specifications are finished, application programmers write the programs to cause the data to be provided to the user.

The logic is similar to the logic of programs written to process the data for any other business data processing application. The major difference is in the language required to manipulate the data base. Each data base system has its own data manipulation language (DML). Since this language is not standardized, a new data manipulation language must be learned by the programmer for each data base management system in which he or she programs. The work of the application programmer is described briefly in the data manipulation language portions of Chapters 5, 6, and 7.

Of all the players on our scorecard, the application programmer's function is the one most likely to change in the near future. The reasons for this change will be presented in Chapter 7.

End Users

In the day-to-day working of a data base management system, quite often the purpose for installing it is lost by individuals who become so involved in the tuning and performance of the software that they forget that it was created to be an aid to performing the functions of the business. But end users rarely forget: They see the data base management system as an automated method to perform their work. Nor do they ascribe any magic or mystical powers to it, as the other players may. The end users look upon the data base management system as another tool they use to accomplish the day-to-day functions of their jobs.

Although they are not a subject of this book, end users are actually the most important people involved with a data base management system. It is the job of the other players to ensure that the users continue to view the data base management system as just another tool, like an electronic calculator or typewriter. Every effort should be made to ensure that the data base environment does not interfere with the end users in accomplishing the business of the enterprise.

1.6 SUMMARY

Data processing has changed dramatically over the past 30 years. The changes have been evolutionary—gradual rather than dramatic. Processing data with conventional files fulfilled a need that existed during the decade of the sixties. As users are exposed to data processing, they find additional ways to use the services. Many different departments within an organization now require access to the same data. With conventional file processing, data is often duplicated in multiple files. Often, data is stored in different formats in each of the files in which it is stored. On occasion, data stored in multiple

Figure 1.5 Advantages and disadvantages of data base management systems.

ADVANTAGES	DISADVANTAGES
Data independence	Size—very large
No unplanned redundant data	Complex
Data security	High cost
Data integrity	Increased hardware requirements
Economy of scale	High impact of failure

files does not agree and time has to be expended to resolve these differences. And if two different departments share data on the same file, a potential security exposure exists.

Processing with a data base management system offers a number of advantages. The location of the data base management system within the software chain provides data independence. With a data base management system, data can be stored in one location and accessed by many different departments; there is no unplanned redundant data. A software mask within the data base management system removes security exposures that exist when using conventional files. A data base management system provides data integrity. Economy of scale can be achieved by installing a data base management system at a central site, where it can be supported by a group of highly trained technicians.

In the Old West, where a bar was a place to socialize, the saloon often had a sign hanging on the front window that advertised a free lunch. But of course the free lunch never truly existed; it was paid for out of the price of the beverages consumed. Likewise, data base management systems—or any other tool in data processing—do not come free; there are always compromises—concessions in one area for the sake of benefits in another. For example, to gain the benefits, data base management systems became quite large and therefore complex. Increased costs are incurred through the large number of hours to develop the software and the computer resources required to support the system. And the end users have placed all their eggs in one basket: A failure in the data base management system or any related hardware or software will prevent many users from accessing the data base until the problem is corrected. The advantages and disadvantages of data base management systems are summarized in Figure 1.5.

Of the personnel needed to ensure the successful operation of a data base management system, three of the four positions are within the Data Processing Department. The systems engineer installs, tunes, and maintains the software. The data base administrator performs the coordination and quality control roles and is the center of all design efforts. The application programmer must provide the data to the end user in a "user friendly" manner. The end users—the only position outside the Data Processing Department—work with the data base management system in the same manner in which they used a pencil and paper 40 years ago.

REVIEW QUESTIONS

1.1 List five problems associated with storing and retrieving data using conventional access methods.

1.2 List five advantages gained by using a data base management system.

1.3 List five disadvantages of using a data base management system.

1.4 Define *data security* and explain why it is important.

1.5 Define *data integrity* and explain why it is important.

1.6 List the major categories of personnel in a data base environment and describe the function of each.

1.7 Give an illustration to explain why privacy of data is important.

DATA BASE IN THE WORKPLACE

A First Data Base Management System

As Chapter 1 has shown, creating a data base management system is not without risk. The following "war story" comes from a data processing installation which does not have pleasant memories about its first data base management system.

The enterprise was under tight budgetary constraints and wanted to purchase the minimum amount of software that would do the job. Thus, they wanted to integrate the data base management system with existing software. For example, they had a teleprocessing monitor which performed well, and they felt it would not be worthwhile to purchase another to replace it. While this seems a worthwhile goal, it proved disastrous.

A data base management system was selected and installed which contained only the software for data base management, not for a teleprocessing monitor associated with the data base management system. Then the learning experience began.

The data base management system was a well-established package, but it was written many years before, using programming techniques less structured than today's. This meant that the vendor was constantly shipping corrections to problems existing in the software. Correcting errors in the data base software required a systems engineer to spend half of his time just on maintenance, far in excess of the time required to maintain any other software.

The development staff found that learning the functions of the package was very difficult, and they also found it cumbersome to make structure changes to the data bases. Because of the file storage techniques, it was very difficult to estimate the space necessary to store data, since the data storage space was sparsely populated. The vendor was based half a continent away and had attempted to resolve problems over the phone instead of sending a representative on-site. This made problem resolution more difficult. Finally, no security features were included in the software to restrict access to data.

The development of the system had consumed 10 man-months of effort and had at last proceeded to the point where an experimental data base was installed. However, the teleprocessing portion of the data base management system software contained the facilities for automatic back-up and recovery of the data bases, and since this portion of the software was not purchased, no means of automated back-up and recovery existed. To obtain this feature, people at the installation would be forced to write the programs themselves or purchase the teleprocessing portion after all. Either alternative presented an expensive solution to the problem, but production systems are not implemented without back-up and recovery procedures, so one of the alternatives was mandatory.

The manager of the installation felt the data base management system should increase the productivity of his staff. However, he found that the existing package provided an additional layer of complexity but did not make the installation of systems easier. He also felt that data base management systems should be responsive, and while the existing package was responsive most of the time, performance occasionally degraded. To make matters worse, as with most data base management systems, it was rented instead of purchased, and the vendor raised the rental price 30 percent within one year.

With all of these problems, the user decided to stop the development of existing work and to select a new data base management system, despite having expended 10 man-months of effort attempting to install the first system. The new data base management system selected used a completely different structure for organizing and storing data. As a result, none of the technical skills learned using the first data base management system were transferable to the second.

The user is much wiser now, but only after a very expensive education and much frustration to his staff.

2

PHYSICAL STRUCTURES

CHAPTER OBJECTIVES

Upon completion of this chapter, you should be able to:

1. Define the terminology associated with direct access storage devices
2. Describe the processes that occur in an I/O operation
3. List three different record formats and specify the advantages and disadvantages of each
4. Explain the advantages and disadvantages of blocking records
5. Explain the function of sequential, indexed sequential, and direct access file organizations
6. Explain the function of direct and sequential access of files and when each is appropriate
7. Explain the compromises between cost and performance that occur when storing and retrieving data

NEW WORDS AND PHRASES

volume
track
cylinder
seek
seek time
head switching
rotational delay
latency
data transfer rate
count-data
count-key-data
blocking
record descriptor word
block descriptor word
sequential file organization
anticipatory buffering
indexed sequential file organization
overflow area
reorganization
direct file organization
indirect addressing
synonyms
packing density

2.1 CHAPTER INTRODUCTION

Most data base management systems store data on direct access storage devices. This chapter will present an overview of data storage and access on these devices.

We will present the terminology and concepts of direct access storage devices, including the process of blocking records and when and why it is performed. Three different record formats will be presented, along with the applications for each.

Several file organizations are used for storing data. This chapter will present three of the basic organizations and the situations in which each is appropriately used. Each file organization and access method has advantages and disadvantages. You will be challenged to determine which method is appropriate in specific situations.

To achieve maximum performance in data base design, it is necessary to understand the interaction among the data base design, the data base management system storage strategies, and the secondary storage medium.

In later chapters, the techniques used by data base management systems to store data will be presented.

2.2 DIRECT ACCESS STORAGE DEVICE CONCEPTS

There are two types of direct access storage devices (DASD): *drum* and *disk*. Drums tend to be special devices, designed to store and retrieve data very rapidly. Due to their design, their cost is high relative to the amount of data that can be stored. They had a place in the evolution of data processing, but very few exist today. Those still in use are seldom used to store data. Instead, they are used for tasks to improve the efficiency of the operating system. Today, the predominant device to store and retrieve data is disk.

Terminology

Let's review the terminology associated with these devices.

The physical unit in which the recording media is housed is called a *disk drive*. Each disk drive holds one unit of storage media called a *disk pack* or **volume**. Each volume is capable of holding one or more files. In most environments, each volume will hold many files or data sets.

The volume is composed of a series of platters fastened to a shaft in the center that causes all of the platters to rotate together at a high speed. The platters are made of metal and are coated on both the top and bottom surfaces with magnetic oxide.

Data is stored on the platter's magnetic oxide coating by a *read/write head*. There are several read/write heads per disk pack. Generally, one read/write head exists for each recording surface (although some of the newer devices have more than one per surface). All of the read/write heads (except for the newer models) are attached to a single post. The assembled

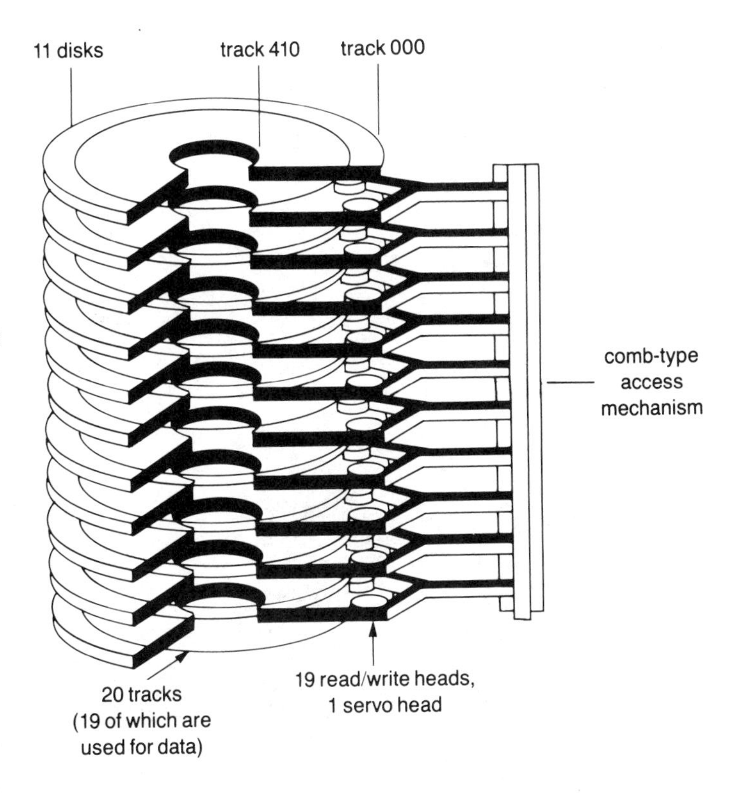

Figure 2.1 **Comb-type access mechanism positioned over each recording surface. (From *Introduction to IBM Direct Access Storage Devices* by Marilyn Bohl. Copyright © Science Research Associates, Inc. 1981. Reprinted by permission of the publisher.)**

device looks very much like a comb (see Figure 2.1).

The read/write heads as a unit are called the *access mechanism*. Since they are fastened to a common post, all of the read/write heads move as a unit. Wherever one moves, the others move with it.

Each read/write head functions rather like an electromagnet. The read/write head electronically encodes data serially on the magnetic surface of each platter as the platter rotates under the read/write head. A **track** is the location on one magnetic surface where data is recorded as the platter makes one complete rotation under the read/write head. Today's technology enables tracks to exist in close proximity. It is not unusual for disk drives to be able to record several hundred tracks of data on one recording surface. Each track recorded is a concentric circle; data is *not* recorded in a spiral fashion as is done on a phonograph record (see Figure 2.2). Each track, from the outermost to the innermost, stores the same amount of data. Data is stored with larger gaps on the outer tracks, due to their larger diameters.

A **cylinder** is composed of all of the recording surfaces on which data can be recorded without moving the access mechanism (see Figure 2.3).

These are the physical parts of storage devices. The actions performed in recording data on disk, which we shall now review, are usually described in terms of movement of the access mechanism and rotation of the recording surface.

When data is written on or retrieved from a disk, several different things influence the amount of time required to transfer data:

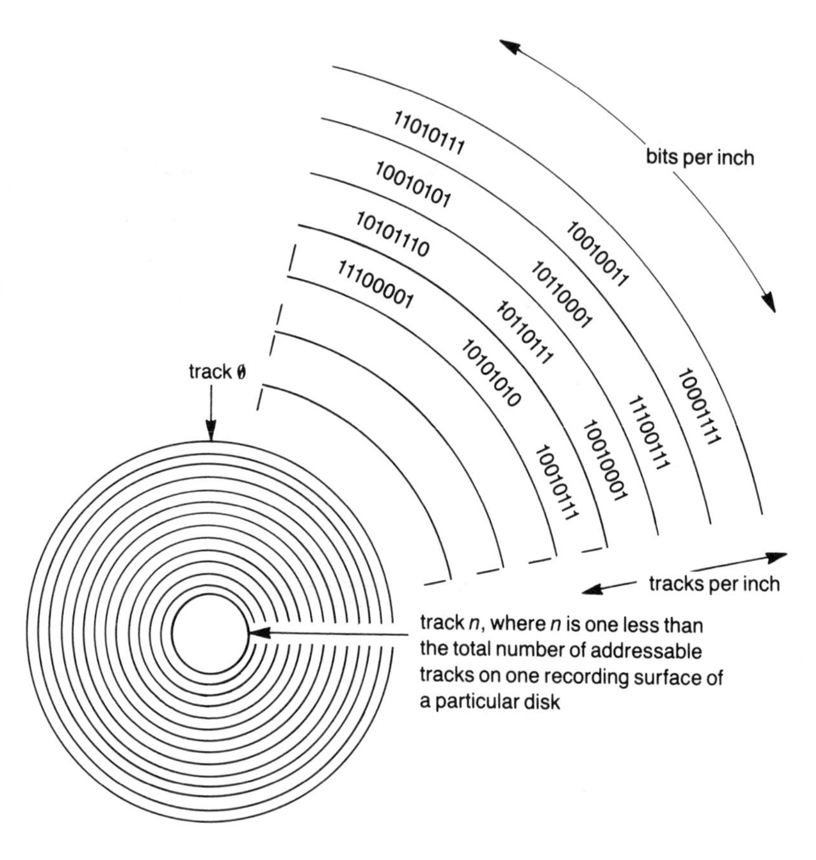

Figure 2.2
Data storage on the tracks of one recording surface. (From *Introduction to IBM Direct Access Storage Devices* by Marilyn Bohl. Copyright © Science Research Associates, Inc. 1981. Reprinted by permission of the publisher.)

1. The access mechanism is moved from the cylinder that it is currently positioned over to the cylinder that contains the data to be read. The process of moving the access mechanism to the desired cylinder is called *seeking*. The amount of time required to move the access mechanism to the correct cylinder is called **seek time** or **access time**.
2. Only one of the read/write heads on the access mechanism can be active at any instant. Therefore, the appropriate read/write head must be activated. This is called **head switching**.
3. The read/write head cannot read data until the correct record comes underneath the head. The time spent waiting for the data to rotate under the read/write head is called **rotational delay** or **latency**.
4. Data is transferred from the device. The speed at which data is transferred from the device to storage is called the **data transfer rate**. The data transfer rate is determined by the rotational speed of the device and the density at which data is recorded.

The time required to accomplish steps one through four above determines the length of time required to transfer data from a disk to primary storage or vice versa.

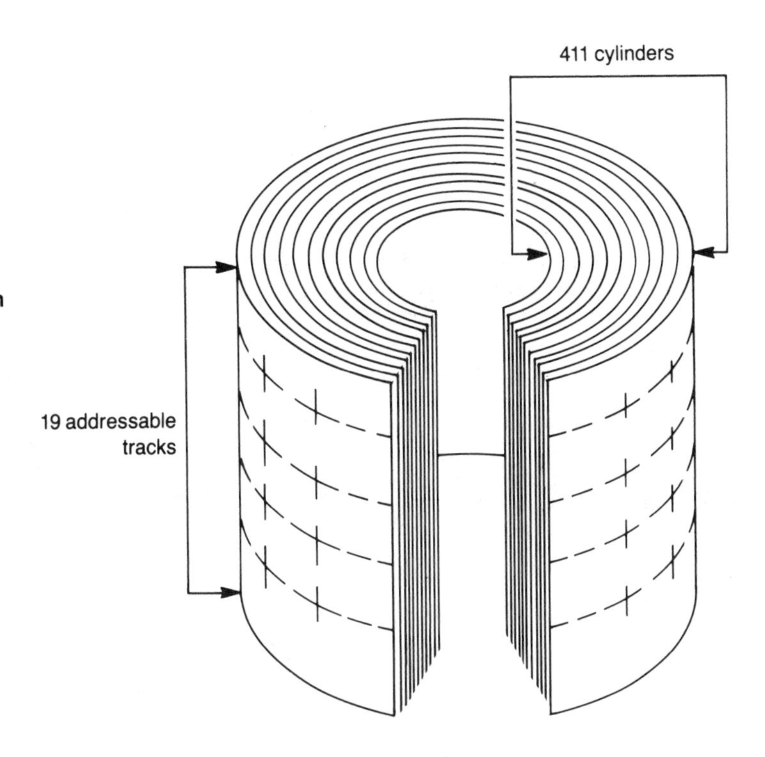

Figure 2.3
Relationship of cylinders and tracks on a single volume. (From *Introduction to IBM Direct Access Storage Devices* by Marilyn Bohl. Copyright © Science Research Associates, Inc. 1981. Reprinted by permission of the publisher.)

To maximize performance, the data base designer attempts to minimize the time required for a read or write operation. Of the four steps listed, only two can be effectively manipulated by the designer. The data transfer rate is determined by the hardware; it cannot be changed by the designer. The time required for head switching is negligible, since it occurs at the speed of electricity. The remaining two functions—rotational delay and seeking—are electromechanical operations. Any time a mechanical operation is performed rather than an electric one, the time necessary to complete the events increases significantly. Thus, to improve performance, the designer must reduce or eliminate the mechanical motion of these two events.

Rotational Delay

Rotational delay, or latency, is directly affected by the sequence in which data is stored or retrieved. Example B1 illustrates.

Example B1
Rotational Delay at Radio Station WACKO

Radio station WACKO has just received the latest hits from the new-wave group the Electric Purple Flatnotes: *Me, You, Them,* and *Lovers.* These four songs are stored on one track of a disk volume in alphabetic sequence.

To retrieve the songs in alphabetic sequence, the access mechanism seeks the correct cylinder. After the access mechanism is correctly positioned, the appropriate head is switched on. After the data rotates under the head, the first song, *Lovers,* is retrieved. When the last byte of data for *Lovers* has been transferred to storage, the read/write head is positioned immediately before the record for *Me.* The record for *Me* is read, followed by *Them,* and *You* (see Figure 2.4). The data has been retrieved with one seek. Rotational delay occurred only before the first song, *Lovers.* Rotational delay did not occur between records, since the songs were stored in the sequence in which they were to be retrieved, and thus the read/write head was positioned prior to the read as a result of reading the previous record.

After a week, the songs make the Top-40 chart. Radio WACKO now wishes to retrieve the records in the sequence they appear on the chart. The number-one record on the chart is *You.* Thus, this is the first record to be retrieved.

Again the access mechanism seeks the correct cylinder and the ap-

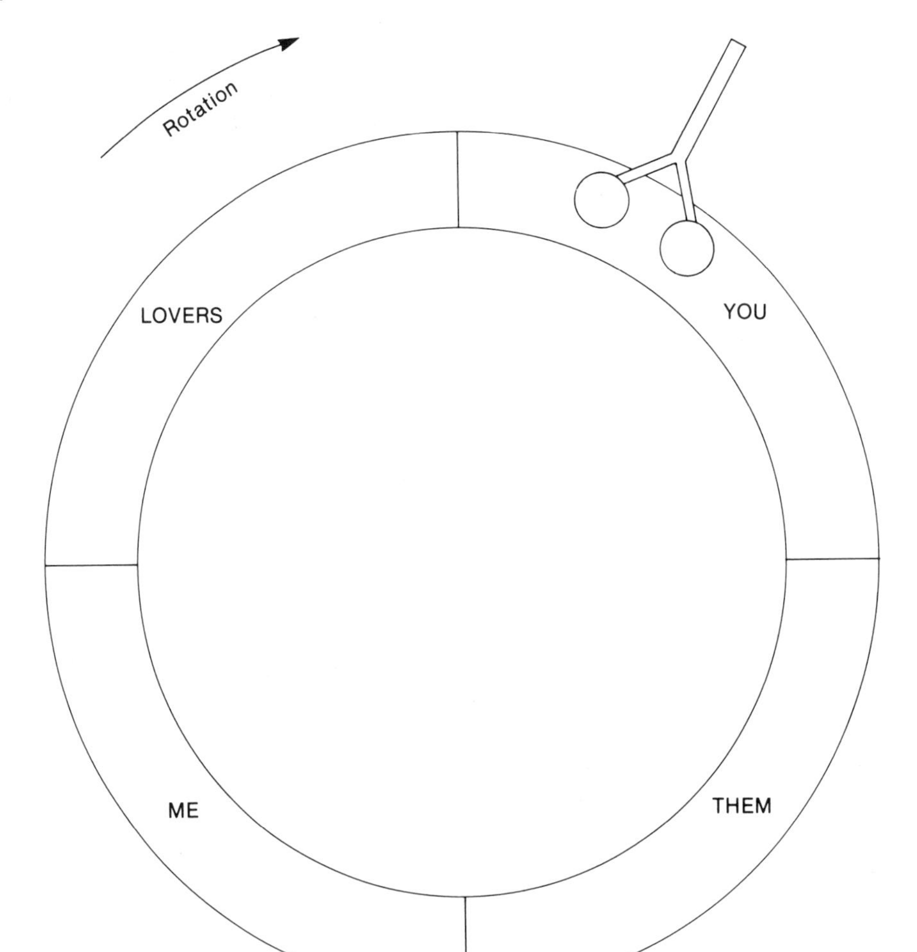

Figure 2.4
Four records stored on one track.

propriate head is switched on. Now the device must wait until the data passes under the read head. The next record on the Top-40 is *Them.* It is positioned halfway around the track from *Lovers* (this is the position of the track after the record for *You* has been read). The device must again wait for one-half of a rotation until the record for *Them* passes under the read head. The next record on the Top-40 is *Me.* After the record for *Them* is read, the read head is positioned at the beginning of the record for *You,* so the device must again wait for one-half of a rotation until the record for *Me* passes under the read head. The last record to be retrieved is *Lovers.* It is positioned halfway around the track from *Them* (this is the position after the record for *Me* has been read). The device must again wait for one-half a rotation until the record for *Lovers* passes under the read head.

When the records were retrieved in the order they were stored, rotational delay occurred only for the first record. Since the position of the record is unknown in such situations, it was assumed that the record is one-half a rotation from the desired record. In reality, it may have been immediately before the read head, just after it, or any place in between. In the second week, the same data was accessed, but in a different sequence. This time, a total of two rotations (one-half a rotation for each record) were required to obtain the desired data.

The sequence in which data is stored and retrieved on a track has a significant impact on the length of time required for input/output (I/O) operations. For an IBM 3350 disk pack, the rotational delay for a full rotation is 16.7 milliseconds. If the exact position of the read/write head in relation to the desired record is unknown, one-half a rotation is assumed to be required to place the data under the read/write head. This is termed the average rotational delay; it is 8.4 milliseconds for an IBM 3350. This sounds like a small amount of time to wait, but it becomes significant if thousands of records must be read from a file. Thus, when the designer has a choice in the sequence in which data is stored, he or she should ensure it will be stored in the same sequence in which it will be retrieved.

Seek Time

The same effort that is applied to reducing rotational delay should be applied to reducing seek time. When a file is stored on disk, it is desirable to store on the same cylinder all of the records that would be accessed together.

In Example B1, if all of the records on the Top-40 chart were stored on disk, they would require more than one track. If the designer attempted to place all of the data on the same recording surface, a seek would be required after each track is read to locate the data on the next track, because the next track would be on a different cylinder. In the example, four records fit on one track; thus, 10 seeks are required to retrieve all of the Top-40 songs. But if the data was stored on successive tracks within the same cylinder, and if there were at least 10 recording surfaces per cylinder, all of the records could be retrieved with a single seek. Seek time would be reduced from 10 occurrences to one.

For an IBM 3350, seek time from one cylinder to the cylinder immediately adjacent to it is 10 milliseconds. The seek time from the outermost cylinder on a disk to the innermost cylinder is 50 milliseconds. The average seek time for an IBM 3350 is 25 milliseconds. Just as with rotational delay, the total seek time required to transfer the data from a disk to storage can be significant if it is not properly controlled. The rule-of-thumb is to, if possible, store on the same cylinder records that will be retrieved together, or else store them on adjacent cylinders.

Track Layout

Records are stored on a direct access storage device in serial fashion along each track. If a track were cut at a defined point and stretched out, it would appear as in Figure 2.5. Refer to Figure 2.5 in the following discussion.

Each track has a starting point called an *index point,* identified by the software. There are no physical markings that enable the human eye to identify them. Two different types of information are recorded on each track: administrative information and the user data itself. Administrative information is used by the access methods to store and retrieve the user data. Administrative information is used for such things as identifying the location where the data is stored (that is, the cylinder, the head or recording surface, and the record number of that user record on a track).

The *home address* follows the index point. It is administrative information used to identify the cylinder and the head (or track) number of this track and the condition of the track. The number of cylinders and tracks on a direct access storage device depends upon the manufacturer and the model number of the device. The capacity is a nominal capacity, since additional tracks are provided as spares. It is not necessary to discard an entire disk pack because one track is damaged. If a track is damaged, it is marked as defective and an alternate track is assigned to replace it. A flag byte in the home address indicates when a track is defective and whether it is a primary or alternate track.

The *track descriptor record* (Record 0) contains administrative information and follows the home address. The track descriptor record is used as a cross reference between the primary track and the alternate track if the primary track has been damaged. It also contains administrative data about user data on the track.

User data is stored after Record 0. It may be stored in two different formats: *count-data* or *count-key-data.* The *key area* is a separate physical area on disk. It is a data field that is unique within a file and can be used to search for a specific record in the file. If the data does not contain external keys, it is stored using the count-data format; otherwise, the count-key-data format is used. As shown in Figure 2.5, the *count area* contains fields for a flag byte, the cylinder number, the head (or track) number, the relative record number, the key length, the data length, and cyclic check characters. The flag byte, cylinder, and track number fields contain essentially the same information as the flag byte in Record 0. The *relative record*

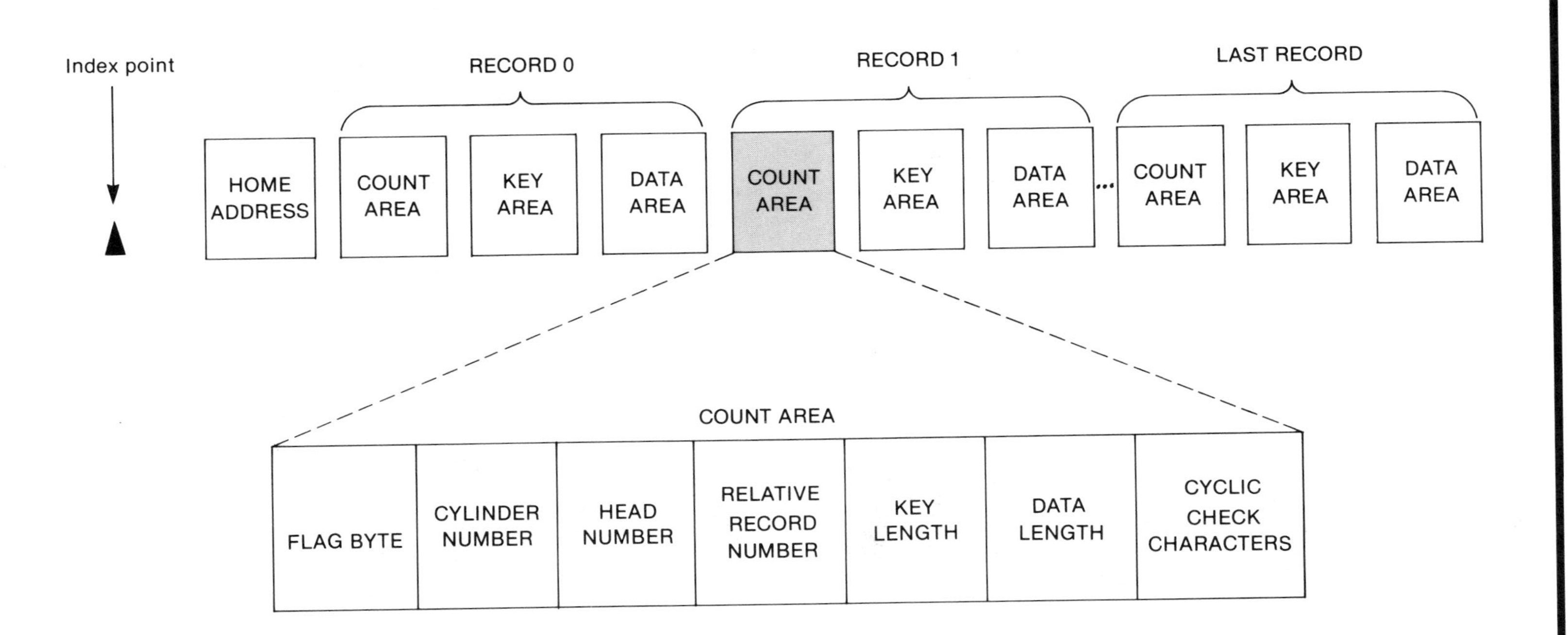

Figure 2.5 Track layout showing count-key-data format for storing data.

number field is a one-byte field that contains the ordinal position of this record on the track, stored as a binary number (from 1 to 255). If the count-key-data format is used, the key field contains the length of the key area; otherwise, it will be zero. The data length field contains the length of the *data area* that follows. The cyclic check characters contain data used to verify that data is read properly, similar to the use of a longitudinal check character on magnetic tape. As we shall see later, the data from the count area and key area is used by the file access methods to retrieve data.

When using state-of-the-art data processing tools, each time the application program is ready to process another record, it issues an instruction such as a READ instruction in COBOL. The READ instruction causes a request to the access method to be generated. (As you recall from Chapter 1, an access method is a set of programs that provides device independence to the application program. It is a part of the operating system and contains all of the instructions necessary to move data from primary storage to secondary storage, or vice-versa.) The access method creates a program of its own, which is provided to the channel to execute against the appropriate device. The desired record as determined by the count area and/or key area is retrieved (if it exists) and placed in storage. The process is reversed in a WRITE operation.

In Figure 2.6, the application program has completed processing Record A. To obtain the next record to be processed, the program issues a

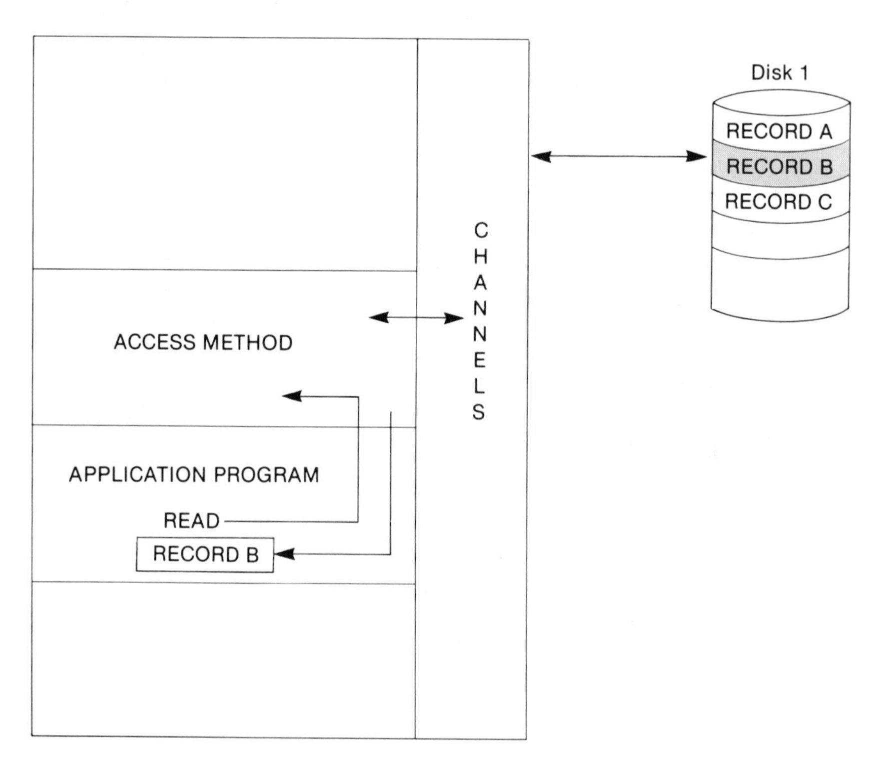

Figure 2.6 Schematic of an I/O operation, showing the relationship among the application program, the access method, and the channels.

READ instruction, which causes the access method to be invoked. The access method builds a channel program requesting Record B. The channel program is executed, causing Record B to be transferred from Disk 1 to primary storage. The access method provides Record B to the application program, which then processes the record.

Track Capacity

The number of records that can be stored on one track can be calculated using a formula provided by the equipment manufacturer. Most manufacturers provide a table that speeds the process. Figure 2.7 is an example of such a table.

The table has two major column headings: Bytes per Record and Number of Records. The Bytes per Record column is subdivided, based on whether the record is stored Without Keys or With Keys. Each of these columns is further subdivided to specify a minimum and maximum length.

To use the table, the length of the physical record is compared to the minimum and maximum values. When the row is found that has a minimum value less than or equal to the physical record length and a maximum value greater than or equal to the physical record length, the corresponding number is read from the Number of Records column. For example, if the length of the physical record is 100 bytes and is stored with keys, the Bytes per Record column is searched until the row with 97 as a minimum value and 103 as a maximum value is found. The value in the Number of Records per Track column shows that 52 records can be stored on one track.

Blocking

Administrative information may take a significant percentage of storage capacity if the data records are small. The amount of administrative information can be reduced by **blocking**.

The higher the number of count, key, and data areas on a track, the less data that can be stored, because one count, one key, and one data area are required each time data is transferred to secondary storage. The number of count, key, and data areas can be reduced by grouping two or more data records and writing them in one transfer operation. This is blocking: the process of storing multiple data records (logical records) in a physical record in secondary storage. Thus, *blocking records can significantly add to the amount of data that can be stored on a track.*

When records are blocked, the number of additional logical records that can be stored on a track can also be determined from the track capacity table (Figure 2.7). If 23 logical records, each 100 bytes long, are stored in a physical record, the physical record length is 2300 bytes. By examining the Bytes per Record with Keys column in the track capacity table, we find the entry containing 2140 bytes as a minimum and 2483 as a maximum. The corresponding entry in the Number of Records per Track shows that 7 physical records can be stored on a track. Since each physical record contains 23 logical records, a total of 161 records (7 × 23) can be stored on a track when blocked, versus 52 unblocked—a dramatic difference.

BYTES PER RECORD				NUMBER OF RECORDS		
Without Keys		With Keys		Per Track	Per Cylinder	Per Drive
Min.	Max.	Min.	Max.			
9443	19069	9361	18987	1	30	16650
6234	9442	6152	9360	2	60	33300
4629	6233	4547	6151	3	90	49950
3666	4628	3584	4546	4	120	66600
3025	3665	2943	3583	5	150	83250
2566	3024	2484	2942	6	180	99900
2222	2565	2140	2483	7	210	116550
1955	2221	1873	2139	8	240	133200
1741	1954	1659	1872	9	270	149850
1566	1740	1484	1658	10	300	166500
1420	1565	1338	1483	11	330	183150
1297	1419	1215	1337	12	360	199800
1191	1296	1109	1214	13	390	216450
1099	1190	1017	1108	14	420	233100
1019	1098	937	1016	15	450	249750
948	1018	866	936	16	480	266400
885	947	803	865	17	510	283050
829	884	747	802	18	540	299700
778	828	696	746	19	570	316350
732	777	650	695	20	600	333000
691	731	609	649	21	630	349650
653	690	571	608	22	660	366300
618	652	536	570	23	690	382950
586	617	504	535	24	720	399600
556	585	474	503	25	750	416250
529	555	447	473	26	780	432900
503	528	421	446	27	810	449550
479	502	397	420	28	840	466200
457	478	375	396	29	870	482850
437	456	355	374	30	900	499500
417	436	335	354	31	930	516150
399	416	317	334	32	960	532800
382	398	300	316	33	990	549450
366	381	284	299	34	1020	566100
350	365	268	283	35	1050	582750
336	349	254	267	36	1080	599400
322	335	240	253	37	1110	616050
309	321	227	239	38	1140	632700
297	308	215	226	39	1170	649350
285	296	203	214	40	1200	666000
274	284	192	202	41	1230	682650
263	273	181	191	42	1260	699300
253	262	171	180	43	1290	715950
243	252	161	170	44	1320	732600
234	242	152	160	45	1350	749250
225	233	143	151	46	1380	765900
217	224	135	142	47	1410	782550
208	216	126	134	48	1440	799200
201	207	119	125	49	1470	815850
193	200	111	118	50	1500	832500

Figure 2.7 Track capacity table for an IBM 3350 disk drive, native mode. (Courtesy IBM Corporation.)

BYTES PER RECORD				NUMBER OF RECORDS		
Without Keys		*With Keys*		*Per Track*	*Per Cylinder*	*Per Drive*
Min.	*Max.*	*Min.*	*Max.*			
186	192	104	110	51	1530	849150
179	185	97	103	52	1560	865800
172	178	90	96	53	1590	882450
166	171	84	89	54	1620	899100
159	165	77	83	55	1650	915750
153	158	71	76	56	1680	932400
147	152	65	70	57	1710	949050
142	146	60	64	58	1740	965700
136	141	54	59	59	1770	982350
131	135	49	53	60	1800	999000
126	130	44	48	61	1830	1015650
121	125	39	43	62	1860	1032300
116	120	34	38	63	1890	1048950
112	115	30	33	64	1920	1065600
107	111	25	29	65	1950	1082250
103	106	21	24	66	1980	1098900
99	102	17	20	67	2010	1115550
95	98	13	16	68	2040	1132200
91	94	9	12	69	2070	1148850
87	90	5	8	70	2100	1165500
83	86	4	4	71	2130	1182150
79	82			72	2160	1198800
76	78			73	2190	1215450
72	75			74	2220	1232100
69	71			75	2250	1248750
66	68			76	2280	1265400
62	65			77	2310	1282050
59	61			78	2340	1298700
56	58			79	2370	1315350
53	55			80	2400	1332000
50	52			81	2430	1348650
47	49			82	2460	1365300
45	46			83	2490	1381950
42	44			84	2520	1398600
39	41			85	2550	1415250
37	38			86	2580	1431900
34	36			87	2610	1448550
32	33			88	2640	1465200
29	31			89	2670	1481850
27	28			90	2700	1498500
25	26			91	2730	1515150
23	24			92	2760	1531800
20	22			93	2790	1548450
18	19			94	2820	1565100
16	17			95	2850	1581750
14	15			96	2880	1598400
12	13			97	2910	1615050
10	11			98	2940	1631700
8	9			99	2970	1648350
6	7			100	3000	1665000
4	5			101	3030	1681650
2	3			102	3060	1698300
1	1			103	3090	1714950

2.3 RECORD FORMATS

Data can be stored using three different formats: **Fixed length record format, variable length record format**, or **undefined length record format**. The format of the records determines how it will be stored on DASD, as well as determining some of the responsibilities of the programmer.

As seen in the preceding section, administrative information precedes each physical record written to secondary storage. In the following discussion, records will be presented with keys, since this represents the more complex case. However, each example could be represented without keys if they were unnecessary. If records are represented without keys, the key area is omitted.

Fixed Length Records

When fixed length records are used, all records in the file have the same length. Fixed length records are used when there is one occurrence of each non-key field or a predictably fixed number of non-key fields in each record of the file. A payroll file is a type of file that uses fixed length records.

A payroll record typically contains fields for an employee number, name, address, pay rate, and year-to-date withholding. Every record in the file contains the same number of fields. When fixed length keyed records are stored unblocked, the key is stored in the key area and is not repeated in the data area to save space. When they are blocked, the key of the highest record in the block is placed in the key area and the key must also be imbedded in each logical record in the block, so the logical record can be identified when it is processed (see Figure 2.8a and 2.8b).

Variable Length Records

Variable length records are used when one or more fields are repeated a variable number of times within a record. For example, students take a variable number of courses during their college careers. If a system were developed to store a student's name, student identification number, and each course taken, the length of the record would depend on the number of courses each student has taken. This data can be stored in a fixed length record if the record is long enough to hold the maximum number of courses taken by any given student. However, this arrangement wastes space. It would be necessary to reserve space for the maximum number of courses, even for students who only take one course. To save space, variable length records are used.

Variable length records have a prefix to inform the processing program of the length of the record. This prefix is called a **record descriptor word** (RDW). The record descriptor word includes the length, in bytes, of all of the fields in the record, including the record descriptor word itself (see Figure 2.8c).

Variable length records may also be blocked. It is necessary to include the length of the block within the physical record. The block is prefixed with a field containing the length of the block. This field is called a **block**

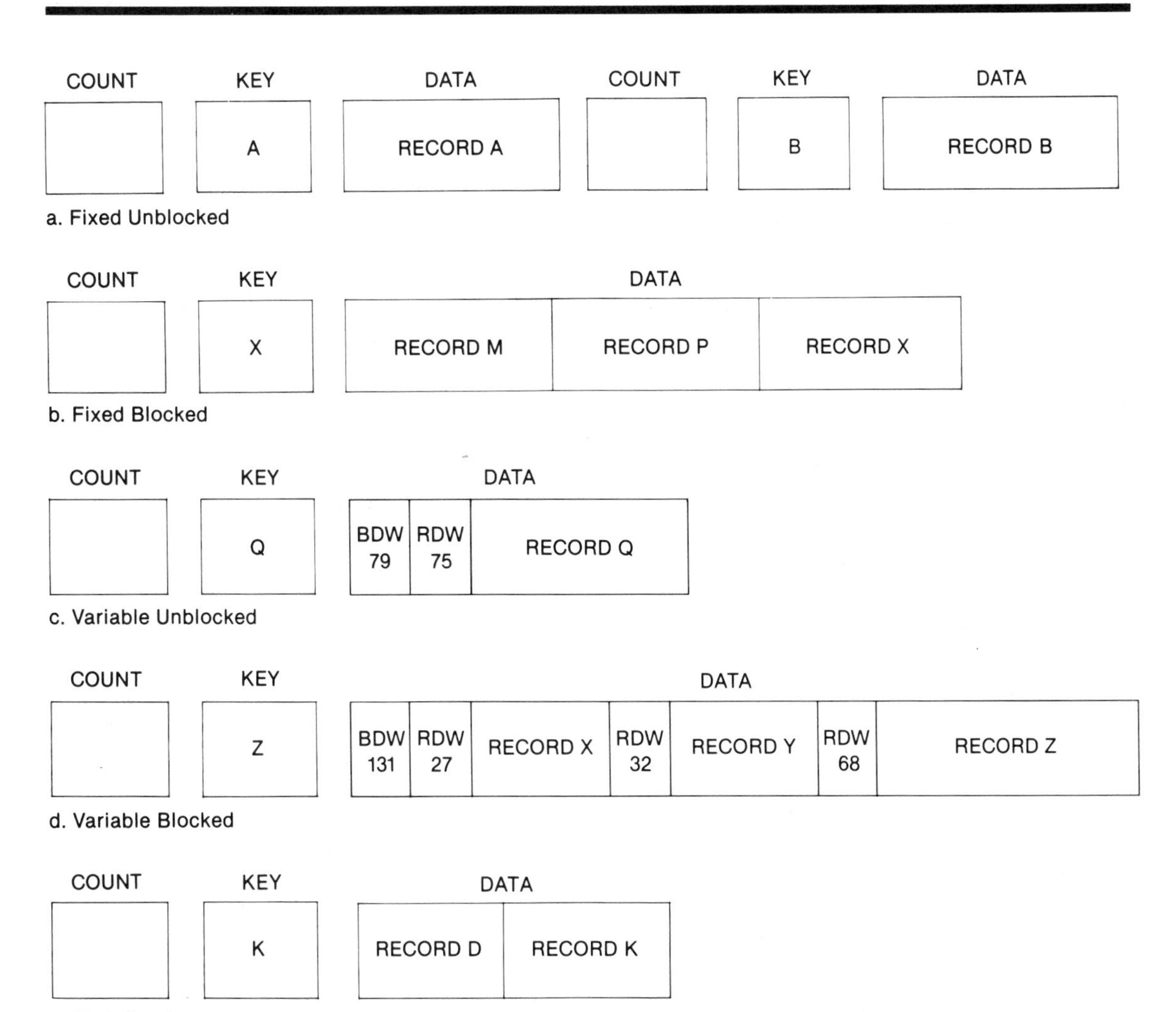

Figure 2.8
Fixed, variable, and undefined record formats.

descriptor word (BDW). The block descriptor word contains the length of all records in the block, as well as the block descriptor word itself. An idiosyncrasy of variable length records is that the block descriptor word is stored with records that are blocked (see Figure 2.8d), as well as with those that are *not* blocked (see Figure 2.8c). In Figure 2.8, Record Q is 71 bytes long, Record X is 23 bytes long, Record Y is 28 bytes long, and Record Z is 64 bytes long. The record descriptor word and the block descriptor word are each 4 bytes long.

Undefined Length Records

Fixed length and variable length records have fixed rules that govern the way they are handled by the access method. In some situations, it is more efficient to include instructions for manipulation of the records in the application program itself. For instance, let's say that Acme Widgets accepts orders for seven different models of widgets. The model number for each widget contains information about its manufacturing process. The manufacturing process for each of the seven models requires a fixed amount of data to describe the components of the model. Each model has a different number of components, so the record lengths for the data to represent each model are different. Once the model number is known, the length of the record is known. In this situation, space would be wasted if a record descriptor word were included with each record. Data in this format is better represented using records with an undefined record length (see Figure 2.8e).

An undefined record length does not mean that the length of the record is unknown; rather, it means that the data is sufficiently unique that the user can handle the length of the records through instructions in the program. It is not desirable to allow the operating system to block or unblock the records. Undefined records are stored, with the length specified in the count area and the key of the highest record or only record in the key area. The application program must handle all further data manipulation.

2.4 FILE ORGANIZATION

The mechanics of storing data on a direct access storage device have been presented in previous sections. The process is usually transparent (that is, only the end result is known; the means may change without affecting the end result) to application programs, so it is not generally given much attention. However, the application program is dependent upon the file organization used to store data. Therefore, the programmer is forced to base development of his or her program upon the **file organization** used. In addition, the file organization used has great impact on the performance of a system.

There are three basic file organizations, each linked to a way in which data is organized in secondary storage: **sequential file organization, indexed sequential file organization**, and **direct file organization**. These three basic organizations are not the only ones available; other organizations have been developed, based on the techniques used in these organizations, with improvements developed to overcome specific deficiencies. Once you understand the three basic organizations, you will have a firm foundation for understanding the functions of other access methods.

Sequential File Organization

Sequential file organization is the first one taught to students of data processing, for it is the easiest to learn.

In sequential organization, each record is stored in sequence by its key field in secondary storage. The record is physically adjacent to the records having the next higher or lower key. All of the records are stored based on physical adjacency.

To maintain a file that is stored using sequential organization, every

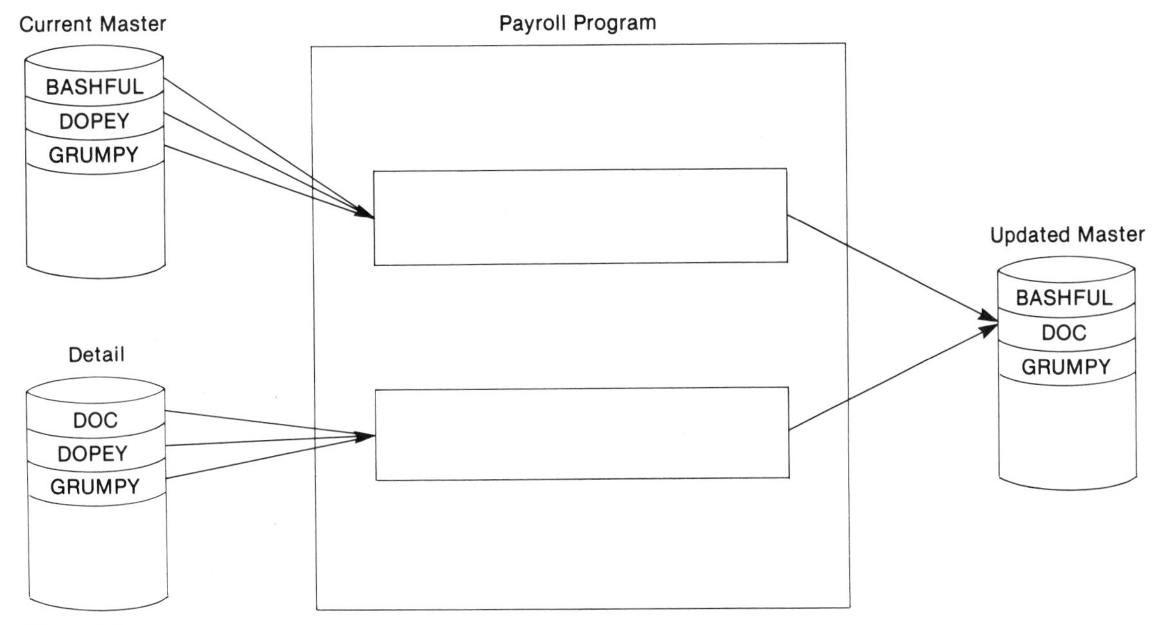

Figure 2.9
Maintenance of a sequential payroll file for the Seven Dwarfs Mining Company.

record in the file must be read and rewritten to a new location. Figure 2.9 shows the maintenance of a file using sequential organization as discussed in Example C1.

Example C1
Sequential Organization of the Seven Dwarfs Mining Co. Payroll File

Let's examine some payroll operations for the Seven Dwarfs Mining Company.

The first record of the payroll file is a record for Bashful. The first record of the detail file is for the addition of a record for Doc. Records of both files are read into storage. Since the record for Bashful will not be processed in this update, it is written directly to the updated master file, and the next record on the current master file, Dopey, is read into storage. Doc's record is lower in sequence than Dopey's, so it is written to the updated master file. The next detail record is read. It indicates that the record for Dopey is to be deleted. The record for Dopey is not written to secondary storage. The next record, Grumpy's, is read from the current master file. Then Grumpy's record is read from the detail file. The detail record is to update Grumpy's pay rate. This field is changed in storage and then is written to the updated master file.

The remainder of the file is processed in this manner. Every record in the file is read, processed, and if not deleted, written to the updated master file. If a record is not updated, it is read from the current master file and written to the updated master unchanged.

Blocking. To understand its impact on performance, you should think about sequential file organization in terms of the work necessary to read each record into storage:

The application program requests the services of the access method. The access method builds the channel program. The channel causes the appropriate device to be selected. The access mechanism seeks to the correct cylinder. The device waits for the appropriate record to pass beneath the read/write head. The count (and key) areas are read. The data is transferred to storage.

The interface between the application program and the access method uses relatively few resources, but the rotational delay to retrieve the next record is significant. If the application program made fewer interfaces with the access method, and if the rotational delay could be reduced, the time required for the program to execute would also be reduced. One technique to reduce both interfaces and rotational delay has already been presented in this chapter—blocking.

When records are blocked, many records can be transferred at once, so both the number of interfaces with the access method and the number of times rotational delay will occur will be reduced.

Anticipatory buffering. **Anticipatory buffering** is another technique that can increase performance when processing sequential files.

As previously stated, processing sequential files is predictable. One of the rules of sequential processing is that every record in the file must be processed. Anticipatory buffering uses this rule to improve performance.

Assume that the Seven Dwarfs Mining Company payroll file is blocked, three records to a block. Without anticipatory buffering, the records for Bashful, Doc, and Dopey would be read into storage when the application program opens the file. After all three of these are processed, the payroll program would request the next block of records (Grumpy, Happy, and Sleepy). The program would then wait until these records were transferred from secondary storage to main storage. The amount of time this program waits can be reduced and possibly eliminated by using anticipatory buffering.

A buffer is a temporary storage area for data. When processing a sequential file, the next event can be anticipated. Thus, the access method can fill an empty buffer with the next data records in sequence. (A buffer becomes empty whenever the data it contains has been processed.)

Let's place the records for Bashful, Doc, and Dopey in the first buffer at the time the file is opened (see Figure 2.10). Using anticipatory buffering, the second block of records can be placed in a second buffer. After the application program processes the records for Bashful, Doc, and Dopey, it can immediately begin processing the records in the second buffer for Grumpy, Happy, and Sleepy. The program does not have to wait for the data to be transferred from secondary storage. While the program is processing these records, the access method can begin its work of filling the buffer that contained the data which was previously processed. The records for Sneezy, White, and Zack can be obtained from secondary storage and placed in the first buffer, while the application program is processing the records in the

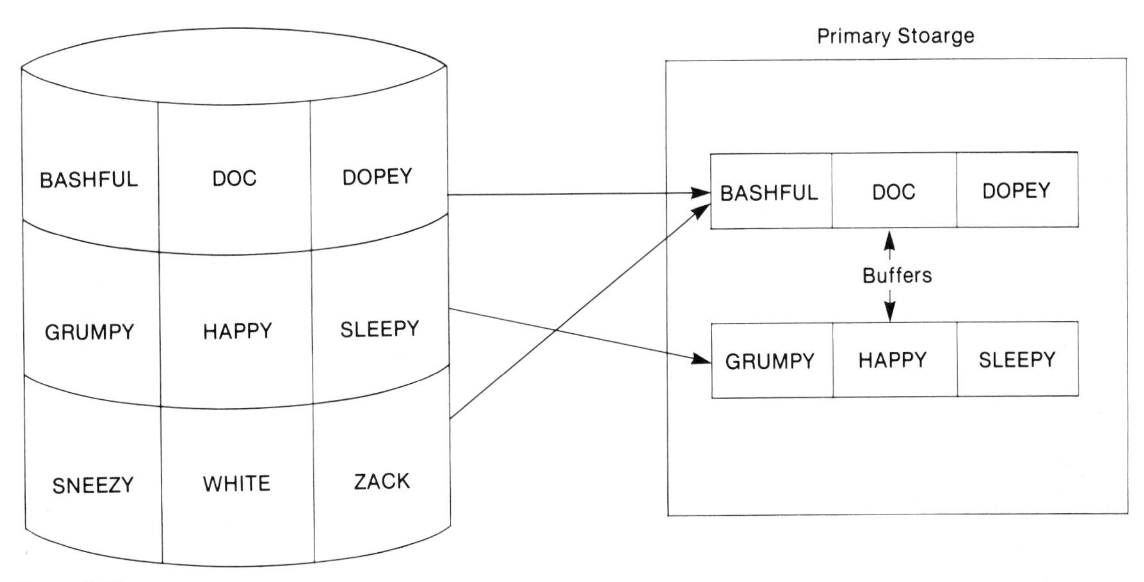

Figure 2.10 Anticipatory buffering at the Seven Dwarfs Mining Co. improves performance with sequential file processing.

second buffer. Since the transfer of data is overlapped with the program execution, the application program spends less time waiting, and the time it takes to execute is reduced.

Summary. Sequential file organization can be the fastest organization for processing data when most of the records in the file are to be maintained during an update run. Blocking records and anticipatory buffering allow maximum throughput using this organization.

However, if only a small number of records in the file are to be updated, much time is wasted reading and writing records not necessary to the update process. If it is necessary to obtain the record for a particular individual or item, the processing is very slow since it is necessary to read all of the records prior to the desired record. For example, if Sneezy's payroll record is the only record to be updated at the Seven Dwarfs Mining Company, the records for Bashful, Doc, Dopey, Grumpy, Happy, and Sleepy must all be read before the record for Sneezy is obtained.

Thus there is a need for a way to retrieve a record without retrieving all of the records that precede it. The method is called *direct* or *random processing*. When this type of processing is required, an alternate file organization is needed.

Indexed Sequential File Organization

Indexed sequential file organization is an attempt to retain the advantages and eliminate the disadvantages of sequential file organization. Example A2 shows how an indexed sequential file organization works.

	Track 1	Track 2	Track 3	Track 4	
Track 0	Track 1 High Record = 7	Track 2 High Record = 34	Track 3 High Record = 64	Track 4 High Record = 175	TRACK INDEX
Track 1	1	5	6	7	PRIME AREA
Track 2	17	28	32	34	
Track 3	45	51	63	64	
Track 4	75	90	97	175	
Track 5					OVERFLOW AREA

Figure 2.11
Indexed sequential file organization: A parts inventory at Acme Widgets.

Example A2
Indexed Sequential File Organization of a Parts Inventory File at Acme Widgets

Figure 2.11 contains one cylinder of data for a parts inventory file at Acme Widgets. For clarity, only the key field of each record is shown. At first glance, this is very similar to a sequentially organized file, but the difference exists on the very first track (Track 0).

The first track of each cylinder is where the track index is maintained. The index maintains the key of the highest record on each track. The index functions just like the index in the back of this book. To find the first page in this book where blocking is presented, look up "blocking" in the index. To find the record with a key of 97, the track index is read, looking for the first track in which the key of the highest record on a track is greater than or equal to 97. The key of the highest record on Track 4 is 175. If Record 97 exists in this file, it must be on Track 4. Track 4 is then searched by key to find the record for 97.

The track index thus eliminates one of the disadvantages that existed with sequential files, because it enables us to retrieve records randomly. Of course, records in a file stored using the indexed sequential organization can also be accessed sequentially, following the records in their physical sequence. Indexed sequential organization is the only one of the three basic file organizations that allows access both sequentially and directly.

Cylinder index and master index. In Example A2, we only dealt with the track index. However, if the file were very large, a great deal of time would be necessary to read the track index on every cylinder to find the desired record. For that reason, a higher-level index called a *cylinder index* exists. The cylinder index contains one entry for the highest key on each cylinder. Once this is known, the track index can be searched to find the correct track.

If the file is even larger, the time to search the cylinder index could also become excessive. For files of this magnitude, an even higher-level index called a *master index* is created. The master index resides in primary storage and is searched first. It points to the correct area of the cylinder index to search. Then, the search proceeds as previously described.

Updating and deletion. Updating an indexed sequential file reduces execution time in certain circumstances. To update a record that exists on the file, the record is retrieved randomly (as previously described), the desired updates are applied, and the record is written back to secondary storage in the same position from which it was retrieved.

The deletion of records from an indexed sequential file is almost as simple. A special field in the record is reserved as a flag byte. This byte indicates that the record has been deleted. To delete a record, it is first retrieved from secondary storage. Then, the flag byte is updated by the application program, and the record is written back to secondary storage in the same location from which it was retrieved.

A logical question is, why must the record be written to secondary storage if it is being deleted? To answer this question, remember that the record physically exists in secondary storage when it is retrieved, and it continues to exist in secondary storage unless some action is taken. However, the access method considers the record to be deleted. Therefore, if in the future a request is made for a record with that key, the access method indicates that the record does not exist. This process is preferable to the alternative of physically deleting the record, which would require rearranging all of the records in secondary storage that follow the deleted record.

Adding. The update and deletion of records in an indexed sequential file are relatively straightforward. The addition of records is somewhat more complex.

When a file is stored using the indexed sequential organization, secondary storage is divided into a prime area and an overflow area. Records are maintained in sequence by physical adjacency in the prime area. All records are placed in the prime area when the file is created. The *overflow area* is used to store records that do not fit on a track when records are added. In Figure 2.11, Tracks 1 through 4 are reserved for the prime area, and Track 5 is reserved for the overflow area. Example A3 illustrates addition of a record in an indexed sequential file.

Example A3 Adding a Record in the Indexed Sequential File Organization at Acme Widgets

To add Record 33 to the Acme Widgets parts inventory file (Figure 2.11), the correct physical location of the record is first determined. For this file, Record 33 must be placed after Record 32 and before Record 34, and so Record 33 is written in the location where Record 34 was previously stored. Now, Record 34 will no longer fit on Track 2. Therefore, Record 34 is written to the first available location in the overflow area.

Figure 2.12 shows some additional information in the track index. A

	Track 1 High Record = 7	Track 2 High Record = 33	Track 3 High Record = 64	Track 4 High Record = 175
Track 0	Overflow High = 0 Next = 0	Overflow High = 34 Next = 34	Overflow High = 0 Next = 0	Overflow High = 0 Next = 0
Track 1	1	5	6	7
Track 2	17	28	32	33
Track 3	45	51	63	64
Track 4	75	90	97	175
Track 5	34			

Figure 2.12 Addition of one record to an indexed sequential parts inventory file at Acme Widgets.

track index contains two different types of information: the key of the highest record that *physically* exists on the track, and the key of the highest record in overflow for that track (the key of the highest record that *logically* exists on the track). In Figure 2.12, after the addition of Record 33, the highest record that physically exists on the track is Record 33. The track index has been updated to reflect this. Record 34 is the first record in the overflow area for this track. The overflow entry has been changed to indicate this. The overflow record also contains a pointer showing the location of the next logical entry on Track 2, which is Record 34.

Any future additions to the file will follow the same procedure. If Record 29 is added to the file, it falls in sequence between Record 28 and Record 32. Record 29 is added in the prime area in the physical location where Record 32 was previously stored (see Figure 2.13). Record 32 is moved to the next position. Now, Record 33 will no longer fit on Track 2, and it is placed in the overflow area. The track index is updated to show the movements of the records. Note that Record 34 is the highest record in overflow. The overflow pointer does not point to Record 34, but to Record 33 instead. Records in the prime area are maintained in physical sequence, just as they were when the file was stored using sequential organization. Records in the overflow area are maintained in logical sequence, using pointers.

All tracks on one cylinder share the same cylinder overflow area, so the records in the overflow might not be stored in physically adjacent positions as in Example A3. The amount of space reserved for overflow must be the same for each cylinder. To determine the space required, the designer must know the maximum number of records that will be added within one cylinder between reorganizations. If an unusually large number of additions occur on one cylinder, a separate overflow area called **independent overflow** may be established to hold records that do not fit in the prime area. This reduces the amount of space reserved for overflow on each cylinder, but a seek is required to store the overflow record, and so processing time is increased. One indexed sequential file may use both a cylinder overflow area and an independent overflow area.

	Track 1 High Record = 7	Track 2 High Record = 32	Track 3 High Record = 64	Track 4 High Record = 175
Track 0	Overflow High = 0 Next = 0	Overflow High = 34 Next = 33	Overflow High = 0 Next = 0	Overflow High = 0 Next = 0
Track 1	1	5	6	7
Track 2	17	28	29	32
Track 3	45	51	63	64
Track 4	75	90	97	175
Track 5	34	33		

Figure 2.13 Addition of subsequent records to an indexed sequential parts inventory file at Acme Widgets.

Let us summarize what we now know about indexed sequential file organization. Indexed sequential file organization solves some of the maintenance problems of sequential file organization. Records are randomly retrieved, updated in place, and easily deleted using the indexed sequential organization. When records are added to an indexed sequential file, ones that do not fit in the prime area are placed in overflow and chained together logically. When a record stored in the overflow area is retrieved, the chain of pointers from the track index through the overflow area is followed to obtain the desired record. If it were necessary to randomly retrieve Record 34 (Figure 2.13), the track index would be searched. Record 34 logically exists on Track 2, but it is stored in the overflow area. The first record in the overflow area for Track 2 is Record 33. Record 33 contains a pointer to Record 34. Record 34 is then retrieved and processed. However, depending upon the location of the record in overflow, this process will cause a certain amount of additional rotational delay, and if an independent overflow area is used, additional seeks will be required. Both of these are undesirable.

Reorganization. The performance of an indexed sequential file organization can be improved through a process called **reorganization**. When performance degrades using indexed sequential organization, it is due to the chasing of chains of records through the overflow area. This chasing can be eliminated temporarily by creating a new file and sequentially reading all of the records that exist logically and copying them to the prime area. Deleted records are read from the old file but are not written to the new file. This process creates a new file with all records in the prime area.

Figure 2.14 shows Figure 2.13 after reorganization. Records 1 through 32 have been retrieved in sequence from the existing file and written in sequence on the first two tracks in a new area. Record 33 has been retrieved from the overflow area in the existing file and written in sequence on Track 3 in the new area; likewise for Record 34. Records originally on Track 3 in

	Track 1 High Record = 7	Track 2 High Record = 32	Track 3 High Record = 51	Track 4 High Record = 90
Track 0	Overflow High = 0 Next = 0	Overflow High = 0 Next = 0	Overflow High = 0 Next = 0	Overflow High = 0 Next = 0
Track 1	1	5	6	7
Track 2	17	28	29	32
Track 3	33	34	45	51
Track 4	63	64	75	90
Track 5				

Figure 2.14 Reorganization of an indexed sequential parts inventory file at Acme Widgets.

the existing file have been written following Record 34. The process would continue until the prime area for the first cylinder is filled. Records 97 and 175 would be placed on the first track of the next cylinder, and so on.

Direct File Organization

Indexed sequential organization provides a technique to randomly access records without reading all of the records that precede the desired record. This permits faster access to selected records than can be obtained using sequential file organization. However, the effort required to obtain a record randomly could be great if long overflow chains were followed. There are some applications in data processing that cannot tolerate the wait time to obtain a record that occurs when using indexed sequential processing. These applications need a faster method to obtain records randomly. Direct file organization is geared to these applications.

The objective of direct file organization is to obtain the desired record on the first access of secondary storage. To accomplish this, an address for the record is established, based on the record's key. A number of methods are available to do this. The two common ones are presented in this section: **direct addressing** and **indirect addressing** (or *hashing*).

Direct addressing. Directly addressed files, for which every record key can be converted to an address on disk, allow the retrieval of a record with one I/O operation. Directly addressed files are maintained using two different methods.

The first method is based upon the characteristics of the key field and the record. The key field must be numeric and the record format must be fixed length. Using space calculations similar to the ones in the track capacity table in Figure 2.7, the number of records that can be stored on each track can be determined. The number of records per track is then divided into the key of the record. The quotient determines the track on which the record will be stored, and the remainder plus one (remember, user data is not stored in Record 0) determines the record number on the track where the record will be stored. Each record key is mapped onto a unique location

Figure 2.15 Mapping of a record key onto disk using direct addressing.

```
                11   ← Relative track number
Records     27|300   ← Record key
per track      297
               3 + 1 = 4   ← Relative record
                             number
```

on disk. In Figure 2.15, the number of records stored on a track is 27. The key of the record to be stored is 300. The quotient is 11, the relative track on which the record is stored. The remainder is 3; plus 1 gives 4, the relative record number on the track where the record is placed.

This procedure has two benefits. First, the processing and the number of I/O operations needed to obtain the data will be minimal. Second, since record location is dependent upon a unique numeric key, the records will be stored in sequence; this is extremely unusual for a file stored using the direct organization. On the other side of the coin, this method works only with numeric keys, and space must be reserved on disk to hold every key that could possibly exist. Thus, this is another example of compromise in data processing: Very fast access time is achieved in exchange for wasted space.

The second direct addressing method is a cross-reference list, where each record is stored at the next available location on disk. The address of the location is made known to the user, who keeps track of the location in which each record is stored. When the user desires a record, he or she determines its location and uses the location as a key to retrieve the data. Keys containing alphabetic and numeric fields can be used with this method.

Figure 2.16 illustrates a cross-reference list and also points out a drawback of the procedure—it is not always user-friendly. In Figure 2.16, record 300 is added to the file in the next available location, Location 7. This address is provided to the user. Whenever the user updates record 300, he or she accesses the record by specifying the location in which the record is stored, not by specifying the key of the record. This is a worst-case example of the cross-reference list: Instead of the data processing system being tailored to the user, the user must learn the data processing system. This method of using a cross-reference list permits high storage densities, but it is not user-friendly.

The cross-reference list can also be implemented with the cross-reference stored on disk. To retrieve a specific record, the cross-reference list is searched to find the entry which contains the location of the record. Then, the record is retrieved. This method is user-friendly but has performance problems similar to those of indexed sequential file organization.

Indirect addressing. Methods more commonly used to access data from secondary storage involve the conversion of the key field to an address on a secondary storage device. Since these methods, as a group, are characterized by manipulation of the key to obtain an address, they are called indirect

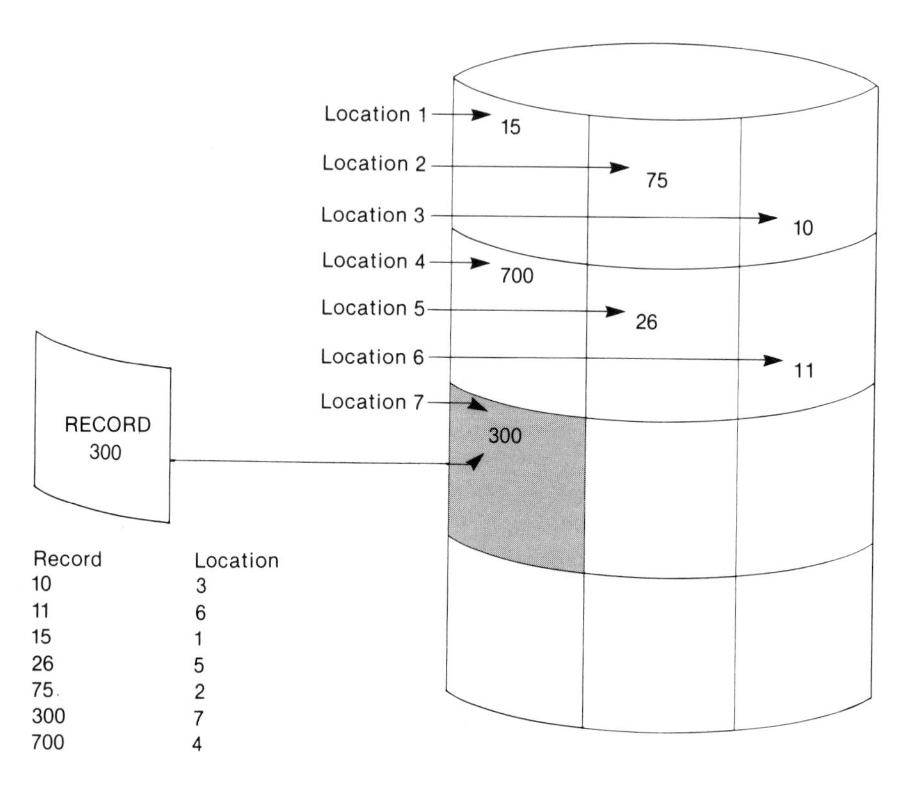

Figure 2.16
Direct addressing using a cross-reference list.

addressing methods. The manipulation is performed by an address conversion algorithm.

It is easy to be overwhelmed by the number of methods that may be used for indirect addressing. Keep the objective of direct file organization in mind: Each method is simply a means of storing or finding a record in secondary storage with the minimum number of I/O operations.

Using indirect addressing, the key can be of any length and can contain alphabetic or numeric characters. Since the number of combinations of characters used for a key field, such as an individual's name, are infinite, and the number of secondary storage locations in which the data can be stored are finite, sometimes address conversion routines will provide the same secondary storage address for two different key fields. When this occurs, the record first stored at the location is called a *prime record* or *home record.* The second and all subsequent records with the same target address are called **synonyms.** The goal of a good address conversion algorithm is to develop no more than 20 percent synonyms.

In Figure 2.17, the address conversion algorithm specifies that Record 13 is to be stored in Location 7. Record 12 is currently stored at that location. Record 13 is a synonym and must be stored at a different location. Location 8 is vacant, so Record 13 is stored there. A pointer is placed in Record 12 to indicate the location where the synonym is stored. When Record 13 is

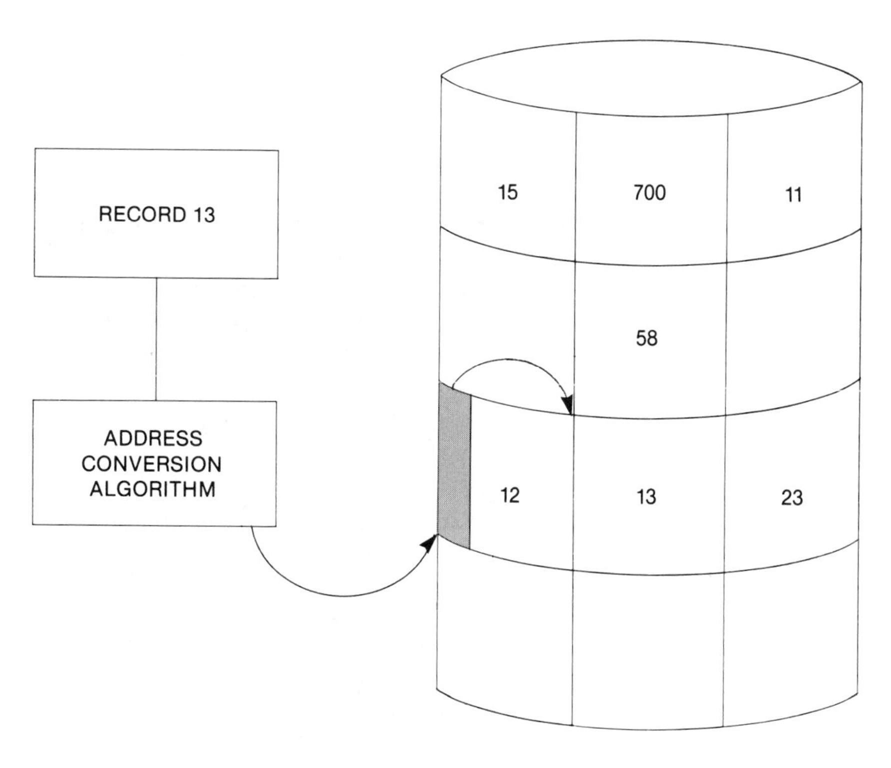

Figure 2.17
Storage and retrieval of synonyms.

retrieved, the address conversion algorithm converts the key of the record to Location 7. The record at Location 7 is then retrieved. Since Location 7 contains Record 12, the pointer in this record is followed to Location 8. The record at Location 8 is retrieved and processed.

Figure 2.17 shows only one synonym. However, synonym chains can extend through several storage locations. If the record stored in Location 8 was not the desired record, it would contain a pointer to the next synonym in the chain. This chain would be followed until the desired record is found. As can be seen in this illustration, synonyms are undesirable because of the additional I/O operations required to obtain the desired record.

When using indexed sequential file organization, you will recall, space (the overflow area) is reserved for records to be added to the file at a later date. Using direct organization, space is reserved *over and above* the amount needed to store the data. The additional space is used to minimize the number of synonyms that will be generated. **Packing density** is a percentage—the amount of space necessary to store the data, as a percent of the total amount of space allocated for the data. The rule-of-thumb packing density to minimize synonyms is 80 percent.

There are several methods of address conversion. The objective of each method is to take the key field of the file and manipulate it to store and retrieve a record with as few I/O operations as possible. Since synonyms will exist, the practical target is an average of 1.2 I/O operations per record.

The performance of an address conversion technique is related to the specific characteristics of a given file's key. Thus, the process of determining the best technique should be repeated for every file. The most common address conversion techniques are the *division/remainder* method, *folding*, and *radix transformation*.

Division/remainder. The division/remainder method is simple, and it usually provides good results.

First, using the record length, a track capacity table (Figure 2.7), and the packing density, the number of storage slots in the file can be determined. A prime number (a number divisible only by itself and one) close to but less than the number of storage locations is selected and divided into the key field of the record. The remainder will be a number between zero and the prime number. The remainder is divided by the number of records per track. The quotient from this second division represents the track on which the record is stored. The new remainder, plus 1, is the relative record number.

Figure 2.18 shows the division/remainder technique for indirect addressing to develop a relative track and record address. By researching the data, it is determined that 20 locations are needed to store the data (only 7 of those locations are filled in this illustration). To achieve an 80 percent packing density, space is allocated to hold 25 records; Record 0 is not used. The number 23 is a prime number close to 25. Dividing the key by this number forces the remainder to be a number between 0 and 22.

Figure 2.18a shows the calculations to determine the address at which a record is stored. For instance, the key of 350 is divided by 23, producing a quotient of 15 and a remainder of 5. The remainder 5 is divided by the number of records per track (5). This provides a quotient of 1 and a remainder of 0. The quotient (1) specifies the track address. The remainder (0) plus 1 specifies the relative record number.

Figure 2.18b shows the location where the records are stored. Note that Record 126 hashes to the same location as Record 2058. Record 126 is a synonym and is stored as close as possible to its home address. Record 403 hashes to the same location where Record 126 is stored. From this you can see that it is possible for records which are synonyms to cause other synonyms to be generated.

Folding. Using the folding method, the key is divided and the digits rearranged. The storage address is obtained by summing the groups of rearranged digits.

In Figure 2.19, two different arrangements of the key are used. In the first arrangement, the key is divided in half. The first four digits are added to the second four digits. The sum of these two numbers is 6099. This is used as the relative address to store the record. In the second arrangement, alternate digits are grouped to form two numbers, 1346 and 2782. These

Figure 2.18
Storage of records using the division/remainder technique.

Record Key	Division of the Key by a Prime Number	Division of the Remainder by the Number of Records on a Track	Relative Track Address	Relative Record Number
115	5 R=0 23⟌115	0 R=0 5⟌0	TRACK=0	RECORD=1
350	15 R=5 23⟌350	1 R=0 5⟌5	TRACK=1	RECORD=1
4621	200 R=21 23⟌4621	4 R=1 5⟌21	TRACK=4	RECORD=2
2058	89 R=11 23⟌2058	2 R=1 5⟌11	TRACK=2	RECORD=2
42	1 R=19 23⟌42	3 R=4 5⟌19	TRACK=3	RECORD=5
126	5 R=11 23⟌126	2 R=1 5⟌11	TRACK=2	RECORD=2
403	17 R=12 23⟌403	2 R=2 5⟌12	TRACK=2	RECORD=3

a. Division/remainder address calculations.

	Record 0	*Record 1*	*Record 2*	*Record 3*	*Record 4*	*Record 5*
Track 0		115				
Track 1		350				
Track 2			2058	126	403	
Track 3						42
Track 4			4621			

b. Records in secondary storage.

Record key = 12374862

Record key divided in half

1237
4862
6099

Sum of alternate digits

1346
2782
4128

Figure 2.19
Folding of the key to obtain a relative address on disk.

two numbers are added. The result, 4128, is used as the relative address to store the record.

The method by which the digits are grouped and summed is determined by the designer, who must analyze several methods and decide which one generates the smallest number of synonyms for a particular file.

Radix transformation. Using the radix transformation method, the key field is represented as a number in a numbering system with a different base. The key is then transformed to the numbering system. The appropriate number of digits are selected as the relative address for the record to be stored. In Figure 2.20, the record key of 978123 is transformed to a number of base 11. The resultant number, 1562740, contains more digits than are required. Excess digits to the left are dropped. In this example, only four

Figure 2.20
Radix transformation to obtain a relative address.

Record key = 978123

$$
\begin{aligned}
& (9 \times 11^5) + (7 \times 11^4) + (8 \times 11^3) + (1 \times 11^2) + (2 \times 11^1) + (3 \times 11^0) \\
&= (9 \times 161{,}051) + (7 \times 14{,}641) + (8 \times 1{,}331) + (1 \times 121) + (2 \times 11) + (3 \times 1) \\
&= 1{,}449{,}459 + 102{,}487 + 10{,}648 + 121 + 22 + 3 \\
&= 1{,}562{,}740
\end{aligned}
$$

~~156~~2740 = 2740

digits are needed to develop a relative record address, so 2740 is used as the relative storage address.

2.5 SUMMARY

Performance is one of the most important criteria applied to data base management systems. The methods used to store and retrieve data on secondary storage have a significant impact on performance. Three basic file organizations are used to store data: sequential, indexed sequential, and direct.

Sequential organization provides high performance when all records (or most records) in the file are accessed. Large blocking factors and anticipatory buffering can improve performance. Sequential organization also requires less space on secondary storage to store data—only space for the records in the file need be reserved. Negatively, records can only be processed sequentially (they cannot be retrieved randomly). To add, change, or delete a record requires rewriting the entire file.

Indexed sequential organization provides high performance when random access to individual records in a file is needed *and* there is a requirement to process the file sequentially. If the file is accessed most often in a sequential manner, large blocking factors and anticipatory buffering can be used to improve performance. Due to the indexes used and the overflow areas, performance will not be as fast as in sequential organization. If the file is accessed randomly most often, small blocking factors are used. Anticipatory buffering is not used for random processing, since the next record to be obtained cannot be determined. The indexed sequential organization is the only one of the basic three that may be accessed randomly or sequentially. Records can be added, changed, and deleted without rewriting the entire file. Negatively, indexed sequential organization uses an overflow area for additions to the file. If the number of additions is large, chaining through records in the overflow area can be time consuming. Then, a reorganization of the file is necessary to restore performance. Use of the overflow area causes space to be allocated that is not used, and this wastes space on secondary storage.

Direct organization provides high performance when a single record is written to or retrieved from secondary storage. This organization is the fastest for random retrieval of data. Negatively, data cannot be retrieved sequentially—it must be sorted to present it in sequence. Synonyms can degrade performance. If performance is severely degraded, a reorganization of the file is necessary. The rule-of-thumb for a packing density is 80 percent. Records cannot be blocked unless the application program handles the blocking and deblocking of records.

Each of the three basic organizations can give maximum performance under specific conditions. A file organization that performs best under *all* conditions does not exist. The designer must have an intimate knowledge of the data to be used in a given application, including how often it will be accessed, in what sequence, and the importance of each sequence. At that point, the designer will select the file organization that provides the greatest number of benefits and the minimum number of disadvantages.

REVIEW QUESTIONS

2.1 Define the terms *track, cylinder,* and *volume.*

2.2 Explain each of the following terms: (a) seek time; (b) head switching; (c) rotational delay; (d) data transfer rate.

2.3 List three different record formats and specify the advantages and disadvantages of each.

2.4 Explain how the blocking of records affects performance. Explain when blocking is advantageous and when it will slow performance.

2.5 Explain the major characteristics of sequential, indexed sequential, and direct file organizations.

2.6 Explain how direct and sequential access of files each functions and when each is appropriate.

2.7 Explain the compromises between cost and performance that occur when storing and retrieving data.

2.8 When using the direct file organization, what is the difference between direct and indirect addressing?

2.9 What conditions necessitate the reorganization of an indexed sequential file to improve performance?

2.10 Why is it desirable to keep synonyms at a minimum when using direct file organization?

2.11 Is the reorganization of a direct file beneficial? Why?

2.12 If a file contains 7500 records and the desired packing density is 75 percent, what is the number of records for which the file must be allocated?

2.13 A decision has been made to use the indexed sequential file organization for a payroll system. What conditions must exist for this to be a good file organization for this application?

2.14 Which file organization requires the least space to store a file in secondary storage? Why?

3

APPLIED DATA STRUCTURES

CHAPTER OBJECTIVES

Upon completion of this chapter, you should be able to:

1. List two different functions that can be accomplished using linked lists
2. List three advantages of storing data using logical structures rather than physical structures
3. Explain the disadvantage of using multiple links for a file
4. Explain and schematically draw data structures represented as tree structures
5. Schematically represent the addition and deletion of records from a tree structure
6. Explain and schematically draw data structures represented as networks

NEW WORDS AND PHRASES

linked lists
ring structures
inverted files
binary search
tree structure
root
preorder traversal
hierarchical pointer
child pointer
twin
twin pointer
network
loop
cycle

3.1 CHAPTER INTRODUCTION

To truly appreciate the facilities made available by a data base management system, one must understand the type of processing that occurs when conventional file access methods are used.

Human beings have a tendency to order their environment. This desire for order has extended to the fundamental rules for the processing of data.

Traditionally, to obtain order, data has been placed in a *physical* sequence based on a sequence field or key such as social security number. For example, two of the three most frequently used conventional access methods—sequential and indexed sequential—depend upon the data appearing in a physical sequence. But today, to satisfy society's information needs, the end user is more interested in the *logical* sequence of the data. The end user does not usually care about the manipulation required to provide the data in that sequence, but as a student of data processing, you must. In this chapter, we will explore the differences in processing that occur when using logically ordered data rather than physically ordered data. The performance of each technique will be examined, and additional techniques to improve performance will be presented. Two new storage strategies—tree structures and networks—will be presented. Even though manual methods are used in our discussions, the conclusions we will reach apply to both manual and automated procedures.

Keep in mind that in the following figures, you will see the entire file used in the example at a glance, but if this were in fact an automated system, the computer would only be able to "see" one item or record at a time. To gain a better understanding of the automated process, you might use two sheets of paper to cover all records except the current one in each example. As the example presents each record, move the paper down to expose that record.

3.2 PHYSICALLY ORDERED LISTS

Maintenance of data using physically ordered lists is the most straightforward method. In physically ordered lists, each record is stored physically adjacent to the record with the next higher key field. Physically ordered lists have their place in data processing; you should understand when to use them and when other techniques should be used.

Figure 3.1 presents a list of several presidents. This data is in a random sequence. Let us say that in a history class, the students must refer to the presidents in sequence by the time period they held office. The results of this change in sequence are shown in Figure 3.2.

To change the order of the list, it was necessary to rewrite it from beginning to end. This is not a large effort for six records, but if there were 500 or 1000 or 100,000 records, a much larger effort would be required.

If the data collected on a particular president (assume Herbert Hoover) was not necessary and that individual was to be deleted, the list would have to be rewritten, as in Figure 3.3. To add an individual to a physically ordered list, the order or position of the record to be added must first be determined. Then, the list will be rewritten with the added record in the proper physical sequence. If Theodore Roosevelt is the president to be added, he will be fourth in the list (see Figure 3.4).

Abraham Lincoln
Dwight Eisenhower
Herbert Hoover
George Washington
William Howard Taft
John Kennedy

Figure 3.1
List of presidents in random order.

Since physically ordered lists depend upon each record being physically adjacent to the record with the next higher key, any addition or deletion from a file necessitates rewriting the entire file, even if only one record is changed. If the sequence field is changed, the record must be deleted from its original position and added to a new position. If a single woman, Mary Smith, was elected president, and she married John Jones after entering office, and she decided to change her name to Mary Smith-Jones, the record for Mary Smith would be deleted from the file and a record for Mary Smith-Jones would be added.

Figure 3.2
List of presidents arranged in order of year inaugurated.

George Washington
Abraham Lincoln
William Howard Taft
Herbert Hoover
Dwight Eisenhower
John Kennedy

Figure 3.3
List of presidents arranged in order of year inaugurated, with Herbert Hoover deleted.

George Washington
Abraham Lincoln
William Howard Taft
Dwight Eisenhower
John Kennedy

Figure 3.4
List of presidents arranged in order of year inaugurated, with Theodore Roosevelt added.

George Washington
Abraham Lincoln
William Howard Taft
Theodore Roosevelt
Dwight Eisenhower
John Kennedy

3.3 LINKED LISTS

Use of Pointers

In each of the preceding examples of physically ordered lists, even minor manipulation of data required many records to be processed. **Linked lists** significantly reduce the effort required to change the order of the lists.

Linked lists use pointers, or links, to maintain the logical sequence of records, instead of physically rearranging an entire file. In this section each of our previous operations on the presidents lists will be repeated using presidents lists chained together by numbers.

We will begin by taking our random order list and putting it in sequence by inauguration year. In Figure 3.5, the random order list in Figure

Figure 3.5
List of presidents using a linked list. This is a reproduction of Figure 3.1.

FIRST = . . . Abraham Lincoln
Dwight Eisenhower
Herbert Hoover
George Washington
William Howard Taft
John Kennedy

FIRST = 4	Abraham Lincoln
	Dwight Eisenhower
	Herbert Hoover
	George Washington
	William Howard Taft
	John Kennedy

Figure 3.6
List of presidents using a linked list. The label FIRST contains the number of the record (4) that is logically first in the list.

3.1 has been reproduced and an entry called FIRST has been added. The tag FIRST will tell the viewer the position of the beginning of the list. Thus, in Figure 3.6, the tag FIRST followed by the number 4 shows that the first president to take office was the fourth person in the list, George Washington. The number 4 is the pointer to indicate the logical beginning of the list. In Figure 3.7, the number 1 has been added before George Washington, showing the ordinal position in the list of the next president to take office, Abraham Lincoln. In Figure 3.8, the number 5 precedes Abraham Lincoln, indicating that William Howard Taft, the fifth person in the physical list, is the next president in sequence.

This process continues until each record has a pointer in front of it, pointing to the next president in the list (see Figure 3.9). The record for John Kennedy is preceded by a 0. This identifies the last record in the list. By following the pointers, the presidents can be viewed in order of their terms in office.

When storing data on secondary storage media, the data can only be placed in one physical sequence. In Figure 3.9, the *physical* sequence has not changed from the original sequence presented in Figure 3.1. However,

FIRST = 4		Abraham Lincoln
		Dwight Eisenhower
		Herbert Hoover
	1	George Washington
		William Howard Taft
		John Kennedy

Figure 3.7
List of presidents using a linked list. The number 1 preceding Washington identifies Lincoln as the next president in the list.

FIRST = 4	5	Abraham Lincoln
		Dwight Eisenhower
		Herbert Hoover
	1	George Washington
		William Howard Taft
		John Kennedy

Figure 3.8
List of presidents using a linked list. The number 5 preceding Lincoln identifies Taft as the next president in the list.

Figure 3.9
List of presidents using a linked list. This is the final linked list, with all pointers updated.

FIRST = 4		
	5	Abraham Lincoln
	6	Dwight Eisenhower
	2	Herbert Hoover
	1	George Washington
	3	William Howard Taft
	0	John Kennedy

the *logical* sequence—that is, the sequence in which the data is viewed—is the same as in Figure 3.2.

Deletion of Records

When using linked lists to delete a record, the pointer to the record to be deleted is altered so that it does not point to the deleted record. In Figure 3.9, William Howard Taft contains a pointer to the record for Herbert Hoover, and Hoover contains a pointer to the record for Dwight Eisenhower. To remove the record for Hoover from the linked list, the pointer from Taft is altered to point to Eisenhower (see Figure 3.10). The record for Hoover still physically exists in the list, but it has been logically deleted: Since records are accessed by following links, and since none of the links point to Hoover, his record will never be accessed and therefore does not logically exist. Thus, deletion of a record has been accomplished through maintenance of pointers, without rewriting the entire physical list.

After the record for Hoover is deleted, the space where this data was stored can be reused the next time it is necessary to add a record to the file.

It is also possible to use more than one set of links for a physical list. Figure 3.11, which will be discussed thoroughly next in relation to free space maintenance, shows the use of multiple links for one physical list. The second link is the free space pointer.

Free Space Maintenance

In Figure 3.11, the list has been extended with additional records that are identified as FREE. Such records can be created in two ways. First, when the file is created, space may be reserved for future growth. (Using linked lists, it is not necessary to rewrite the entire file when a record is added; therefore, it is necessary to plan for future growth and reserve space for it when the file is created.) Second, records may occupy these positions at some

Figure 3.10
List of presidents using a linked list. The record for Herbert Hoover has been logically deleted by rearranging the pointers.

FIRST = 4		
	5	Abraham Lincoln
	6	Dwight Eisenhower
	2	Herbert Hoover
	1	George Washington
	2	William Howard Taft
	0	John Kennedy

Figure 3.11
List of presidents using a multiple linked list containing a free space pointer in addition to the pointer used for logical ordering.

prior time during the life of the file; during file maintenance, these records are deleted, allowing this space to be reused.

Let us now see how this space can be reused. In Figure 3.11, a new link has been added to keep track of any free areas, or free space, in the list. The first available free space is the third record in the list, where Herbert Hoover was logically deleted by removing all pointers to that record. By changing the free space pointer to point to this record, this area can be reused when a new record is added to the list. The third record points to the next available free space, located at the seventh slot in the file. The seventh record points to the next available free space at the eighth slot in the file, and so on. Note that the ninth position is the last available free space in the file and therefore contains a 0, just as was done with the earlier linked list to indicate the end of the list.

At this point, two different but interrelated logical lists exist. If presidents are deleted from the list, the number of records linked together by year of inauguration will decrease and the number of records in the FREE list will increase. As we shall see in the next example, this process is reversed when records are added to the list of presidents.

Addition of Records

The addition of records to the list is almost as simple as the deletion of a record. In Figure 3.12, Theodore Roosevelt has been added to the list. To accomplish this, the free space pointer was examined to find the first available area that could be used. The free space pointer pointed to the third record (the record for Herbert Hoover, which was deleted). Since this was the first available free space in the file, the record for Theodore Roosevelt was placed in the third position in the list. The list then contained six active records. The free space pointer had to be updated to point to the seventh record, since this was the next record to be used to store an additional record. Back in Figure 3.4, Theodore Roosevelt was placed in sequence between Taft and Eisenhower. To maintain this relationship in Figure 3.12, the entry for Taft has been updated to point to the third record. The pointer for Theodore Roosevelt points to the next president, record number two.

Figure 3.12
List of presidents using a linked list. The record for Theodore Roosevelt has been added and the free space pointers updated.

FIRST = 4
FREE = 7

5	Abraham Lincoln
6	Dwight Eisenhower
2	Theodore Roosevelt
1	George Washington
3	William Howard Taft
0	John Kennedy
8	Free
9	Free
0	Free

Ring Structures

Addition or deletion of a record in a linked list requires less effort than the same operations with a physically ordered list. With the techniques that have been demonstrated thus far, in order to find any given record in the list, it is necessary to start at the FIRST pointer and follow all of the pointers until the desired record is found. Another technique is available that allows the list to be searched forward until the desired record is found. This technique is called a *circular linked list,* or a **ring structure**.

The ring structure derives its name from the structure of the list. If the pointers are followed from the beginning, the records in the list will be presented in a circle, or ring. The only modification required is to change the pointer of the last logical record from a 0 to the same number that is in the tag FIRST entry. In Figure 3.13, a circular linked list permits a forward search for the desired record regardless of the current position in the list. If the current position was at Abraham Lincoln, and the desired record was John Kennedy, the pointer would be followed from Lincoln to William Howard Taft, from Taft to Theodore Roosevelt, from Roosevelt to Dwight Eisenhower, and from Eisenhower to John Kennedy.

Figure 3.13
List of presidents using a linked list. A circular linked list has been created by modifying the pointer of the last logical record in the list to point to the first record in the list.

FIRST = 4
FREE = 7

5	Abraham Lincoln
6	Dwight Eisenhower
2	Theodore Roosevelt
1	George Washington
3	William Howard Taft
4	John Kennedy
8	Free
9	Free
0	Free

Figure 3.14
List of presidents using a linked list. An additional set of links has been added to view the list in a second sequence.

FIRST = 4	5	Abraham Lincoln	4
FREE = 7	6	Dwight Eisenhower	3
	2	Theodore Roosevelt	5
	1	George Washington	6
	3	William Howard Taft	1
	4	John Kennedy	2
	8	Free	
	9	Free	
	0	Free	
LAST = 6			

3.4 MULTIPLE LINKED LISTS

Our recent illustrations have shown the advantages of using linked lists. One disadvantage of using linked lists appears when a record at the end or near the end of the linked list is desired. For example, imagine a beauty contest in which the title of Miss Galaxy is awarded, followed by the first, second, and third runners-up. Of course, this would be anticlimactic. The usual order would be to present the third runner-up, followed by the second and the first runners-up, and finally "Miss Galaxy." A result like this—data ordered from last to first—can be achieved by using linked lists with *backward pointers.*

Figure 3.14 contains the same data as Figure 3.13, but with both forward and backward linked list pointers. To find the last record in the list, follow the LAST pointer to the sixth record in the list, John Kennedy. To find the next-to-the-last record, follow the pointer from Kennedy to the second record (Dwight Eisenhower), and so on. This list can now be viewed in reverse order by following the links that begin using the LAST pointer. The new set of links added follow the same procedures that were followed when we began chaining from the FIRST pointer. The only difference is that the records are being viewed in the opposite sequence.

Recovering a Damaged File

The addition of backward pointers not only reduces the effort required to find a record at or near the end of the list, but it also provides another advantage. If a record in the middle of the list is accidently damaged or destroyed, and only the forward pointers existed, the remainder of the data would be lost. The use of both forward and backward pointers enables the file to be recovered, except for the actual damaged record.

Imagine that the third record in the list is destroyed. First, the forward

Figure 3.15
List of presidents using a linked list. The links have been modified to delete the record for Herbert Hoover.

FIRST = 4	5	Abraham Lincoln	4
FREE = 3	6	Dwight Eisenhower	5
	7	Herbert Hoover	5
	1	George Washington	6
	2	William Howard Taft	1
	0	John Kennedy	2
	8	Free	
	9	Free	
	0	Free	
LAST = 6			

pointers are followed until the damaged area is encountered. Then the backward pointers are followed until the damaged area is again encountered. After following both chains, all records except the actual damaged area can be recreated.

Impact of Multiple Links

By adding links to a file, we are able to view the file in as many different sequences as the number of links in the file. This greatly reduces the amount of file manipulation required to view the file in multiple sequences. However, this is not a panacea to cure the ills of the world! For example, each of the links for a file must be updated whenever a record is added or deleted. Figure 3.15 shows the work that must be done to delete one record (Herbert Hoover, again) from the list.

The FIRST pointer points to the fourth record in the file, George Washington. But Washington is not the record to be deleted. The forward pointer from Washington points to the first record in the file, Abraham Lincoln. Forward pointers are followed, record by record, until the record for Herbert Hoover is obtained. This is the record to be deleted.

The FREE pointer contained a 7, indicating that the first free space was the seventh record in the file. Now, the FREE pointer is updated to point to record 3. The free space chain is completed by placing the 7 (originally located in the FREE pointer) as the prefix in the third record.

The forward pointer from Herbert Hoover points to the second record in the file, Dwight Eisenhower. The pointer from Hoover is stored for future use. The backward pointer from Hoover is stored and this is followed to obtain the record for William Howard Taft. The forward pointer from Hoover's record that was stored for future use is now placed in Taft's record. Taft now points to Dwight Eisenhower. The forward pointer is followed to obtain the record for Eisenhower. The backward pointer in the record for Eisenhower is changed to point to the fifth record in the file, William Howard Taft.

The data for Herbert Hoover physically remains in the list, but no pointers point to that record (except FREE), so this record does not logically exist.

This illustration vividly demonstrates that the use of links is not free. The costs incurred are the pointer maintenance required whenever records are added or deleted.

3.5 INVERTED FILES

The close of the preceding section was not an attempt to deter you from using linked lists, or even multiple linked lists. In fact, today's environment *demands* multiple data sequences for a file. The caution is to use these structures judiciously. Early in this book, it was stated that data processing has required a series of compromises since its origins. Linked lists, or even multiple linked lists, are a compromise that can be more desirable than physical lists on many occasions.

The techniques presented thus far have shown different logical views of data stored in one physical sequence. However, to obtain the desired record, all of the records between the current position in the file and the desired record had to be accessed. With a small file and the hardware currently available, this is not a problem. But often, files today are very large, containing thousands or even hundreds of thousands of records. The end user would have to wait a long time for a record to be retrieved, working with files of this size. Clearly, a means is needed to rapidly retrieve any given record based on a predetermined key.

One approach is to make a copy of the key field in a separate and supplemental file, called an **inverted file.** The link to a record in the prime file is stored with the key field in the inverted file. The inverted file requires less space for each record; therefore, more records will fit in storage, which speeds the process of searching for records randomly.

Sequential Inverted Files

Figure 3.16 shows the inverted file that places the presidents in sequence by inauguration date. To find the president that was inaugurated in 1953, the first block of records is read into storage. This block is searched sequentially, looking for a 1953 inauguration date. A 1953 inauguration date is not found in the first block. The second block of records in the inverted file is read into storage and the search repeated. This time, 1953 is found. Stored with this record is a link (2) that yields the location of the record for Eisenhower. The link is followed to the primary file, and the primary record for Eisenhower is obtained.

Figure 3.16
Sequential inverted file containing inauguration dates and a link to the record in the prime file.

1789–4	1861–1	1909–5
1901–3	1953–2	1961–6

Figure 3.17
Binary search of the inauguration dates of presidents to access the date of 1909.

	1789	4
	1797	7
	1829	9
	1845	13
	1849	11
	1850	15
	1861	1
First probe →	1865	8
	1877	12
	1885	14
	1889	16
Second probe →	1901	3
Fourth probe →	1909	5
Third probe →	1933	10
	1953	2
	1961	6

With the inverted file, two objectives have been accomplished. First, the primary file can be processed in sequence by the key field that has been established in the inverted file. In the illustration, the records in the primary file can be presented to the user in sequence by inauguration date. Each record in the inverted file is read to obtain the link for the primary file. The link is followed to the primary file and the corresponding record is presented. This is merely a modification of the techniques used with linked lists in the preceding section.

Second, using inverted files, the speed with which a record can be randomly retrieved from the primary file is increased, since the records in the inverted file are shorter than the records in the primary file. Thus more records can be searched with fewer I/O operations than would be required to search the primary file to obtain the same record.

Although performance is improved, this technique is still not fast enough to satisfy current demands for anything other than very small files. However, this technique can be expanded in several ways to reduce the time to randomly retrieve data from large files. These methods include binary search, the indexed sequential inverted file, and the direct inverted file.

Binary Search

Binary search is a technique to reduce the time required to obtain a record randomly using large files. This technique requires the key field of the file to be in sequence in either ascending or descending order. The number of records in the file must be known. The search does not begin with the first record in the file; instead, it begins with the record at the file's midpoint.

In Figure 3.17, the desired record is the one for the president who was inaugurated in 1909. The number of records in the table is 16; therefore, the table's midpoint is Record 8, and the eighth record in the table is the first one examined. It contains an inauguration date of 1865, which is lower than the desired date of 1909. Thus, the record containing an inauguration date of 1909 must be in the second half of the table, if it exists.

The midpoint of the second half of the table is found. This point is 12

[(8 + 16)/2]. The twelfth record is examined and found to have a value of 1901, again lower than the desired value. The desired record must follow this record.

The midpoint of the remaining portion of the table is found. This point is 14 [(12 + 16)/2]. The fourteenth record in the file is examined and found to have a value of 1933, greater than the desired record. The midpoint of the portion of the file that has not been searched (between 12 and 14) must be found. This point is 13 [(12 + 14)/2]. Record 13 is searched and found to contain the desired date, 1909. The pointer from the inverted file is followed to the primary file and the record for Taft is obtained.

When using binary search, the file (or table) must be in either ascending or descending sequence. Each point to be searched is chosen so it divides the unsearched entries in half. If the file is in ascending sequence and the current record being examined has a value higher than the desired value, the next search will be in the direction of the beginning of the table. If the current record has a value lower than the desired value, the next search will be in the direction of the end of the table. In the preceding illustration, the second and third searches were in the direction of the end of the table because the preceding values examined were lower than the desired value. The fourth search was in the direction of the beginning of the table because the preceding value examined was greater than the desired value.

On the surface, binary search appears to require more effort than was required before, due to the small number of records in the file. The greater the number of records in the file, the more efficient this technique becomes. To prove this to yourself, use both serial and binary search techniques to find the 501st record in a file that contains 1000 records.

Indexed Sequential Inverted File

The inverted file may be stored using an access method that has direct access capabilities, such as the indexed sequential access method. Also, the key field and the link to the primary file can be stored in an inverted file by using the indexed sequential access method. The records are stored using the conventional techniques for this access method.

Using indexed sequential organization to store the inverted file has two benefits. First, the indexed sequential file can be read sequentially. Each time a record is obtained from the inverted file, the link is used to obtain the corresponding record from the primary file. Thus, this technique allows the user to view the primary file in sequence, according to the sequence of the inverted file. Second, a record from the inverted file can be obtained randomly. Then, a record from the primary file can be obtained using the key of a record in the inverted file.

To find the desired record, the access method examines the cylinder index to determine the cylinder that contains the record. Then the track index is searched to determine the track that contains the record. Finally, the track is searched to obtain the desired record in the inverted file. The link in this record is used to obtain the record in the primary file. If the files being searched are very large, this again reduces the effort required to find the desired record.

Direct Inverted File

The technique just described may not be fast enough to service applications with the most stringent requirements. For systems in which data must be accessed in minimal time, the inverted file may be stored using the direct file organization. Using this technique, you are unable to view the primary file in the sequence of the link field, because the direct organization does not provide for sequential access of the data. However, random access of a record by its link field is extremely fast.

The key of the desired record is presented to a randomizing algorithm which converts the key to the address of the record in the inverted file. If an efficient algorithm is used, the desired record in the inverted file could be retrieved in an average of 1.25 file accesses. Again, the link field from the record in the inverted file is used to access the record from the primary file.

3.6 TREE STRUCTURES

The techniques presented thus far access data when the same data is to be represented in multiple sequences. Such techniques show no relationship between the data items, except for the order in which the data is presented. However, these basic techniques can be expanded to give additional meaning to the data, so that besides having an alternate sequence to the data, we can see a relationship between two or more data items. The first technique used to establish this relationship is called a **tree structure**. Since this technique will likely be new to you, the terminology associated with it will be presented first. This will be followed by a presentation of the uses of this construct.

Tree structures resemble the depiction of a family tree. As with a family tree, they are normally viewed from the top to the bottom. The highest level in a tree structure is called the **root** node, the root record, or the root segment. The root node is also called a *parent*. The root can and usually does have nodes below it, called *children* of the root. The children, just as in real life, can become parents and also have children.

Preorder Traversal

In Figure 3.18, Node A is a root node and a parent. Nodes B and C are children of Node A. Node B has three children (Nodes D, E, and F), and therefore is a parent in its own right. Note that every node (except the root) has exactly one parent.

Nodes within a tree structure are connected to each other by pointers, as was done in linked lists. The simplest arrangement of pointers would occur when a tree structure is processed from the beginning to the end, accessing all of the nodes in the structure. Node A contains a pointer that points to Node B, the child that exists at the next level down and left-most within the structure. Node B contains a pointer to Node D, the child that exists at the next level down and left-most within the structure. Node D has no children, therefore it points to Node B's next child, Node E. Node E has no children, therefore it points to Node B's next child, Node F. Node F has

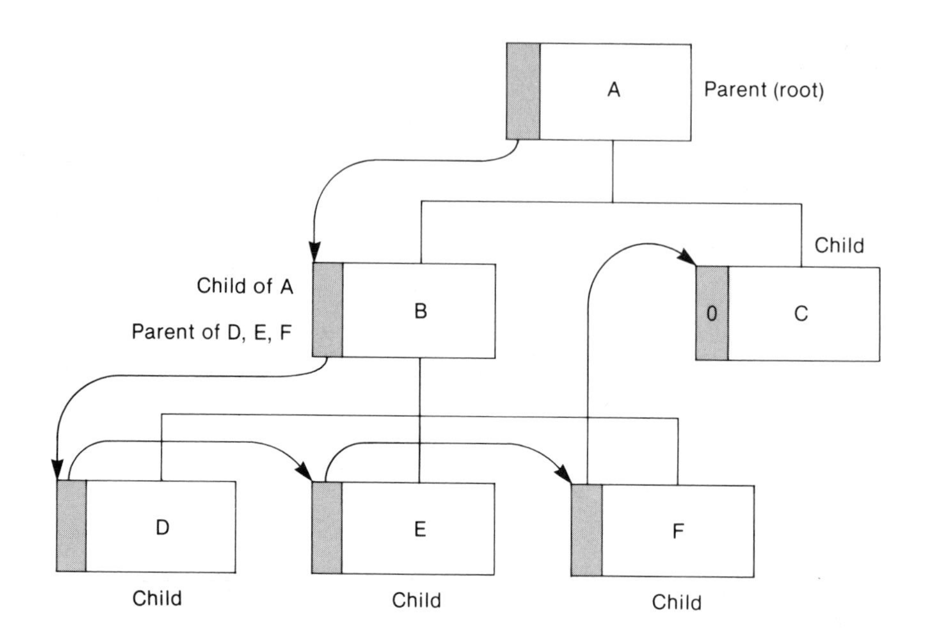

Figure 3.18
A tree structure using hierarchical pointers.

no children, therefore it points to Node C, which is Node A's next child leftmost in the tree. This process continues through all of the children of Node A. The process of obtaining all of the nodes in a tree in this fashion is called **preorder traversal.** It is usually done when a backup copy of a data base is desired. The pointers used to maintain data in a preorder traversal sequence are called *hierarchical pointers.*

Tree structures can be *unbalanced* or *balanced.* The illustration just presented is an unbalanced tree. In an unbalanced tree, each node may have a different number of children, and the root length varies depending upon the number of children.

Binary Trees

Binary trees are a special kind of balanced trees; each node can have only two children and two pointers. They can be used to randomly search for a child in the tree if the children have been added in a random sequence. The root is accessed first. To obtain any record, the value of the key of the record retrieved is compared to the desired record. If the record retrieved is not the desired record, one of the two pointers is followed, based on the value of the key of the current record. If the desired child has a key lower than the key of the root, the pointer to the child on the left is followed. If the desired child has a key higher than the key of the root, the pointer to the child on the right is followed. The same procedure is followed when each succeeding child is retrieved, until the desired child is obtained.

Figure 3.19 represents a binary tree with record key fields 1, 2, 3, 4, 5, 6, and 7. To obtain Record 5, the tree is entered at Record 4. The desired record key of 5 is greater than 4, so the pointer to the record with a higher key value is followed, the pointer to Record 6. Record 6 has a higher key

Figure 3.19
A binary tree for rapid access to any node in the tree.

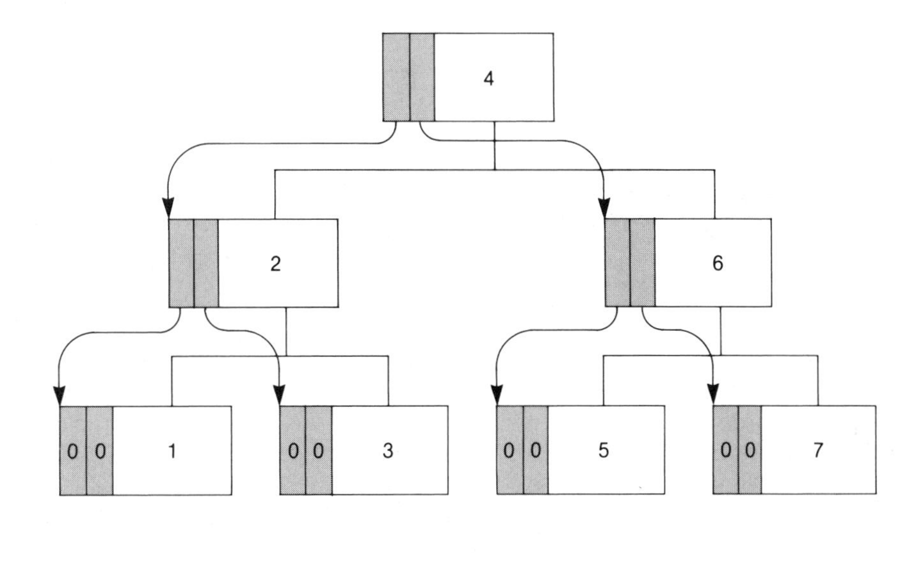

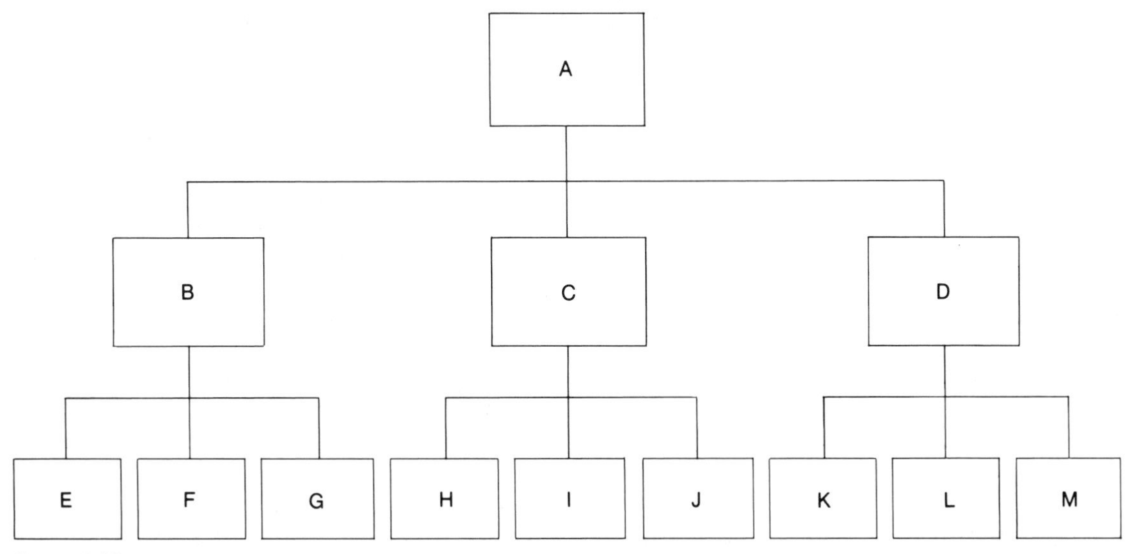

Figure 3.20
A balanced tree.

than the desired record, so the pointer to a record with a lower key value is followed and Record 5 is retrieved.

The binary tree is so easy to implement, it is sometimes used for data bases on microcomputer systems.

Balanced Trees

Figure 3.20 represents a balanced tree structure. In a balanced tree, each node has the same number of children. Children are added from the left to the right until each level is filled. This process repeats itself at each level. Like binary trees, balanced trees are also rather simple to represent in secondary storage. Since each node has the same number of children, the node can be stored as a fixed length record.

Storing Variable Length Records in Tree Structures

Tree structures provide an effective way to store data when multiple occurrences of one field or record occur for every occurrence of another field or record. Example D1 illustrates.

Example D1
Storing Variable Length Records in a Tree Structure at the Zenith Medical Group

The task at hand for the Zenith Medical Group is to maintain data about its doctors throughout a metropolitan area. Each doctor treats many patients and performs service at one or more offices and hospitals. If conventional files were used, the most likely technique would be to create a variable length record containing data about the doctor, each of the locations at which he or she practices, and data for each patient. One occurrence of the data appears in Figure 3.21.

The same data can be stored in a tree structure, as shown in Figure 3.22. The records for data about the doctor occur at the root node. The node for doctor has two different types of children. One child type is the location of practice data. The other child type is patient data. One occurrence of the data for this tree structure is shown in Figure 3.23.

Note in Figure 3.23 that several locations of practice (one child type) are shown. When multiple occurrences of data exist for one child type, each occurrence of that child type is called a *twin*. Twins exist for each child type of the doctor node. The doctor node itself will be a twin, because this tree structure is being used to collect data for the many doctors of the Zenith Medical Group. The data for each doctor would be represented in the same fashion. Each doctor would be a twin of those that precede.

Child and Twin Pointers

If we were interested in all of the data in this tree structure, we could use hierarchical pointers, as was done for preorder traversal. If, on the other hand, we are interested only in selected data, other types of pointers exist to simplify processing.

For example, the root node for doctor may contain a pointer (called a *child pointer*) to the first occurrence of each child type. Each twin would contain a pointer to the next occurrence of the same child type. These pointers are called *twin pointers* (what else would you expect?). Example D2 illustrates the use of child and twin pointers.

DOCTOR	OFFICE	OFFICE	HOSPITAL	PATIENT	PATIENT		PATIENT
DR. JOHN SMITH	111 FIRST STREET	222 SECOND STREET	GOOD SAMARITAN	JOE DOAKS	JANE JONES		SAM WINKLE

Figure 3.21
A variable length record used to store repeating fields for the Zenith Medical Group.

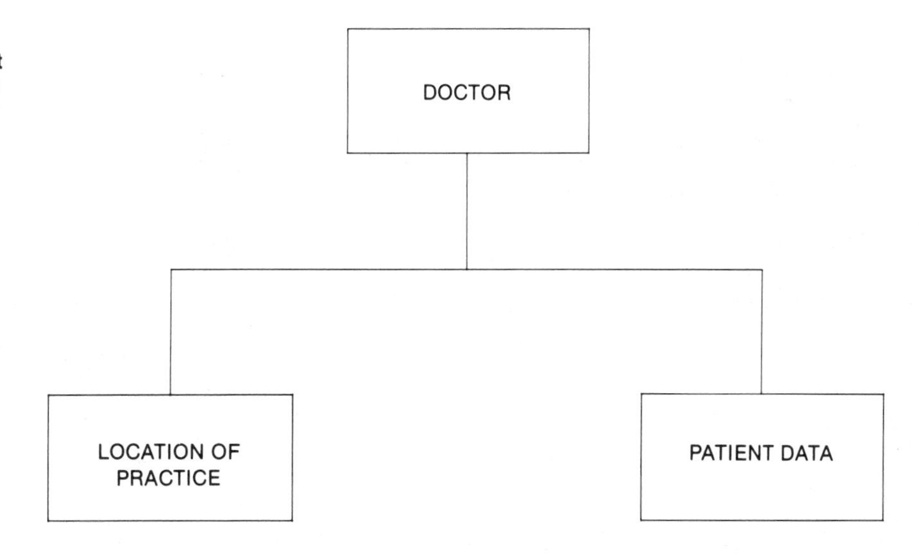

Figure 3.22
Tree structure to depict the relationship of data for a doctor with many locations of practice and multiple patients.

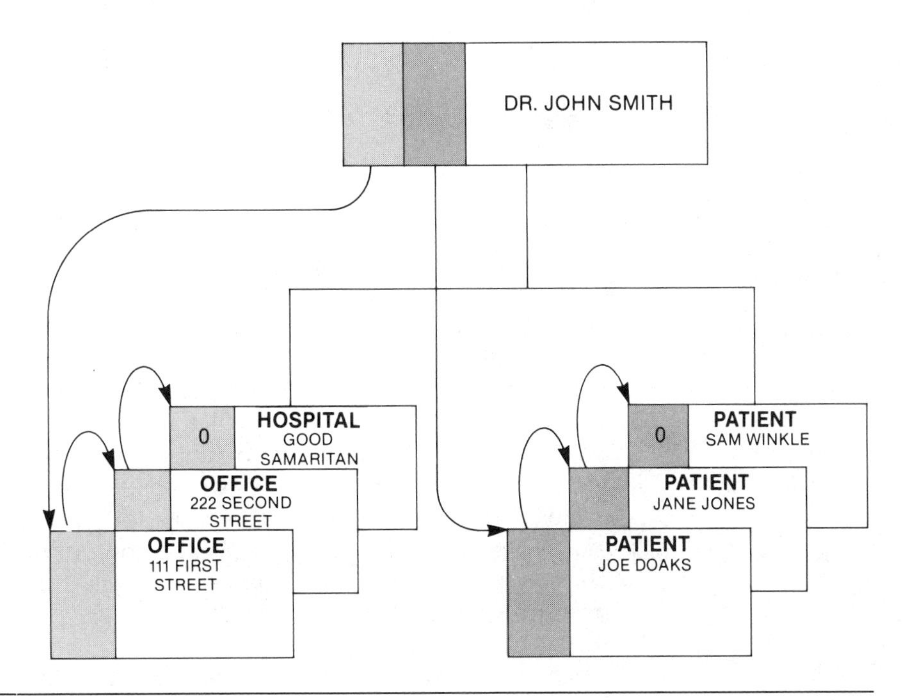

Figure 3.23
One occurrence of a tree structure for one Zenith Medical Group doctor with many locations of practice and multiple patients.

Example D2
Child and Twin Pointers as Used by the Zenith Medical Group

The Zenith Medical Group wants to determine the type of case most often treated by its doctors. Since they do not desire data concerning location of practice, the child pointer to this data is not used. Instead, the child pointer to the patient data is used. The child pointer from Dr. John Smith to patient Joe Doaks is followed, and the malady for which Doaks is being treated is obtained. Then, the twin pointer stored with the record for Doaks is obtained and followed to patient Jane Jones. This process is repeated until all of the necessary data is obtained.

Figure 3.24
A tree structure with one doctor with one office location and no patients.

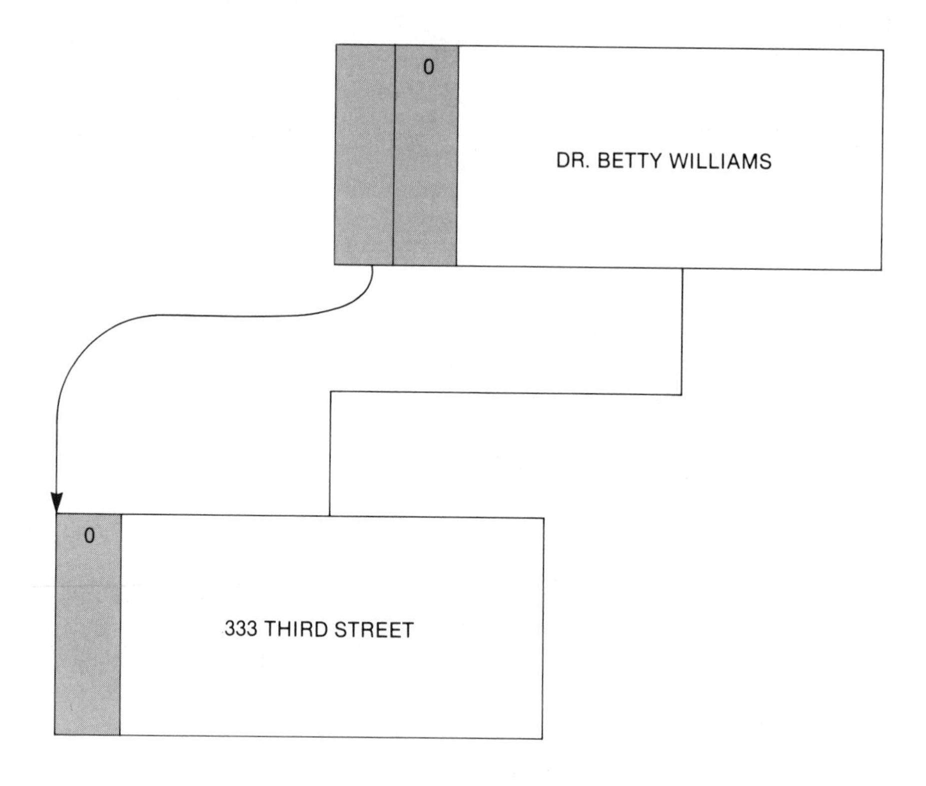

Using a tree structure with child and twin pointers, it is not necessary to retrieve records for a child type that does not contain data to solve the problem at hand. Note that the last twin of each child type in Figure 3.23 contains a 0 in the twin pointer location to indicate that no other records of that type follow. If a new doctor, Betty Williams, joined the medical group she might at first have only one office location and no patients. This would be indicated by a child pointer pointing to the record with the location of her office (see Figure 3.24). The twin pointer for location would contain a 0, indicating that no other office locations follow. The child pointer pointing to patients would also contain a 0, indicating that no nodes presently exist. Thus, as you can see, a good deal of flexibility is achieved by using a tree structure with child and twin pointers.

Deletion of Records in a Tree Structure

Deletion of records using a tree structure with child and twin pointers is easily accomplished. Example D3 depicts the processing to be performed.

Example D3
Deletion of Records in a Tree Structure at Zenith Medical Group

Dr. John Smith closed his office at 222 Second Street. The twin pointer in the record for location 111 First Street is altered to point to the record for Good Samaritan Hospital (see Figure 3.25). (Records are deleted in tree structures in the same manner as they were using linked lists.)

Figure 3.25
Tree structure showing the deletion of the record for an office location at 222 Second Street.

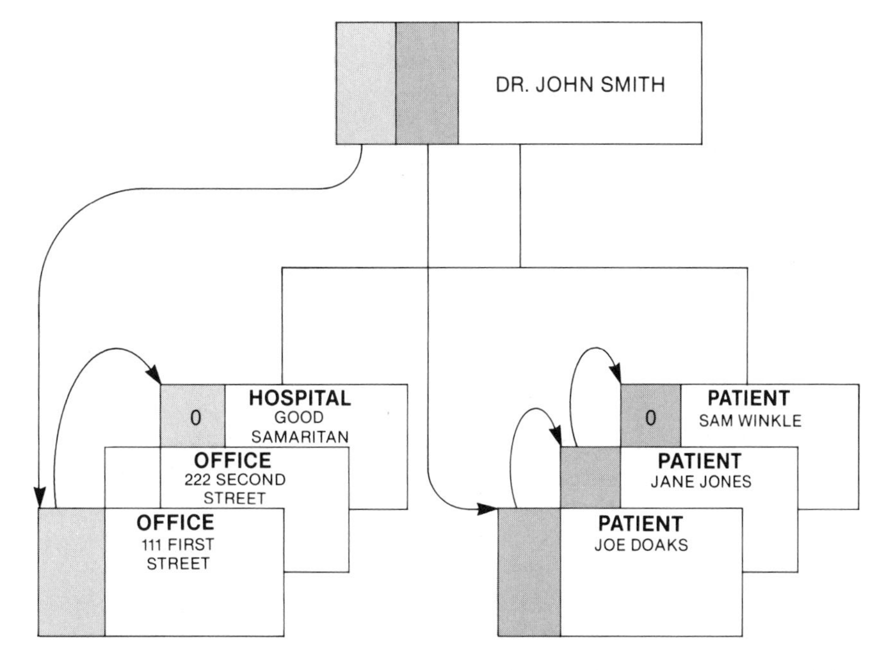

If Dr. Smith were to stop practicing altogether, his record at the root level would be deleted in a similar fashion. The twin pointer from another twin at the root level would point to the record that followed Dr. Smith. This is what one would expect, based on the methodology presented thus far. However, note the implications of this process. Since Dr. Smith has been deleted, all of his children are also deleted, for a child cannot exist without a parent. (Having children is hereditary. Chances are, if your parents did not have any children, you will not have any children either!). The result of this process is logically correct. If Dr. Smith has stopped practicing, he will have neither locations at which he practices, nor will he have any patients.

Addition of Records to a Tree Structure

The addition of records in a tree structure follows the same pattern as for linked lists. Example D4, which illustrates this process, makes two assumptions. First, assume all patients will be processed in alphabetic order. Second, Dr. Smith has not closed an office after all, and in fact his practice is enlarging.

Example D4
Addition of Records to a Tree Structure at the Zenith Medical Group

A new patient, Judy O'Connor, is treated by Dr. Smith. The record for O'Connor will be added in the next available location in the data base (free space pointers will be used, as for linked lists). The child pointer is followed from Dr. Smith to the first patient. Then the twin pointers are followed until the correct location for Judy O'Connor is found. The twin pointers are altered to point to O'Connor in alphabetic sequence (See Figure 3.26). Each record has now been placed in the correct logical sequence through the use of pointers.

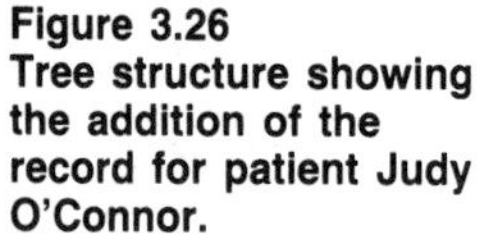

Figure 3.26
Tree structure showing the addition of the record for patient Judy O'Connor.

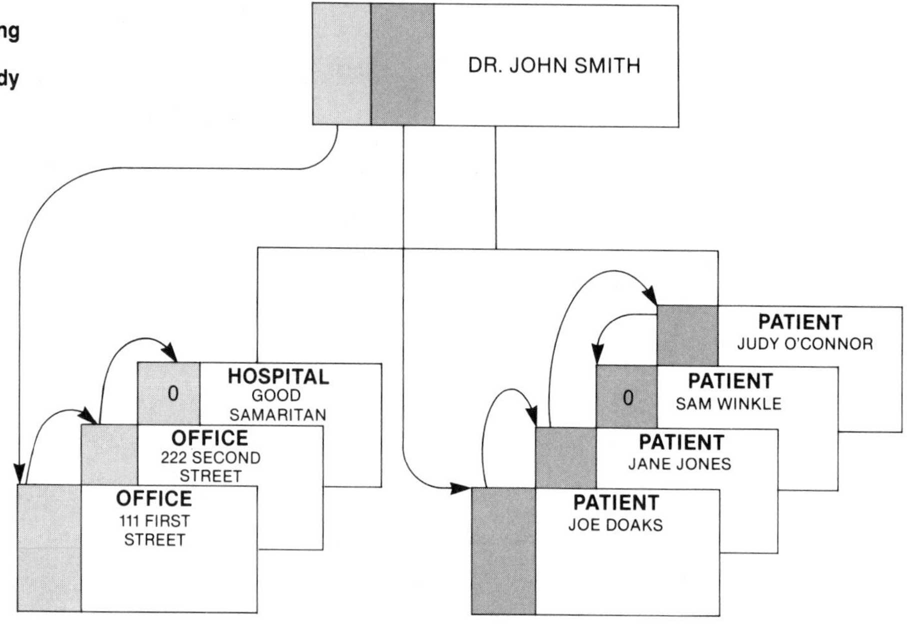

The Zenith Medical Group examples have been drawn schematically to show the relationships between parents, children, and twins. Each record has been presented as if it were physically adjacent to the one preceding it. However, this is not necessarily the way in which records are physically stored. If a direct access storage device were used to store the data, each record would be stored in the next available storage location, regardless of physical position, just as they were with linked lists. The examples will continue to be drawn schematically here, but keep in mind, the schematics do not represent the physical locations in which data is stored.

3.7 NETWORK STRUCTURES

In the early days of data processing, it was not uncommon to determine the requirements of a system and then design the system to fit the hardware and software available. Times have changed. Over the years, it has been recognized that users should not have to change their method of doing buisness to fit a data processing system. Instead, the data processing system should be tailored to meet the needs of the user.

Simple Networks

Certain data relationships cannot be represented in a straightforward manner using tree structures. Remember, in a tree structure, each child can have only one parent.

Figure 3.27 depicts a data relationship in which data is maintained about recording stars, the hit songs they have made famous, and their albums. The

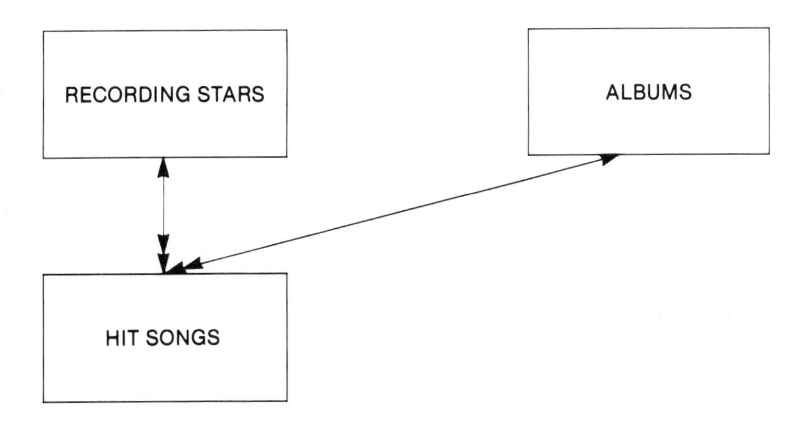

Figure 3.27
Simple network structure. The child has two parents.

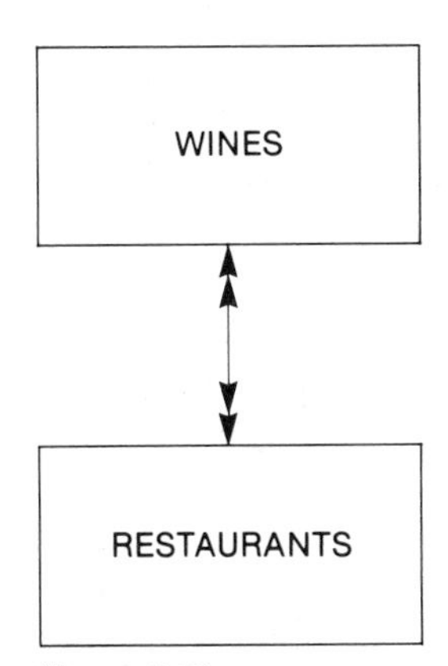

Figure 3.28
Complex network structure. A "many-to-many" relationship exists between child and parent.

data structure uses arrows to show the relationships. A single arrowhead represents a "one-to-one" relationship; a double arrowhead represents a "one-to-many" relationship.

In the left side of the structure, the relationship is consistent with the rules governing tree structures. A one-to-many relationship exists between a recording star and his or her hit songs. However, the child "songs" has two parents: "recording stars" and "albums." This violates the rules for tree structures. Instead, it falls within the realm of a network structure.

In a network structure, each child is capable of having more than one parent. The relationship in Figure 3.27 is called a *simple network*, because the child has a one-to-one relationship with each parent. Each recording star performs many songs. Each song is performed by only one recording star. Each album contains many songs. Each song is recorded on one album.

Complex Networks

Network structures need not be simple. In Figure 3.28, a many-to-many relationship exists. Each wine is served at many restaurants; each restaurant serves many wines. This is a *complex network*, because a many-to-many relationship exists between the child and parent. (This relationship has also been called a *group marriage* by James Martin in his book *Computer Data-Base Organization.*)

Complex networks are difficult to store. Some data base management systems can represent simple networks, but not complex networks.

Loops

Network structures have two special implementations—*loops* and *cycles.*

In a loop, a record has a relationship with itself. The most common example of this implementation is a bill of material processor. Example E1 shows how a manufactured product such as an automobile can be represented.

Example E1
A Loop at the Epic Motorcar Company

The Epic Motorcar Company builds fine automobiles. An automobile is made of many components, such as wheels, engine, and chassis. Each of the components can be further broken down into other components. An engine is composed of a carburetor, heads, block, pistons, and so on. A carburetor can in turn be broken down into floats, nuts, bolts, and gaskets. A loop structure provides a convenient technique to logically represent this process without having to specifically describe each component. Figure 3.29 shows the Epic Motorcar loop.

Each occurrence of a record in the loop structure in Figure 3.29 is the same record type. Figure 3.30 shows specific occurrences of the structure in Figure 3.29. In Figure 3.30, automobile, wheels, engine, chassis, carburetor, heads, block, and pistons are all occurrences of the same record type: COMPONENT. In the loop structure, the first child of the occurrence of automobile is wheels, but wheels is the same record type as automobile, so it is stored at the same level within the structure. Engine and chassis are twins of the record for wheel. The engine can be subdivided into other components. The first component, or child, of the engine record is the carburetor. Heads, block, and pistons are all twins of the carburetor record and are components, so they are stored at the same level. This process is repeated until each component is subdivided into its lowest level of detail.

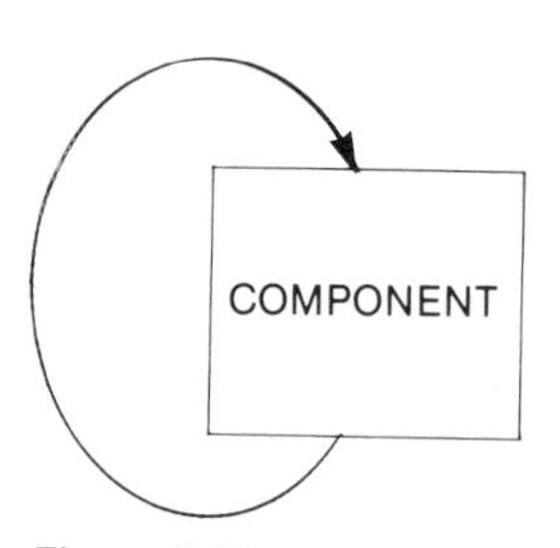

Figure 3.29
Loop structure in which each component has a subassembly at the same level.

Cycles

The other special implementation of a network structure is a cycle. In a cycle, a record has as its child a record that is higher in the structure than itself (its antecedent).

Figure 3.31 illustrates a cycle for computer repair technicians. Today's computers are extremely complex. To check the hardware when a problem occurs, one or more technicians may be called in, depending on the type of problem. Each technician has multiple pieces of test equipment. The test equipment is driven by computers. Thus, the cycle repeats itself, and the record type TEST EQUIPMENT has as its child the record type COMPUTERS, which occurs in the structure two levels above the record type TEST EQUIPMENT.

Example F1, illustrated in Figure 3.32, describes an occurrence of the basic structure depicted in Figure 3.31.

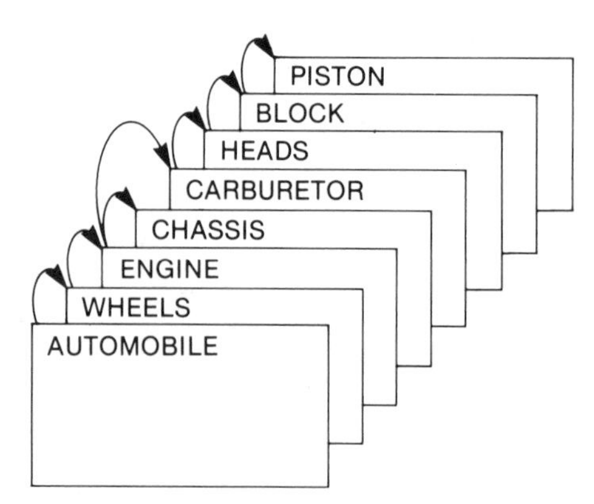

Figure 3.30
Occurrences of a loop structure showing the subassemblies for specific components.

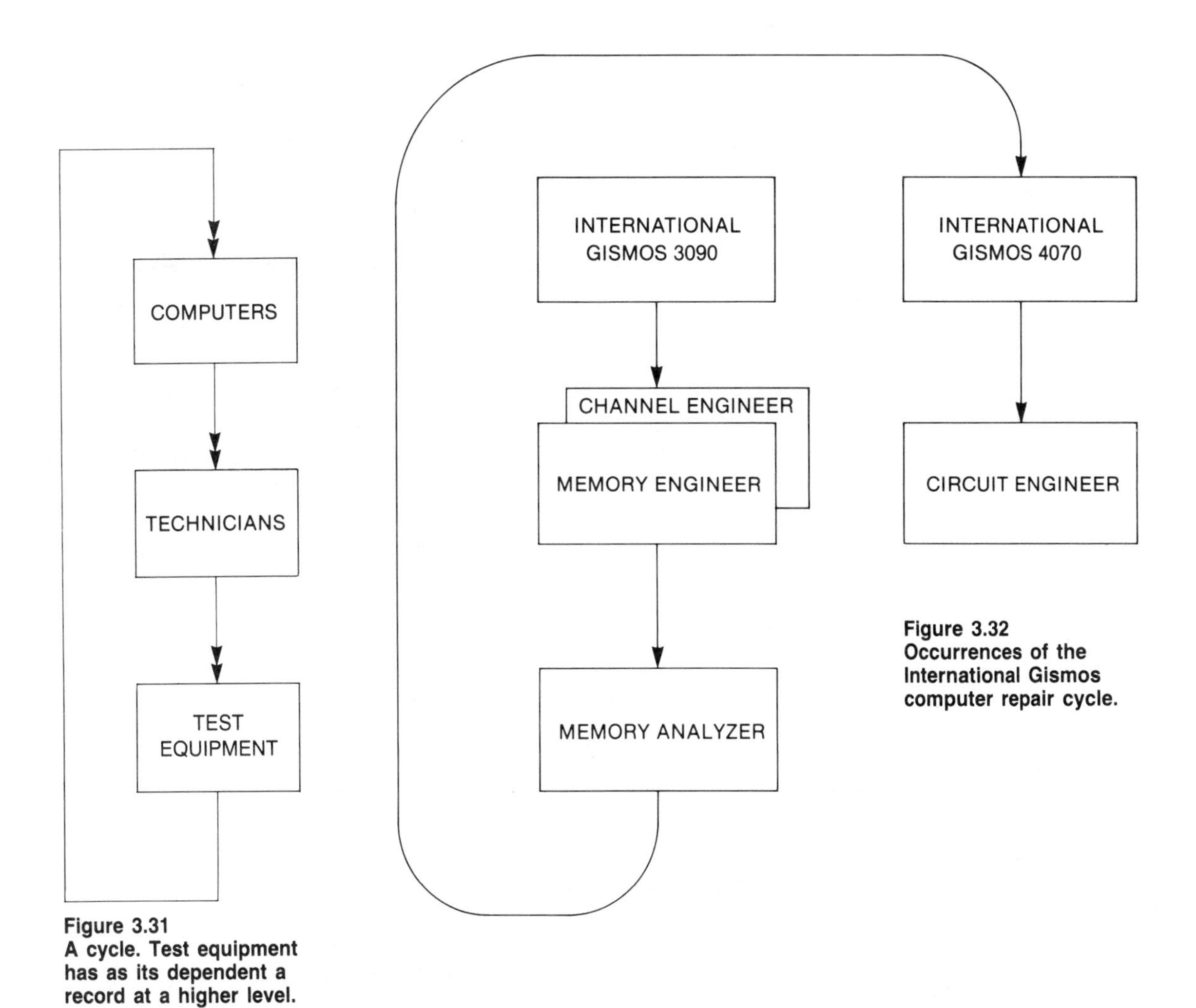

Figure 3.31
A cycle. Test equipment has as its dependent a record at a higher level.

Figure 3.32
Occurrences of the International Gismos computer repair cycle.

Example F1
A Cycle: The International Gismos Computer Repair

The International Gismos 3090 computer is serviced by two different technicians: a channel engineer and a memory engineer. The engineer responsible for the proper functioning of the memory has a piece of test equipment which is a memory analyzer. The memory analyzer uses an International Gismos 4070 computer to test the functioning of the memory. The International Gismos 4070 is also serviced by a series of technicians, one of whom is a memory engineer. Thus, the child of the memory analyzer record is another computer which is the same record type as one of its ancestors. The child belongs to a different occurrence of the same structure.

Cycles and loops are special network structures used to simplify data relationships. In the next chapter, the means by which data is defined to the data base management system is presented. When loops and cycles exist, the effort required to define them to the data base management system is greatly reduced.

3.8 SUMMARY

When data is stored using an access method that requires the data to be in a physical sequence, the entire file must be read and rewritten to perform maintenance. This is true even if only one record is changed.

Use of linked lists to store data significantly reduces the number of records that must be updated in maintenance. Use of multiple links for one file allows the user to view the file in many sequences without having to alter the file's physical sequence. However, using linked lists (even multiple lists) to view a file means the records must be processed in sequence until the requested record is found—a time-consuming and thus often unacceptable procedure. By using an inverted file, records in the primary file can be accessed directly, allowing data to be accessed by the user in minimal time.

Tree structures allow the data to be accessed in sequence when it is necessary to obtain all the data within a structure. By using child and twin pointers, selected data can be obtained without having to process all of the records in a file. Tree structures force some restrictions upon the ways in which data can be represented. For example, trees only provide for one parent for each child record. Network structures, however, allow multiple parents to exist for each child.

All these techniques are used in combination with access methods to provide different logical views of data without changing the physical structure of the data to match *every* user's view.

REVIEW QUESTIONS

3.1 List two advantages of using forward and backward linked lists.

3.2 List three advantages of storing data using linked lists rather than storing data using physically ordered lists.

3.3 List one disadvantage of using multiple links on one file.

3.4 Assume you are to supervise a new car sales campaign. Draw a tree structure to depict each sales location, the car models available at that location, and the salespeople who work at each location. Specify the types of pointers to be used. Defend your solution.

3.5 Assume you work for a newspaper and write a sports column. You wish to automate the system that provides background information for your column. Draw a network structure that will show all of the teams, the players who play on each team, and the name of each player's agent. Also, you wish to be able to find all of the players represented by an agent. Is this a simple or complex network? Why?

3.6 When using tree structures, what advantage is provided by child pointers?

3.7 When using tree structures, what is the effect on a child when its parent is deleted?

3.8 What is the difference between a simple network and a complex network?

3.9 What are two special implementations of the network structure?

3.10 Name and explain the function of one procedure that may be used to recover a damaged file.

3.11 What is another name given to a circular linked list?

3.12 What is the purpose of using inverted files?

3.13 If a tree structure is retrieved in a preorder traversal sequence, what does this mean?

4

DATA MODEL OVERVIEW

CHAPTER OBJECTIVES

Upon completion of this chapter, you should be able to:

1. Define the term *data definition language* and explain why it is important to data base management systems
2. Define the term *schema* and explain the generic terminology for global data definition
3. Define the term *subschema* and explain the generic terminology for describing restricted views of data
4. Understand the language used to manipulate data within a data base management system and cite the reasons for its existence
5. Name the three data models used to categorize data relationships and identify the design characteristics of each

NEW WORDS AND PHRASES

data definition language
data manipulation language
data models
relational model
schema
subschema
binding
navigation

4.1 CHAPTER INTRODUCTION

Adding a field to a record or changing the length of an existing field in a conventional file sounds at first like a trivial task. In fact, it can be a complex and time-consuming process. Such changes are common when new subsystems are added to existing applications. To make these changes successfully, a programmer first analyzes the documentation to determine which programs access the file. The source programs are then changed to account for the modifications being made, compiled, and tested. All programs that access the file which contains the changed field must be changed, whether or not the program accesses the changed field. Finally, the file is changed to include the modifications.

Changes of this nature usually involve production jobs. All of the changes must be synchronized at the completion of a processing cycle for the application. In large-scale applications, hundreds of programs may be involved in the change. Thus the change can consume a great deal of time and effort—effort diverted from the development of new applications.

By placing the definition of the data in the data base management system, much of the effort is automated. Then, only those programs that manipulate the changed data need be recompiled to account for the change. A tool called a *data dictionary* (which will be discussed in Chapter 8) is used to determine which programs need to be changed. Some data base management systems also have utility programs to facilitate the change. Thus, use of a data dictionary and utility programs reduces the time required to make changes in a data base management system.

Data base management systems are extremely complex software packages. To discuss them, we will break them down into functional components and explain each component separately, rather than deal with them *in toto*. Two major functional components are the **data definition language** and the **data manipulation language**.

The data definition language (DDL) is used to define the location, length, and format of the data elements, the position of each element within the data structure, and the security of each data element. The DDL can, in turn, be subdivided into two subfunctions: the definition of the schema and the definition of the subschema (see Figure 4.1).

The data manipulation language (DML) is a set of commands to cause data to be stored and retrieved by a data base management system. Programming languages use verbs or macro instructions to cause data to be transferred between application programs and secondary storage. Data base management systems provide more-powerful data manipulation verbs than are provided with conventional file access methods. These verbs, taken as a group, are called the data manipulation language.

Three major data models are used to classify processes and terminology for data representation and manipulation. The *hierarchical data model* is used to describe data relationships involving tree structures. The *network data model* is used to describe data relationships involving network structures. The *relational data model* uses tabular structures to represent data relationships.

This chapter is an introduction to the basic concepts of these three data models. Each of the data models is explored in turn in more detail in Chapters 5, 6, and 7, with specific illustrations of the DDL and the DML for each model.

The academic and professional communities have not agreed upon a consistent set of terminology to describe data. Because the COBOL language

Figure 4.1 Schematic of the components of data base management system software.

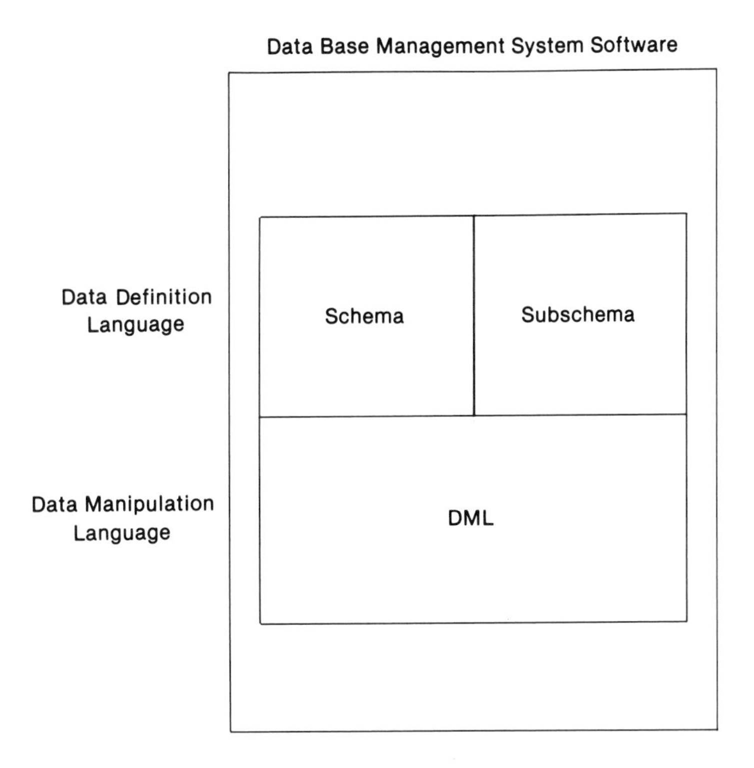

has been standardized by the American National Standards Institute (ANSI), this book will use COBOL terminology as a frame of reference whenever possible.

4.2 DATA DEFINITION LANGUAGE

When using programming languages other than machine language, the length, location, and format of every data element the program references is symbolically defined. The compiler determines the addresses and lengths of each data element defined and generates the machine instructions necessary to manipulate the data. Since the data base management system provides the software to access the data base, it, like a COBOL program, must know the names of the elementary items used and the location, length, and format of the data associated with a given data name. Data base management systems not only have the same basic requirements as a language like COBOL in order to describe the physical structure of the data base, but also require additional definitions.

Data base management systems give us the ability to present data in logical sequences, in addition to the physical sequence in which the data is stored. The data base management system creates these logical structures based upon the control statements in the DDL.

Figure 4.2
Record Description from a COBOL program.

```
01  STUDENT-RECORD.
    05  STUDENT-NAME           PIC X (30).
    05  STUDENT-ID             PIC 9 (9)   COMP-3.
    05  FILLER                 PIC X (10).
    05  STUDENT-ADDRESS        PIC X (60).
    05  STUDENT-MAJOR          PIC X (15).
    05  STUDENT-BIRTH-DATE     PIC X (6).
```

The term **schema** is used to describe the logical view of data. Traditionally, data design is separated into two phases. In the first phase, the data needed to support an application is grouped into records within a file. The data relationships are specified in the record layouts for each file as it is designed. In the second phase, the file design is superimposed upon the file organization and the secondary storage media.

The same process is followed when dealing with data base management systems, as is emphasized throughout this book. Phase one, the description of the data relationships independent of any consideration of the physical storage, is termed the **logical structure**. Phase two, the logical structure superimposed on the access method and the secondary storage media, is termed the **physical structure**. Throughout this book, data structures are described first in terms of their logical structure, then their physical structure.

Data base management systems provide data security by restricting the data an application program is allowed to view, as well as by restricting the data manipulation the program may perform. The term **subschema** describes the application program view of the data. The definition of the schema and the subschema are the major components of the DDL.

Data Definition with Conventional Files

In a COBOL program, an entire division of the program is devoted to the definition of the data as it exists in secondary storage. Example G1, illustrated in Figure 4.2, describes data definition of a Record Description entry for a student record at Blue Whale College.

Example G1 Data Definition at Blue Whale College with Conventional Files

Before data can be manipulated in the Procedure Division, the location, length, and format of the data must be defined in the Data Division. Figure 4.3 shows a data name table depicting information needed by a COBOL compiler.

The location counter is set to relative Location 0 when the beginning of the record is encountered by the compiler. The compiler saves the data name STUDENT-NAME in the data name table. Since the location counter con-

Figure 4.3
Table relating data name to storage of data.

DATA NAME	LOCATION	LENGTH	FORMAT
STUDENT-NAME	0	30	Display
STUDENT-ID	30	5	Packed
STUDENT-ADDRESS	45	60	Display
STUDENT-MAJOR	105	15	Display
STUDENT-BIRTH-DATE	120	6	Display

tains 0, STUDENT-NAME is located at relative Location 0.

The number 30 indicates that the data is 30 characters long, and so the location counter is incremented by 30. PIC X identifies this elementary item as any allowable character from the ASCII or EBCDIC character set.

The next data name encountered is STUDENT-ID. The compiler gives this data name relative Location 30 in the data name table, the number in the location counter when this item is encountered. PIC 9 and usage COMP-3 indicate that this is a numeric item stored in packed decimal format. The number 9 in the picture clause indicates that nine characters are to be stored. Nine characters stored in a packed decimal format are stored in five positions. Therefore, STUDENT-ID is given a length of 5 bytes. The location counter is incremented by 5, giving a total of 35.

The next item has a data name of FILLER. This is an indication to the compiler that the data in this location is not referenced by this program. The location counter is incremented by 10, the value in the picture clause. The definition of this item allows the compiler to calculate the total length of the record and to calculate the offset to the next elementary item.

This process continues until all of the elementary items in the STUDENT-RECORD are defined. Compare the data name table in Figure 4.3 with the record description in Figure 4.2. (The name FILLER is not included in Figure 4.3 because the data in this location is not referenced by the application program.)

When a data name is referenced in the Procedure Division, the compiler uses the data name table to find the characteristics of the data to be manipulated. Whenever STUDENT-NAME is referenced, 30 bytes of alphanumeric data, beginning at relative Location 0, are accessed. Whenever STUDENT-ID is referenced, the compiler generates instructions to retrieve 5 bytes of numeric data represented in packed decimal format beginning at relative Location 30. If the data stored at this location is compared with other numeric data stored in a different format, the compiler generates instructions to place both data items in the same format when the comparison takes place.

This process takes place in every program. When a file is manipulated by many programs, it is not unusual for the record descriptions to be stored in a separate file. They are copied into each program that manipulates the file when the program is compiled, in order to standardize documentation of the file and also to ensure that no errors are made in the record definition. This definition must exist in the program when it is compiled in order for the correct locations and lengths to be calculated. As previously noted, whenever the length of a record changes, all programs that access the record must change to account for the changed record length. While Example G1 is specific to the COBOL language, other programming languages function similarly.

Schema Definition

Example G1 illustrates data definition with conventional files. A similar process takes place with data base management systems, although the actual DDL used differs with each data base management system. (Examples of the

DDL used to define each data item will be provided in later chapters for each data model.)

The schema within the DDL contains a definition of a name (which is associated with specific data) and the length and format of the data. In addition, the schema describes the relationship between records within the total data structure.

A major difference between conventional file definition and the DDL is the time period in which data is bound to the application program. **Binding** is the connecting of the description of the data to the data itself. In Example G1, the binding of the data to the application program occurred at the time the program was compiled. However, recall that in Chapter 1, we presented data base management systems as a layer of software between the application program and the access method; since the data is defined to the data base management system, the binding of the data to the application program occurs when the program is executed, when a data base management system is used. This provides greater flexibility than with conventional files, and it allows the data structure or the storage medium to be changed with minimal impact on the application program.

Logical Data Structures

End users need to see data in multiple sequences. The DDL describes logical data structures to provide multiple data sequences and to provide multiple data relationships. Logical data structures will be presented in more detail in future chapters. For now, let's say they are somewhat similar to the sequence of the data as it is seen when obtained through an inverted file.

Example G2 shows how data is accessed in more than one sequence. Use of both conventional files and a data base management system is illustrated, for comparison.

Example G2 Multiple Sequence Data Access at Blue Whale College, Conventional Files vs. a Data Base Management System

In the system installed at Blue Whale College to maintain data about students, a social security number field is used to uniquely identify each student. (Other colleges might use a student identification number field.) This is necessary to ensure that each student is credited with the correct grades and charged the correct tuition. The student name is not used for identification, since duplicate names may exist; for example, there might be two Karen Schaefers. However, students are not normally identified by social security number in a classroom. They are accustomed to being addressed by name. Traditionally, instructors are given a class roster which lists students in sequence by surname. This is one of the many situations that exist in which data is presented to the end user in more than one sequence.

If Blue Whale College uses conventional files, the data is stored in one physical sequence (such as social security number) and sorted into as many different sequences as dictated by the end user. Sorting the data consumes considerable time, given the very large files of a college.

If, on the other hand, the college changes to a data base management system, the data is stored in one physical sequence. Inverted files (similar techniques could be used) now present alternate sequences required by the end user. Sorting is no longer required, thereby reducing the amount of time to provide alternate sequences. Inverted files are created through entries in the definition of the schema in the DDL. This is transparent to existing application programs; they are unaware of the physical structure of the data base.

Subschema Definition

The subschema is a separate and distinct part of the DDL. The subschema defines the data structure which an application program is permitted to view; thus the subschema is sometimes called the *application program view* of the data. The subschema defines a portion of the data defined in the schema, ranging from one field to the entire data structure.

Each application program has a different purpose, and so the operations performed by the program require different types of data manipulation. In the subschema definition, the application program is granted the authority to view and update the data needed to accomplish the purpose for which the program was written. The subschema definition serves two purposes. First, it simplifies the data structure as viewed by the application program. Therefore, the application programmer need not be aware of the entire data structure and can concentrate on the portion of the data structure needed to satisfy the task at hand. Second, the subschema definition increases data security. Let us amplify this second point.

Data must be secured against unauthorized access. With a data base management system, the data base administrator determines which data an application program is allowed to view, then authorizes the use of the data through control statements in the subschema. Functionally, this is accomplished by providing the application program only a subset of the data in secondary storage or providing the data in an arrangement different from the way it physically exists. The data base management system examines the subschema definition for the application program before providing data to the program. If an application program attempts to access data for which it is not authorized, the data base management system generates an error indication.

The subschema also limits the functions the program can perform against the data base. In Figure 4.4 a tree structure depicts the data relationships between students, sports, cars registered on campus, and tickets. But a report program written to—for example—print mailing labels to be attached to course catalogs has no need to access the records containing data about sports, cars, or tickets. Therefore, the subschema is defined to restrict the program's access to the student record. The view of the data base, as seen by this application program, is shown in Figure 4.5. This program is unaware that any records other than the STUDENT record exist. If the program attempts to access an occurrence of another record in the data base, such as an occurrence of the CAR record, it will be given an error indication.

The subschema definition provides additional security. It limits the functions a program can perform against a data base. Typically, four func-

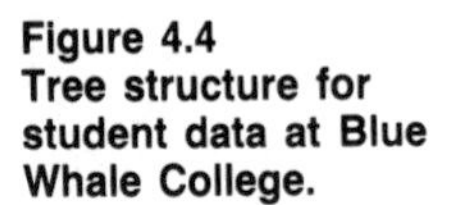

Figure 4.4
Tree structure for student data at Blue Whale College.

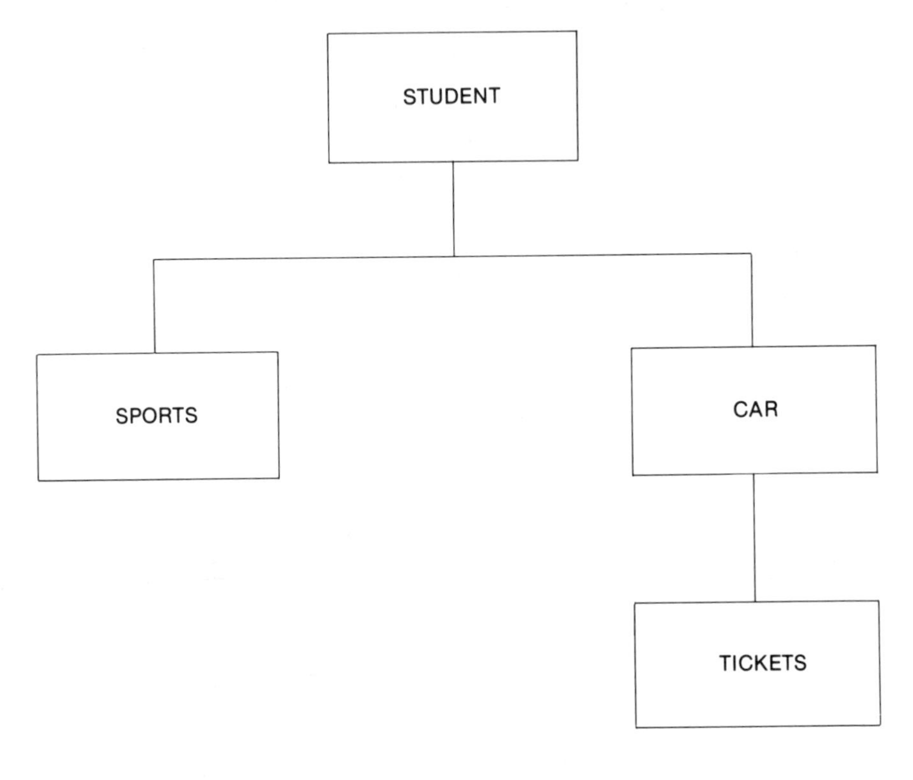

Figure 4.5
Mailing label program view of student tree structure at Blue Whale College. Note: Shaded record types cannot be viewed by the mailing label program.

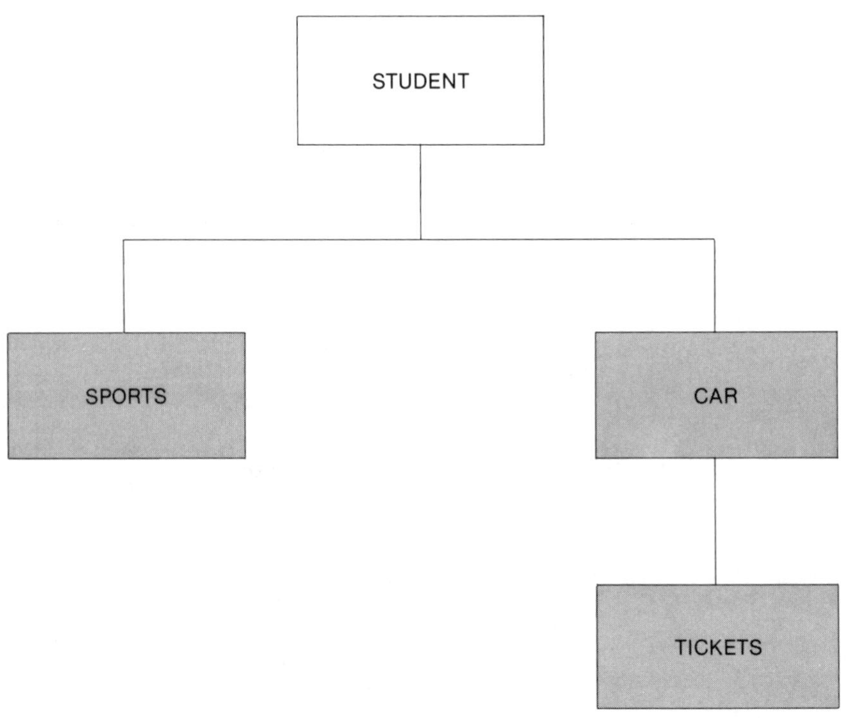

tions can be defined: READ, UPDATE, ADD, and DELETE. Any one, or any combination of the four, may be specified for each application program. In Figure 4.5, the only function to be performed is to provide mailing labels. Student data is not updated, added, or deleted. The DDL for the subschema contains parameters to restrict this program to READ operations only. If any other operations are attempted, the program is given an error indication.

The application program's view of the data and the functions the program is permitted to perform are defined external to the application program through the subschema. They can be changed any time before the application program is executed, without recompiling the program. They will be in effect at the time the program executes. The binding of the logical view and the security occurs at program execution time. A different subschema may be generated for every application program regardless of the number of programs that access a data base. Due to the number of different logical views, and execution time binding, this is a flexible tool for administering data security.

4.3 DATA MANIPULATION LANGUAGE

Because the data base management system manipulates the data, a set of commands is needed to enable the programmer to direct the system to store and retrieve data.

Languages such as COBOL have two basic verbs, READ and WRITE, which are used to transfer data to and from secondary storage. For conventional files, instructions to select and process specific data are included in the application program. A data base management system, on the other hand, achieves higher performance through its data manipulation language (DML), the collection of verbs available in a data base management system to access, update, and store data.

In data base management systems based on the hierarchical or network models, the DML permits the application program to travel from the occurrence of the record which it is processing to an occurrence of some other record in the data base. In later chapters, we will explain why the programmer must know the current location in the data base and determine which path to follow to obtain the next record to be processed. For now, an illustration of the procedure (Example G3) should suffice.

Example G3
Use of DML at Blue Whale College

At Blue Whale College, a data base management system is now in place. An application program has just retrieved an occurrence of the STUDENT record in the structure shown in Figure 4.4. The objective of the program is to determine the number of tickets received by each student; the application program achieves this by proceeding through the occurrences of the CARS record type to the occurrences of the TICKETS record type.

The application program must know the path to take to travel from point A (STUDENTS) to point B (TICKETS); this is known as **navigation** through the data base.

Data Manipulation with Conventional Files

To understand how the DML works, you must understand the difference in function between conventional file processing and data base management systems when searching (as in Example G3) for data in secondary storage.

When an application program manipulates data using conventional file organizations, the program issues a READ or WRITE verb. The compiler generates the instructions to make the request through the access method and to point to a buffer, within the boundaries of the application program, where the access method returns the data (see Figure 4.6). The application program accesses every candidate record. The program contains instructions to determine whether or not the record meets the criteria specified. Many records are accessed, but only a subset are actually processed.

To illustrate, let us imagine using conventional file access techniques at a college to produce a listing of students who are over 21 years old and have a zip code of 21040.

The application program reads every candidate record in the file, as in the following skeleton program:

```
     READ STUDENT-DATA.
     PERFORM PROCESS-STUDENT-DATA
         UNTIL ALL-RECORDS-ARE-READ.
     STOP RUN.
 PROCESS-STUDENT-DATA.
     IF AGE IS GREATER THAN 21
         AND ZIP-CODE EQUALS '21040'
         PERFORM WRITE-REPORT.
     READ STUDENT-DATA.
```

The application program requests a record from the access method through the READ statement, obtains the record, and places it in the buffer designated by the application program. The application program then compares the age and zip code of the student against the specified criteria. If the candidate record meets the criteria, the record is printed; otherwise, the next record in sequence is examined and the process is repeated.

Data Manipulation with a Data Base Management System

In many cases, DML removes the need for the application program to include the instructions to select a given item. Instead, by using parameters in the DML, the application program specifies the criteria for the required records. The data base management system returns only the records that meet the criteria to the application program.

Figure 4.6
a. Access to data using conventional files.
b. Access to data using a data base management system.

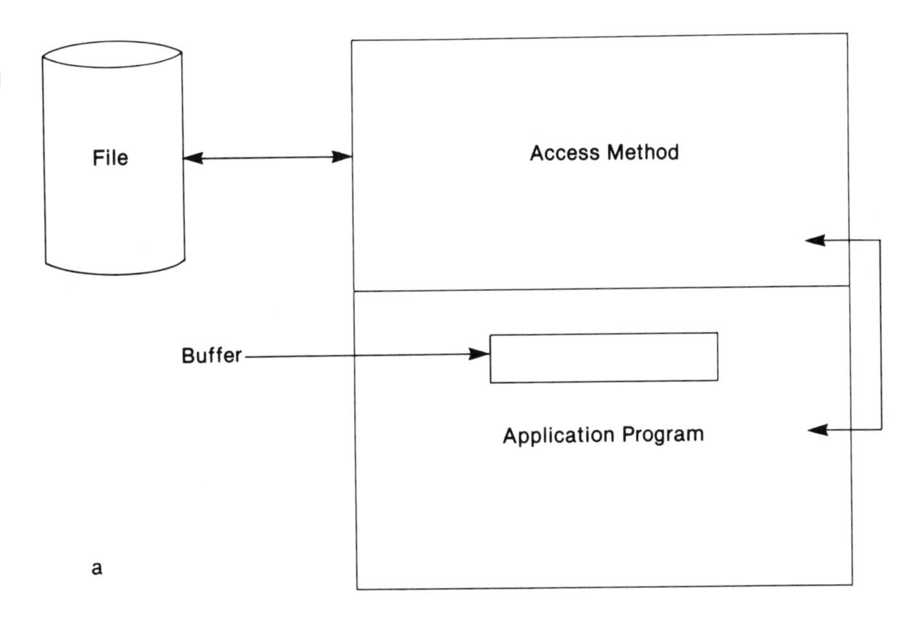

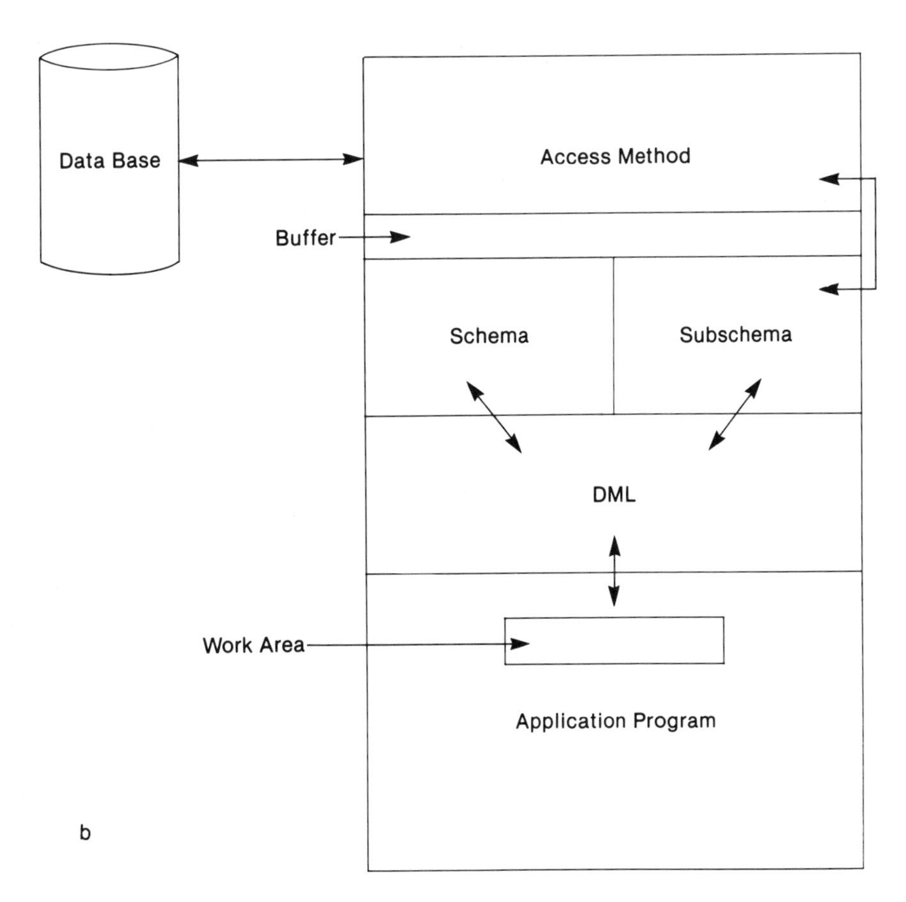

Example G4 demonstrates how DML is used in the data base management system at Blue Whale College.

Example G4
Data Manipulation at Blue Whale College

Figure 4.6b adapts Figure 4.6a, showing the schematic of the process for the same program, except in the data base management system environment at Blue Whale College. The application program uses a DML verb, the data name, and the desired value of the data, as in the following program skeleton:

```
    PERFORM
        PROCESS-STUDENT-DATA
        UNTIL END-OF-DATA-BASE.
    STOP RUN.
PROCESS-STUDENT-DATA.
    SELECT * FROM STUDENT
        WHERE AGE > 21 AND
        ZIP-CODE = 21040.
```

SELECT * FROM STUDENT WHERE . . . is the DML command to the data base management system. The DML portion of the data base management system interprets the DML command to determine the function requested. The subschema is examined to find whether the application program has the authority to issue the command. If the program is not authorized for the DML command, it is given an error indication. If the command is authorized, the data base management system interrogates the schema to determine the structure of the data base.

The data base management system then requests a record from the data base through the access method. The access method obtains the specified record and places it in the data base management system's buffer. The system examines the record in the buffer for the criteria specified by the application program. If the record does not meet the criteria, the data base management system formulates a new request to the access method for the next record to be examined. This is repeated until a record that matches the criteria is found or until the data base management system determines that the record requested does not exist.

If the record is found, the system strips the pointers from the data and presents the requested data in a work area (sometimes called an I/O-AREA or USER-WORK-AREA) specified by the application program. If the requested data is not found, an error indication is passed to the application program.

The data base management system reduces the number of instructions needed in the application program, which in turn reduces the time to produce the completed program. It does not necessarily remove the need for searching data; it merely changes the location where the search is performed. Although development time is reduced, such a feature must be used judiciously, due to its effects on overall system performance; the DML commands may appear trivial in relation to the application program, but they are in fact powerful. A single command can cause an entire data base to be searched, consuming a significant amount of time due to the pointers chased and the corresponding seek time and rotational delay.

It is important to remember that the application program is unaware of any pointers that exist within the data base. If the application program were provided pointers to request data and used them, it would not be possible to change the physical or logical structure of the data without making corresponding changes to the application program.

4.4 DATA MODELS

As we stated in the chapter introduction, three major data models are used to represent data relationships: hierarchical, network, and relational.

Hierarchical

DL/I will be presented in this book as an example of hierarchical, or tree, data models, because it is the most widespread data base management system using this model. DL/I is a portion of IMS, which is a program product marketed by IBM.

Network

The Data Base Task Group (DBTG) uses the network data model to represent data relationships. The DBTG is a task group of the CODASYL Programming Language Committee, which is responsible for the development of COBOL. The task group's intent is to develop a data base management system similar to COBOL—a system that is machine independent. Standardization has not yet occurred. However, some vendors, such as Cullinet with its IDMS, market data base management systems based on DBTG specifications. IDMS is used in this book to demonstrate the features of the DBTG proposal.

Relational

The relational data model represents data relationships as tables. The relational model is couched in complex mathematical notation, and this terminology is unfamiliar to the average data base management system student. The original terminology is presented in this book, but it will be followed by an explanation in terms familiar to most students.

The traditional data manipulation language of the relational model was relational algebra and relational calculus. However, the current trend is to provide entries in a table using English-like statements and to eliminate mathematical procedures for manipulation. SQL, the data manipulation language for an IBM data base management system, reflects this trend. SQL will be used in this book to demonstrate relational models.

Because of its power and ease of use, the relational model is likely to be the data base model of the future.

A Framework for the Evaluation of Data Models

Each data model has characteristics that differentiate it from others. Chapters 5 through 7 present each of the three data models in detail. As you progress through the next three chapters, keep the comparison framework shown in Figure 4.7 in mind. At the end of Chapter 7, the characteristics of all three data models will be reexamined with respect to this framework.

Figure 4.7 Framework for the evaluation of data models.

	HIERARCHICAL	NETWORK	RELATIONAL
Representative system			
Definition of data building blocks			
Representation of logical data structures			
Data independence			
DML commands			
Means of data base navigation			
Navigator			
Performance			
Additional pointers available to improve performance			
Security			
Security officer			
Responsibility for adding data to the data base			
Modification of data structure			

4.5 SUMMARY

Data base management systems can be divided into two major functions: the data definition language (DDL) and the data manipulation language (DML). The DDL can be subdivided into two additional components: the schema and the subschema.

The schema defines the logical structure of the data base. The subschema increases data security by defining the application program view of the data and limiting the functions the application program can perform against the data base. Since this occurs at the time the program is executed instead of at the time the program is compiled, it also increases flexibility in manipulating data, without affecting the application program.

The DML is a vehicle for the application program to request data from the data base management system. Through parameters, it can reduce the instructions needed in application programs to select records for processing.

The three basic data models are presented in this book to describe data relationships. DL/I, a data base management system marketed by IBM, will be used to illustrate processing with the hierarchical model. IDMS, a data base management system marketed by Cullinet, will be used to illustrate processing with the network model. SQL, the data manipulation language for a data base management system marketed by IBM, will be used to illustrate processing with the relational model.

REVIEW QUESTIONS

4.1 Define the term *data definition language* (DDL). Explain why DDL is used in a data base management system.

4.2 Name the two components of DDL and explain the function of each.

4.3 What is data binding? Explain the differences between data binding in conventional files and data base management systems.

4.4 Explain the procedure to add a field to a record, using conventional files. Explain the procedure to add a field to a record, using a data base management system. Why is this difference important?

4.5 Why is data security important?

4.6 What feature of a data base management system enhances data security? What are two techniques used to accomplish this?

4.7 How are alternate data sequences provided when using conventional files? When using a data base management system?

4.8 What is the purpose of a data manipulation language (DML)?

4.9 How can the DML shorten program development time?

4.10 Are the pointers used to maintain data relationships made available to application programs? Why or why not?

4.11 Name the three major data models used to represent data relationships in data base management systems. What are the important characteristics of each?

4.12 What is the reason for attempting to standardize data base management systems?

DATA BASE IN THE WORKPLACE

Successful Installation of a Data Base Management System at a State University

At Gonswago State University, systems were in place to perform basic functions such as mailing grade reports, but the users wanted more.

They wanted on-line systems for credit registration, with which they could ensure that a student had completed a prerequisite before being allowed to register for a course. They wanted to ensure that there were no time conflicts between the course for which the student was registering and courses for which the student had already registered. If all of the courses for which the student wished to register were full, they wanted to be able to determine the courses previously completed by the student and the unfilled courses which remained outstanding to complete the student's program of study, so they then could recommend alternate courses to the student. They believed that these on-line systems would result in fewer occurrences of courses dropped and added, which would reduce administrative costs during registration.

The director of data processing purchased a data base management system and a fourth-generation data manipulation language, which is a language in which the user specifies the data desired and the data manipulation to provide the data is determined by the software. The Data Processing Department developed a system for the university library using the data base management system and the fourth-generation language in three days.

Their next efforts with the data base management system were to develop a system for the Continuing Education Department and a system for credit registration. Both systems use the same data base, but the users require different functions. The credit registration system is Gonswago's most important one, since the university revenues depend upon the number of students enrolled for courses. During registration, the dean must evaluate the classes being offered. In one day, the dean must decide which classes will run, which ones will be cancelled, and which ones will be combined. The information needed to make such decisions must be accurate and up-to-date. It is not recommended for any installation to tackle its most important system using an unfamiliar and complex tool, yet, this is a case which was very successful.

Their practice now is to prototype systems where a function is designed and programmed and presented to the user for evaluation. Users identify the portion of each response with which they are satisfied and also identify those areas which they would like to see improved. If minor changes are required, the programmer redesigns those areas and presents the changed programs for additional user evaluation. If the users are totally dissatisfied, the entire system is scrapped, and the programmer starts over from the beginning.

Using a fourth-generation data manipulation language, little development time is wasted in this effort. Simple systems can be written quickly and given to the user to experiment with. Since users have the system designed to their exact specifications, they are more likely to use the system. Using the fourth-generation language, Gonswago's Data Processing Department has programmed major systems which were demonstrated to the user at the end of a week and fully implemented at the end of two weeks.

As a result of their success, all new development is performed with the fourth-generation language. COBOL, the language previously used for development, is not even considered for new development. They are so happy with the product, the director of data processing says that he and his staff have forgotten how to spell COBOL.

5

HIERARCHICAL DATA MODEL

CHAPTER OBJECTIVES

Upon completion of this chapter, you should be able to:

1. Read a DBD and construct the corresponding tree structure
2. Read a PSB and construct the corresponding application program view of the data
3. Describe why logical structures are needed in the hierarchical model and demonstrate how redundant data is eliminated using logical structures
4. Describe how DL/I manipulates data with its DML

NEW WORDS AND PHRASES

DBD
PSB
SSAs
segment
hierarchical path
physical data base record
segment sensitivity
logical structures
segment code
physical parent
physical child
logical child
logical parent
intersection data
calls

5.1 CHAPTER INTRODUCTION

In this chapter, we will discuss hierarchical data models in detail by focusing on IBM's DL/I, an acronym for Data Language I. DL/I is a part of an IBM product called IMS and is the portion which performs data base storage and retrieval.

DL/I and other hierarchical models represent data only as tree structures; network structures are not allowed. The schema definition is provided to the data base management system through a data base definition (DBD). The subschema definition is provided through a program specification block (PSB).

In DL/I, instead of a READ verb as in COBOL, the command to obtain data from the data base management system is the GET command. Instead of the WRITE verb, the INSERT command is used to add new data to the data base, and the REPLACE command is used to change data. The DELETE command is used to remove data from the data base. Segment search arguments (SSAs) are used to identify a specific segment to be processed.

5.2 DATA DEFINITION LANGUAGE

DBD

The schema (schema is not, however, a DL/I term) is represented through a data base definition (DBD). The DBD describes the length, location, and format of each data element to be accessed by DL/I. The term **segment** describes related fields grouped together and presented to the application program as a unit. This is similar to the unit of data called a record in conventional file processing. The DBD describes the position of each segment within the tree structure and includes statements to describe the physical representation of data in secondary storage.

The PSB is used to describe the subschema (also not a DL/I term). The PSB contains the names of each segment a program has the authority to access. The application program is said to be *sensitive* to each segment specified in the PSB. The hierarchical structure described in the PSB is called the *application program view* of the data.

After the control statements in the DBD are coded, the DBD is assembled in the same manner as a program written in assembly language. The output from the assembly is stored for future use. The process of assembling and storing the DBD statements is called a *DBD generation,* or a DBDGEN. It describes the physical characteristics of the data base, the place of each segment within the tree structure, and the fields the programmer will refer to when accessing data. This definition is somewhat similar to the Data Division entries in a COBOL program. Any segment that DL/I must retrieve is defined within the DBD. Any fields that DL/I must search are also defined in this process. If data is omitted from the definition, DL/I cannot search the data base to find specific values for those fields.

Example G5
Tree Structure for the Student Data Base at Blue Whale College

Figure 4.4, the tree structure for student data at Blue Whale College, is reproduced for your convenience as Figure 5.1. The root segment contains fields of data about the student: name, student identification number, address, major, and so on.

Some students participate in one or more sports at the college; the SPORTS segment contains data about each sport in which the student participates. Some students have access to one or more vehicles; the next child in hierarchical sequence (CAR) contains

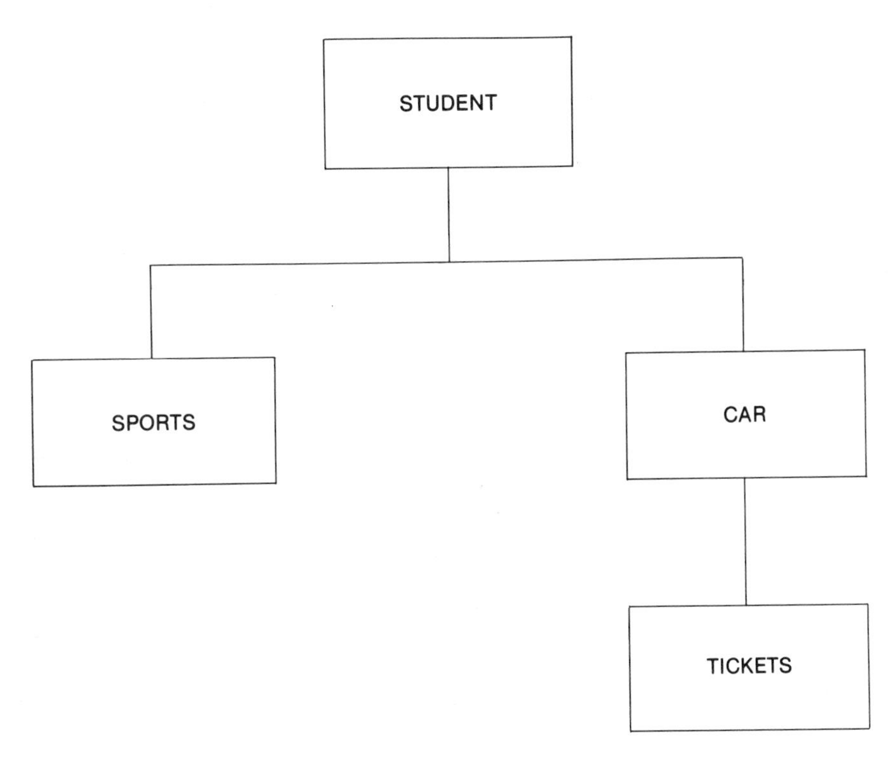

Figure 5.1 Reproduction of student data structure from Figure 4.4.

a list of the vehicles the student has registered to park on campus. The last segment (TICKETS) contains a list of the tickets given for violations for each vehicle. Figure 5.2 shows one occurrence of the data.

The DBD for the tree structure described in Figure 5.1 is provided in Figure 5.3. The DBD is made up of several types of statements. The first statement, which begins with DBD, identifies the beginning of a data base definition. This statement contains the name of the data base (NAME=STUDENT) and the access method used to access the data base. (DL/I access methods are discussed in Module A, which follows Chapter 5.) In DL/I, information about the physical structure (the access method, the physical record length, and so on) is separated from the definition of the logical structure, which follows it.

The DBD statement is followed by a series of SEGM statements. Each SEGM statement defines the characteristics of the segment and the segment's location within the tree structure. Each SEGM statement may be followed by none, one, or more FIELD statements. FIELD statements identify the sequence field and the fields that the application programs will ask DL/I to search. Should it be necessary to add new search fields, this can easily be accomplished by repeating the DBD generation and adding the new field.

The first segment in Figure 5.3 is named STUDENT (NAME=

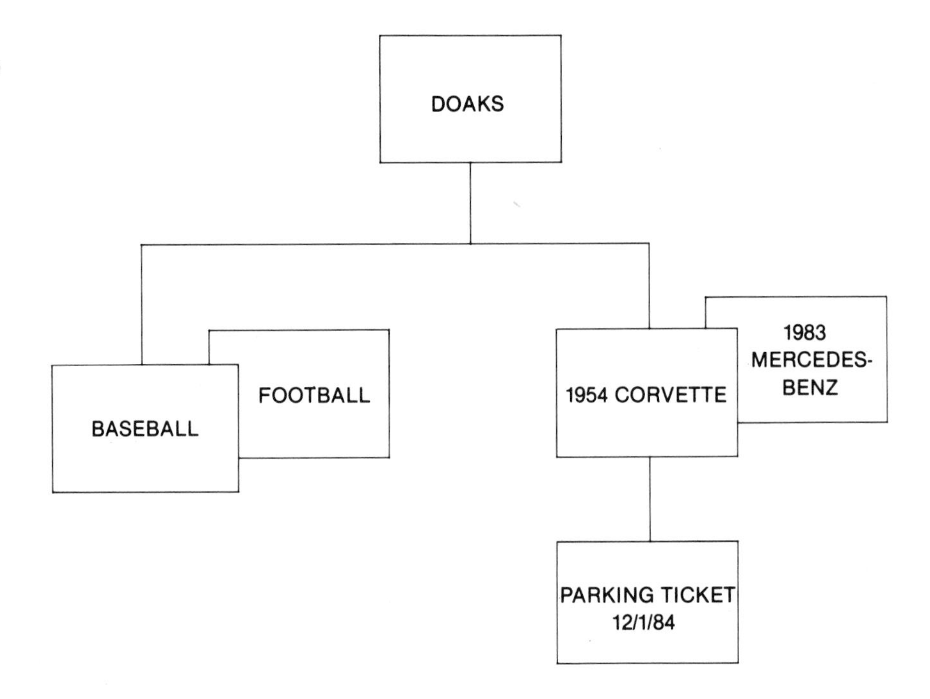

Figure 5.2
One occurrence of the data in the Student Data Base.

STUDENT). The parameter PARENT=0 means there are no segments in the data base higher than this segment; therefore, it is the *root segment.* The BYTES=250 parameter specifies the total length of this segment. SID, the name of the first FIELD statement after the STUDENT segment, is defined as a sequence (SEQ) field (NAME=(SID,SEQ,U) for the STUDENT segment. As new segments are added, they are placed in logical sequence based on the value of this field in a segment, as was done in Example D4 in Chapter

Figure 5.3
DBD for Student Data Base.

```
DBD     NAME=STUDENT,ACCESS=HIDAM

SEGM    NAME=STUDENT,PARENT=0,BYTES=250
FIELD   NAME=(SID,SEQ,U),START=31,BYTES=5,TYPE=P
FIELD   NAME=SNAME,START=01,BYTES=30,TYPE=C
FIELD   NAME=ADDRESS,START=46,BYTES=60,TYPE=C

SEGM    NAME=SPORTS,PARENT=STUDENT,BYTES=125
FIELD   NAME=(SPORTNAM,SEQ),START=15,BYTES=12,TYPE=C

SEGM    NAME=CAR,PARENT=STUDENT,BYTES=90
FIELD   NAME=(MAKEMODL,SEQ),START=5,BYTES=27,TYPE=C

SEGM    NAME=TICKETS,PARENT=CAR,BYTES=65
FIELD   NAME=(DATEKIND,SEQ),START=1,BYTES=13,TYPE=C

DBDGEN
FINISH
END
```

3. The U, for unique, in the NAME parameter tells DL/I not to permit two occurrences of the STUDENT segment to have the same value in SID. If a program attempts to add a segment which has the same value as an existing segment, DL/I will give an error indication to the program. Compare the format of the remainder of the FIELD statements with the COBOL definitions in Figure 4.2. Also note that the fields may be defined in any sequence in DL/I and that the STUDENT-MAJOR and STUDENT-BIRTH-DATE fields are not defined, because DL/I will never be requested to search for specific values of these fields.

The next SEGM in Figure 5.3 is named SPORTS. In Figure 5.1, the SPORTS segment is the first segment to the left on the second level. The DBD in Figure 5.3 reflects this, since SPORTS is the first segment defined with a parent of STUDENT (PARENT=STUDENT).

The next SEGM statement is named CAR. It is on the second level to the right of SPORTS in Figure 5.1. The DBD in Figure 5.3 reflects this, since CAR is the second segment defined with a parent of STUDENT (PARENT=STUDENT). SPORTS and CAR are two different children who have the same parent. The CAR segment contains the fields to describe the vehicle the student registered to park on campus.

The last segment presented in Figure 5.3 is named TICKETS. It is the only segment at the third level in Figure 5.1. Its parent is CAR (PARENT=CAR), a second-level segment. The field that follows in Figure 5.3 describes the offense for which the ticket was presented.

DL/I searches for segments having specified values in certain fields, as was described in our discussion of DML processing in Chapter 4. Note that the lengths of all of the fields specified do not add up to the total length of the segment. The only fields that must be defined in FIELD statements in the DBD are those that DL/I will be requested to search to find specific values. It is not necessary or even desirable to define every field in a segment. DL/I must build a table to determine the location of each field named in a FIELD statement. If fields are named which are not sequence or search fields, this causes the size of the table to be increased needlessly to hold definitions which are not used.

The order of the SEGM statements is important in a DBD. The SEGM statements are specified in hierarchical sequence which allows DL/I to develop a segment code that prefixes each segment when it is stored. The segment code is a number that identifies the segment type in preorder traversal sequence and is used internally by DL/I. The STUDENT segment has a segment code of 1; the SPORTS segment, 2; the CAR segment, 3; and the TICKETS segment, 4. DL/I uses the segment code to determine which segment within a tree structure it has obtained. DL/I allows a maximum of 255 different segment types and 15 levels to be specified in a single DBD.

The data base has four different segment types, STUDENT, SPORTS, CAR, and TICKETS. It has two different **hierarchical paths**. A hierarchical path is all of the segments from the root segment to the lowest-level segment in a tree along one leg of the tree structure. One hierarchical path is through the STUDENT and SPORTS segments. The second hierarchical path is through the STUDENT, CAR, and TICKETS segments.

After the DBDGEN is performed, DL/I uses it to store data within the data base. Data must be initially stored by a special program called a *load program.* The load program presents DL/I with a root segment, followed by the dependent segments in hierarchical (preorder traversal) sequence for each occurrence of a root. For example, when the data described in Figure 5.2 is initially loaded, the application program presents the segment for the student Doaks. The next segment presented is the first occurrence of the SPORTS segment, baseball. The next segment is for the second occurrence of the SPORTS segment, football. Next, the first occurrence of the CAR segment is presented, a 1954 Corvette. The next segment presented is for a ticket obtained on 12/1/84. The next segment is for the second car registered, a 1983 Mercedes-Benz. This completes the data for the first student.

The root segment along with all of its dependent segments is called a **physical data base record.**

PSB

The PSB describes the data as it is seen by the application program. The PSB is implemented in much the same manner as the DBD. First, a series of statements is completed, describing the view of the data required by the application program. These statements are assembled and stored for future use by DL/I. The assembly and storage process is called a *PSB generation,* or PSBGEN. This view is a subset of the segments described in all of the DBDs accessed by this program. The PSB contains one or more program communication blocks (PCBs). Each PCB describes the segments that the application program is permitted to access in one data base. A program is not permitted to access a segment not defined in a PSB.

Figure 5.4 shows the PSB definition for the mailing label program presented in Chapter 4 (see Figure 4.5). The mailing label program needed to view just one segment in the data base. This PSB defines one sensitive segment (SENSEG NAME=STUDENT), the STUDENT segment. Regardless of the number of segments that exist in the data base, this program will never be aware that any segments other than the STUDENT segments exist. If the program attempts to access the SPORTS segment, or any other segment except the STUDENT segment, it will be given an error indication. PROCOPT=G specifies the processing option (the type of data manipulation) the mailing label program may perform. DL/I permits five different processing options—G, I, R, D, and A—which stand for get, insert, replace, delete, and all, respectively.

The number of segments included with the PSB are a function of the processing needs of the application program. The data base administrator

Figure 5.4
PSB definition for mailing label program.

```
PCB      TYPE=DB, DBDNAME=STUDENT
SENSEG   NAME=STUDENT, PROCOPT=G
PSBGEN   LANG=COBOL, PSBNAME=MAILABEL
```

includes all of the segments required by the application program in the PSB. If the requirements of the application program change, the PSB can be modified to meet the new requirements.

5.3 LOGICAL DATA BASE STRUCTURES

DL/I stores data as hierarchies, but data does not always occur as hierarchical structures. Certain data relationships evolve as networks. Although networks cannot be represented directly in DL/I, they can be converted to hierarchical, or tree, structures by duplicating data. Since duplicate (redundant) data is undesirable, DL/I eliminates the redundant data with pointers called *logical pointers.*

The tree structure presented in Example G5 was the first phase of an information management system installed at Blue Whale College. Over a period of time, additional phases are installed. As each system is installed, it should provide minimum disruption to existing systems.

The system has four phases. The first phase, as was presented in Example G5, was designed to capture and maintain student data. The second phase is to store data concerning the courses taken by the student. The third phase is to provide a class roster for the instructor. The fourth phase is to mail student grades at the end of the semester. Examples G6, G7, G8, and G9 show the evolution of the data base in the life of the project. This evolution does not affect existing application programs. The manipulation of the data base by the application program will be presented in the next section, 5.4 Data Manipulation Commands.

Example G6
Adding Phase Two at Blue Whale College

To add the data for the second phase at Blue Whale College (data concerning the courses taken by students), the structure of the data base is changed. An additional segment is added to provide data about the courses taken by each student (see Figure 5.5). The COURSE segment is added to the right and below existing segments in the tree structure. By doing this, the COURSE segment can be added with no change to existing programs. Figure 5.5 shows the one-to-many relationship between the student and the courses taken, in addition to the one-to-many relationship that previously existed between students and car registrations, and between students and sports.

Redundant Data

The new relationship in Example G6 and Figure 5.5 causes an undesirable situation: redundant data. In the student-course relationship, occurrences of the COURSE segment are duplicated. For instance, if 30 students are taking course DP209, Data Base Management Systems, one occurrence of the course exists for every student taking the course. To change the description of a course in the COURSE segment, the STUDENT segment is accessed and the child pointers in the STUDENT segment are followed to the COURSE seg-

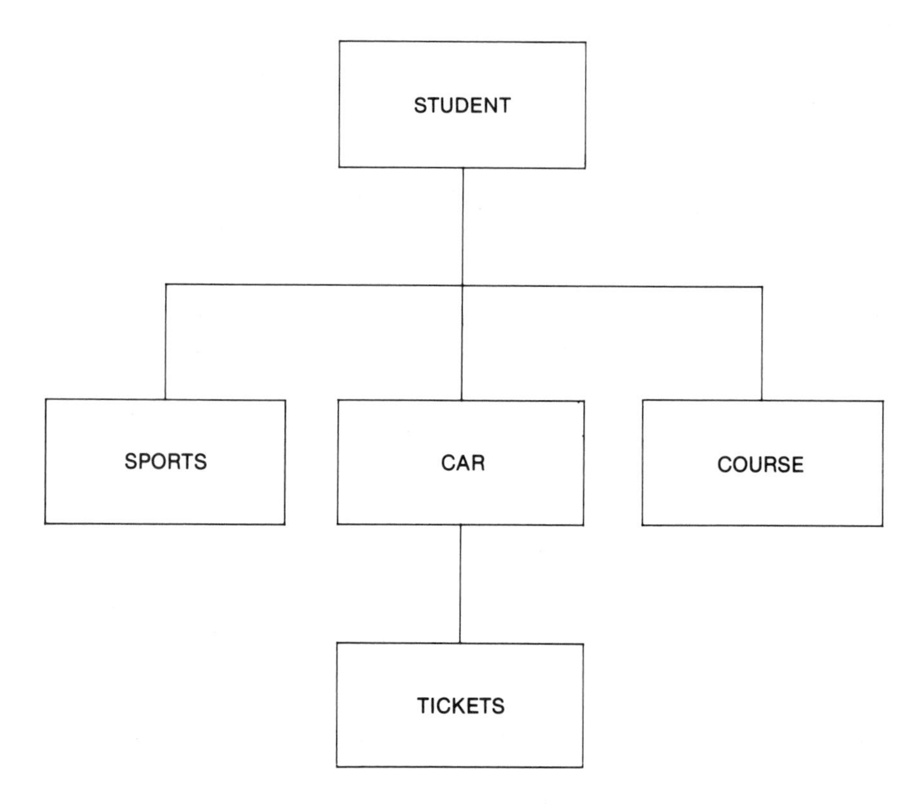

Figure 5.5 Student data structure at Blue Whale College after adding the COURSE segment.

ment. If the student is taking a course whose description is to be changed, the description of the course in the COURSE segment is changed; otherwise, the COURSE segment is accessed but not processed. To ensure that the description of a course is changed in every occurrence of the COURSE segment, every student in the data base and every course taken must be accessed. This is inefficient.

Figure 5.6 illustrates the problem in more detail. It depicts three occurrences of the data for a new relationship. (Since DL/I follows child pointers from the STUDENT segment to the COURSE segment, the segments for SPORTS, CAR, and TICKETS have no bearing on this example; they have been omitted for clarity.) To change the description of course DP209 from Introduction to Data Base Management Systems to Understanding Data Base Management Systems, pointers are followed to the COURSE segments. The segment for Doaks is obtained, and the child pointer pointing to the first COURSE segment for Doaks is followed. Each COURSE segment is examined to determine if it is for DP209. After each course is examined, the twin pointer in the COURSE segment is followed to the next twin. Doaks is taking DP209, so the description of this course in the COURSE segment is changed. The COURSE segments for courses taken by Jones are searched in the same manner. Jones is not taking DP209; therefore, no segments are updated. The segments for Adams are searched. Adams is taking DP209, so the description of the course is changed. In this process, DL/I reads the data for six courses

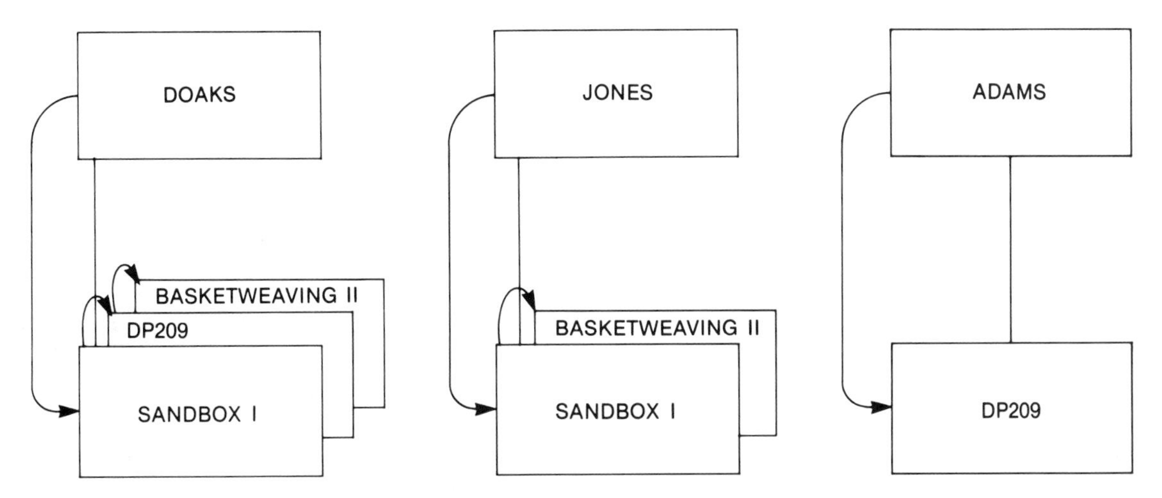

Figure 5.6
Three occurrences of the student-course data.

searching for segments to be updated. Only two segments are updated, but the same update is applied twice! Clearly, this is undesirable.

Logical Pointers

DL/I eliminates redundant data by placing the COURSE segments in a separate data base, the COURSE data base. Now two separate data bases exist: the STUDENT data base shown in Figure 5.1 and the COURSE data base. Through a logical DBDGEN, DL/I provides a logical view of the data that existed in Figure 5.5. A logical DBDGEN creates a logical data base by specifying data relationships between two segments normally in more than one data base.

The terminology associated with this data relationship is important. The STUDENT segment is now called the **physical parent**. The terminology for this segment has not changed, but now the emphasis is on the word *physical*. The segment where the course data was stored in Figure 5.5 is now called the **physical child** of the physical parent and a **logical child** of the COURSE segment. In this example, the logical child segment does not contain any data. Instead, it contains two pointers. First, a twin pointer points to the next physical child for this parent. Second, a logical parent pointer points to the segment where the course data is stored. The segment pointed to is called the **logical parent**. The course data is stored only once in the COURSE segment in the COURSE data base. This is an example of a unidirectional logical relationship, since the logical parent pointers point only in one direction.

Example G7 shows how this process avoids redundancy in our Blue Whale College illustration.

Example G7
Use of Logical Pointers to Eliminate Redundancy at Blue Whale College

To eliminate redundant data, Blue Whale College installs logical pointers. Figure 5.7 shows the system structure as it physically exists. The data relationship between students and courses is still present. However, to determine the courses taken by Doaks, logical parent pointers are now followed from the logical child to obtain the data for the courses. The physical child pointer

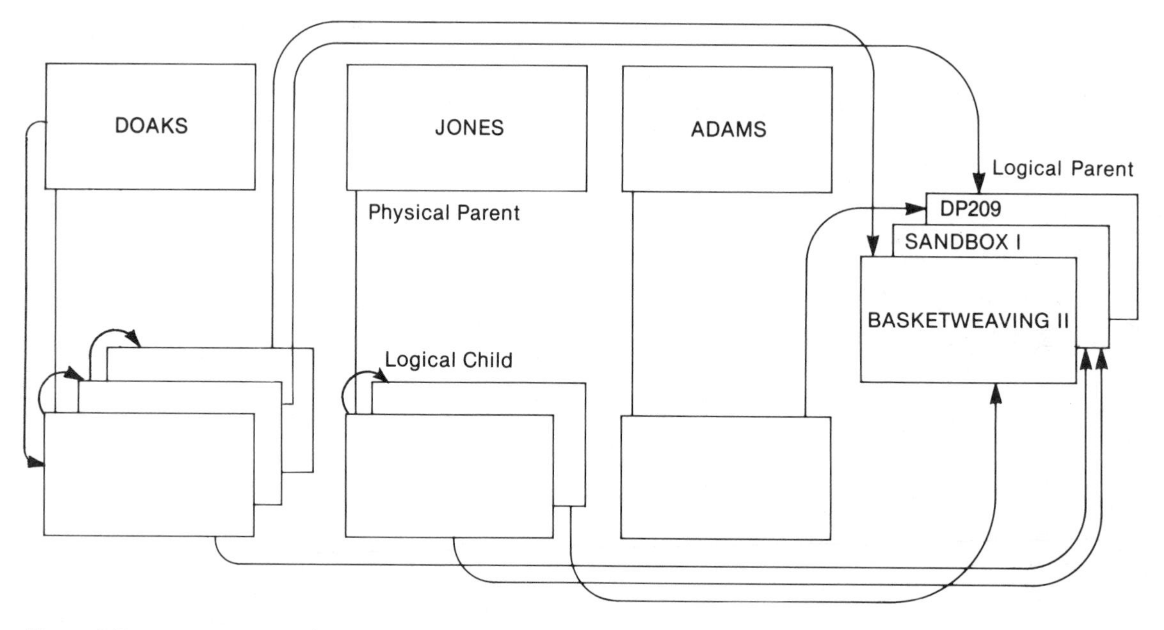

Figure 5.7
Unidirectional logical relationship between students and courses.

in the root segment for Doaks points to the first occurrence of the COURSE segment. This segment contains two pointers. One points to the location where the data for the course Sandbox I is stored in the COURSE data base. The second pointer points to the next occurrence (twin) of a COURSE segment for Doaks. No data is lost in the logical relationship, and pointers are used to eliminate redundant data.

The COURSE segments can now be changed with a single update. The COURSE segments in the COURSE data base are searched for course DP209. When the COURSE segment is obtained, the description is changed. Since this is the only place the data for courses is stored, the new description is obtained when pointers are followed to obtain data.

Bidirectional Logical Relationships

To install the third phase at Blue Whale College (class rosters for instructors), the data base must represent a one-to-many relationship between courses and students. If this structure were implemented in conjunction with the previous structure, it would form a complex network (see Figure 5.8). Since networks are not permitted in DL/I, an alternative design is necessary. Example G8 illustrates how it is installed.

Example G8
Adding Phase Three at Blue Whale College

In the design necessary at Blue Whale College because DL/I cannot represent network structures, the one-to-many relationship between courses and students is expressed by Figure 5.9a, and the previous relationship is shown in Figure 5.9b. The complex network of Figure 5.8 has been restructured into two tree structures by duplicating data.

But this recreates the redundant

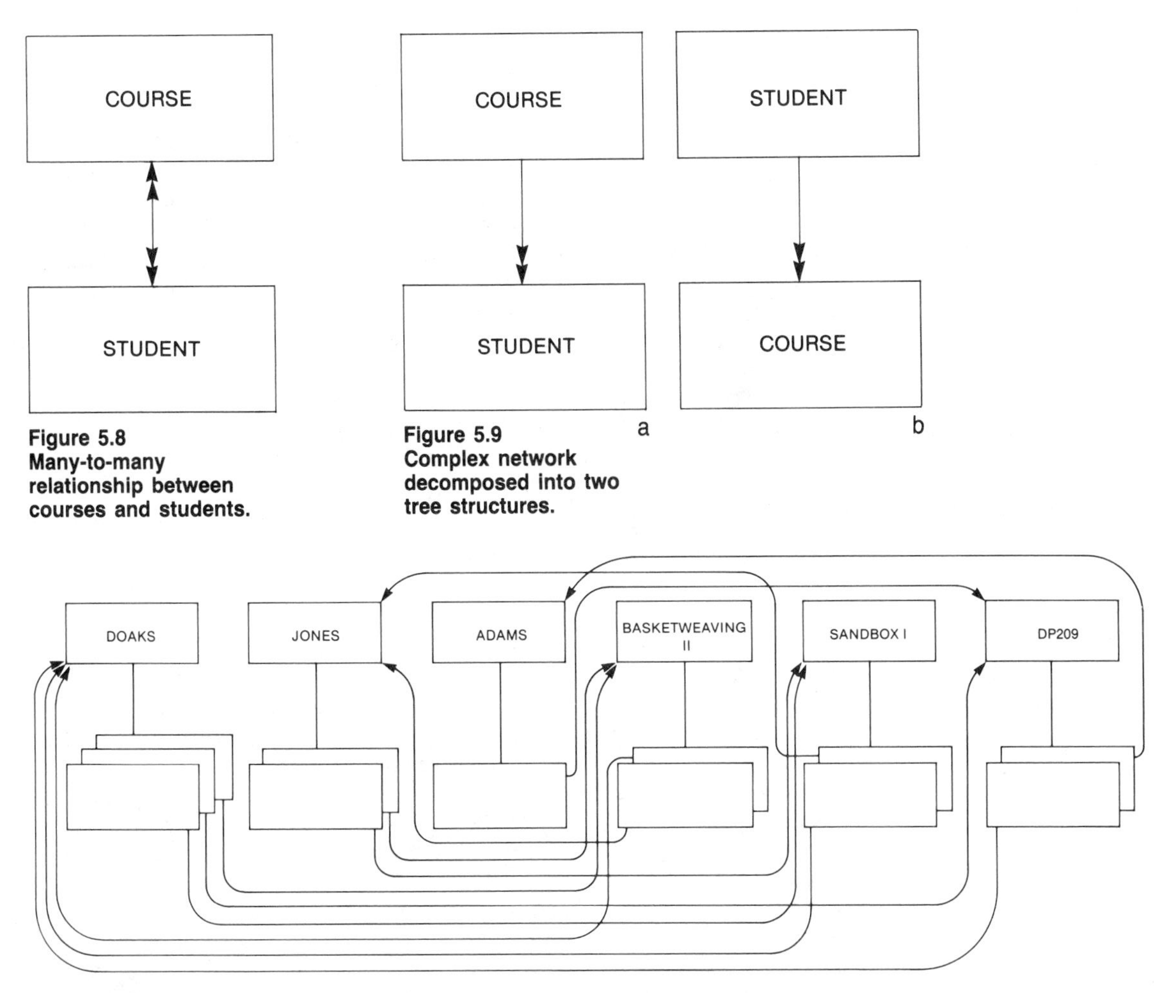

Figure 5.8
Many-to-many relationship between courses and students.

Figure 5.9
Complex network decomposed into two tree structures.

Figure 5.10
Bidirectional logical relationship for the many-to-many relationship between students and courses.

data problem, for the data for students is duplicated in the course-student relationship. If a student changes his or her name, every COURSE segment and every student in each course must be accessed to find the student whose name is to be changed. This, as in the previous phase, is undesirable.

The solution is again logical pointers, created through a DBDGEN. DL/I takes the data from two separate data bases and connects it through logical pointers. This is called a *bidirectional logical relationship,* since the two segments are logically related to each other. Each physical parent has a logical child that points to the other.

Figure 5.10 shows three occurrences of the data structure to represent the student-course and course-student relationships. Doaks is taking three courses: Sandbox I, DP209, and Basketweaving II. Jones is taking Sandbox I and Basketweaving II. Adams is taking one course, DP209. On the right, the course-student relationship is shown. In this structure, the data for the students is not stored in the segments that are children of the courses. Instead, a pointer is stored to point to the location of the actual data. To obtain the data for the courses taken, DL/I follows the child pointer from DP209 to its first STUDENT segment, Doaks. To obtain the data for Doaks, the logical parent pointer from the logical child Doaks is followed to logical parent Doaks in the STUDENT data base. DL/I obtains the data for Doaks from this segment. DL/I then follows the twin pointer (omitted for clarity) from the logical child Doaks to the next STUDENT segment, the logical child for Adams. Again, DL/I follows the logical parent pointer to the STUDENT data base to obtain the student data for Adams.

Using logical pointers, data duplication has been eliminated. The data for each course and each student is stored only once. Any reference to the course is made through logical pointers. Since all references are through pointers, only one segment needs to be modified to effect a change to a field. No other changes are necessary. Each child segment under a student points to a logical parent where the data is actually stored.

Intersection Data

The fourth phase at Blue Whale College expands the data base to include a system to mail student grades at the end of the semester.

Example G9 Adding Phase Four at Blue Whale College

In implementing grade mailing at Blue Whale College, a question first arises as to the placement of the field that contains the grade. It cannot be placed in the physical COURSE segment; since many logical child segments point to the COURSE segment, there would be no way to determine which student obtained the grade. Nor can it be placed in the physical STUDENT segment; since many logical child segments point to the STUDENT segment, there would be no way to determine what course the grade was obtained in. It must be placed in one of the logical children: in the logical child for the COURSE segment under the STUDENT segment, or in the logical child STUDENT segment under the COURSE segment.

Either parent, by itself, is not sufficient to make the data meaningful. Data that is stored in a logical child involved in a logical relationship is called **intersection data** (see Figure 5.11). In this example, GRADE obtains its meaning from both of its parents, STUDENT and COURSE. In a bidirectional logical relationship, when an application program adds or changes intersection data in one logical child, DL/I automatically duplicates the change in the other logical child.

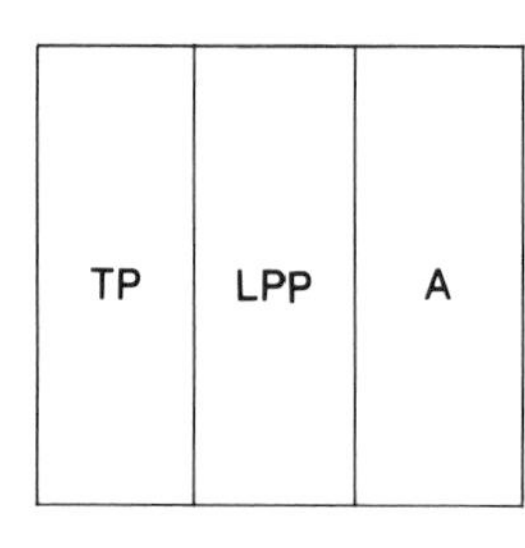

Where:
TP = Twin pointer
LPP = Logical parent pointer
A = Grade

Figure 5.11 Logical child segment showing the pointers and the intersection data for grade.

5.4 DATA MANIPULATION COMMANDS

DL/I contains a series of DML commands to access the data from the data base management system. Since a request from a COBOL program to DL/I is accomplished through a COBOL call verb, the DML commands are referred to as **calls.** Six different calls are available to obtain data: Get Unique (GU), Get Hold Unique (GHU), Get Next (GN), Get Hold Next (GHN), Get Next Within Parent (GNP), and Get Hold Next Within Parent (GHNP). "Hold" notifies DL/I that the application program may update the segment retrieved. This is important in the on-line environment. The reasons for the use of the hold calls will be explained in Chapter 9, which discusses the on-line environment. Three other DML calls—Insert (ISRT), Replace (REPL), and Delete (DLET)—are used for data base maintenance.

The calls are used in conjunction with the DBD and PSB definitions to obtain the segment to be processed. DL/I verifies the authority of each program to issue the command before data is presented. However, the description of this verification will be omitted from the following examples for simplicity. Each call causes one segment to be returned to the application program. However, the call has been replaced by the command itself in the following examples, to show the coding of the command.

Special operands called *command codes* allow multiple segments to be returned for each command issued. They are, however, the exception rather than the rule, and we will not discuss them here. After each command is issued, DL/I returns a status code to indicate the success or failure of the command. It is the responsibility of the application program to test the status code after each command is issued.

Application programs operate on logical data structures: the view of data as seen through the PSB. One hierarchical path is operated on at a time. First, an application program requests data from DL/I by issuing a call statement. Four different parameters are passed to DL/I on the call statement:

1. The first parameter is the function code, which describes the type of request being made.
2. The second parameter is a PCB mask indicating which PCB of the PSB the program is using.
3. The third parameter is the address of an I/O-AREA in the program where DL/I places the requested segment.
4. The fourth parameter is a segment search argument (SSA), which further describes (qualifies) the segment being requested.

SSAs (the fourth parameter) are optional. A maximum of 15 SSAs can be used in one call; one SSA per level in a hierarchical path. SSAs can be qualified or unqualified. Unqualified SSAs specify the segment type being requested. Qualified SSAs specify the name of a key field or search field in the DBD and the value of the data in the segment requested.

Get Unique

The Get Unique (GU) call directly obtains any sensitive segment that can be uniquely identified within the data base. It is the only DL/I call that can go forward and backward to retrieve a segment. For example, to obtain the data for the student who has a student identification number 123456789, the following command would be issued:

```
GU STUDENT(SID    = 123456789)
```

GU is the function code to request a specific occurrence of the data. Following GU is the SSA that uniquely identifies the requested segment. STUDENT is the name (from the SEGM NAME=STUDENT in the DBD) of the segment requested. SID is the name of the key field (from the FIELD statement under the SEGM statement in the DBD) to be searched. 123456789 is the value of the SID desired. However, the SSA is not limited to values of the key field. DL/I will search for a segment based on any field defined in a FIELD statement in the DBD.

Get Next

The Get Next (GN) call performs sequential retrieval of segments in a data base. It may be issued with or without qualifiers. Let us say, for example, that the PSB is defined such that the application program is only sensitive to the COURSE segment in the COURSE physical data base. The following call, repetitively issued, obtains a list of all of the courses in the data base:

```
    PERFORM GET-NEXT-COURSE
        UNTIL NO-MORE-ARE-FOUND.
GET-NEXT-COURSE.
    GN
    PERFORM TEST-STATUS.
    IF GN-STATUS-IS-OK
        PERFORM PRINT-COURSE.
```

Note that it is not necessary to qualify this call, since the program is only sensitive to the COURSE segment. DL/I fetches the next occurrence of the COURSE segment in the data base each time the command is issued. DL/I returns a status code to the application program to indicate when the end of the data base is reached.

If the application program is sensitive to more than one segment, an occurrence of each segment to which it is sensitive is presented in hierarchical sequence each time the call is issued. If the application program wanted to obtain every occurrence of every segment in the data base (a highly unusual request), the GN call could be issued repetitively until the end of the data base is reached.

If the application program is sensitive to multiple segments in the data base, the GN call must be qualified to specify which segment the application program desires. The call is modified as follows to obtain every course when the program is sensitive to multiple segments:

```
    PERFORM GET-NEXT-COURSE
        UNTIL NO-MORE-ARE-FOUND.
GET-NEXT-COURSE.
    GN     COURSE.
    PERFORM TEST-STATUS.
    IF GN-STATUS-IS-OK,
        PERFORM PRINT-COURSE.
```

Get Next Within Parent

After the application program issues the command to DL/I, DL/I searches the data base for the requested segment. DL/I uses one of a series of access methods to find the location of the desired segment and present it to the application program in an I/O-AREA. In addition to presenting the data, DL/I also "remembers" the position in the data base where the segment was obtained. This is called *establishing parentage.* The position in the data base is used with subsequent commands.

The Get Next Within Parent (GNP) call sequentially retrieves segments. It is normally used to obtain all of the occurrences of a given segment type for a parent. The GNP call would find all of the courses taken by all of the students by issuing the following commands:

```
    PERFORM GET-NEXT-STUDENT
        UNTIL NO-MORE-ARE-FOUND.
GET-NEXT-STUDENT.
    GN     STUDENT.
    PERFORM TEST-STATUS.
    IF GN-STATUS-IS-OK
        PERFORM PRINT-STUDENTS-NAME
        PERFORM GET-NEXT-COURSE
            UNTIL ALL-COURSES-ARE-PROCESSED.
GET-NEXT-COURSE.
    GNP COURSE.
    PERFORM TEST-STATUS.
    IF GNP-STATUS-IS-OK
        PERFORM PRINT-COURSE-NAME.
```

GNP is the command to request all of the occurrences of a given segment type for a parent, one at a time. COURSE is the name of the segment to be obtained from the data base. Recall that the COURSE segment is stored in a separate data base and connected by pointers. This has no impact on the application program, since the application program is unaware of the storage strategies used to store the data. DL/I follows the pointer from the physical parent to the first logical child for COURSE. DL/I knows from the DBD that the data resides in a separate location. DL/I follows the logical parent pointer to the COURSE data base, fetches the data, and presents it to the application program. Each time the application program repeats this command, DL/I follows twin pointers to the next child of the parent and follows pointers to the logical parent, COURSE. The application program may repeat the process until no more COURSE segments for the specified student exist. Then DL/I returns a status code to the application program indicating that the last occurrence of the child for the specified parent has been processed.

Get Hold

A segment must be retrieved from DL/I with the "Hold" form of one of the previous Get calls before a segment can be deleted or replaced. DL/I does not permit a segment to be deleted or replaced if it has been obtained with one of the other Get calls.

Replace

The Replace (REPL) call changes data within a segment. After the application program obtains the data with the "Hold" form of one of the Get calls, it modifies the data that has been placed in its I/O-AREA.

Let's examine the statements executed to change an address. After a GHU command is issued for student 123456789, the application program changes the address for the student in the I/O-AREA, using the following commands:

```
GHU    STUDENT(SID    =123456789)
PERFORM TEST-STATUS.
    IF GHU-STATUS-IS-OK
        PERFORM CHANGE-ADDRESS
        REPL
        PERFORM TEST-STATUS
        IF REPL-STATUS-IS-OK
            PERFORM UPDATE-SUCCESSFUL.
```

REPL is the DML function code to replace a segment. Any data within the segment may be changed, except the key field. To change a key field, the segment with the old key must be deleted and a segment with the new key added.

Delete

The Delete (DLET) call removes an occurrence of a segment from the data base. For example, let's remove the DP209 COURSE segment for student 123456789 from the data base. The application obtains the segment with Get Hold calls and then issues the delete command as in the following statements:

```
GU STUDENT(SID     =123456789).
PERFORM TEST-STATUS.
IF GU-STATUS-IS-OK
    PERFORM GHNP COURSE(COURSKEY=DP209)
    PERFORM TEST-STATUS
    IF GHNP-STATUS-IS-OK
        DLET
        PERFORM TEST-STATUS
        IF DLET-STATUS-IS-OK
            PERFORM UPDATE-SUCCESSFUL.
```

The GU call navigates to the correct student, 123456789. The GHNP call navigates to the correct COURSE segment, DP209. DLET is the call to delete a segment. In this example, DL/I performs one of two actions depending on how this segment was obtained. If the course is obsolete and if it is obtained from the COURSE data base, the course is deleted. If the course is an active course and is being dropped by the student, the child segment which contained a pointer to the COURSE segment is deleted and the actual COURSE segment remains in the data base. DL/I has a series of INSERT, REPLACE, and DELETE rules (specified in the DBD) that govern the action taken with segments involved in logical relationships. The rules that determine which action will take place are specified in the DBDGEN by the data base administrator. In any case, regardless of the rules specified, the view seen by the application program does not change.

Insert

The last DL/I call is Insert (ISRT), which adds new segments to the data base. This is also the call used to load a data base (to place data in the data base for the first time). When a data base is loaded, the application program inserts segments, one at a time, in hierarchical sequence. When segments are added to an existing data base, the application program specifies the SSAs to define the position in the hierarchical sequence where the segment is placed. For example, to add an occurrence of a SPORT segment for student 123456789 the following call is issued:

```
ISRT STUDENT(SID     =123456789)
    SPORT
```

ISRT is the function code to add a segment. STUDENT is the name of the parent segment for the segment to be inserted. SID=123456789 identifies which parent segment is to be used. SPORT is the name of the segment to be added. The data to be stored is taken from the I/O-AREA in the application program.

5.5 SUMMARY

DL/I uses hierarchical structures to represent data. The schema is defined through a DBD. The subschema is defined through a PSB. DL/I cannot represent complex networks directly; it does so by reducing networks to tree structures by duplicating data, then using logical pointers to eliminate the redundant data.

Nine data manipulation commands are available. GU, GHU, GN, GHN, GNP, and GHNP are used to retrieve segments. ISRT adds new segments. DLET removes segments. REPL replaces segments in the data base after they have been modified in the application program I/O-AREA.

REVIEW QUESTIONS

5.1 What is the process used to define the schema in DL/I? The subschema?

5.2 Draw the tree structure defined in the following DBD:

```
DBD    NAME=CARMAKER,ACCESS=HDAM
SEGM   NAME=CARMAKER,PARENT=0,
       BYTES=1500
FIELD  NAME=(COMPNAME,SEQ,U),
       START=2,BYTES=33,TYPE=C
FIELD  NAME=ADDRESS,START=163,
       BYTES=74,TYPE=C
FIELD  NAME=TYPECODE,START=1203,
       BYTES=6,TYPE=X
SEGM   NAME=MAKE,PARENT=CARMAKER,
       BYTES=180
FIELD  NAME=(MAKEKEY,SEQ,U),
       START =150,TYPE=C
SEGM   NAME=MODEL,PARENT=MAKE,
       BYTES=90
FIELD  NAME=(MODLNAME,SEQ)START=1,
       BYTES=12,TYPE=C
SEGM   NAME=DEALER,PARENT=MAKE,
       BYTES=130
DBDGEN
FINISH
END
```

5.3 Draw the application program view of the tree structure defined in the following PSB:

```
PCB     TYPE=DB,
        DBDNAME=CARMAKER
SENSEG  NAME=CARMAKER,PROCOPT=G
SENSEG  NAME=MAKE,PROCOPT=G
SENSEG  NAME=DEALER,PROCOPT=GIR
PSBGEN  LANG=COBOL,
        PSBNAME=DEALERS
```

5.4 What function does the PROCOPT parameter in a PSB perform?

5.5 Who controls the statements included in DBDs and PSBs?

5.6 To develop a new relationship between students and the courses they are taking, what procedure would be performed? What programs would be changed? How does DL/I solve the problem of redundant data?

5.7 Complex networks exist in everyday data relationships, but DL/I does not permit network structures. How is this problem resolved?

5.8 What is intersection data? Give an example of how it is used.

5.9 What are the DL/I commands used to retrieve data? What commands must be used if the data is to be updated?

5.10 What is the only DL/I command that can move both forward and backward in the data base?

5.11 What is an SSA? How do they reduce the amount of work required by the application programmer?

5.12 An application program is sensitive to both the STUDENT and the SPORTS segments. A GU command has been issued to obtain the first occurrence of the STUDENT segment in the data base. If an application program issued the following commands repetitively, would the result be the same?

GN SPORT

GNP SPORT

5.13 What DML command must be issued before a DLET or REPL call?

5.14 What is the purpose of the "U" in the FIELD statement NAME=(SID,SEQ,U)?

5.15 What fields must be defined in the FIELD statements in a DBD?

DATA BASE IN THE WORKPLACE

The Hierarchical Data Model at Acme Widgets

We have already been introduced to Acme Widgets in Examples A1, A2, and A3 in Chapters 1 and 2.

Acme Widgets is a large corporation, having a workforce of over 10,000 employees who work on assembly lines in geographically dispersed locations. It is not a surprise that an extensive effort is needed to manage the workforce.

Prior to automating the personnel system, personnel recordkeeping was dispersed across many locations. When an employee was hired, the initial employee record was created at the employment office. When an employee started to work, additional entries were kept at the location where the employee worked. Also at the work location, each time an employee was trained to perform a new job, a skills entry was made in the employee's record. Common job skills were needed at multiple locations, so employees were permitted to move from one location to another to work at the jobs of their choice, limited only by the contract negotiated between the union and management. As employees were moved from one location to another, their personnel records were mailed to that location.

Employees were assigned to specific jobs at each location, based on their seniority and their job skills. Instead of a typical tree structure organization, each employee had multiple paths to the most desirable jobs. Because of the rules of the labor contract and the paths to jobs of higher responsibility and earnings, the process of scheduling an employee to a job was very complex. A scheduling clerk at each work location spent an entire day each week scheduling individuals in the jobs they would work in the coming week.

If an employee had an unscheduled absence, it was recorded on the employee record, and the supervisor had to fill the vacancy with the next employee who had contractual rights to work the job. When one employee was assigned to fill a vacancy, the vacancy created by the employee moving up had to be filled. The process cascaded from the original vacant position until the lowest jobs were filled. If the supervisor placed an employee in a lower-paying job than the employee was entitled to by the labor contract, Acme was obligated to pay the employee the wage difference. Since the supervisors had to make immediate decisions involving complex contract rules, they of course made unintentional errors.

When employees transferred from one work location to another, their records did not always follow immediately. This further complicated the scheduling process, since an accurate record of employee skills was not always on hand. On one occasion, an employee was assigned a job for which he did not have the necessary skills. While on the job, he made an error which caused over a quarter of a million dollars damage to the assembly line.

The sheer cost of administering records for all employees and moving the data from one location to another was a major problem for Acme. Records existed in the dispensary, in the employment office, in each work location office, and in the accounting department. Each location was hesitant to give up its records about an employee, so they made copies of information that they thought important. All employee information was not sent from one location to another when an employee changed work locations, and data was duplicated in multiple work locations. Occasionally, records were not sent at all. Each area had a partial picture of the employee data, but no one area contained all of the data for an employee.

Since there were many different uses for employee data, the employee records were accessed in multiple sequences. The employee record was accessed by employee number for job scheduling, vacations, and so on. It was accessed by social security number to provide information to government agencies and by employee name when someone outside the work location had to contact the employee.

Thus Acme faced several problems with this manual system:

1. A complete set of records did not exist in any one location.
2. When employees moved from one work location to another, their records did not follow them in a timely manner. Therefore, administrative decisions were made without adequate information.

3. Because of the way in which the system was administered, Acme paid out differential wages and the costs to repair damaged equipment.
4. Since there were no immediate checks on the accuracy of the data, long periods of time elapsed before an error was corrected.
5. Since data was required in multiple sequences, extensive time was required to resequence the data for reports.
6. A huge staff was needed to administer the volumes of personnel data. This prevented them from performing other tasks they were assigned.

Acme attempted to automate the system by running batch reports from conventional files on a daily basis and mailing the reports, like a newspaper, to all work locations. Each location read the reports looking for information about employees at their work location. Then they manually copied information from the batch reports onto their employee records. This was an improvement over the manual system, since a master copy of the employee data was stored at a central location and since the data could be resequenced using the computer. However, each work location continued to keep its own records because it would take them 24 hours or more to inquire about employee data. Also, since the report was 24 hours old when it was received, it was not completely trusted; each location knew additional information had been added since the report was generated. The massive effort that went into keeping personnel records was propagated instead of reduced.

Acme tried to purchase the software for a personnel system, but their requirements were different from those fulfilled by standard personnel systems. Therefore, Acme developed an on-line personnel recordkeeping system using a data base management system based on the hierarchical data model. It was implemented as an inventory system for people. Well over 500 programs were written to develop it.

The new system has provided a number of benefits:

1. Management at Acme can immediately determine the location at which each employee works, along with biographic data about the employee. Anyone at any work location, having the proper authority, can access and update the data base.
2. The complex relationships implanted in the data base management system permit the data to be accessed in multiple sequences without the resequencing which was previously necessary.
3. Since data is validated when it is entered, the number of errors has decreased dramatically.
4. Since the data is both timely and accurate, manual record keeping has been eliminated.
5. Since data is stored once and accessed on-line, the staff has adequate time to perform jobs they neglected under previous systems.

6. Due to on-line access, the skills of each employee can be verified prior to placing an employee on a new job. This reduces the chances of injury to the employee and damage to the assembly line.
7. Acme has a scheduling system which generates not only the weekly crew schedules, but also performs the rescheduling made necessary by an unscheduled absence.
8. Using a fourth-generation programming language, ad hoc queries can be made by clerks who do not have formal training in data processing.

A final benefit is that the new system has provided Acme with data about employment costs. Since the assembly of widgets is a labor intensive process, a major cost of doing business is the cost of labor. Acme now has an additional tool to manage it.

MODULE A

PHYSICAL STORAGE OF DATA IN DL/I

MODULE OBJECTIVES

Upon completion of this module, you should be able to:

1. Explain how DL/I logical structures are physically stored
2. List the considerations for the physical storage of data
3. Describe when each of the four hierarchical access methods is appropriately used to provide efficient data storage and retrieval

NEW WORDS AND PHRASES

HSAM
HISAM
HDAM
HIDAM
symbolic key
secondary index
bit map

A.1 MODULE INTRODUCTION

Chapter 5 presented the logical structures used to store data using DL/I. This module couples the logical structures with the DL/I access methods to store data. DL/I offers the data base administrator four different access methods to store and retrieve data sequentially, directly, or sequentially part of the time and directly the remainder of the time.

Each access method is designed to provide rapid access in a specific environment. The data base administrator must choose one of the four access methods to provide the best performance to either the most important end users or the greatest number of end users, if they are all of equal importance.

All DL/I access methods are hierarchical. HSAM is the Hierarchical Sequential Access Method, which is designed for sequential access to the entire data base. HISAM is the Hierarchical Indexed Sequential Access Method; it provides sequential access to the root and dependent segments and direct access to root segments. HDAM, the Hierarchical Direct Access Method, provides direct access to both root and dependent segments, with no sequential access. HIDAM, the Hierarchical Indexed Direct Access Method, provides direct access to root and dependent segments and sequential access to root segments.

The DBDGEN described in Chapter 5 is the vehicle to specify not only the desired access method, but also details about the environment in which the data is physically stored—items such as device type, physical record length, and block sizes.

The following sections present parallel information about each access method: the environment in which each access method is best used, an example of the way segments are stored, the manipulation provided on behalf of DL/I function codes, and the relation of each access method to the performance criteria we specified in Chapter 2.

A.2 HIERARCHICAL SEQUENTIAL ACCESS METHOD (HSAM)

We shall present HSAM first, because it is the easiest to understand of the four methods.

The logical structures presented in Chapter 5 are stored sequentially in preorder traversal sequence. HSAM is designed to provide fast sequential access to every segment in the data base. HSAM is the only DL/I access method that can be used with magnetic tape.

Since HSAM data bases use sequential organization, its uses with DL/I are severely limited. DLET and REPL calls are not permitted. ISRT calls can only be issued to create a new HSAM data base. Logical relationships are not allowed. Pointers are not used.

Each segment has a two-byte prefix. The first byte is the segment code; the second byte is a delete byte. DL/I identifies each segment type by the segment code prefix stored with the segment. Since DLET calls are not permitted, the delete byte is not used but exists for compatibility among DL/I access methods.

HSAM is designed for sequential access only. (A technique for random retrieval also exists but is considered so inefficient, I have never seen it used.) HSAM data bases store data in fixed-length records. The major decision to be made is the length of the physical record: The data base administrator must determine the most efficient physical record size for a given data base. Since the length of segments within a physical data base record can vary greatly, consideration is also given to the amount of unused space at the end of a physical record.

One or more segments are stored in each physical record in HSAM data bases. Example G10 illustrates use of HSAM at Blue Whale College.

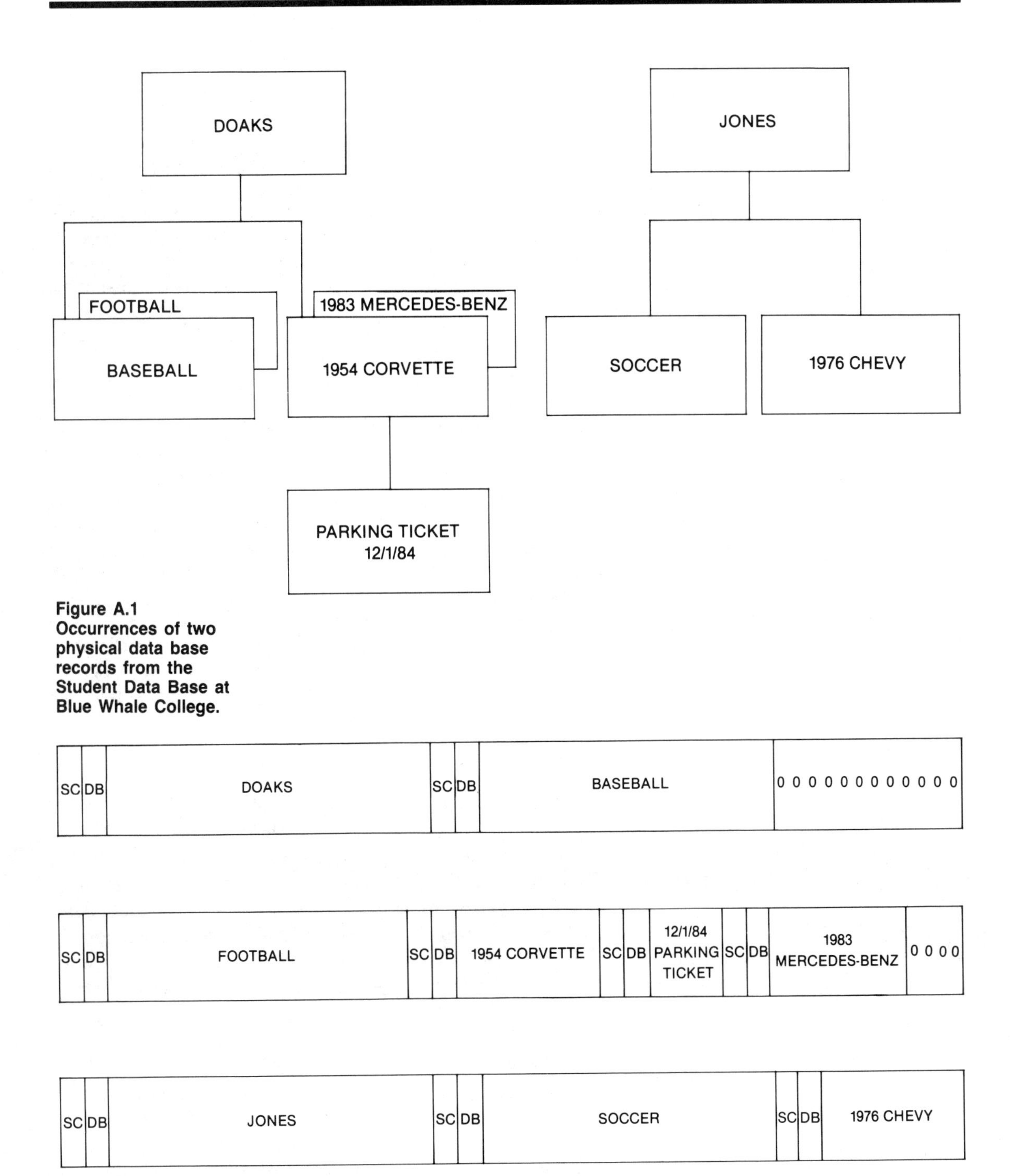

Figure A.1
Occurrences of two physical data base records from the Student Data Base at Blue Whale College.

Figure A.2
Two physical data base records stored using HSAM.

Example G10 HSAM at Blue Whale College

Figure A.1 presents occurrences of two physical data base records to be stored at Blue Whale College using HSAM. The STUDENT segment occupies 250 bytes, the SPORTS segment 125 bytes, the CAR segment 90 bytes, and the TICKET segment 65 bytes. (A physical record length of 471 bytes has been selected for this example to illustrate the storage of segments in each physical record. In practice, a much larger record size is normally used. Also, student name is used as the key for the STUDENT segment. In practice, a field which would guarantee uniqueness would normally be used.) Segments are stored in preorder traversal sequence. Occurrences of data for the tree structure we introduced in Chapter 5 in Example G5 are mapped onto a secondary storage device using HSAM. The root segment for Doaks is placed in the first physical record (see Figure A.2). The next segment in hierarchical sequence is baseball. This is placed as the second segment in the first physical record. The total length of the segments just stored is 379 bytes: 250 bytes for Doaks + the segment code and delete byte = 252 bytes; 125 bytes for baseball + the segment code and delete byte = 127 bytes. The segment for football is 127 bytes long, which does not fit in the first physical record. Therefore, only the segments for Doaks and baseball are placed in the first physical record, and the balance of the record is padded with binary zeros.

The segment for football is placed in the second physical record, followed by the segments for a 1954 Corvette, a 12/1/84 parking ticket, and a 1983 Mercedes-Benz. The total length of these segments with their segment codes and delete bytes is 378 bytes.

The next segment, for Jones, does not fit in the second physical record, and so the second physical record is padded with binary zeros and written to secondary storage. The segments for Jones, soccer, and a 1976 Chevy are written to the third physical record. These segments require exactly 471 bytes, so padding bytes are not necessary.

An HSAM data base is manipulated using the GU, GN, GNP, and ISRT function codes. Segments are retrieved from an HSAM data base with the GU, GN, and GNP function codes. The combination of these function codes permits the application program to perform *skip sequential processing*—the ability to skip to a desired sequence of records and process sequentially from that point. The GU function code is used to select the first segment to be processed, while the GN or GNP function code is used to process additional segments sequentially. Remember, this is a sequential access method. Even though the application program skips many segments to obtain the desired segment, DL/I still reads every segment between the current segment and the desired segment.

The ISRT function code is only permitted when creating a new HSAM data base. HSAM data bases are usually created in the same manner as magnetic tape files are created using a conventional sequential file organization. The current HSAM data base is read. If segments are not changed, they are ISRTed to an updated HSAM data base. If the segment is changed, the segment from the current HSAM data base is retrieved, changes are applied in a work area called the program I/O-AREA, and the changed segment is ISRTed

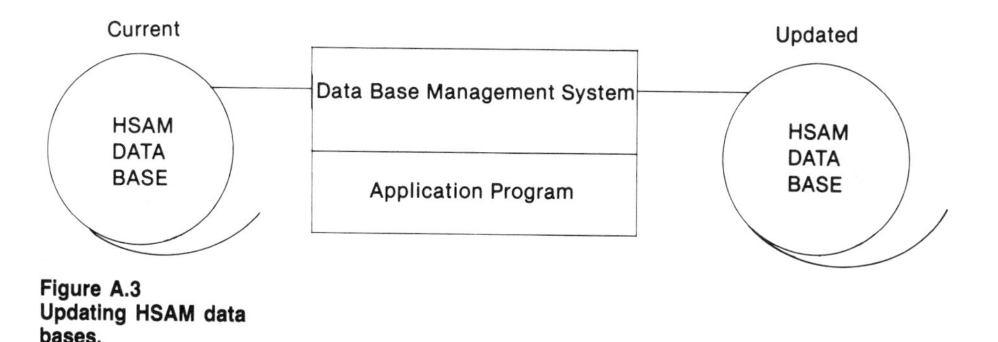

Figure A.3
Updating HSAM data bases.

into the updated HSAM data base. If segments are to be deleted, they are retrieved from the current HSAM data base, but never written to the updated HSAM data base. Figure A.3 illustrates this process.

Due to their sequential processing characteristics, HSAM data bases are best used in applications such as a history retirement data base. History retirement data bases are used when segments are no longer active in a production data base but the data is too valuable to permanently delete. It can be deleted from the production data base and added to an HSAM history data base. Since very few data base applications read the entire data base, HSAM is not often used.

HSAM data bases have the access and retrieval characteristics of sequential files. Faster sequential performance is achieved by using techniques we described in Chapter 2. HSAM permits anticipatory buffering, but not blocking. However, the effects of blocking can be achieved by increasing the physical record length when creating a new HSAM data base.

A.3 HIERARCHICAL INDEXED SEQUENTIAL ACCESS METHOD (HISAM)

HISAM provides fast sequential processing of the root and dependent segments and provides random retrieval of root segments. The restrictions that exist with HSAM data bases are eliminated in HISAM: All DL/I function codes can be used, and HISAM data bases may participate in logical relationships.

HISAM data bases combine the logical data structures we discussed in Chapter 5 with the physical data storage techniques of conventional ISAM files. It is important to keep this in mind, since the hierarchical features of DL/I cause the addition of root segments to be handled differently than with just ISAM. HISAM data bases have a primary data set and an overflow data set. In the primary data set, each segment is stored physically adjacent to the next segment in hierarchical sequence. Segments in the overflow data set are maintained in hierarchical sequence through a combination of physical adjacency within a block and direct address pointers between blocks. Example G11 shows how HISAM would be used at Blue Whale College.

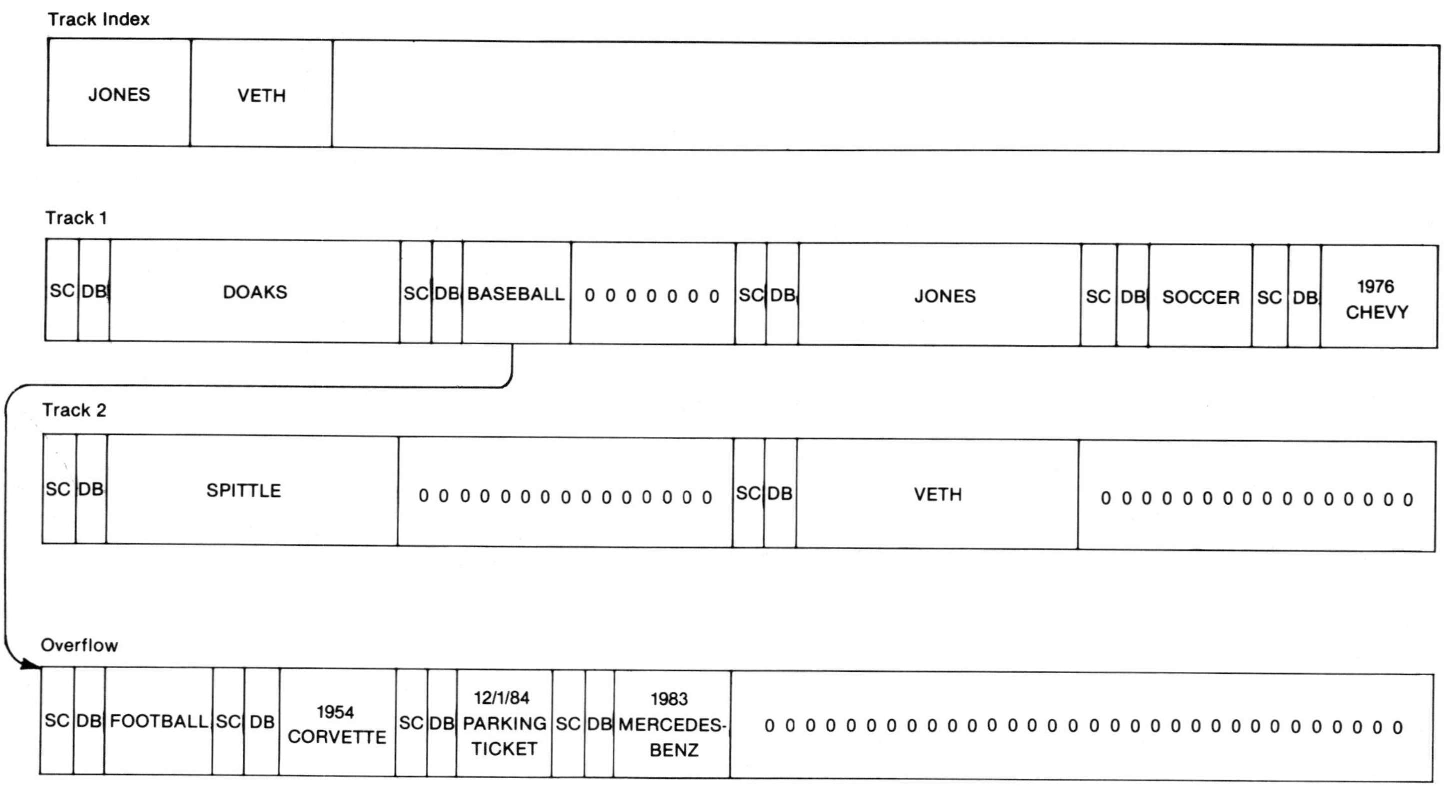

Figure A.4 Four physical data base records stored using HISAM.

Example G11
HISAM at Blue Whale College

In Figure A.4, occurrences of data for the tree structure from Example G5 (Chapter 5) are mapped onto a secondary storage device using HISAM. The logical record length is again 471 bytes to allow comparison with HSAM (Example G10). Two logical records are stored in each physical record, and there is one physical record per track. As with HSAM, the root segment for Doaks and the segment for baseball fit in the first logical record. Since HISAM uses fixed-length records, the balance of the first logical record is padded with zeros and is written to the primary data set.

The remainder of the dependent segments for Doaks fit in the next logical record. Again padding is added to the balance of the record. The second logical record, containing the balance of the dependent segments for Doaks, is written as the first logical record in the overflow data set and maintained in sequence by a direct address pointer from the logical record in the primary area.

The physical data base record for Jones fits in one logical record. This logical record is written in the primary data set. Since this physical record contains the root segment having the highest key on Track 1, an entry is created in the index to indicate this.

Two new occurrences of the STUDENT segment are included in this example to further demonstrate the manner in which segments are stored. Spittle and Veth are new students. They do not have any dependent segments. Each root is stored in a separate logical record on Track 2, and the index entry is updated.

When dependent segments are added, other dependent segments move to maintain physical adjacency to the next hierarchical segment. When Jones takes up lacrosse, this segment is added after the root segment. Now, the segments for soccer and the 1976 Chevy no longer fit in this logical record. These segments are placed in the next available logical record in the overflow data set. The logical record is chained in hierarchical sequence by direct address pointers from the logical record for Jones in the primary data set.

When the root segment for Roksiewicz is added, it is chained by a direct address pointer in the record for Spittle (see Figure A.5). When root segments are added, they are also placed in a separate logical record in the overflow data set. These records are also chained in hierarchical sequence by direct address pointers from the logical record in the primary data set.

The direct address pointer chains become longer with each root segment added and with each dependent segment that does not fit in the primary data set. Direct address pointers that chain physical records are not the segment pointers described in Chapter 3. There are no segment pointers in a HISAM data base. All hierarchical relationships are maintained by physical adjacency.

All DL/I function codes can be used to access and manipulate an HISAM data base. When a qualified GU function code is issued, DL/I searches the index to obtain the root segment, similar to the manner in which a record is obtained using ISAM, as shown in Chapter 2. If a dependent segment is desired, DL/I sequentially processes the dependent segments, using the segment code to determine the hierarchical position of each segment processed, until the desired segment is located. If the desired segment is not

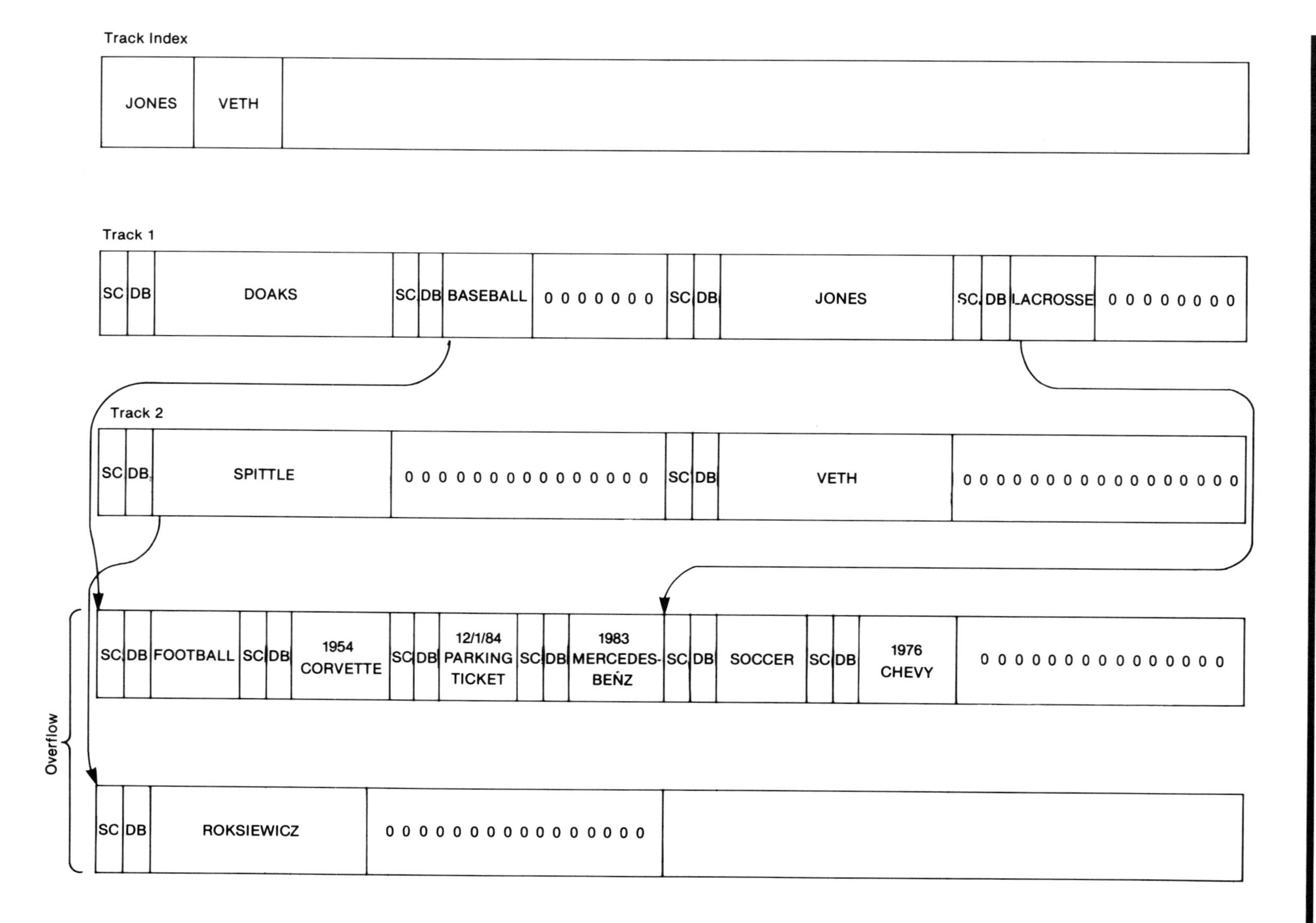

Figure A.5 Addition of segments using HISAM.

Figure A.6
The symbolic key for the occurrence of the soccer segment owned by Jones.

JONES	SOCCER

in the primary data set, direct address pointers are followed to the overflow data set and records are searched until the desired segment is found.

When a segment is deleted, the delete byte is altered, indicating deletion. The segment is not physically removed from secondary storage until the data base is reorganized.

With HISAM, since segments move when other segments are added, child, twin, hierarchical, or other segment pointers are not used to maintain logical relationships. Instead, a symbolic key of the desired segment is stored. **Symbolic keys** are the concatenated keys (keys placed end-to-end) of all the segments in the hierarchical path of the desired segment. The symbolic key for the soccer segment under the root for Jones contains the key of the root for Jones (Jones plus 19 spaces) and the key of the soccer segment (soccer plus 6 spaces) (see Figure A.6). When DL/I searches for this segment using a symbolic key, the length of the key for each segment can be determined from the DBD. With the symbolic key provided, DL/I searches for a root segment with a key of Jones. After locating the correct occurrence of the root, the next 12 characters (soccer plus 6 spaces) are compared to the key of each SPORTS segment until the correct segment is located.

HISAM data bases have many of the performance characteristics of conventional ISAM files. They are best used when the number of additions is small and when random retrieval of root segments and sequential processing of dependent segments is required. If most of the data base access is sequential, performance can be improved with high blocking factors. When many segments are inserted in the data base, performance degrades due to the chaining of records in the overflow data set. Performance is also degraded when a large number of segments are deleted. Since segments are not removed from the data base at the time they are deleted, DL/I still accesses these segments but does not return them to the application program. As with conventional ISAM files, performance is restored when the data base is reorganized.

Due to their indexed sequential processing characteristics, HISAM data bases are best used in applications such as, for example, a company where the payroll data base is a two-level structure with the employee data in the root segment and job history segments as dependent segments. Every other week, the entire data base is processed to develop the employees' paychecks. In an emergency, the name and phone number of a person to be contacted must be retrieved from the root segment immediately. A clerk in the Personnel Department can randomly obtain the root segment containing this information and make the phone call. In this company, most processing is sequential, yet some random processing capabilities exist.

A.4 HIERARCHICAL DIRECT ACCESS METHOD (HDAM)

HDAM provides fast and direct access to the root and dependent segments. The key of the root segment is processed by a randomizing module to provide a storage address similar to the direct organization described in Chapter 2. Sequential processing is possible only under unique circumstances: if the randomizing module manipulates the key field in such a manner that the roots are placed in physical sequential order in the data base. This rarely occurs. HDAM does not have the restrictions imposed by HSAM: All DL/I function codes can be used and HDAM data bases may participate in logical relationships.

HDAM data bases combine logical data structures with the physical data storage techniques of direct files. HDAM data bases are stored in one data set that is divided into two areas. The first area, the root addressable area, contains root segments and dependent segments. The second area, the overflow area, contains dependent segments that do not fit in the root addressable area.

The DBDGEN specifies the format of secondary storage. The root addressable area is composed of fixed-length physical records called *blocks*. The DBDGEN specifies the number of blocks in the root addressable area. The balance of the data set is for the overflow area. Each block in the root addressable area contains an area called a *root anchor point* or *RAP*, reserved for pointers to root segments (see Figure A.7). The number of root anchor points per block is also specified in the DBDGEN. After a block size is chosen, the number of physical data base records stored in a block is determined. The number of RAPs per block is equal to the number of physical data base records to be stored in a block.

The location where each physical data base record is stored is determined by the randomizing module. The key field of each root segment is presented to the randomizing module, which develops a block number and a RAP number. DL/I stores the root segment in the specified block. The RAP points to the location within the block where the root is stored. Dependent segments are stored in the same block as the root, if possible, to improve performance when later retrieving segments. Hierarchical relationships between segments are maintained by pointers.

If the segments for a physical data base record were stored in adjacent blocks, they would occupy the location where new root segments could randomize to, thereby causing synonyms. DL/I allows the data base administrator to specify, through a parameter in the DBDGEN, the maximum number of bytes to be stored consecutively. If this value is exceeded, the balance of the physical data base record is stored in the overflow area. This technique reduces synonyms caused by unusually long physical data base records.

Example G12 shows how HDAM would be used at Blue Whale College.

Figure A.7
Format of secondary storage using HDAM.

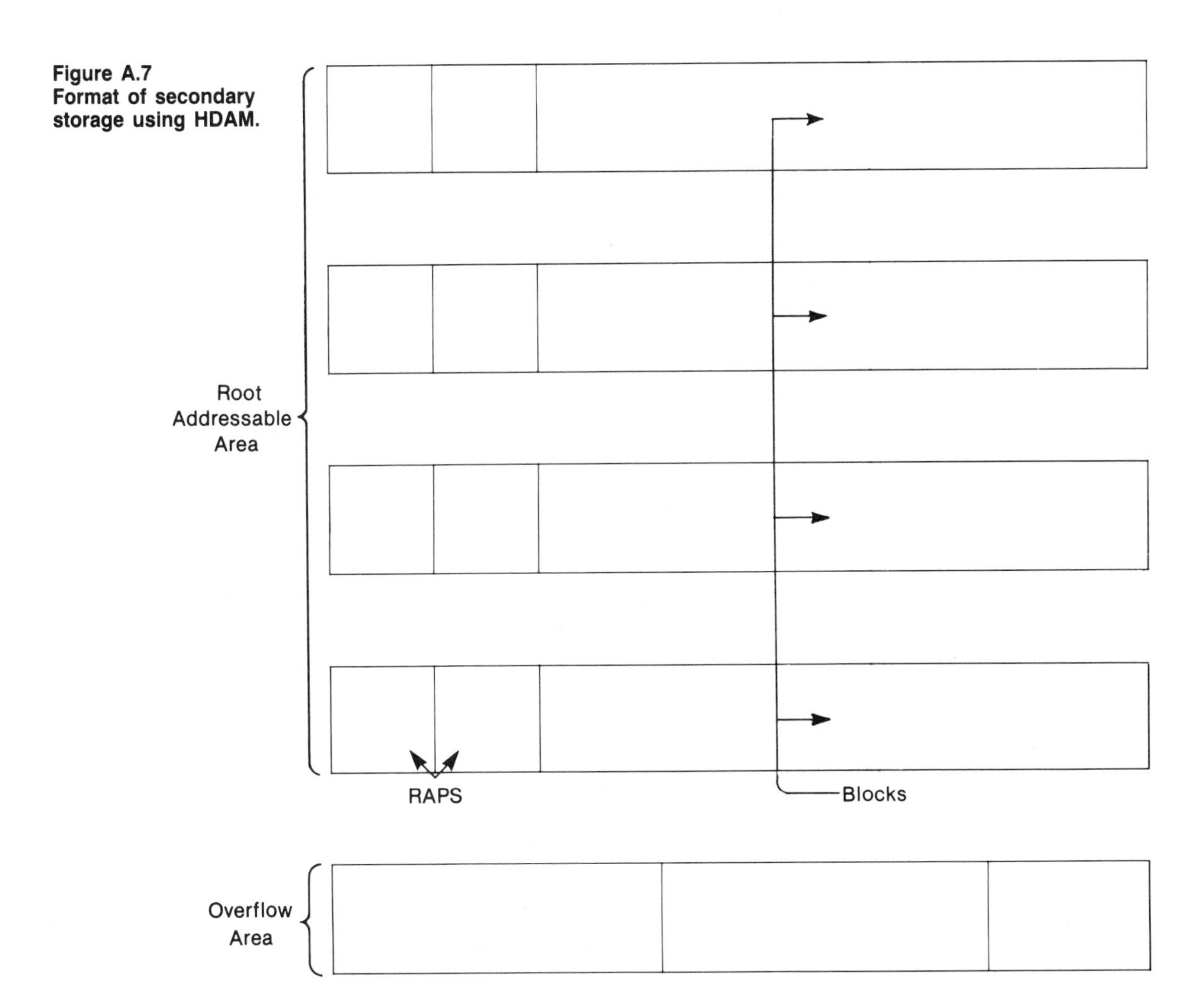

Example G12
HDAM at Blue Whale College

In Figure A.8, occurrences of data for the tree structure in Example G5 (Chapter 5) are mapped onto a secondary storage device using HDAM. The number of bytes consecutively inserted at one time is 471, to be consistent with Examples G10 and G11. The key for Doaks randomizes to Block 2 RAP 2. The segments for Doaks and baseball fit in 471 bytes and are stored in Block 2. The segment for football, when added to the length of the previous segments, does not fit in the block. It is placed in the overflow area and is pointed to by its twin, baseball. The second RAP in Block 2 points to the root segment for Doaks. The root segment for Jones randomizes to Block 1 RAP 1 and is stored in its entirety in that block.

In this example, child and twin pointers connect segments. Several types of pointers can be used. Each type of pointer improves performance with a specific access pattern. After learning the access patterns for the data base, the data base administrator determines which pointers are most beneficial

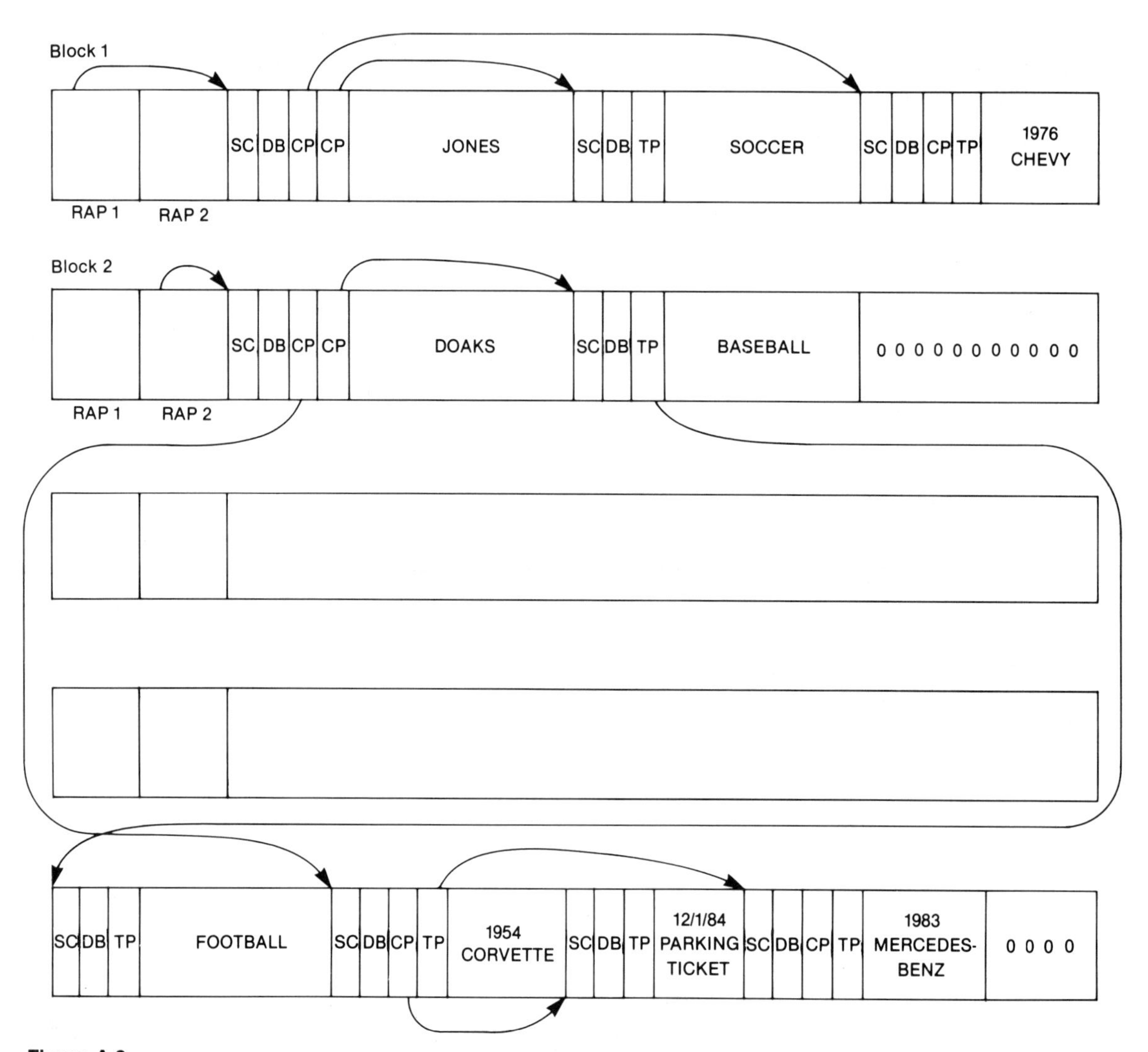

Figure A.8
Two physical data base records stored using HDAM.

for a specific data base. The type of pointers desired is then specified by the data base administrator in the DBDGEN.

All DL/I function codes can be used with HDAM. If a qualified GU were issued for Doaks, the randomizing module randomizes to Block 2 RAP 2, and the segment for Doaks is retrieved with one I/O operation. If the application program requests a CAR segment, child pointers from the root segment are followed to obtain that segment. In this example, dependent segments are in the same blocks, so no additional I/O operations are necessary. With longer physical data base records which span many blocks, child pointers are used to go directly to the block containing the desired data. This eliminates the retrieval of all unnecessary dependent segment types between the root segment and the child type of the desired segment.

HDAM is used for rapid random retrieval of root and dependent segments, and when there is no requirement for sequential retrieval. Performance is degraded when long synonym chains occur. Performance can sometimes be restored by reorganizing the data base. Sometimes the randomizing algorithm must be changed to restore performance.

Due to its direct processing characteristics, HDAM data bases are best used in applications such as, let's say, the reservations system at Fly-By-Nite Airlines. Fly-By-Nite has developed a reservations system with a root segment and two different child types. The root segment contains fields for flight number, departure and arrival times, and destination. One child type contains data for cargo to be transported, while the other child type contains data for passengers. When a person books a flight, the root segment for the flight is randomly obtained and flight information is given. The child segment for passenger seats is searched until an open seat is found. The passenger segment is updated with the name of the passenger. Since a passenger seat is desired, segments for cargo are bypassed through the use of child pointers, thus speeding the update process. Note that this data base cannot be processed sequentially.

A.5 HIERARCHICAL INDEXED DIRECT ACCESS METHOD (HIDAM)

HIDAM provides direct and sequential access to root segments and direct access to dependent segments. It is similar to the cross-reference list approach to direct access described in Chapter 2. Direct access is not as fast as HDAM, since the index data base is searched to find the location where the root is stored. HIDAM combines the storage techniques used in HISAM and HDAM. Again, the restrictions that exist in HSAM have been eliminated in HIDAM: All DL/I function codes can be used and HIDAM data bases may participate in logical relationships.

HIDAM data bases are composed of two separate data bases: the data base where the data is stored and an index data base which acts as a cross-reference list to the root segments in the data base. The data base is a series of consecutive blocks where data can be stored. It does not have a root addressable area or an overflow area. The load program inserts segments in hierarchical sequence, just as with HSAM. The data base administrator can reserve space, called *free space,* in the data base through parameters in the DBDGEN. Free space can be used to add segments added after the initial load of the data base has been completed.

Each time a root segment is added to the data base, an entry is created in the index data base. The index data base is a root-only HISAM data base. Each root segment contains the key field of the root segment in the primary data base and a pointer to the location where the root is stored in the primary data base. The root segment is placed in the most desirable block in

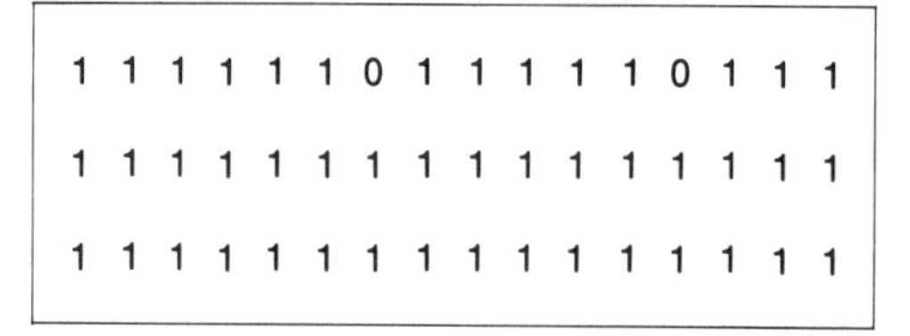

Figure A.9
Bit map showing available free space in all blocks except 7 and 13.

the data base. DL/I has a complex space management algorithm to determine which block is most desirable. The objective of the algorithm is to write the segment with the minimum rotational delay and seek time.

Both of the direct access methods—HDAM and HIDAM—attempt to place new segments next to segments with which they are referenced. If space in that block is not available, DL/I must find a block with sufficient space to accommodate the new record. If, for example, DL/I examined secondary storage to find a block with sufficient free space, performance would degrade because of the time taken to perform the search. Instead, DL/I uses bit maps to manage free space. A **bit map** is a control block which maps available free space within the data base with a series of ones and zeroes. Each one or zero represents a corresponding block within the data base (see Figure A.9). The bit is set to one if the block has sufficient free space to store the longest segment length within the data base, and to zero if it does not. In Figure A.9, all blocks except the seventh and the thirteenth have sufficient free space to store the longest segment in the data base, and thus their bits are set to one. By referencing the bit map, DL/I can determine the most desirable block to store a segment without having to perform I/O operations to examine each block.

Example G13 illustrates use of HIDAM at Blue Whale College.

Example G13
HIDAM at Blue Whale College

In Figure A.10, occurrences of data for the tree structure in Example G5 (Chapter 5) are mapped onto a secondary storage device using HIDAM. The block length used is 589 bytes with 20 percent free space. This means 471 bytes are available to store segments. Thus, this example may be easily compared to Examples G10, G11, and G12. (Convenient calculation, isn't it?) Segments are added in hierarchical sequence. The segments for Doaks and baseball are placed in the first block, as was done in the examples of the three previous access methods. With the free space specified, the next segment, football, and those that follow it do not fit in the first block and are placed in the second block. An entry is placed in the primary area of the index data base for the root segment, Doaks. The segment for Jones and its dependents fit in the third block, and an entry for Jones is placed in the index data base.

This procedure is followed until the data base is loaded. Then additional segments are added in the most desirable block, and segment pointers are used to place them in hierarchical sequence. Figure A.11 shows the insertion of the lacrosse segment for Jones. Lacrosse is placed in the free space in the same block that contains the seg-

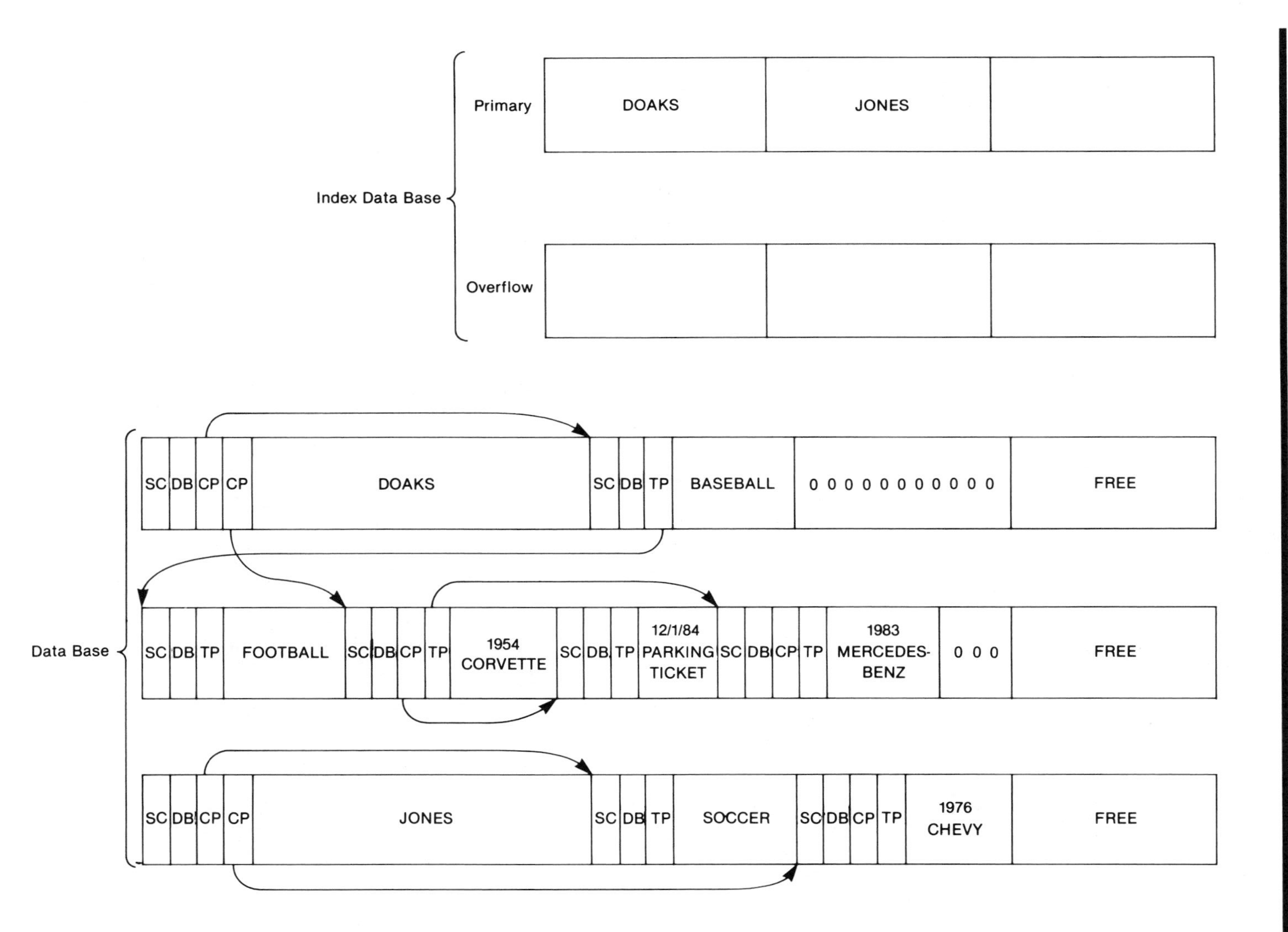

Figure A.10 Two physical data base records stored using HIDAM.

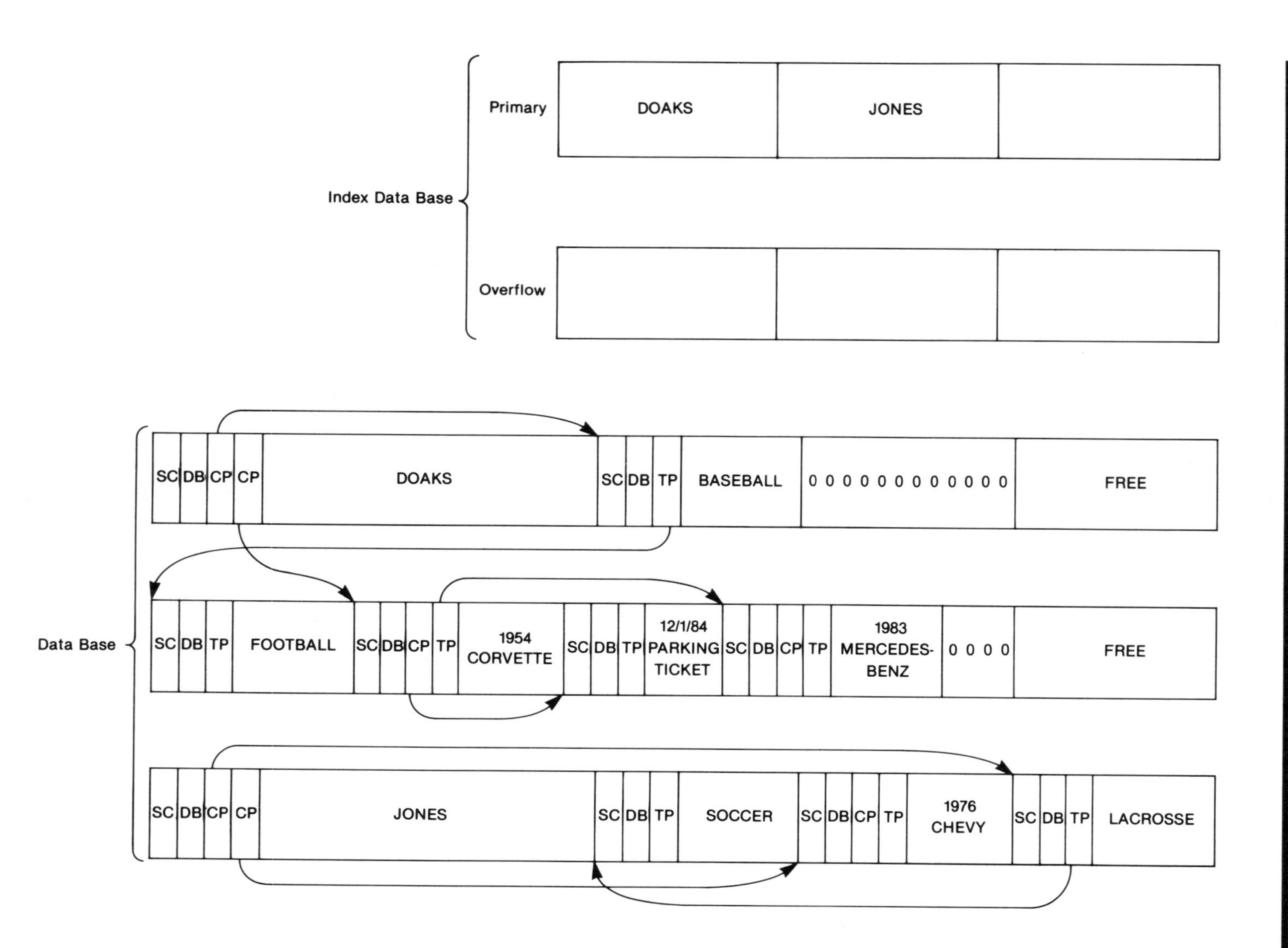

Figure A.11 Addition of a dependent segment in a HIDAM data base.

ment for soccer. It is maintained in logical sequence by twin pointers. Note that the segments are not in sequence by physical adjacency as occurred with the hierarchical sequential access methods (HSAM and HISAM). However, due to the free space reserved when the data base was loaded, all of the sports played by Jones can be retrieved with one I/O operation. If free space were not reserved, the segment for football would be in a different block, and two I/O operations would be necessary to retrieve the sports segments for Jones.

Using the hierarchical direct access methods (HDAM and HIDAM), segments do not move once they are stored, so direct address pointers can be used to point to the location where segments are stored.

HIDAM data bases have performance characteristics of both conventional ISAM files and direct files. Using HIDAM, root segments can be accessed directly by going to the HISAM index data base to determine the location of the desired root. If a large number of root segments are added, overflow chains increase in length and degrade performance. Reorganization of the HISAM index data base restores performance. This technique allows roots to be accessed directly or sequentially, just as with the ISAM access method. Direct access of the root is not as fast as with HDAM, due to the access of the index data base. Sequential processing of the dependent segments is not as fast as HSAM or HISAM, since pointers must be chased to present the dependents in sequence instead of physical adjacency.

Due to its indexed-sequential and direct-processing characteristics, HIDAM data bases are best used in applications such as an order entry data base. International Gismos, for example, has a two-level order entry data base. The root segment contains fields for order number, customer name and address, and so on. A child segment contains one segment for each item on the order. It contains fields for the description, quantity, ship-by date, etc. When the customer inquires about the order status (which is the primary purpose of this data base), a specific root segment is randomly obtained. Each individual order item can be examined to determine its status. Weekly, the entire data base is read sequentially to generate a shipping status report for the coming week.

A.6 SECONDARY INDEX

DL/I provides for a facility called a *secondary index* to access the segments for any DL/I data base organization (except HSAM) in more than one sequence. A secondary index is the DL/I terminology for the inverted file structures presented in Chapter 3.

The secondary index is used when there is a requirement to access data in more than one sequence or to provide rapid access to data when the key field is unknown. The secondary index functions in a manner similar

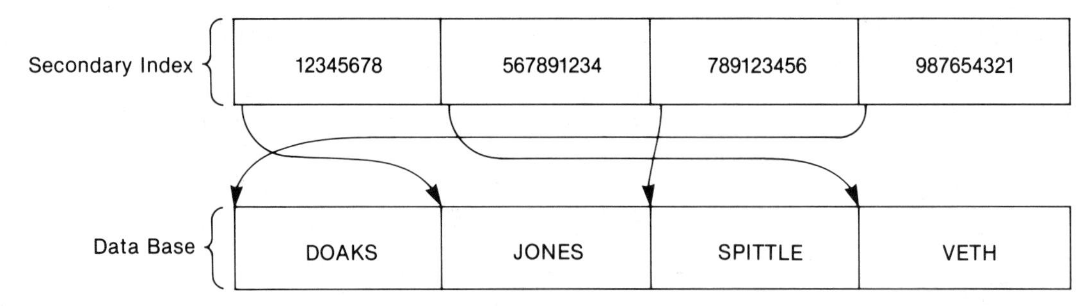

Figure A.12 Using a secondary index to provide alternate data sequences.

to the HISAM index for a HIDAM data base. The difference is that the HISAM index for a HIDAM data base is based on the key field of the root segment, and only one HISAM index exists for a HIDAM data base. The secondary index, however, can be built on any field specified within a segment and is created through a DBDGEN. The indexed segment can be at any level in the data base; it does not have to be a root segment. Each secondary index provides access to segments in a different sequence than is provided in the key sequence.

The data base administrator creates as many secondary indices for a segment as he or she feels are necessary. They are used to eliminate the sorting of data in the multitude of sequences needed by the end user. Figure A.12 demonstrates the use of a secondary index with the Student Data Base. In previous examples, student NAME was the key field for the data base (and it was assumed to be unique). During registration, the student is identified by a number, not by name. This requires a means to access the student in a different sequence than that in which the data is stored. The access must occur in a short period of time. When a student registers for a course, the secondary index is searched to find the student number. Once found, the segment also contains a pointer to the segment containing the full data about the student in another data base. The pointer may be a direct pointer, if the data base pointed to is a hierarchical direct data base (HDAM or HIDAM), or it may be a symbolic pointer, if the data base pointed to is a hierarchical index sequential data base (HISAM). By following this pointer, the full segment is retrieved.

The secondary index requires additional overhead, for it must be updated every time the source field is added, changed, or deleted. The benefit is the short access time needed to find the segment when the primary key of the segment is unknown. This is yet another example of compromise to satisfy a specific need. Constant overhead is absorbed on a continuing basis to provide rapid access or an alternate access sequence to a segment in an on-line environment.

A.7 SUMMARY

DL/I offers four different access methods to provide high performance when data bases are accessed sequentially, directly, or a combination of sequen-

Figure A.13 Summary of DL/I access methods.

	HSAM	HISAM	HDAM	HIDAM
Primary access to root	Sequential	Sequential	Direct	Direct
Secondary access to root	—	Direct	—	Sequential
Access to dependent segments	Sequential	Sequential	Direct	Direct
DL/I function codes	All but REPL and DLET Insert only to new data base	All	All	All
Logical relationships permitted?	No	Yes—must use symbolic pointers	Yes	Yes
Facilities to improve performance	Anticipatory buffering Increase physical record length	High block sizes Reorganization	Good randomizing algorithm Direct pointers	Reorganize index data base Direct pointers

tially and directly. HSAM provides the fastest performance when every segment in the data base is accessed and all accesses are sequential. HISAM provides the fastest performance when most accesses of the root and dependent segments are sequential and there is a secondary requirement for random retrieval of root segments. Neither HSAM or HISAM use pointers to obtain dependent segments. Hierarchical relationships are maintained through physical adjacency of segments.

HDAM provides rapid random retrieval of root and dependent segments. With a randomizing module that generates a minimum of synonyms, a root segment can be retrieved with one I/O operation. HDAM does not provide for sequential processing. HIDAM provides for fast random retrieval of root segments. It is slower than HDAM because an index is searched to determine the location where the root segment is stored. Direct access to dependent segments using the hierarchical direct access methods (HDAM and HIDAM) is faster than using the hierarchical sequential access methods (HSAM and HISAM). This is due to the use of child and twin pointers that allow DL/I to bypass the retrieval of unwanted child types when performing direct access of dependent segments.

The four DL/I access methods are summarized in Figure A.13.

While the DL/I access methods are flexible, they lack a basic attribute desirable in a data base management system: They do not allow complete data independence for the application program. For example, the results the application program obtains are different when issuing repetitive GN calls for root segments to the same data base stored using HDAM or HIDAM. HIDAM presents the segments in ascending root key sequence. HDAM presents the segments in the sequence they are stored. This does not diminish the effectiveness of DL/I. It does mean that application programs may require changes if the access method changes.

REVIEW QUESTIONS

A.1 Name the four DL/I access methods.

A.2 Which DL/I access method provides the fastest performance when the access pattern for the data base is primarily sequential, but random access to the root segment is occasionally needed?

A.3 Which DL/I access method provides the fastest performance when the access pattern for the data base is primarily random, and no sequential access is necessary?

A.4 Which DL/I access method provides the fastest performance when the access pattern for the data base is primarily random, and some sequential processing is needed?

A.5 Which DL/I access method provides the fastest performance when the access pattern for the data base is primarily sequential and used mainly for historical data?

A.6 From the secondary storage techniques presented in Chapter 2 to speed performance, give one technique to improve performance for HDAM. For HSAM. For HISAM. For HIDAM.

A.7 Which DL/I access methods do not use segment pointers to maintain hierarchical data relationships? Which do?

A.8 Which DL/I access method most closely resembles conventional sequential file processing?

A.9 What is a symbolic key? When logical relationships are established, which DL/I access method *must* have symbolic keys pointing to its segments? Why?

A.10 To save mailing costs when mailing student grades, STUDENT segments are accessed in sequence by zip code. What DL/I tool is available to provide this sequence without sorting student segments in zip code sequence?

6

NETWORK DATA MODEL

CHAPTER OBJECTIVES

Upon completion of this chapter, you should be able to:

1. Explain the terminology associated with the network (Data Base Task Group) model
2. State the relationship between a DBTG schema and the corresponding network structure
3. Read a DBTG schema and construct the corresponding network structure
4. Read a DBTG subschema and construct the corresponding program view of the data
5. Describe the similarities and differences between hierarchical and network structures
6. Explain the function of each DBTG data manipulation command

NEW WORDS AND PHRASES

CODASYL
DBTG
data item
record
set
currency indicators
locking

6.1 CHAPTER INTRODUCTION

Today, without standardization of data base management systems, the selection of a system is a long-range commitment by an organization. Data base management system software from each vendor is different, and often it is only for a specific type of hardware. When a data base management system is installed, hundreds of thousands of hours are spent developing application systems around the software. To change to different software or a different CPU requires a significant amount of time for conversion of the application systems to execute under the new system. Any conversion effort reduces the human resources available for new development, and most installations already have a backlog of requests for new development without the burden of a conversion.

If standardization were to take place, it would provide great flexibility to data processing installations. Standardization would allow an enterprise to change computer hardware, software, or even data base management system software without a massive conversion effort. The Data Base Task Group made an early attempt at standardization of data base management systems, similar to the work performed for the COBOL programming language.

Background of the Data Base Task Group Model

Data base management systems first appeared commercially in the late 1960s. Earlier, in May 1959, CODASYL (the Conference on Data System Languages) had been established as an informal voluntary organization comprised of COBOL users and manufacturers of computer equipment. The CODASYL committee was responsible for the COBOL specifications accepted as a national standard by the American National Standards Institute (ANSI).

The CODASYL Programming Language Committee created a group called the List Processing Task Force to develop a means to incorporate list processing techniques in file management. The List Processing Task Force examined many data base and file systems in order to draft language specifications. In 1967, the committee changed its name to the Data Base Task Group (DBTG). The network data model presented in this chapter is based on the DBTG specifications. The terms *network data model* and *DBTG model* will be used interchangeably.

In October 1969, the Association for Computing Machinery published the *DBTG Report* on behalf of CODASYL. From the time of the 1969 report until the next one in 1971, 179 proposals for changes and extensions were received by the DBTG. The 1971 report accepted 130 of these proposals, including proposals for three distinct languages: a schema data description language (schema DDL), a subschema data description language (subschema DLL), and a data manipulation language (DML). The 1971 report was criticized because the DDL did not provide a high degree of data independence, since it gave the application program access to system control information, making application program changes necessary if the data structure or the physical storage characteristics were changed.

In 1971, the CODASYL Executive Committee created the Data Description Language Committee (DDLC), which was given the responsibility for the development of a schema DDL independent of any high-level programming language. At the same time, the Programming Language Committee was given the responsibility for the development of the subschema DDL and the DML within COBOL. Several additional reports have been issued, the most recent in 1981.

The American National Standards Institute, which is responsible for standards in the United States, has not yet accepted the DBTG proposal as a national standard. Even so, several data base management systems have been developed based on part of the DBTG specifications.

Approach

This chapter presents the major features of the DBTG model. The DBTG model DDL operates on building blocks called data items, records, and sets. Trees, simple networks, and complex networks are decomposed to form sets. The application program uses the DML to navigate through the sets in a data base. The DML uses the verbs READY, FIND, GET, MODIFY, STORE, ERASE, CONNECT, DISCONNECT, and FINISH to allow the application program to navigate.

While the terminology applied to the network model is considerably different from that applied to the hierarchical model, a number of the basic functions are remarkably similar. The building blocks of the DBTG model are similar to some of the building blocks of the hierarchical model. We will compare the terminology of the network model to the terminology of the hierarchical model whenever possible.

6.2 LOGICAL DATA STRUCTURES

As in the presentation of DL/I in Chapter 5 and Module A, our presentation of the DBTG model will be divided into two sections. This chapter deals with the logical structures, independent of the physical storage of the data. Module B will present an example of the logical structures superimposed on the physical storage medium.

Basic Terminology

Understanding the concepts of the DBTG model begins with definition of the terminology of each of the building blocks: data items, records, and sets.

As Figure 6.1 shows, the basic unit of data is the **data item**, the smallest unit of data that can be updated by an application program. It is comparable

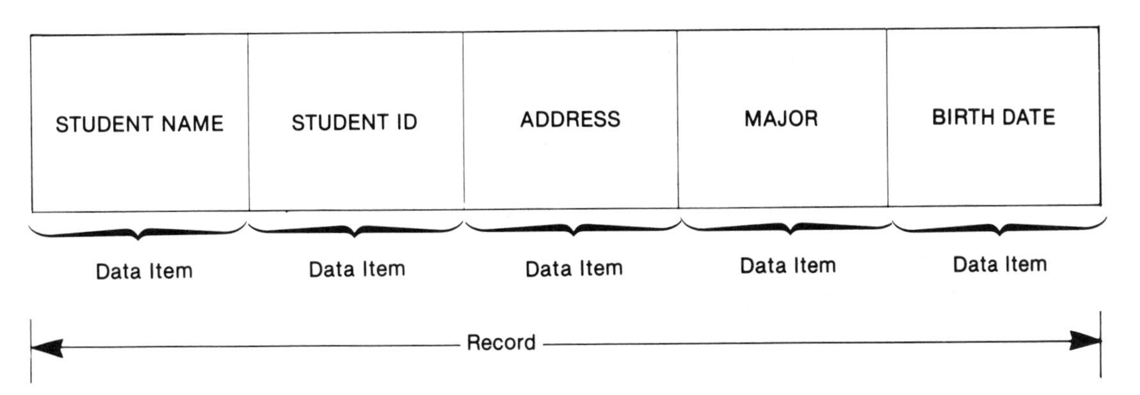

Figure 6.1
DBTG record with data item subdivisions.

to a field in DL/I. In this example, student name, student ID, address, major, and birth date are data items.

Record is the term used to describe a series of related data items. It is similar to a record in a COBOL program. A record is similar to a segment in DL/I, the unit of data that the data base management system presents to the application program for manipulation.

The third building block in the DBTG model is the **set**, which we shall now discuss in detail.

Sets

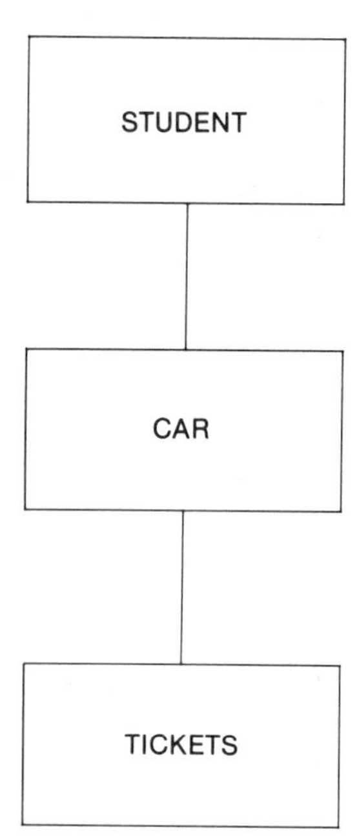

Figure 6.2 (*above*) One path of a hierarchical structure.

Any tree structure, regardless of the number of levels, can be decomposed into a series of two-level structures. The number of two-level structures required for the decomposition is one less than the number of levels in the original tree structure. Figure 6.2 shows one path of our Blue Whale College tree structure from Figure 4.4. One-to-many relationships exist between the STUDENT record and the CAR records and between the CAR record and the TICKETS records.

The hierarchical structure shown in Figure 6.2 can be decomposed into two two-level structures, as in Figure 6.3. Now the CAR record type exists in two different two-level structures. The relationships depicted are logical structures, not physical structures. As in the decomposition of hierarchical structures, this does not mean that data in the CAR records is duplicated. The decomposition of trees into two-level structures is simply a technique to describe data relationships in the network model. Redundant data is eliminated through the use of pointers implemented in the physical structure.

Figure 6.4 shows occurrences of the CAR record type for the STUDENT-CAR and the CAR-TICKETS sets. Occurrences of the CAR record type resemble a schematic of a data communications network. Figure 6.4 demonstrates how redundant data is eliminated, and it vividly demonstrates how the network model acquired its name.

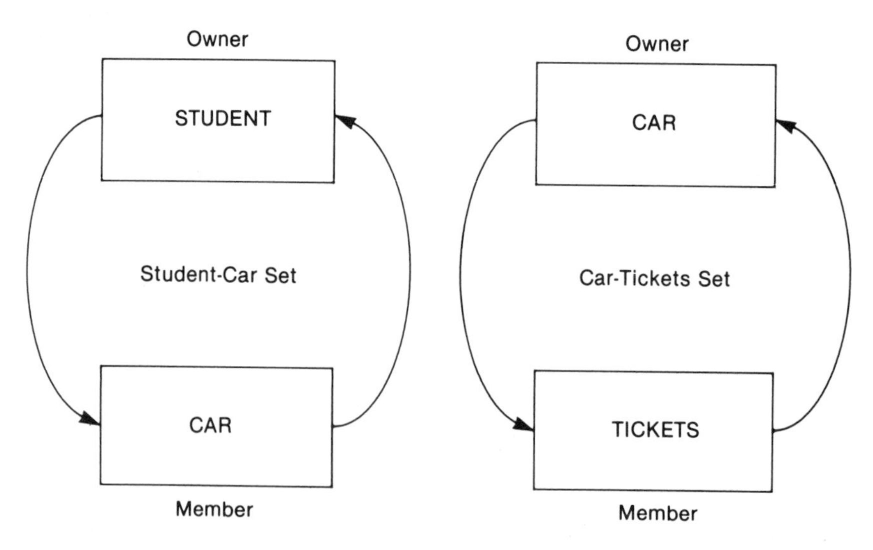

Figure 6.3 (*right*) Decomposition of a tree structure into two-level structures (sets).

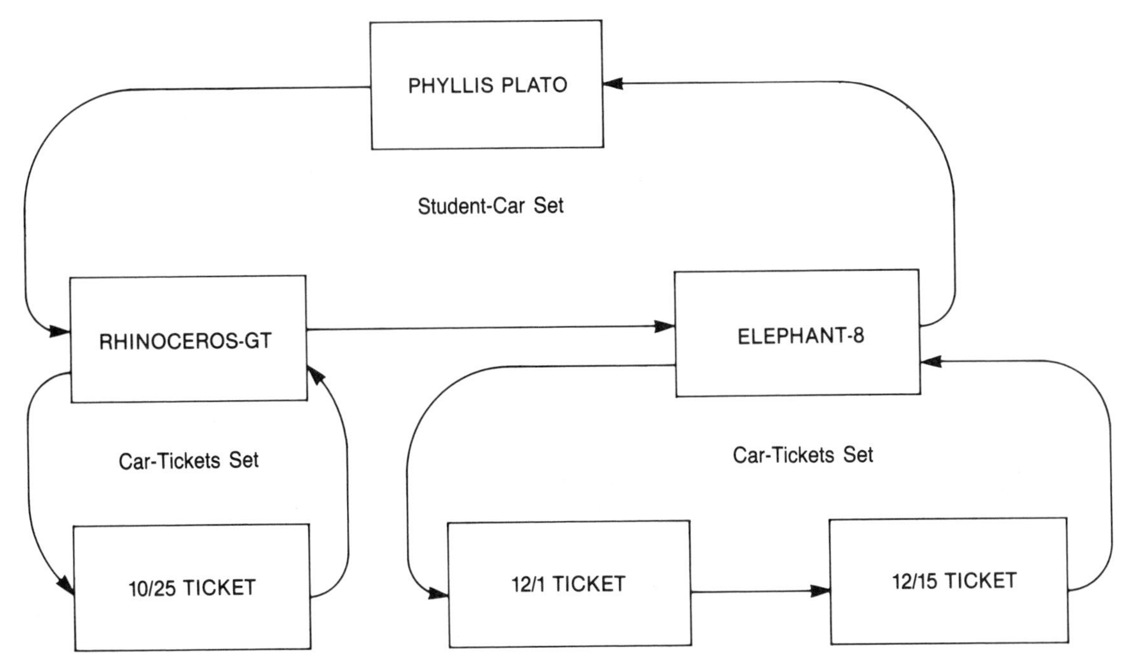

Figure 6.4 Occurrences of the STUDENT-CAR and CAR-TICKETS sets.

In the DBTG model, each data relationship consists of a two-level structure. Each two-level structure is called a set. (This is not a set in the mathematical sense.) Each set represents a one-to-many relationship between two record types. Figure 6.3, representing the data structure, shows the relationship between record types. Figure 6.4, representing occurrences of the data, shows the relationship between records. Note the distinction between record types and occurrences of records.

Each set is identified by a name, such as STUDENT-CAR. A set contains a record type defined as the owner of the set—STUDENT, in our example. The owner record type is usually, but not always, shown at the top level of each set. The second level in each set is occupied by a record type for the members of a set—CAR, in our example.

The STUDENT-CAR structure in Figure 6.3 shows a one-to-many relationship between each student and the cars driven by the student. The CAR-TICKETS structure shows a one-to-many relationship between a car and the number of tickets against the car. One occurrence of the STUDENT-CAR set and two occurrences of the CAR-TICKET set are shown in Figure 6.4. Phyllis Plato owns two cars: an Elephant-8 and a Rhinoceros-GT (ever wonder why cars are named after animals?). The Elephant-8 has received two parking tickets, one on 12/1 and the other on 12/15. The Rhinoceros-GT has received one ticket on 10/25.

The technique for representing owners and members of a set in DBTG differs from the technique used to represent hierarchical structures. Although the DBTG specifications do not cover the physical storage of data,

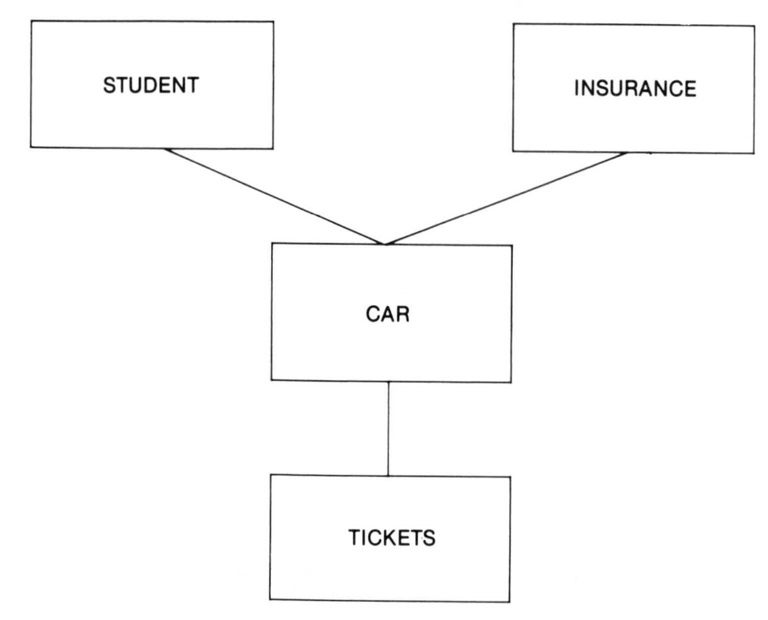

Figure 6.5 Addition of an INSURANCE record type to Figure 6.2.

the DML suggests that a circular (ring) or modified circular structure may be used. Therefore, sets are often represented as ring structures. But the actual physical storage mechanism is unimportant in our discussion, since the diagrams show the logical rather than physical structure of the data.

Simple Networks

Structures presented thus far depict the mechanism for representing tree structures in the network model. The DBTG model can also directly represent simple networks. In Figure 6.5, a new record type has been added to the structure in Figure 6.2, showing the addition of a record type for insurance companies. Each insurance company has a one-to-many relationship to the cars it insures. The CAR record is part of a simple network. It has two parents: the STUDENT record type and the INSURANCE record type.

Simple networks such as the one in Figure 6.5 can be decomposed into sets. Figure 6.6 shows the decomposition of the structure in Figure 6.5 into two sets, STUDENT-CAR and INSURANCE-CAR.

Figure 6.7 shows one occurrence of the INSURANCE-CAR set. Big Bucks Insurance Company is an occurrence of an INSURANCE record type and owner of this occurrence of the INSURANCE-CAR set. The Rhinoceros GT, Elephant-8, and Alligator 2 + 2 are cars and members of the INSURANCE-CAR set.

Figure 6.8 combines the data for Figure 6.4 and Figure 6.7. Each car shown is a member of the STUDENT-CAR set. Each car is owned by two different record types. In Figure 6.8, the record for the Elephant-8 is a member of two different set types: the STUDENT-CAR set and the INSURANCE-

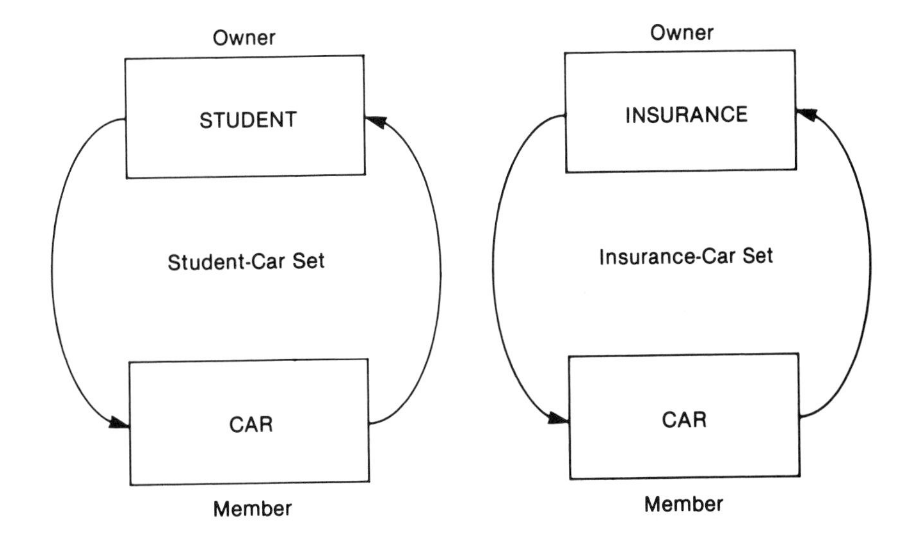

Figure 6.6
Simple network structure decomposed into two sets.

Owner
BIG BUCKS INSURANCE COMPANY
Member
RHINOCEROS-GT
Insurance-Car Set
Member
ALLIGATOR 2 + 2
ELEPHANT-8
Member

Figure 6.7
One occurrence of the INSURANCE-CAR set.

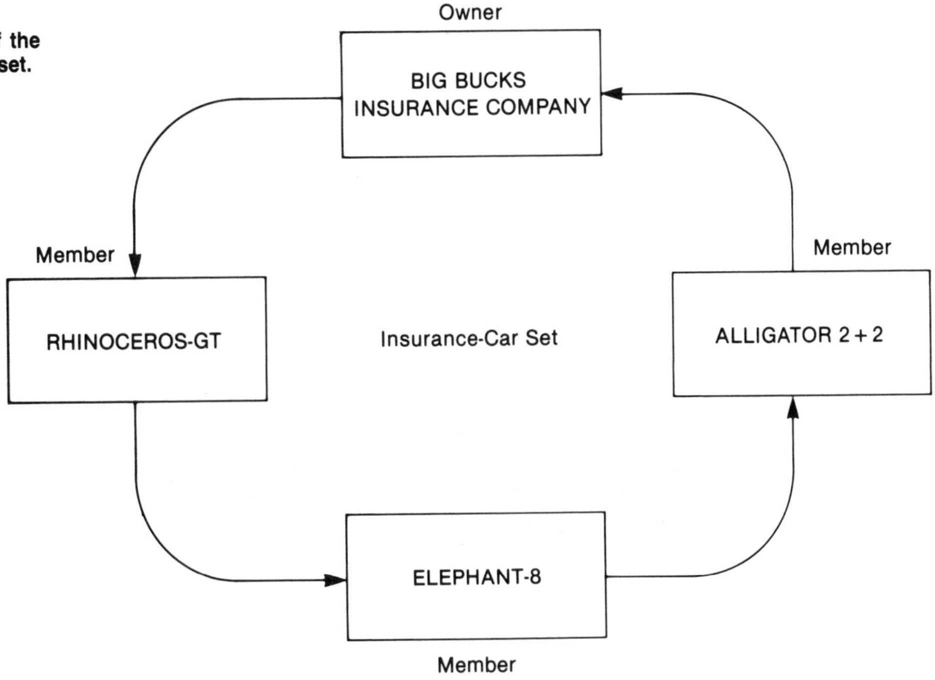

CAR set. In addition, the Elephant-8 is an owner of the CAR-TICKET set. The CAR-TICKET set has two members, a ticket received on 12/1 and a ticket received on 12/15.

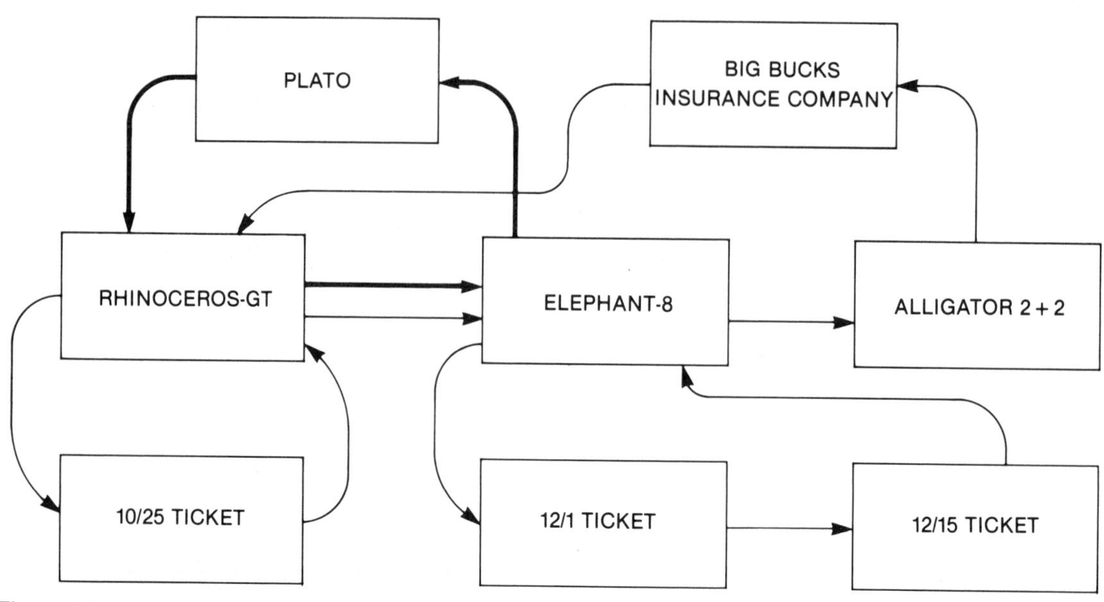

Figure 6.8
Three sets in which Elephant-8 participates.

Complex Networks

Each of the illustrations thus far in this chapter demonstrates a one-to-many relationship between an owner record type and a member record type. In Chapter 5, the relationship between students and classes was presented as a many-to-many relationship, or a complex network. Neither DL/I nor the DBTG model represents complex networks directly. Recall that in DL/I, a logical segment was created containing pointers and intersection data from the two different parent segment types. The DBTG model uses a similar approach to represent complex networks by creating a record type which acts as an intersection record. In Figure 6.9, the COURSE record type contains data concerning courses offered. The CLASS record type is an intersection record. The CLASS record type is a member of two different set types: the COURSE-CLASS set and the STUDENT-CLASS set. The many-to-many relationship between students and courses has thus been decomposed into two one-to-many relationships (see Figure 6.10).

The creation of the COURSE-CLASS and STUDENT-CLASS set types is necessary because the DBTG model does not permit an occurrence of a member record to have more than one owner record in the same set type. In Figure 6.8, the Elephant-8 has two different owners in two different set types. Plato is the owner of the Elephant-8 in the STUDENT-CAR set, and Big Bucks Insurance Company is the owner of the Elephant-8 in the INSURANCE-CAR set. While the Elephant-8 may have two different owners in two different set types, it may not have more than one owner in the same set type.

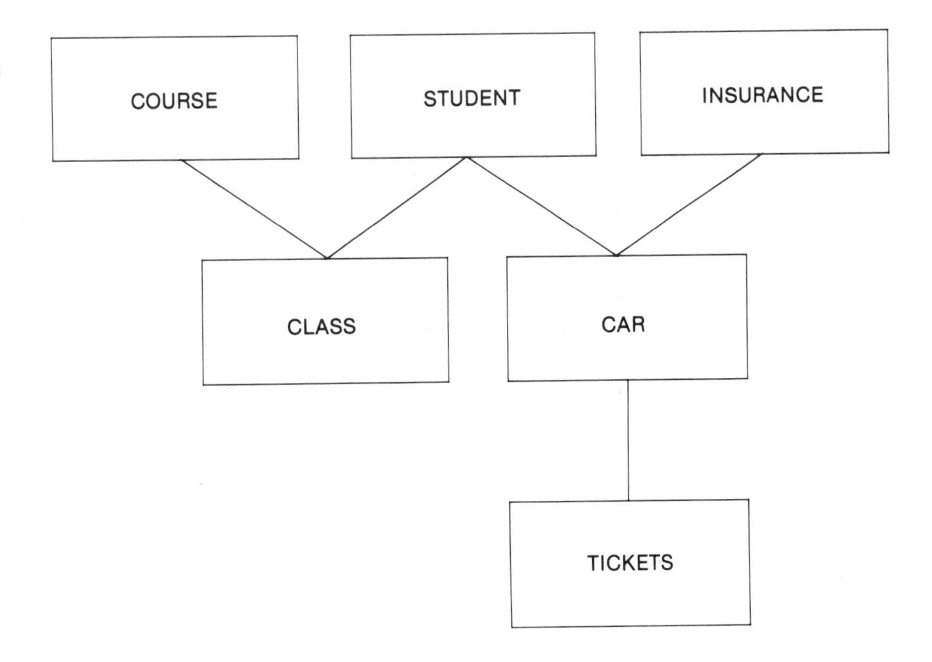

Figure 6.9
Addition of the CLASS record type to the structure in Figure 6.4 to demonstrate the DBTG mechanism for modeling complex networks.

Chapter 5 described a four-phase system to be installed at Blue Whale College. The phases were to (1) capture and maintain student data, (2) record the courses taken by each student, (3) provide a class roster, and (4) mail student grades at the end of the semester. To add new data relationships, the schema had to be updated to reflect the relationships desired. DL/I required the course segments to be placed to the right and below existing segments in the structure to eliminate the need to change programs because of the new data relationships. The DBTG model has no such restrictions. New sets can be created without affecting the structural position of records. All that is required following the change in the schema definition

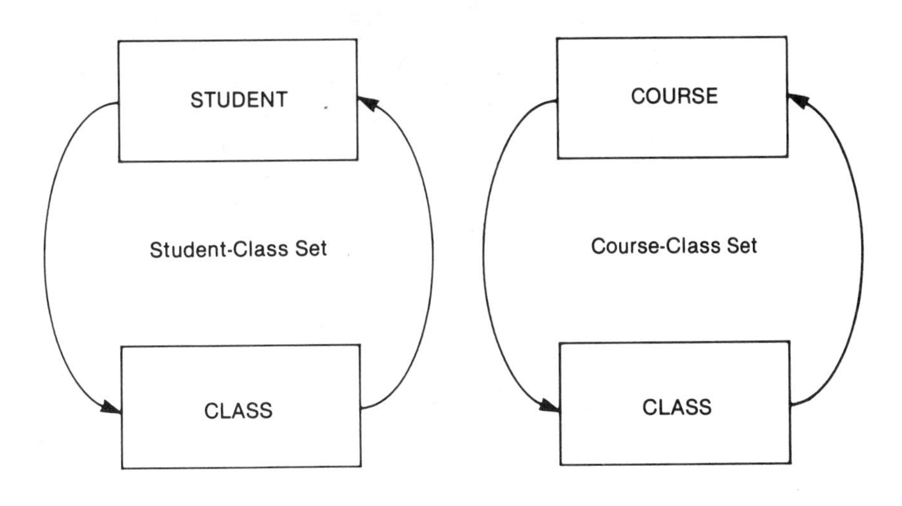

Figure 6.10
Many-to-many relationship between STUDENTS and COURSES represented in two sets with intersection data.

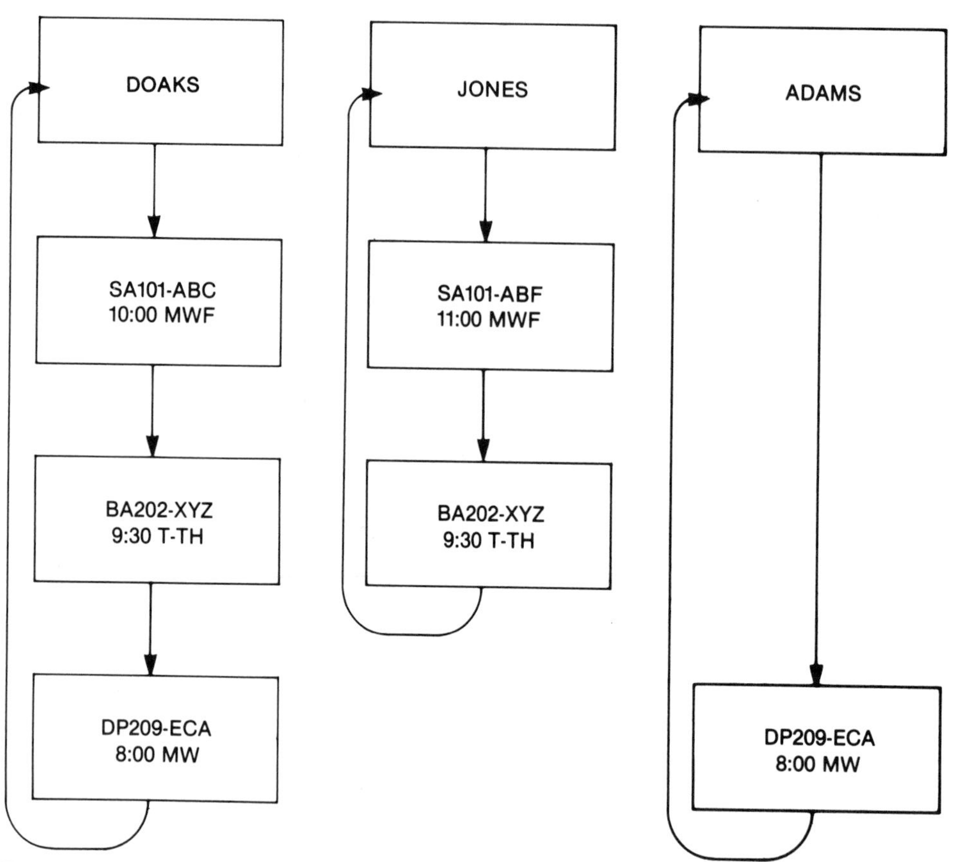

Figure 6.11
Three occurrences of the STUDENT-CLASS set.

is the execution of utility programs to make the physical connections to establish the data relationships. Figure 6.11 illustrates.

Figure 6.11 shows occurrences of the STUDENT-CLASS set. Doaks is the owner of an occurrence of the STUDENT-CLASS set, taking three courses which are members of the set: SA101-ABC, BA202-XYZ, and DP209-ECA. Jones and Adams are also owners of occurrences of the STUDENT-CLASS set. (Figure 6.11 has been drawn in a slightly different format than previous examples so that it may be used in a later illustration.)

Figure 6.12 shows occurrences of the COURSE-CLASS set. Sandbox I is the owner of an occurrence of the COURSE-CLASS set, with two sections which are members of the set, SA101-ABC and SA101-ABF. Basketweaving II and Data Base Management Systems are also owners of members in the COURSE-CLASS set.

Figure 6.13 combines Figure 6.11 and 6.12 and illustrates occurrences of the data relationship (as it applies to the DBTG model) to satisfy the second phase of the system, recording courses taken by students. Many types of pointers may be selected in the DBTG model, as was the case with DL/

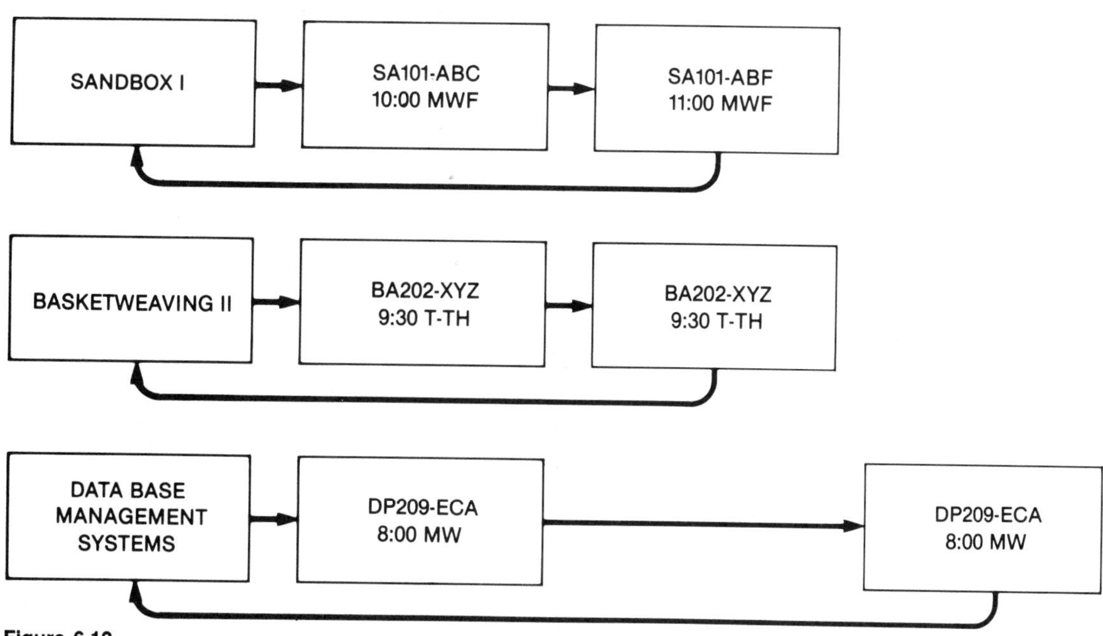

Figure 6.12
Three occurrences of the COURSE-CLASS set.

I. The DBTG model provides for a pointer from each member record to the owner record of the set. (The pointer to the owner record exists in this example but is not shown in Figure 6.13. Only the minimum number of pointers is shown, to improve clarity.) Example G13 describes the implementation of phase two at Blue Whale College, using the DBTG model.

Example G13
Phase Two at Blue Whale College, with DBTG Model

First, a list of courses taken by each student is developed by following a pointer from the student, who is the owner of the STUDENT-CLASS set, to each of the members of the set. After each class record is retrieved, a pointer from the class record, which is a member of the CLASS-COURSE set, is followed to the owner of that set.

In Figure 6.13, a pointer from Doaks points to the first member in the STUDENT-CLASS set, SA101-ABC. The CLASS record for SA101-ABC is obtained. A pointer from the SA101-ABC CLASS record is followed to the owner of that occurrence of the COURSE-CLASS set. The first course Doaks is taking is Sandbox I. The pointer from the SA101-ABC record is followed to the next member in the STUDENT-CLASS set, BA202-XYZ. The pointer from the BA202-XYZ class record is followed to the owner of that occurrence of the COURSE-CLASS set, Basketweaving II. This process is repeated for each class each student is enrolled in, in order to obtain a list of courses each student is taking.

In Example G14, a similar process is followed to provide a class roster, the third phase at Blue Whale College.

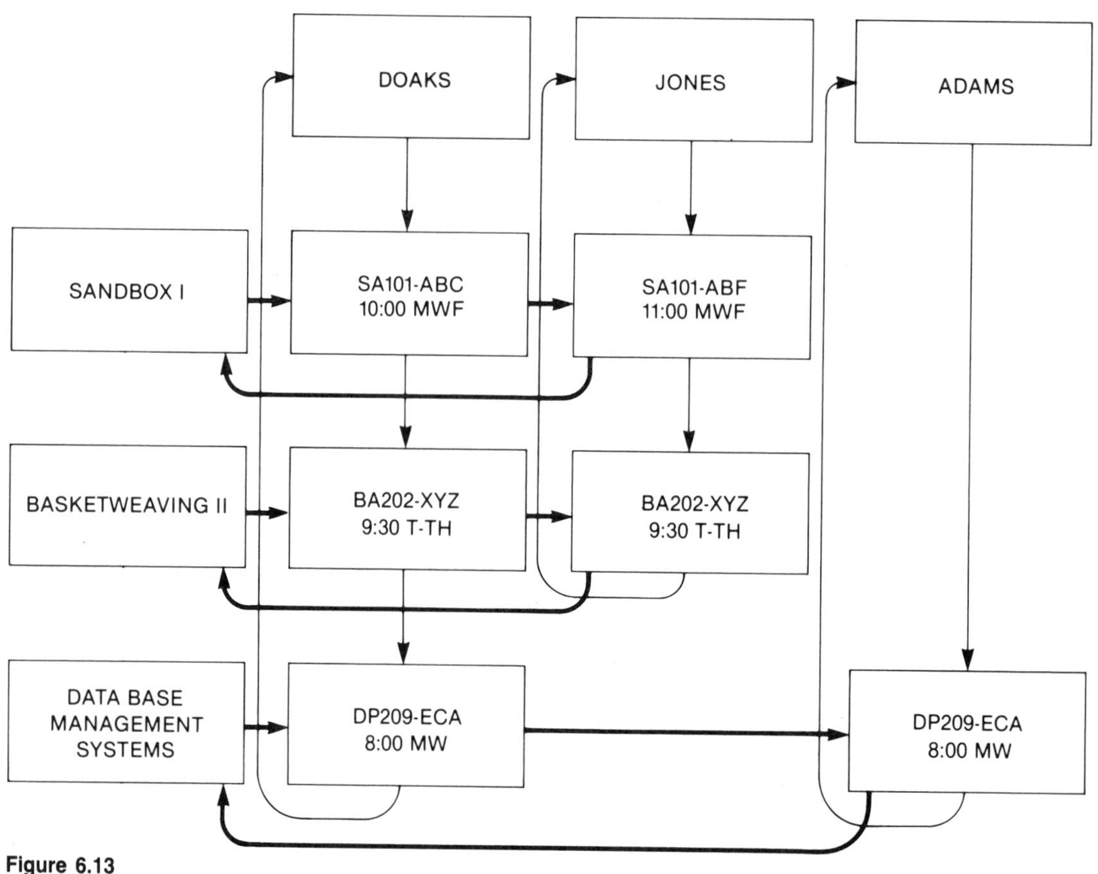

Figure 6.13
Use of an intersection record to represent complex networks.

Example G14
Phase Three at Blue Whale College, with DBTG Model

A pointer is followed from the COURSE record, which is the owner of the COURSE-CLASS set, to each of the members of the set. After the CLASS record is retrieved, a pointer is followed to the owner of that occurrence of the STUDENT-CLASS set.

In Figure 6.13, a pointer is followed from the Sandbox I record to the first member of the COURSE-CLASS set, SA101-ABC. The CLASS record for SA101-ABC is obtained. The pointer in the SA101-ABC record is followed to the owner of the STUDENT-CLASS set, Doaks. The next occurrence of the COURSE-CLASS set is obtained, and the process is repeated for each member of the COURSE-CLASS set until all of the students taking Sandbox I are obtained. This process is repeated for each course until a complete set of class rosters has been developed.

Example G15 depicts the final phase of the system at Blue Whale College, to mail grades from each course to the students.

Example G15 Phase Four at Blue Whale College, with DBTG Model

The grade for each course is stored in the intersection record, CLASS. To retrieve all of the grades for a student, the members of the STUDENT-CLASS set are retrieved. The grade is retrieved from each CLASS record.

6.3 DATA DEFINITION LANGUAGE

Schema

The data definition language (DDL) permits each record type to be placed in a set with other record types through definition of set types in the schema. The schema describes the logical relationship between record types. It also describes the data items within each record type and the relationship of owner and member record types, in order to develop each set. Figure 6.14 shows the schema for the data relationships in Figure 6.9.

SCHEMA NAME

The schema definition performs a function similar to a DBD in DL/I. The SCHEMA NAME clause assigns a name to the schema being described. This is similar in function to that of the DBD NAME= clause in DL/I. The KEY clause identifies the name of the key field used to sequence records. This is a logical rather than a physical sequencing. The DUPLICATES clause performs a function similar to the U in the NAME parameter in the FIELD statement in DL/I and is optional. When used, it requests the data base management system to invoke a checking function to examine each record when stored in the data base. If a program attempts to enter a new record in the data base that has the same value in this field as an already existing record, the program is given an error indication in the data base status field. (More about this in Section 6.4, which discusses the DML in detail.)

RECORD NAME

The RECORD NAME clause assigns a name to the record being described. This is similar in function to the SEGM NAME= clause in DL/I. Each data item within a record is defined following the RECORD NAME clause. The data item name is given, followed by the format of the data item. These data item definitions perform a function similar to that of the FIELD statement in DL/I. They assign a name to the data item and specify the type of data (for example, character or decimal) and the length of the data item.

SET NAME

The SET NAME clause assigns a name to each set. There is no equivalent clause in DL/I; however, sets impose relationships between record types, and in DL/I the PARENT= parameter establishes the relationship between segment types.

In the network model, the relationship between record types is defined by the OWNER and MEMBER clauses, where the OWNER clause identifies the name of a previously defined record type that is the owner of an occurrence of a set, and the MEMBER clause identifies the name of a previously defined record type that is a member of the set.

Figure 6.14
The DBTG schema for the records and sets for the data relationships in which the student is involved.

```
SCHEMA NAME IS COLLEGE-LIFE
  RECORD NAME IS STUDENT
  KEY STUDENT-ID IS ASCENDING
  DUPLICATES ARE NOT ALLOWED FOR STUDENT-ID
    02 STUDENT-ID              TYPE IS DECIMAL      9
    02 STUDENT-NAME            TYPE IS CHARACTER 30
    02 STUDENT-ADDRESS         TYPE IS CHARACTER 30
    02 MAJOR                   TYPE IS CHARACTER 08
    02 BIRTH-DATE              TYPE IS CHARACTER 08
  RECORD NAME IS CAR
  DUPLICATES ARE NOT ALLOWED FOR CAR-SERIAL-NO
  DUPLICATES ARE NOT ALLOWED FOR CAR-LICENSE
    02 CAR-SERIAL-NO           TYPE IS CHARACTER 18
    02 CAR-MAKE                TYPE IS CHARACTER 12
    02 CAR-MODEL               TYPE IS CHARACTER 17
    02 CAR-YEAR                TYPE IS DECIMAL      2
    02 CAR-LICENSE             TYPE IS CHARACTER  6
  RECORD NAME IS TICKETS
    02 TICKET-DATE             TYPE IS CHARACTER  8
    02 OFFENSE                 TYPE IS DECIMAL      6
    02 TICKET-NUMBER           TYPE IS CHARACTER 12
    02 TICKET-STATUS
  RECORD NAME IS INSURANCE
    02 COMPANY-NAME            TYPE IS CHARACTER 43
    02 COMPANY-ADDRESS         TYPE IS CHARACTER 35
  RECORD NAME IS COURSE
    02 COURSE DESCRIPTION      TYPE IS CHARACTER 35
    02 COURSE-ID               TYPE IS CHARACTER  5
  RECORD NAME IS CLASS
    02 COURSE-ID               TYPE IS CHARACTER  5
    02 CLASS-SECTION           TYPE IS CHARACTER  8
    02 CLASS-TIME              TYPE IS CHARACTER 13
SET NAME IS STUDENT-CAR
    OWNER IS STUDENT
    ORDER IS SORTED
    MEMBER IS CAR
    INSERTION IS MANUAL
    RETENTION IS OPTIONAL
    SET SELECTION IS KEY STUDENT-ID
SET NAME IS CAR-TICKET
    OWNER IS CAR
    ORDER IS NEXT
    MEMBER IS TICKETS
    INSERTION IS AUTOMATIC
    RETENTION IS FIXED
    SET SELECTION IS KEY CAR-LICENSE
SET NAME IS INSURANCE-CAR
    OWNER IS INSURANCE
    ORDER IS SYSTEM DEFAULT
    MEMBER IS CAR
    INSERTION IS MANUAL
    RETENTION IS OPTIONAL
SET NAME IS STUDENT-CLASS
    OWNER IS STUDENT
    ORDER IS FIRST
    MEMBER IS CLASS
    INSERTION IS MANUAL
    RETENTION IS OPTIONAL
    SET SELECTION IS KEY STUDENT-ID
SET NAME IS COURSE-CLASS
    OWNER IS COURSE
    ORDER IS LAST
    MEMBER IS CLASS
    INSERTION IS MANUAL
    RETENTION IS OPTIONAL
```

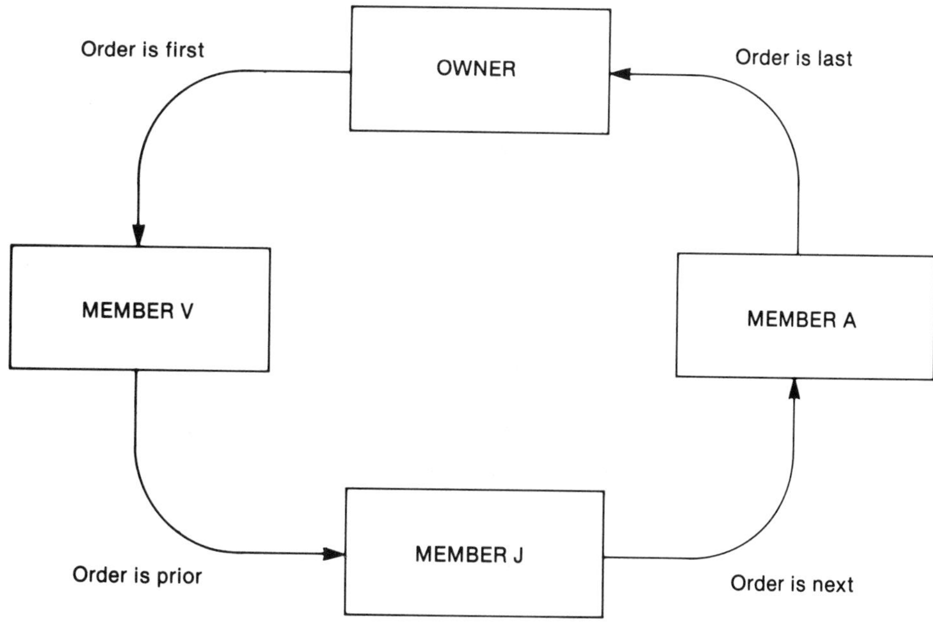

Figure 6.15
Points of insertion of new member records for ORDER clause parameters.

The SET SELECTION clause defines a method for obtaining direct access to an occurrence of a set if the manner to obtain it is not explicitly defined by the application program. No equivalent function exists in DL/I. In the absence of DML commands to connect a car member to an occurrence of the STUDENT-CAR set, the data base management system will use the value of STUDENT-ID to determine in which occurrence of the set the member will be placed.

ORDER

The ORDER clause specifies the logical order in which member records are stored in the set, or it specifies the insertion point where a new member record is to be added. The options for ordering member records within a set are *first*, *last*, *next*, *prior*, *system default*, and *sorted*. When a record type participates in two different set types, it may be placed in a different logical order in each set type.

With the order of last, new member records are added in chronological sequence in a set, with the most recent record added as the last member of the set and immediately prior to the owner record (see Figure 6.15).

When the order is first, member records are placed in reverse chronological sequence, with the most recent record added as the first member of the set and immediately following the owner record (see Figure 6.15).

With an order of next or prior, the application program locates a specific occurrence of a member record, and the new record is stored before (PRIOR) or after (NEXT) the member record. In Figure 6.15, the application program locates record MEMBER-J. If ORDER IS PRIOR is specified, the new member record is placed between records MEMBER-V and MEMBER-J. If ORDER IS NEXT is specified, the new member record is placed between records MEMBER-J and MEMBER-A.

With an order of sorted, the sequence field is specified in the schema definition. During execution of a program, the data base management system places each new member record in the set in sequence by the value of the sequence field.

With an order of system default, the sequence of member records is unimportant to the application program. The data base management system then controls the sequence in which member records are placed in the set.

Note that the ORDER clause only provides for logical sequencing of the members of a set. On some occasions, it is necessary to retrieve the owners of a set in a prescribed sequence. The network model allows for the creation of a special *singular* or *system set* which declares the system to be the owner of the set. Then the owner records, now members of the singular set, can be sequenced without forcing them into a conventional set. Use of a singular set is shown in Section 6.4 (Data Manipulation Language), where it is used only to place occurrences of COURSE records in sequence.

There is not a direct correlation between the ORDER clause and a specific DL/I function; however, in DL/I a combination of the INSERT, REPLACE, and DELETE rules and secondary indices provides a somewhat similar function.

INSERTION and RETENTION

The INSERTION and RETENTION clauses define criteria for storing member records and removing member records from sets. The set insertion status and the set retention status act in combination. The INSERTION and RETENTION clauses also perform a function somewhat similar to that of the INSERT, REPLACE, and DELETE rules in DL/I.

The set insertion status determines whether the application program or the data base management system has the responsibility for placing a member record in an occurrence of a set. The set retention status determines the rules for removing a member record from an occurrence of a set. Once a record is placed in an occurrence of a set, the retention status specifies whether the record must stay in the same occurrence of a set for the rest of its existence, or if it is allowed to move from one set occurrence to another, or if it may be removed from all occurrences of the set and be allowed to exist outside the set.

Set Insertion Status

The set insertion status can be AUTOMATIC or MANUAL. If AUTOMATIC is specified, the data base management system places a member record in the correct occurrence of a set at the time the record is created. If MANUAL is specified, the application program places a member record in the correct occurrence of a set when it is appropriate to do so.

Set Retention Status

The set retention status can be FIXED, MANDATORY, or OPTIONAL. The set retention status determines the removal status of a record.

FIXED means that once a record becomes a member in an occurrence of a set, the record must remain in that occurrence of the set. The record must be deleted and recreated before it can become a member of another occurrence of a set.

MANDATORY means that once a record becomes a member in an occurrence of a set, the record must always be a member in some occurrence of the set. The record can move from one set occurrence to another.

OPTIONAL means that the record can move from one occurrence of a set to another or may be removed from the set. With an OPTIONAL set retention status, the record does not have to be a member of an occurrence of a set.

Example G16 illustrates the use of insertion and retention status at Blue Whale College.

Example G16 DBTG Record Insertion and Retention at Blue Whale College

In Figure 6.14, the set insertion status for the INSURANCE-CAR set is MANUAL. When a student purchases insurance for a car, it is the responsibility of the Policy Maintenance Program to establish the car as a member of the INSURANCE-CAR set. After the car is established as a member of the correct occurrence of the INSURANCE-CAR set, the retention status determines the rules governing whether or not a car may be removed from an occurrence of a set.

Retention for the INSURANCE-CAR is OPTIONAL, for the student may discontinue the insurance from one company and insure the car with another company. Then, the car moves from a member of one occurrence to a member of another occurrence in the INSURANCE-CAR set. Also, a student may drop insurance. Then the OPTIONAL retention status allows the record for car to be removed from the occurrence of the set and stand alone in the data base.

Figure 6.16a depicts the relationship between students, cars, and insurance. Big Bucks Insurance Company insures the Elephant-8, Rhinoceros-GT, and Alligator 2+2. Since this record type is OPTIONAL, Sue Socrates may drop insurance for her car. Thus in Figure 6.16b the Alligator 2+2 record is allowed to stand alone, not part of any occurrence of the INSURANCE-CAR set.

If the state in which the college is located requires every car to be insured, the set retention status would be MANDATORY. Each car must be insured; therefore, it must be a member of some occurrence of the INSURANCE-CAR set. A student can change insurance companies, thereby removing the car from one occurrence of the INSURANCE-CAR set and placing it in a different occurrence of the set. However, a CAR record would not be allowed to exist if it were not a member of some occurrence of the INSURANCE-CAR set.

In Figure 6.16c, Socrates changes insurance companies. The CAR record is removed from the occurrence of the set owned by the Big Bucks Insurance Company and is placed in an occurrence of a set owned by Slippery Sam's Insurance Company.

Let us now turn our attention to the CAR-TICKET set. In Figure 6.14, the set insertion status for the CAR-TICKET

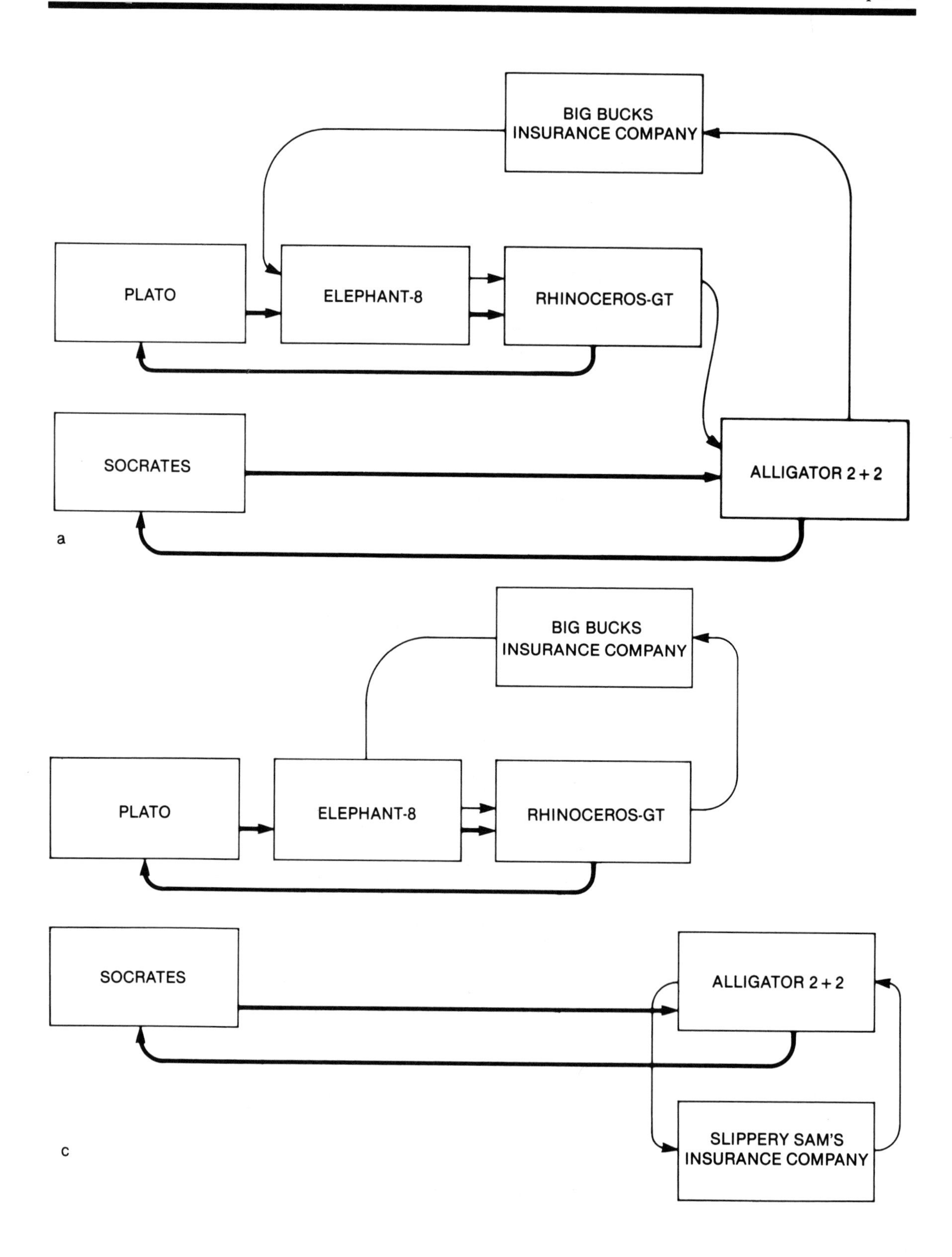
BIG BUCKS
INSURANCE COMPANY
PLATO
ELEPHANT-8
RHINOCEROS-GT
SOCRATES
ALLIGATOR 2 + 2
a
BIG BUCKS
INSURANCE COMPANY
PLATO
ELEPHANT-8
RHINOCEROS-GT
SOCRATES
ALLIGATOR 2 + 2
SLIPPERY SAM'S
INSURANCE COMPANY
c

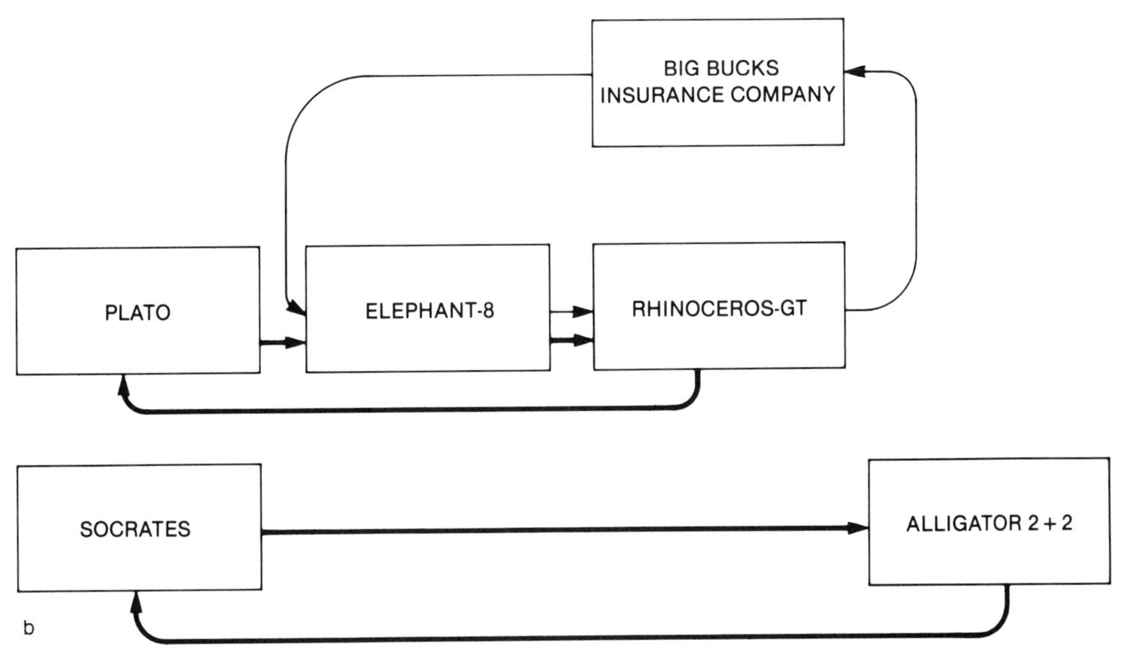

Figure 6.16
a. Data relationship between STUDENTs, INSURANCE, and CARS.
b. Alligator 2+2, with an OPTIONAL retention status, is removed from the INSURANCE-CAR set.
c. Alligator 2+2 moves from the Big Bucks Insurance Company occurrence to Slippery Sam's Insurance Company occurrence.

set at Blue Whale College is AUTOMATIC and the set retention status is FIXED. When a ticket is received, the Ticket Update Program creates a new member record in the CAR-TICKET set. The data base management system establishes the links to insert the record into the appropriate occurrence of the CAR-TICKET set, based on value of the CAR-LICENSE number. Since the set retention status is FIXED, once the record becomes a member of this set, it cannot be removed from this set occurrence. Once a car receives a ticket, the ticket remains outstanding until the ticket is paid. Only then can it be removed from the set. The ticket cannot be transferred from one car to another.

Subschema

The subschema DDL describes the records and sets viewed by the application program and provides a restricted view of the schema. It is not necessary for the subschema to define all of the record types or all of the set types defined in the schema; only the record types and set types needed by the application program are defined. In addition, the data items in a record may be in a different sequence than the data items defined in the schema.

Figure 6.17 shows the subschema for the CAR-TICKET set and the STUDENT-CAR set. Data items, records, and sets may be given different names in the MAPPING DIVISION.

The subschema definition in the DBTG model provides a function similar to that of the PSB in DL/I. But although DL/I allows for the subsetting

Figure 6.17
DBTG subschema for the records and sets in TICKET-PROCESSING.

```
TITLE DIVISION.
SS  TICKET-PROCESSING WITHIN COLLEGE-LIFE.
MAPPING DIVISION.
ALIAS SECTION.
AD  RECORD STUDENT IS CAR-OWNER.
AD  SET CAR-TICKET IS VIOLATION.
AD  STUDENT-ID IS OWNER-ID.
AD  STUDENT-NAME IS OWNERS-NAME.
AD  STUDENT-ADDRESS IS OWNERS-ADDRESS.
STRUCTURE DIVISION.
RECORD SECTION.
01  CAR-OWNER.
    05  OWNERS-NAME           PIC X(30).
    05  OWNERS-ADDRESS        PIC X(60).
    05  OWNER-ID              PIC 9(9).
01  CAR                           ALL.
01  TICKET                        ALL.
SET SECTION.
SD VIOLATION.
SD STUDENT-CAR.
```

of the schema, it does not provide the other facilities available in the DBTG subschema definition language.

Let's look more closely at Figure 6.17. TITLE DIVISION marks the beginning of the subschema definition. TICKET-PROCESSING is the name given to this subschema definition, a subset of the COLLEGE-LIFE schema.

The MAPPING DIVISION is the area where alternate names for data items, records, and sets are defined. Often, several names exist for the same data item. For instance, it is necessary to uniquely identify each student in a college, usually with a student ID number. The student ID number is often the same as what would be called the social security number in another operation. Since different names are associated with the same data item, the MAPPING DIVISION allows the application program to use the name of the data item as it applies to the process performed by the program.

The alias definition (AD) clauses of the MAPPING DIVISION define each alternate name. In Figure 6.17, the subschema definition assigns the CAR-OWNER alias to the record for STUDENT, VIOLATION for CAR-TICKET, and other aliases for several data items within the STUDENT record, where each data item is renamed with a prefix of OWNER(S) instead of STUDENT.

The STRUCTURE DIVISION defines the records and sets to be processed within the subschema. In the CAR-OWNER record, only the OWNERS-NAME, OWNERS-ADDRESS, and OWNER-ID data items are accessed. Thus, an application program is not allowed to change the data items for MAJOR or BIRTH-DATE, since they are not defined in the subschema. (Note also that it is permissible for the order of the data items in the subschema to be different from the order of the data items in the schema.) In addition, only two of the sets defined in the schema are allowed to be accessed in the subschema: VIOLATION and STUDENT-CAR.

6.4 DATA MANIPULATION LANGUAGE

The DBTG data manipulation language (DML) contains commands of READY, FIND, GET, MODIFY, STORE, ERASE, CONNECT, DISCONNECT, and FINISH to interface with the data base management system.

The READY command notifies the data base management system of the intent to access data. The FINISH command notifies the system that the program has completed the processing against the data base. The FIND command locates data. The GET command causes data to be made available to the application program. The STORE command adds new records to the data base. The ERASE command removes records from the data base. The CONNECT and DISCONNECT commands add or remove records from sets but not from the data base.

Each application program has a USER-WORK-AREA that is an interface between the application program and the data base management system. The application program places data to update the data base in the USER-WORK-AREA before requesting the data base management system to make the change. The data base management system places data and status information in the USER-WORK-AREA after the application program issues a request.

The data base management system updates status information to indicate the success or failure of each request. The status information also contains positioning information called **currency indicators.** Although it is not shown in any of the following examples, proper programming practices dictate that the status information be examined after every interaction with the data base management system. If the status information then provides an unexpected status, appropriate error procedures must be followed before processing continues.

Currency Indicators

The DML is used to navigate through the data base. As with navigation in a ship, it is necessary to know both where you are going and your current location. In DL/I, certain DML commands establish parentage—that is, they mark the current location in the data base for future use. In the DBTG model, on the other hand, fields called currency indicators are set aside to mark the current location within the data base.

There is one currency indicator for each record type and each set type defined in the subschema. In the TICKET-PROCESSING subschema we have been discussing, one currency indicator exists for the VIOLATION set, one for the STUDENT-CAR set, one for the CAR-OWNER record, one for the TICKET record, and one for the CAR record. In addition, a currency indicator is reserved for the record most recently accessed during the execution of the program (the *run unit*).

Each currency indicator records information indicating the record most recently accessed. For instance, when the CAR-OWNER record for Phyllis

Plato is accessed, Plato becomes the current record of the CAR-OWNER records or simply "current of CAR-OWNER" and also "current of run."

Each DML command is described in the following paragraphs. The discussion is intended to show the function and power of each command, rather than the use of a specific programming language. Therefore, some poetic license has been exercised and instructions not germane to the explanation of the commands have been omitted. Figure 6.18 shows the currency indicators for each of the commands in our discussion. After each command is issued, examine these currency indicators to determine the effect of each command on them.

READY

The READY DML command prepares the data base management system for access by the program. The following line shows the format of the READY command:

```
READY TICKET-AREA USAGE MODE IS EXCLUSIVE UPDATE.
```

READY TICKET-AREA notifies the data base management system that this program intends to access the area in the data base where the records for students and tickets are stored.

An action called **locking** must be taken to ensure that a record is not updated by two different programs concurrently. Locking is instigated by the word EXCLUSIVE, which indicates that the program requests exclusive control of the records specified while it is executing. PROTECTED may be used in place of EXCLUSIVE. When PROTECTED is used, other programs are permitted concurrent access to the same records, but they are not permitted to update any records accessed. EXCLUSIVE is typically used for update programs, while PROTECTED is typically used for report programs. The PROTECTED and EXCLUSIVE parameters in the network model serve a purpose similar to that of the HOLD form of the GET command in DL/I. (In-depth information about locking is presented in Chapter 9.)

FIND

The FIND command locates an occurrence of a record within the data base and causes the currency indicators to be updated with the location of the record obtained.

Since the FIND command is only a data base navigation aid, it does not cause data to be made available to the application program. The following command causes the data base management system to (attempt to) locate ticket number 123456 in the data base and to update the currency indicators:

```
MOVE '123456' TO TICKET-NUMBER.

FIND ANY TICKET USING TICKET-NUMBER.
```

After the command is issued, the currency indicators in Figure 6.18 show the current of run to be ticket 123456 and the current of TICKET to be ticket 123456.

COMMAND	VIOLATION	STUDENT-CAR	CAR-OWNER	TICKET	CAR	RUN
READY	NULL	NULL	NULL	NULL	NULL	NULL
FIND	123456	NULL	NULL	123456	NULL	123456
GET	123456	NULL	NULL	123456	NULL	123456
MODIFY	123456	NULL	NULL	123456	NULL	123456
STORE	123456	111111111	111111111	123456	NULL	111111111
CONNECT	123456	XYZ789	222222222	123456	XYZ789	XYZ789
DISCONNECT	123456	NULL	222222222	123456	DEF333	DEF333
ERASE	NULL	NULL	222222222	NULL	NULL	ABC123

Figure 6.18 Currency indicators for DBTG data manipulation commands.

Several variations of the FIND command are available to the program, including FIND NEXT, FIND PRIOR, FIND FIRST, FIND LAST, FIND OWNER, FIND DUPLICATE, and a FIND command that can locate a specific occurrence of a member record within an occurrence of a set. An example of this last variation is:

```
FIND SEVENTH TICKET.
```

This command locates the seventh occurrence of the TICKET record within a set.

FIND commands provide the application program with great flexibility and power in locating a specific occurrence of a record. As was shown in Example G13, an application program may enter an occurrence of a set at other than the first record, then use the record as a navigation path to locate a member within one set to process records in another set.

Additional examples of the FIND command are shown with the GET commands which follow, since the FIND command locates data within the data base and updates currency indicators but does not transfer data to the application program.

GET

The GET command follows the FIND command and causes the data located by a FIND command to be made available to the application program. GET causes the record that is current of run to be made available to the application program. Currency indicators are not modified after the issuance of the GET command. The following command causes the data located in the previous FIND command (FIND SEVENTH TICKET) to be made available to the application program in the USER-WORK-AREA:

```
GET TICKET.
```

Let's describe a more common use of the FIND and GET commands. Example G17 returns us to phase three of the Blue Whale College data base system—developing a class roster.

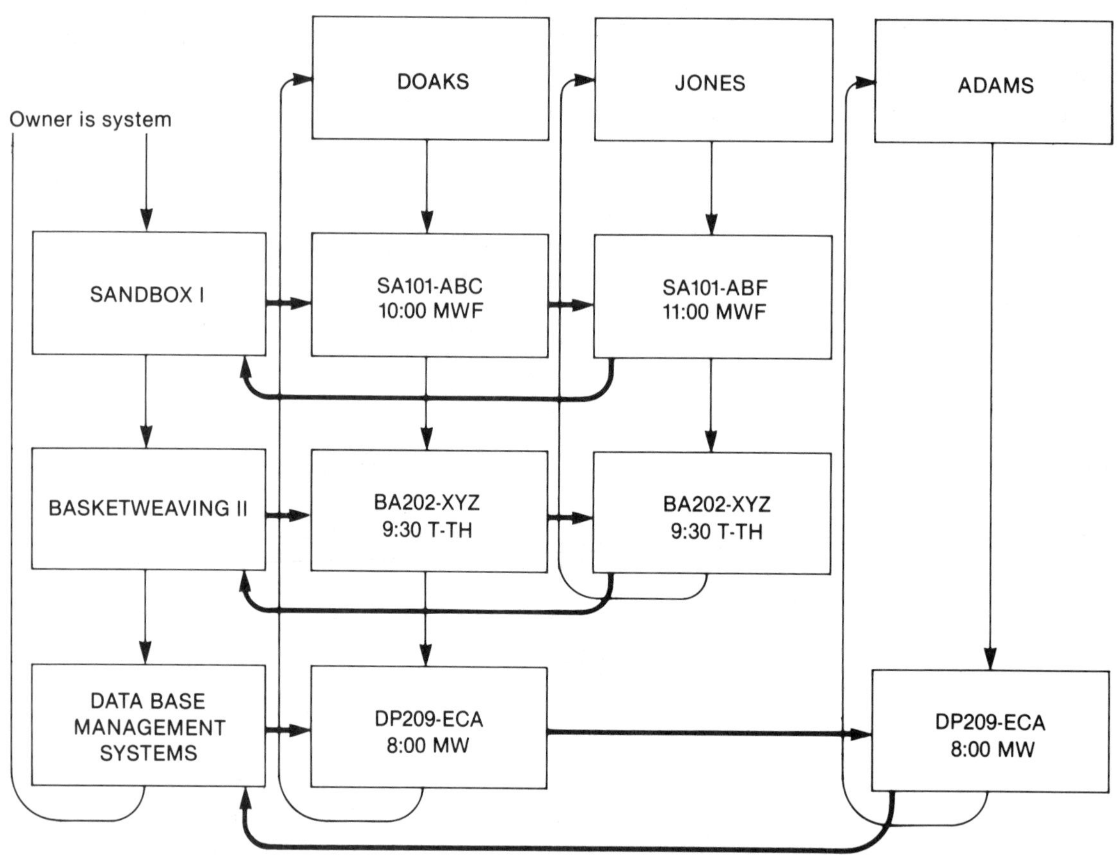

Figure 6.19
Use of a singular set to retrieve occurrences of COURSE in sequence.

Example G17
Use of GET Command in Phase Three at Blue Whale College

Figure 6.13 has been reproduced in Figure 6.19 so that we may illustrate the use of the GET command in phase three at Blue Whale College. The COURSE record type must be in sequence for this processing, and so occurrences of the COURSE record type have been chained together with pointers to provide the desired sequence through a singular set, with the owner of this new set declared as the system.

The commands are presented below. As you review them, examine Figure 6.19 to determine the records which are processed.

Let's see what takes place. In the GET-COURSE paragraph, the program obtains the COURSE record in order to print the course name on the roster. On the first execution of the paragraph, the FIND FIRST COURSE statement is executed to obtain Sandbox I. On subsequent executions, the next course in sequence is located through the FIND NEXT COURSE statement. After the COURSE record is located, it is made available to the application program through the GET COURSE statement.

After the name of the course is printed, the names of all the students in each course are also to be printed. This can be demonstrated beginning with Sandbox I. First, the CLASS record is located in the GET-CLASS paragraph. On the first execution of the paragraph, the FIND FIRST CLASS WITHIN COURSE-CLASS statement is executed, which locates the record for SA101-ABC in the COURSE-CLASS set. Notice that the data in the CLASS record was not needed and was only used for purposes of navigation. The desired data is the student's name, which is located in the owner record type in the STUDENT-CLASS set type. Therefore, the FIND OWNER WITHIN STUDENT-CLASS statement is executed, and the owner of the SA101-ABC record is located in the STUDENT-CLASS set. This is followed by the GET STUDENT statement, which makes the data from the STUDENT record available to the application program. On the next execution of the paragraph, the FIND NEXT CLASS WITHIN COURSE-CLASS statement is executed, which locates the record SA101-ABF. This process is followed repeatedly until all courses and students have been listed.

```
    PERFORM GET-COURSE
        UNTIL ROSTERS-ARE-COMPLETE.
GET-COURSE.
    IF FIRST-COURSE
        FIND FIRST COURSE WITHIN PROGRAM
    ELSE
        FIND NEXT COURSE WITHIN PROGRAM.
    PERFORM CHECK-STATUS.
    IF COURSE-STATUS-IS-OK
        GET COURSE
        PERFORM PRINT-COURSE
        PERFORM GET-CLASS UNTIL LAST-STUDENT IS FOUND
    ELSE
        PERFORM ERROR-ROUTINE.
GET-CLASS.
    IF FIRST-CLASS
        FIND FIRST CLASS WITHIN COURSE-CLASS
    ELSE
        FIND NEXT CLASS WITHIN COURSE-CLASS.
    PERFORM CHECK-STATUS.
    IF CLASS-STATUS-IS-OK
        FIND OWNER WITHIN STUDENT-CLASS
        IF OWNER-STATUS-IS-OK
            GET STUDENT
            PERFORM PRINT-STUDENT.
```

MODIFY

The MODIFY command causes data in the data base to be changed by the data in the application program's USER-WORK-AREA. When a MODIFY command is successfully executed, the record modified becomes the current of run, current of record type, and current of all sets in which it is an owner or a member. The following MODIFY command is used to update the TICKET record after it is made current of run by a FIND command and placed in the USER-WORK-AREA by a GET command:

```
MOVE 'PAID' TO TICKET-STATUS.
MODIFY TICKET.
```

STORE

The STORE command causes a new record to be placed in the data base. If the record to be added is an occurrence of an owner record type, it is simply added to the data base. If the record to be added is an occurrence of a member record type and the insertion status is AUTOMATIC, the data base management system connects the record in the correct occurrence in the set when the record is stored. However, even though the data base management system is responsible for placing the record in the data base and connecting it in the correct occurrence of all sets in which it is an automatic member, it is the application program that is responsible for establishing the currency indicators before the record is STOREd. For instance, if the new record is a member record which is to be first or last, the application program must establish currency indicators specifying the correct occurrence of the owner record. If the new record is ordered NEXT or PRIOR, currency indicators must also be updated to show which member record the next record is prior or next to.

If the record to be added is an occurrence of a member record type and the insertion status is MANUAL, the application program must establish the currency indicators, store the record, and connect the record to the correct occurrence of the set. Currency indicators are then updated to reflect the addition of the new record.

The following command adds a new CAR-OWNER to the data base. The CAR-OWNER record is not a member of any sets.

```
MOVE '111111111' TO OWNER-ID.
MOVE 'SUE SOCRATES' TO OWNERS-NAME.
MOVE '333 THIRD STREET' TO OWNERS-ADDRESS.
STORE CAR-OWNER.
```

CONNECT

Occasions exist when records may be stored in a data base but do not belong to the desired set, or they may belong to a set from which they are to be removed but it is not desirable to remove them from the data base.

For example, the CAR record type belongs to the STUDENT-CAR, CAR-TICKET, and INSURANCE-CAR set types. If a student discontinues her insurance for her car, it is not desirable to delete the occurrence of the car record from every set in which it participates. And if she were adding insurance coverage, the occurrence of the record is already stored in the data base and merely needs to be made a member in the INSURANCE-CAR set type. The CONNECT and DISCONNECT commands place a record which already exists in a data base into an occurrence of a set and remove member records from a set without deleting them from the data base.

The CONNECT command causes records existing in the data base to be connected to a set. CONNECT cannot be used for member records having an AUTOMATIC insertion status, since the data base management system is responsible for inserting these record types into the correct occurrence of the set. Rather, the CONNECT command is issued for member record types with a MANUAL insertion status. MANUAL insertion status is used when the application program contains the decision-making criteria to determine when a member record becomes a member in an occurrence of a set. The application program must cause the currency indicators to reflect the correct occurrence of the set in which the member record is to be connected. Currency indicators are updated to reflect the addition of the record to a set.

In the following example, the FIND command causes the appropriate currency indicators to be set. Note the function of the FIND command: The data for CAR-OWNER is not needed, and so the FIND command's only function is to set the currency indicators. The record connected becomes the current of run, current of its record type, and current of set. The commands cause a new CAR record which is a member of the STUDENT-CAR set to be added to the data base. The STORE CAR statement causes the occurrence of the car record to be stored in the data base. Since the INSERTION status is MANUAL, the new record is connected to the correct occurrence of the STUDENT-CAR set via a CONNECT command:

```
MOVE '222222222' TO OWNER-ID.
FIND ANY CAR-OWNER USING OWNER-ID.
PERFORM CHECK-STATUS.
IF FIND-STATUS-IS-OK
    MOVE 'XYZ789' TO CAR-LICENSE
    STORE CAR
    PERFORM CHECK-STATUS
    IF STORE-STATUS-IS-OK
    CONNECT CAR TO STUDENT-CAR.
```

DISCONNECT

The DISCONNECT command causes a record to be removed from an occurrence of the set. DISCONNECT cannot be used for member records having a FIXED or MANDATORY retention status, for FIXED status and MAN-

DATORY status require the member record type to always be a member of some occurrence of some set. DISCONNECT can only be used for member records having an OPTIONAL retention status.

Before the DISCONNECT command can be issued, a FIND command must be issued to establish the currency indicators. Currency indicators are updated after a successful DISCONNECT command, because currency is nullified in the set in which the record is disconnected. The disconnected record becomes current of run and current of its record type. The following command removes a car record from an occurrence of the STUDENT-CAR set:

```
MOVE 'DEF333' TO CAR-LICENSE.
FIND ANY CAR USING CAR-LICENSE.
PERFORM CHECK-STATUS.
IF FIND-STATUS-IS-OK
    DISCONNECT CAR FROM STUDENT-CAR.
```

ERASE

The ERASE command causes a record to be removed from the data base. Before the ERASE command can be issued, a FIND command must be issued to locate the record to be removed from the data base. Currency indicators are updated after the ERASE command, because currency is nullified for all record types and sets in which the erased record was found. The following command causes a CAR record to be deleted:

```
MOVE 'ABC123' TO CAR-LICENSE.
FIND ANY CAR USING CAR-LICENSE.
PERFORM CHECK-STATUS.
IF FIND-STATUS-IS-OK
    ERASE CAR.
```

The result of issuing the command depends upon the retention status of the sets owned by CAR. In this example, CAR owns one record type, TICKETS. The TICKETS record type has a FIXED retention status. Therefore, the data base management system not only deletes the occurrence of the CAR record with a CAR-LICENSE of ABC123 but also deletes all of the members of the TICKETS record type, since they can only exist as members of a set or not at all.

If the retention status for TICKETS were OPTIONAL, only the CAR record would be deleted. The TICKET member records for the VIOLATION set would be disconnected from the set and would be allowed to exist outside of the set.

If the retention status for TICKETS were MANDATORY, the data base management system would disallow the ERASE for CAR if any member records existed in the occurrence of the set owned by the CAR occurrence with a CAR-LICENSE of ABC123. The member records in the occurrence of this set would have to be deleted or transferred to another occurrence of the set before the ERASE command could be issued.

The result of the ERASE command is not limited to the record types defined in the subschema. ERASE affects *all* the record types that are members of a set owned by the occurrence of the CAR record being deleted. Therefore, it is possible for the application program to delete occurrences of records unknown to the program.

FINISH

When the program has completed execution, it issues a FINISH command for the records specified in the READY command, to inform the data base management system it has completed processing:

```
FINISH TICKET-AREA.
```

6.5 SUMMARY

The concept of data bases was established in the 1960s. Due to the successful standardization of the COBOL language, the data processing community attempted to standardize the features and language of data base management systems. The DBTG model is the result. Acceptance of the DBTG model as a national standard has not yet occurred, but several network data base management systems have been developed based on the specifications from the Data Base Task Group.

The DBTG model represents data as two-level structures called sets. Each set occurrence has one record as the owner of the set and none, one, or more records as members of the set. Tree structures can be represented in sets by decomposing the trees into a series of two-level structures. The DBTG model can represent simple networks directly. In a simple network, each member record may belong to two or more different sets. Therefore, each member may be owned by two or more different record types. The DBTG model cannot represent complex networks directly. However, they can be represented by decomposing them into simple networks and using intersection records to connect the principal records of the complex network.

The schema resembles the COBOL language. It describes the data items, the records, and the data relationships between the sets. Specifications for a set include the owner record type, the member record type, the sequence of the member records within the set, rules for inserting and deleting member records from a set, and a default method for obtaining a member of a set.

The SCHEMA NAME, RECORD NAME, and SET NAME clauses permit the naming of each data building block which is operated upon. The ORDER

DBTG	FUNCTION	DL/I
SCHEMA NAME	Provide a name for the data base	DBD NAME
DUPLICATE	To insure two records having the same value in a specific field are not stored in the same set	'U' in NAME parameter of FIELD statement
RECORD NAME	To name the unit of data transferred between the data base management system and the program	SEGM NAME
DATA ITEM	The smallest unit of data defined	FIELD
SET NAME	Names and defines the relationship between two record types	No equivalent function; similar to PARENT=
ORDER	Places member record occurrences in a logical sequence	Similar to 'SEQ' parameter in FIELD statement and INSERT, REPLACE, DELETE rules
INSERTION	To define the responsibility for connecting a member into a set	Similar to INSERT rules
RETENTION	To define the conditions under which member records are removed from a set	Similar to DELETE rules

Figure 6.20
Summary of DBTG schema definition commands.

Figure 6.21
Summary of DBTG data manipulation commands.

DBTG	FUNCTION	DL/I
READY	Prepares the data base management system for possible update by the application program	Similar to HOLD form of GET command
FIND	Locates an occurrence of a record	GU, GHU
GET	Transfers a record to the application program	GN, GHN GNP, GHNP
MODIFY	Alters a record in a data base	REPL
STORE	Adds a new record to a data base	ISRT
CONNECT	Causes a member record to be made part of a set	—
DISCONNECT	Causes a member record to be removed from a set	—
ERASE	Causes a record to be removed from a data base	DLET
FINISH	Notifies the data base management system the program has completed processing	

clause defines the logical sequence in which member records are stored. The INSERTION and RETENTION clauses define whether the data base management system or the application program has the responsibility for connecting member records to a set and under what conditions member records may be removed from sets. Figure 6.20 summarizes these schema definition commands.

The subschema defines the records within the data base that an application program is permitted to access. The DBTG subschema permits alternate names to be specified for data items, records, and sets.

The network DML commands are READY, FIND, GET, MODIFY, STORE, CONNECT, DISCONNECT, ERASE, and FINISH (see Figure 6.21). The READY command notifies the data base management system of the type of data base access to be performed by the application program. Position in the data base is maintained through currency indicators. The FIND command locates data within the data base. The GET command causes data located by the FIND command to be available to the application program. The MODIFY command causes the data base to be changed by the data in the application program USER-WORK-AREA. The STORE command causes new data to be entered into the data base. The ERASE command causes records to be deleted from the data base. The CONNECT command causes records currently in the data base to become members of a set. The DISCONNECT command causes records to be removed from a set without removing them from the data base. The FINISH command notifies the data base management system that processing has been completed.

REVIEW QUESTIONS

6.1 Draw the network structure defined in the following schema definition.

```
SCHEMA NAME IS WINE-DISTRIBUTION
RECORD NAME IS DISTRIBUTOR
   02 DISTRIBUTOR-NAME
          TYPE IS CHARACTER 30
   02 DISTRIBUTOR-ADDRESS
          TYPE IS CHARACTER 60

RECORD NAME IS RESTAURANT
   02 RESTAURANT-NAME
          TYPE IS CHARACTER 30
   02 RESTAURANT-ADDRESS
          TYPE IS CHARACTER 60
RECORD NAME IS WINE
   02 WINE-NAME
          TYPE IS CHARACTER 22
   02 YEAR
          TYPE IS CHARACTER  4
   02 QUANTITY
          TYPE IS DECIMAL    3
SET NAME IS DISTRIBUTOR-WINE
   OWNER IS DISTRIBUTOR
   ORDER IS LAST
   MEMBER IS WINE
   INSERTION IS MANUAL
   RETENTION IS MANDATORY
SET NAME IS RESTAURANT-WINE
   OWNER IS RESTAURANT
   ORDER IS SYSTEM DEFAULT
   MEMBER IS WINE
   INSERTION IS MANUAL
   RETENTION IS MANDATORY
```

6.2 Draw the application program view of the records defined in the following subschema definition.

```
TITLE DIVISION.
SS  WINE-STOCK WITHIN
       WINE-DISTRIBUTION.
MAPPING DIVISION.
ALIAS SECTION.
STRUCTURE DIVISION.
RECORD SECTION.
01  RESTAURANT.
    02  RESTAURANT-NAME          PIC X(30).
01  WINE.
    02  WINE-NAME                PIC X(22).
    02  QUANTITY                 PIC  9(3).
SET SECTION.
SD  RESTAURANT-WINE.
```

6.3 What process is used to represent tree structures using the DBTG model?

6.4 How are simple networks represented in the DBTG model?

6.5 How are complex networks represented in the DBTG model?

6.6 What is the purpose of the ORDER clause in the schema definition?

6.7 What is the purpose of the INSERTION clause?

6.8 What is the purpose of the RETENTION clause?

6.9 Record type B is a member of set AB. If record type B exists, it must be a member of set AB. What parameter would normally be used for the RETENTION clause?

6.10 Record type B is a member of set AB. The rules that govern when record type B becomes a member of a set can only be determined by an application program. What parameter would normally be used for the INSERTION clause?

6.11 What is the function of currency indicators?

6.12 How many currency indicators are needed in an application program?

6.13 What is the purpose of the status information? When should it be checked?

6.14 What effect does the retention status of FIXED have on the DISCONNECT command?

6.15 What effect does the insertion status of AUTOMATIC have on the CONNECT command?

6.16 Which DML command locates a record but does not make the record available to the application program?

6.17 Which DML command causes a new record to be placed in the data base?

6.18 How did the DBTG model acquire its name?

6.19 What is the purpose of the USER-WORK-AREA?

6.20 What is the basic unit of data made available to the application program?

6.21 What procedure is followed to add new records to an existing schema? How is this different from the procedures in DL/I?

6.22 How does MANDATORY retention status differ from FIXED retention status?

6.23 Does the subschema define all the records updated by an application program? (Trick question!)

6.24 Name a function provided in the DBTG subschema not available in the DL/I subschema (PSB).

6.25 Which DML command updates a record existing in a data base?

6.26 Why is standardization of a data base management system being pursued?

MODULE B

PHYSICAL STORAGE OF DATA IN IDMS

MODULE OBJECTIVES

Upon completion of this module, you should be able to:

1. Explain how DBTG logical structures are physically stored within IDMS
2. Discuss the considerations for the physical storage of data
3. Explain the techniques used to provide efficient data storage and retrieval

NEW WORDS AND PHRASES

data dictionary
area
location mode
CALC
VIA
page
line index
space management pages

B.1 MODULE INTRODUCTION

Chapter 6 presented the logical structures of the DBTG (network) model. This module presents the techniques used in a network model to store and retrieve logical data structures in secondary storage.

The DBTG model is a group of specifications for a proposed national standard; it is not a functioning data base management system. IDMS, an actual commercial implementation based on the DBTG specifications, will be used in this module to illustrate the physical storage of data. IDMS is not the only data base management system based on the network model, but it is representative of data base management system software based on the DBTG specifications, and it has been in use for a number of years. Marketed by the Cullinet Corporation, IDMS is based on the DBTG model specifications that appeared in the 1971 report. Some of the specifications in the

1971 report have been deleted from later reports issued by the CODASYL Data Description Language Committee, but IDMS retains the original features in its software.

As with DL/I, when using IDMS the data base administrator must choose among a number of options to satisfy user requests. The data base administrator develops a storage strategy based on his or her knowledge of the access patterns of the users of the data base.

The device media control language (DMCL) and the schema data definition language are the vehicles to describe the environment in which the data is physically stored. The data base administrator defines the logical data relationships and some of the parameters for the physical data structures in the schema. The schema is compiled and then stored in a **data dictionary**—a library on secondary storage in which data is described. (More about the data dictionary in Chapter 8.) The DMCL specifies the amount of data to be transferred between primary and secondary storage. The DMCL is compiled and stored for use during application program execution.

IDMS stores data using several of the techniques we presented in previous chapters, including hashing, linked lists, and secondary indexes using the BDAM or VSAM access methods. BDAM is a direct file organization. VSAM is an access method that offers sequential, indexed, and direct operations.

B.2 PHYSICAL STORAGE OF DATA USING IDMS

Areas

An application program must specify an **area** in which IDMS is to store a record. Areas were presented in the early DBTG reports, but they have not been included in more recent reports. An area may contain one or more files, or a file may contain one or more areas. The data base administrator determines which of the preceding is used. Areas allow a data base to be subdivided to improve performance.

Example A4 illustrates how the use of areas can improve performance.

Example A4
Use of IDMS Areas at Acme Widgets

Periodically, a government agency requests Acme Widgets to provide a list of employees who have worked in a specific area of the manufacturing plant and may have been exposed to hazardous chemicals. Every employee record in the data base, whether for an active employee or one who is retired, is interrogated to produce this report.

On a daily basis, the Personnel Department accesses and updates employee records for active employees. If data for both groups of employees was stored in one area, the daily programs would require additional seek time and rotational delay to bypass records for inactive employees. Areas allow the two types of records to be segregated.

The Personnel Data Base may be subdivided into two areas within the same file (see Figure B.1). Area A contains active employee records. Area B contains records for inactive em-

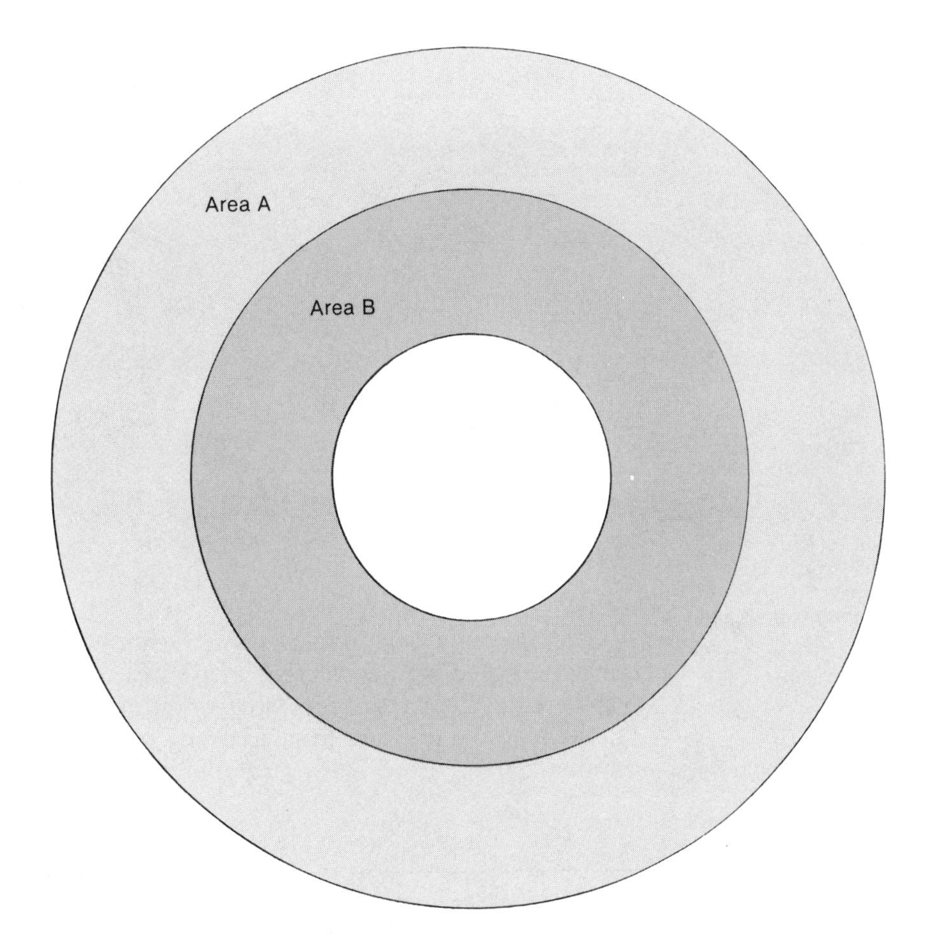

Figure B.1 Storing two areas in one file.

ployees (employees that are laid off or retired, not employees who are lazy!).

During periodic processing to satisfy the government requests, both areas are accessed to generate the required reports. But during daily processing, only Area A is accessed. Thus, during daily processing, the number of records traversed in search of a desired record is reduced by segregating records into areas.

During the 1960s and early 1970s, disk drives with removable disks were prevalent. The use of removable disks could allow Acme Widgets to reduce its expenditures for hardware in Example A4 by removing inactive data from disk drives when it is not being used. Since data for inactive employees is only needed periodically, each area can be placed in a separate file. Placing Area A on a disk separate from Area B would allow the disk containing Area B to be removed until needed (see Figure B.2). This would allow a different disk to be placed on the disk drive when the disk containing Area B is not mounted. Thus, fewer disk drives would need to be purchased to satisfy Acme Widgets' direct access storage requirements.

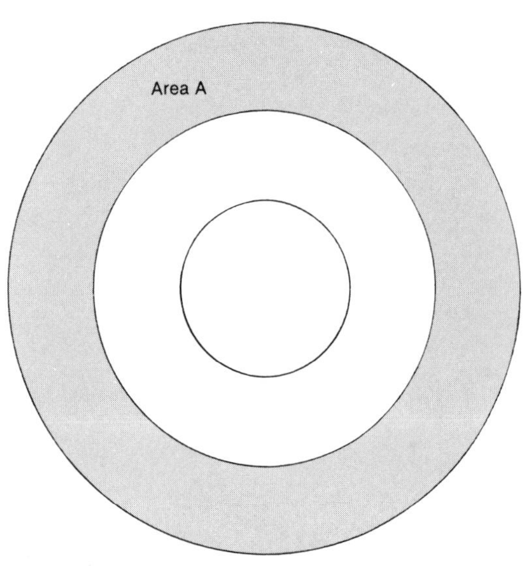

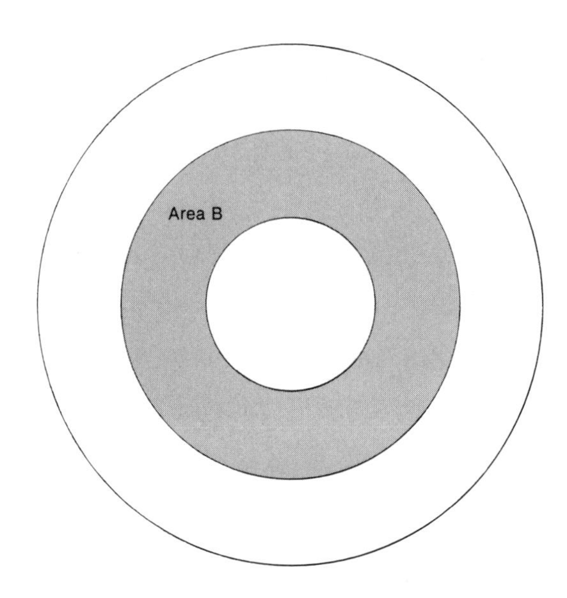

Figure B.2 Storing two areas in two files.

Areas can also be used as a security tool. Records of one record type may be stored in two different areas, Area C and Area D. The data base administrator can restrict the access of a program to a specific area, thus preventing the program from accessing protected data. Example A5 illustrates.

Example A5 Areas Used for Security at Acme Widgets

At Acme Widgets, the PAYROLL record type is stored in both Area C and Area D. Payroll records for employees below the vice-presidents are stored in Area C. Payroll records for employees who are vice-presidents and above are stored in Area D.

The data base administrator permits the weekly Payroll Program to access the records in Area C to perform standard payroll processing. Even though the records in Area D have the same format as the records in Area C, the weekly Payroll Program is denied access to Area D because management has deemed this information to be confidential.

Since the application program must specify which area IDMS is to use to store a record, a change to the data structure may require a change to the application program. This low degree of data independence is what caused areas to be deleted from the DBTG model. Continuation of this feature in IDMS allows users to operate existing programs. If this feature were deleted from IDMS, every application program would require a conversion to delete the use of areas.

Page

Each area is subdivided into a number of **pages.** A page is the unit of data transferred between primary and secondary storage. Normally, one or more

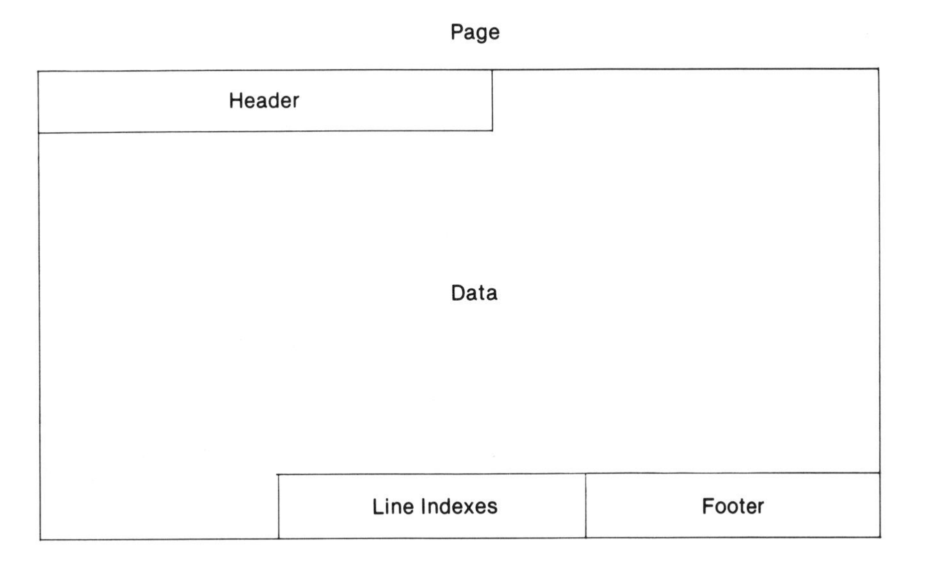

Figure B.3
Anatomy of a page.

records plus IDMS control information are placed in a page. The number and size of the pages is specified in the DMCL.

Each page within an area is given a sequential number. The IDMS control information in each page includes a header, data, line indexes, and a footer (see Figure B.3).

The *header* contains control information for the page (see Figure B.4). The first field in the header contains the page number (value 3333 in Figure B.4). The page number is followed by pointers for a system-owned set called a CALC set. Each page in the data base contains a CALC set, whose members are all user record types with a CALC location mode. These pointers are followed by a space-available count field which indicates the number of bytes of space available in the page.

The *footer* occupies the last 16 bytes of each page. It contains a field for the page number (value 3333 in Figure B.4), the line space count (value 16), and the line 0 index. The line space count specifies the number of bytes used for the line index and the footer. The line 0 index accounts for the space used by the system record for the CALC set. Additional line indexes are added in reverse order at the end of a page. One line index exists for each record in the page, to identify the location of the record.

Location Mode

A **location mode** must be specified for each record type, to identify which technique IDMS is to use to store a record. IDMS offers three location modes: CALC, DIRECT, and VIA. The choice of location mode is made in the schema.

With a CALC location mode, a data item is specified which contains a key. IDMS hashes the key to provide a target page number within an area in which the record is to be stored. CALC provides rapid direct access to a record.

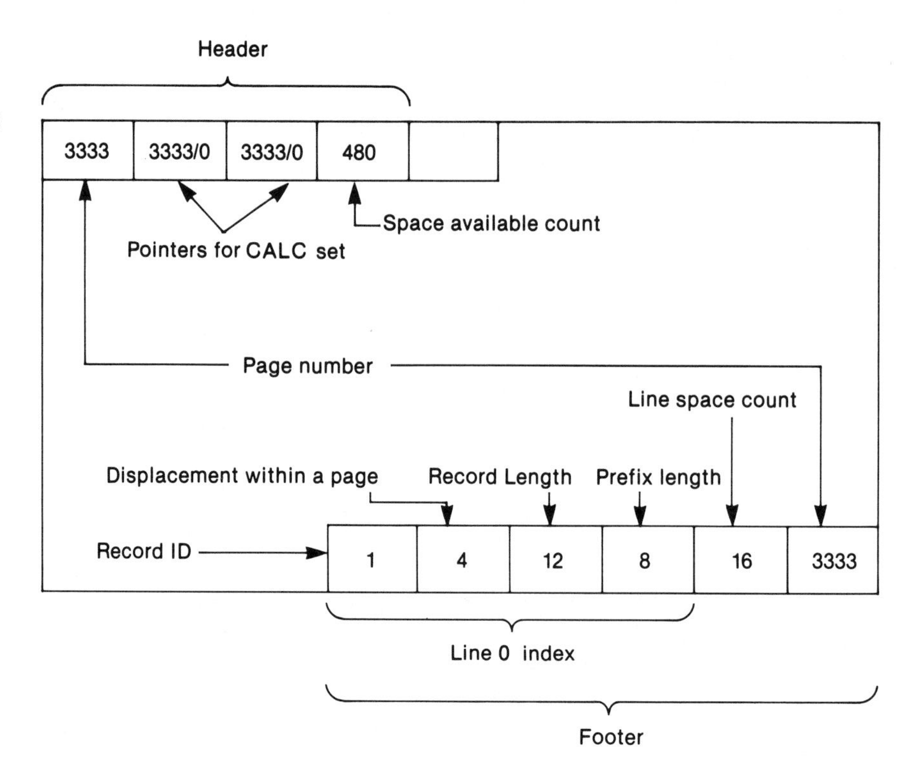

Figure B.4
PAGE 3333, showing values of the header, footer, and line 0 index for an empty page.

With a DIRECT location mode, the application program specifies the target page number for the page in which the record is to be stored. DIRECT provides improved performance when a critical application has a known and constant access pattern to a record type.

With a VIA location mode, IDMS stores the record as close as possible to the record's owner in the specified set. VIA provides improved performance when one record type is accessed through its relationship to an owner record type.

Physical Storage Mechanism

The logical structure for Blue Whale College shown in Figure 6.13 has been reproduced in Figure B.5 to demonstrate how IDMS stores the logical structures in secondary storage. In the examples that follow, each page is 512 bytes long: The COURSE records are 317 bytes, the CLASS records require 100 bytes, and the STUDENT records require 250 bytes.

The COURSE record type described in Chapter 6 was an owner record type which did not participate as a member in any sets. In the schema, these records were defined with a CALC location mode (not shown in Figure B.6). IDMS hashes the key for Sandbox I to PAGE 3333 (see Figure B.6), and so the record for Sandbox I and its prefix are placed after the header in PAGE 3333. A line index is created for Sandbox I. The line index contains the displacement from the beginning of the page (value 16), the length of the record (325), and the length of the prefix (value 8). Then, the amount of

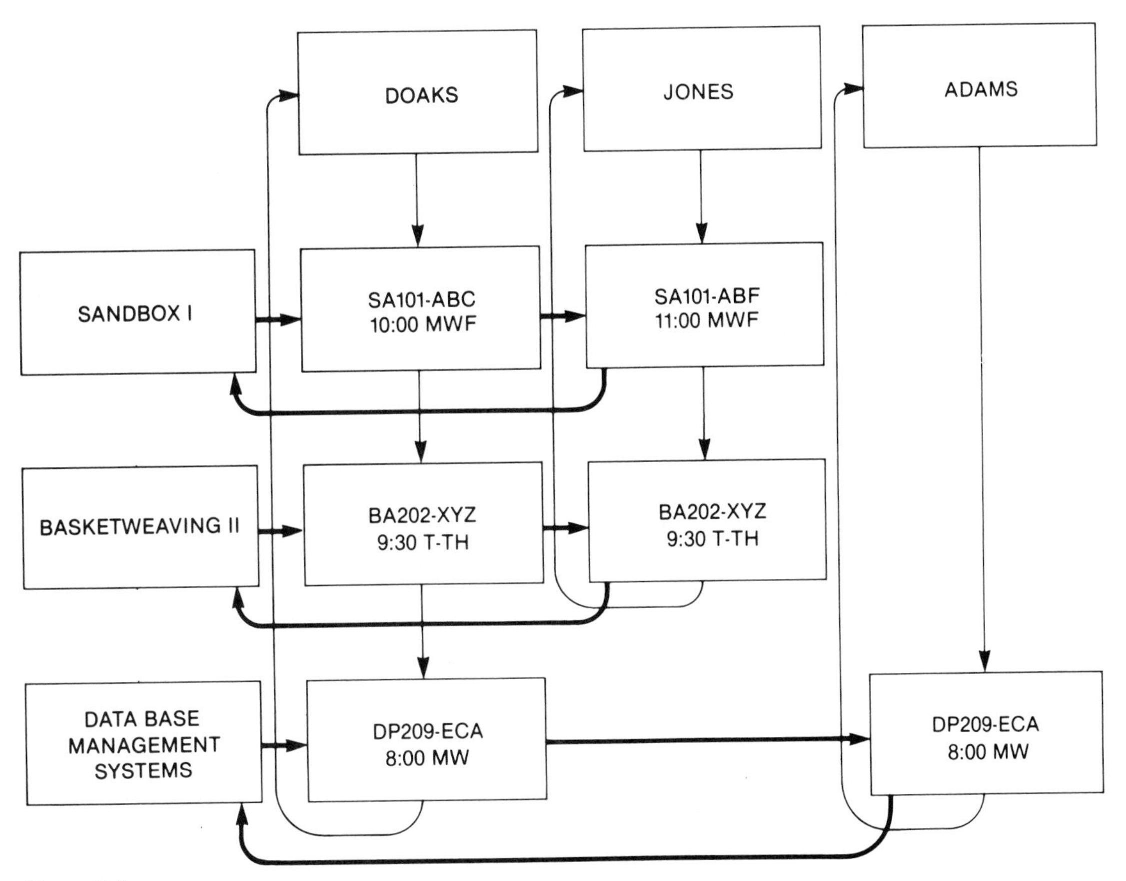

Figure B.5
Occurrences of the STUDENT-CLASS and COURSE-CLASS sets.

space available in the page is calculated: 512 (total) − 32 (header and footer and line indexes) − 325 (record and prefix) = 155. The system-set CALC pointers in the header are updated to point to the page (value 3333) and line (value 1) where the record is stored. The record for Basketweaving II hashes to PAGE 2121, and the record for Data Base Management Systems hashes to PAGE 1234.

In this example, IDMS calculated the target page number in which each record was stored. However, in the schema the location mode could be specified as DIRECT, allowing the application program to specify the target page number when a record is stored.

If the pattern of record accesses is well defined, unchanging, and known by the application programmer, improved performance can be obtained by storing records accessed together on the same page. If the records in Figure B.6 are requested, three I/O operations are required to transfer these records to main storage. But if these records are always accessed together, the application program could place them in the same page, using the DIRECT location mode. Then they could be transferred to main storage with only one I/O operation.

Figure B.6
COURSE records stored in three pages.

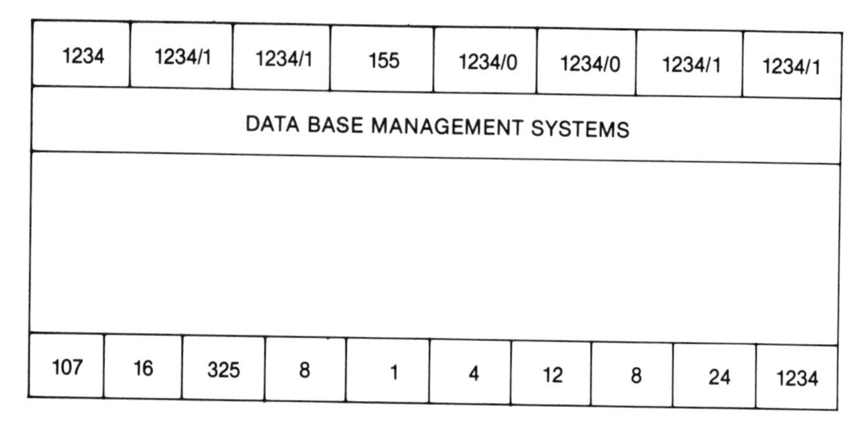

2121
2121/1
2121/1
155
2121/0
2121/0
2121/1
2121/1
BASKETWEAVING II
107
16
325
8
1
4
12
8
24
2121

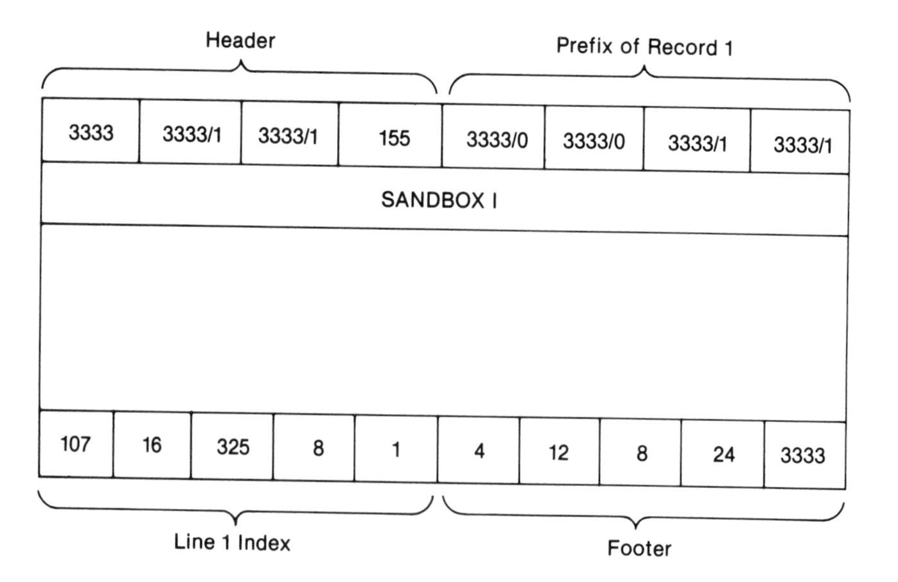

Figure B.7 Storage of CLASS records for one occurrence of the COURSE-CLASS set.

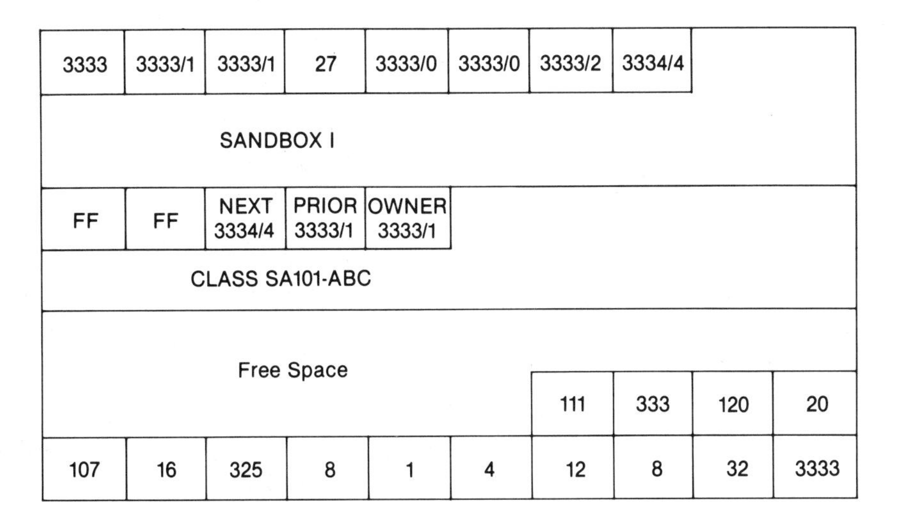

Use of the DIRECT location mode can improve performance in special situations. However, the application program would require changes if the access pattern changed. This low degree of data independence is undesirable, and so the DIRECT location mode is not often used.

In our example, the CLASS record type is the one retrieved most often after obtaining the records for COURSE. The CLASS record type is a member of the COURSE-CLASS set, and the CLASS records have a VIA location mode. They are stored as close as possible to occurrences of the owner of the set. Figure B.7 shows the CLASS record for SA101-ABC stored in a page with its owner, Sandbox I.

The CLASS record for SA101-ABC is stored VIA the owner of the occurrence, Sandbox I, and is stored in PAGE 3333. A line index is created at the bottom of the page. Since this is the second record in PAGE 3333, line 2 index contains control information about this record. The CLASS record for SA101-ABC is 120 bytes long, including the data and the prefix: its prefix is 20 bytes long, and the record is located 333 bytes from the beginning of the page. Note that the space available field is updated to show 27 bytes remaining in this page.

When IDMS attempts to store the CLASS record for SA101-ABF, space is not available in the desired page. Therefore, the record is stored in the next available position, PAGE 3334. Three other records have already been placed on this page and the appropriate pointers updated, and so the CLASS record for SA101-ABF is the fourth record stored in this page. Therefore, the line index for Record 4 is added in reverse order at the end of the page. A similar process is followed for each of the other CLASS records.

In Chapter 2, a rule-of-thumb was given, that records accessed together should be placed on the same cylinder and in the sequence they are accessed, whenever possible. This is the purpose of the VIA location mode, which reduces the number of I/O operations needed to retrieve records accessed together. Because the VIA location mode has been used in our example, when the page containing the COURSE record Sandbox I is transferred to primary storage, it contains the CLASS record for SA101-ABC. When the application program requests the record for SA101-ABC, there is no need to perform additional I/O operations to retrieve the record, because it is already in storage.

When a record participates as a member in more than one set type, it can only use the VIA location mode efficiently for one of the set types in which it is a member. Therefore, it is normally stored with the owner record type with which it is most often accessed.

Pointers

As we previously stated, each record in IDMS is divided into two parts: a prefix area and a data area. The prefix area contains the pointers necessary to maintain the data relationships with other records. The data area contains data to satisfy the requests of the application program.

Each record in IDMS is connected by pointers to the other records in an occurrence of a set. The pointers are composed of the page number and the line number of the stored record. The type of pointers for each set type are specified by the data base administrator in the schema data definition language. The data base administrator can choose from NEXT, PRIOR, and OWNER pointers. Figure B.7 shows the retrieval of records in the COURSE-CLASS set and the use of each of these pointers.

Occurrences of a set are connected by forward circular linked list (NEXT) pointers by default. Figure B.7 shows the use of a circular linked list to connect the owner and member records for one occurrence of the COURSE-CLASS set. In Chapter 6, Figure 6.9 depicted the logical relationships among these records, but now Figure B.7 depicts the physical storage of these relationships with the implementation of NEXT pointers.

In Figure B.7, the prefix of the Sandbox I record contains a pointer to the page and line number (3333/2) of the NEXT record in sequence, class SA101-ABC. The page number in which class SA101-ABC is stored is 3333, and the line number is 2. The prefix of the record for class SA101-ABC contains the page and line number (3334/4) of the NEXT class record, SA101-ABF. Class SA101-ABF completes the circular linked list with a page and line number pointer (3333/1) in the prefix to Sandbox I.

Some applications process member records in an occurrence of a set in chronological order so that each new record is added as the last member in an occurrence of a set. In this case, if a program requests the last member record in an occurrence of a set, IDMS must access all of the member records—using a forward linked list to add or retrieve these records—prior to the desired record before obtaining it. To add another CLASS record in chronological order (that is, LAST) in our example, IDMS would follow the pointers from Sandbox I to SA101-ABC to SA101-ABF. In this short list, two I/O operations (one for PAGE 3333 to retrieve record SA101-ABC, and one for PAGE 3334 to retrieve record SA101-ABF) would be required to find the last record currently in the list. In an operational data base, the number of classes is much larger and the list is correspondingly longer. The larger the number of I/O operations, the longer the time needed to add a new record into an occurrence of a set.

If records are added frequently, the number of records accessed to retrieve the requested record can be reduced by the addition of backward (PRIOR) pointers in the set. Figure B.7 also shows the use of forward and backward pointers to connect the owner and member records for one occurrence of the COURSE-CLASS set. To add a member record to an occurrence of a set, IDMS follows the PRIOR pointer (3334/4) in the owner record (Sandbox I) to the last member record in the occurrence of the set, CLASS SA101-ABF. After retrieving SA101-ABF, the new record is added in the next available location, PAGE 3334, line number 5 (see Figure B.8). The NEXT pointer in SA101-ABF (3334/5) points to the new record, SA101-BVD. The NEXT pointer in SA101-BVD points to Sandbox I (3333/1). The PRIOR pointer in SA101-BVD points to SA101-ABF (3334/4). The PRIOR pointer in Sandbox I points to SA101-BVD (3334/5).

In this example, two pages are retrieved with or without PRIOR pointers, and two I/O operations are needed to add the record for CLASS SA101-BVD. However, the number of I/O operations would be reduced using PRIOR pointers if the number of CLASS records was as great as that found in a typical college or university, records that therefore would be stored in many pages.

When representing complex networks using intersection records, it is not unusual to access a member record from the owner record of an occurrence of one set, and then use the member record to obtain the owner record in an occurrence of a different set. Phase two of the system at Blue Whale College is to determine the courses taken by each student. Example G18 illustrates how this phase is implemented with IDMS.

Figure B.8
Addition of a member record.

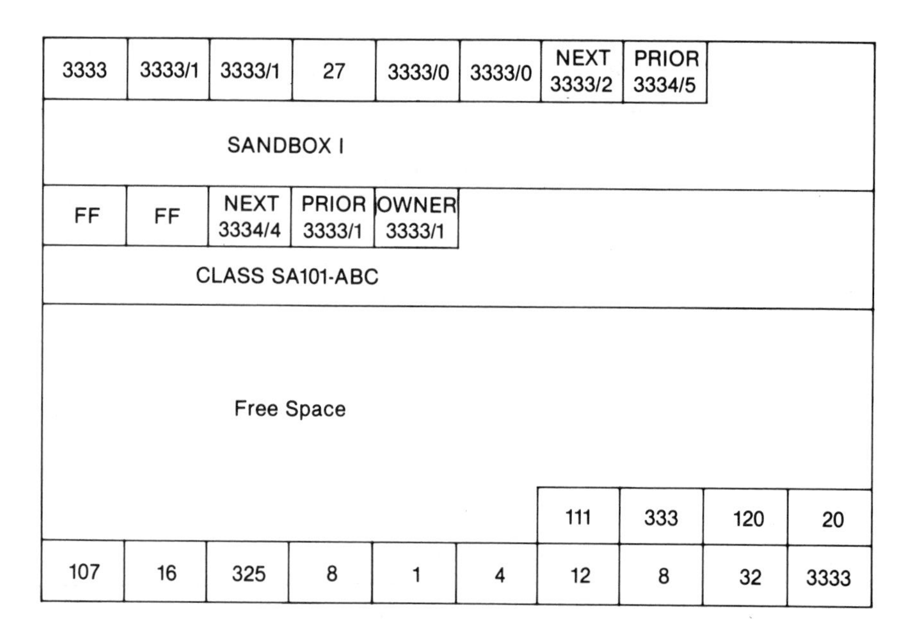

3334
3334/1
3334/3
53
Three Other Records
FF
FF
NEXT 3334/5
PRIOR 3333/2
OWNER 3333/1
SA101-ABF
FF
FF
NEXT 3333/1
PRIOR 3334/4
OWNER 3333/1
SA101-BVD
Free Space
111
295
120
20
111
175
120
20
LINE 3 INDEX
LINE 2 INDEX
LINE 1 INDEX
LINE 0 INDEX
64
3334

Example G18
Phase Two at Blue Whale College, Using IDMS

To determine the courses taken by each student, a member of the STUDENT-CLASS set is obtained. Then the owner of that occurrence of the COURSE-CLASS is obtained by following the NEXT pointers from the current record to the owner record for that occurrence of the COURSE-CLASS set. Figure B.9 shows the pointers that connect the STUDENT record for

Figure B.9
Pointers for the STUDENT-CLASS set.

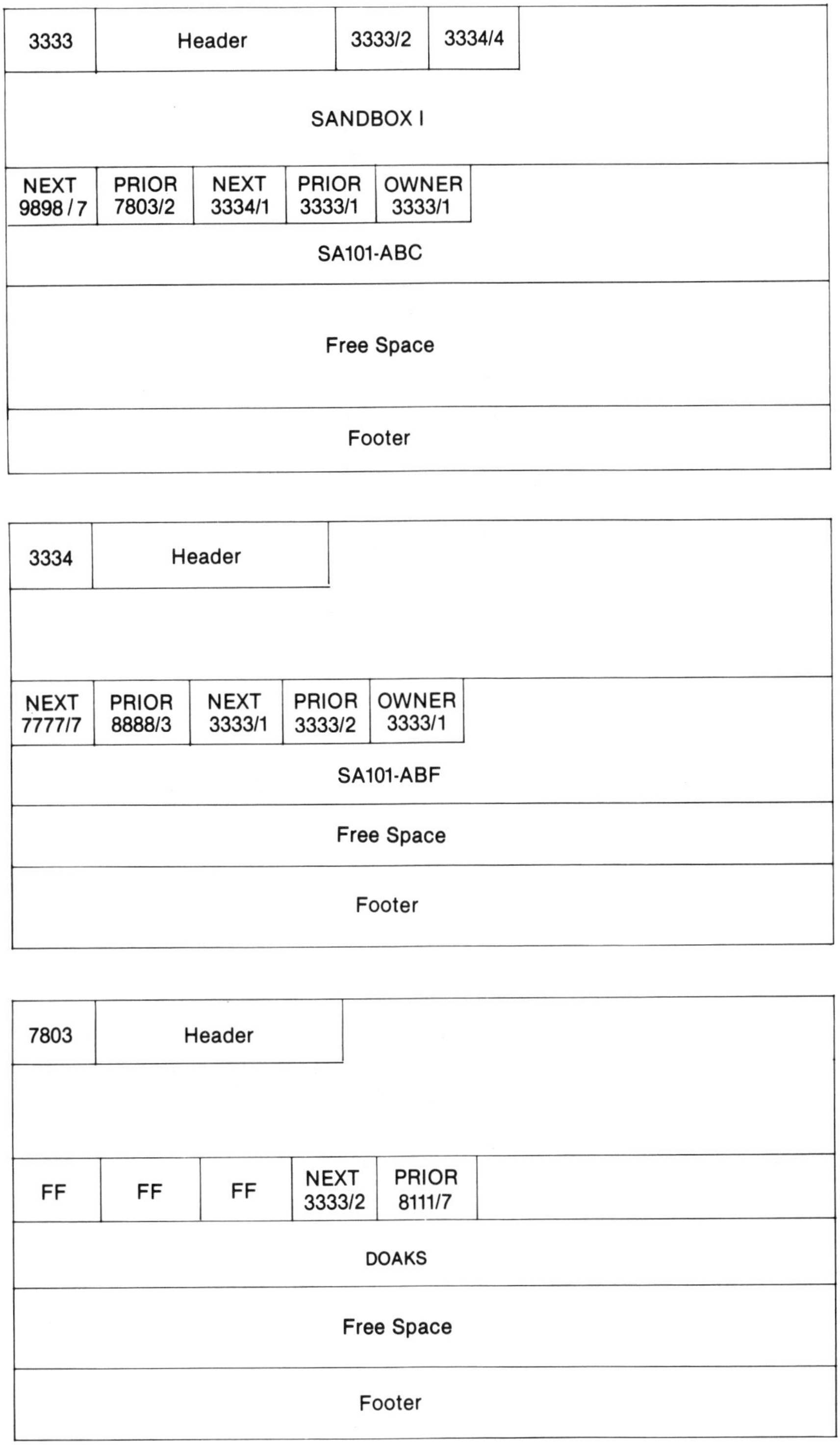

3333	Header	3333/2	3334/4

SANDBOX I

NEXT 9898/7	PRIOR 7803/2	NEXT 3334/1	PRIOR 3333/1	OWNER 3333/1

SA101-ABC

Free Space

Footer

3334	Header

NEXT 7777/7	PRIOR 8888/3	NEXT 3333/1	PRIOR 3333/2	OWNER 3333/1

SA101-ABF

Free Space

Footer

7803	Header

FF	FF	FF	NEXT 3333/2	PRIOR 8111/7

DOAKS

Free Space

Footer

Doaks to the first STUDENT-CLASS record, SA101-ABC. (All unnecessary control information is omitted for clarity.)

To generate a list of all the courses taken by Doaks, the prefix of the record for Doaks contains a NEXT pointer (3333/2) to the page and line number for the first CLASS record in this occurrence of the STUDENT-CLASS set, SA101-ABC. After the CLASS record for SA101-ABC is obtained, forward (NEXT) pointers are followed from SA101-ABC to SA101-ABF (3334/4) to Sandbox I (3333/2). Even though Sandbox I is in the same page as SA101-ABC, when NEXT pointers are used, IDMS must follow the pointer chains through the remainder of the member records for that occurrence to determine that Sandbox I is the owner of this occurrence of the COURSE-CLASS set. Again, the pointer chains followed are much shorter in this example than would normally be experienced with actual data.

If this process is performed frequently, a new pointer, to the owner of an occurrence of the set, can be added. Figure B.9 includes the OWNER pointer for the COURSE-CLASS set. To determine the courses taken by Doaks, the NEXT pointer in the prefix of the record for Doaks is followed to the page and line number (3333/2) of the first member in this occurrence of the STUDENT-CLASS set, SA101-ABC. The CLASS record for SA101-ABC contains an OWNER pointer (3333/1) to the owner of this occurrence of the COURSE-CLASS set. Unlike the situation when NEXT pointers were used, the owner can now be determined directly without following pointers through the remainder of the member records for that occurrence. Thus, use of OWNER pointers reduces the number of I/O operations needed to obtain the owner of the occurrence of the set containing the member record. Thereby, performance is improved.

To obtain the remainder of the courses taken by Doaks, the NEXT pointer (9898/7) for the STUDENT-CLASS set in the prefix of SA101-ABC is followed to class BA202-XYZ (not shown), and the process is repeated.

In the preceding example, the page sizes were made artificially small for clarity. Actually, the size of the page has a significant impact on performance. The best page size is determined by the patterns of access of the data. Recall from Chapter 2 that performance for sequential storage and retrieval improves with large page sizes. For direct retrieval, performance improves with small page sizes, due to the reduced amount of data transferred. Thus, the data base administrator must determine the page size by considering the access patterns of the data.

Space Management Pages

When a record will not fit within the desired page, it is placed in the page closest to the desired location, to minimize seek time. If IDMS sequentially searched each succeeding page to determine whether or not the record will fit, the rotational delay and seek time could be excessive. To reduce the effort needed to find a page with sufficient space to store the record, IDMS contains **space management pages**, which record the amount of free space in an area.

A space management page is one page in length and contains one entry for each page within an area. As many space management pages as necessary to provide one entry for each page in the area are created. When a page is 70 percent full, IDMS finds the entry for that page in the space management page. IDMS updates the corresponding entry for the 70 percent full page in the space management page. In our example, when IDMS searches for the page to store record SA101-ABF, the space management page is searched for the page closest to PAGE 3333 with enough space to store the record. This allows IDMS to use a minimum number of I/O operations to examine a number of pages, searching for free space.

Note that IDMS does not update the space map after each record is stored, but only after a page becomes 70 percent full. If space management pages were updated after each record was stored, the maintenance of the space management pages would require significant effort. Updating an entry on a space management page only when a page is 70 percent full is another technique to reduce the number of I/O operations.

B.3 SUMMARY

IDMS is a commercial implementation of the DBTG specifications for a network data base management system. IDMS is marketed by the Cullinet Corporation. It contains some of the constructs of the early DBTG model that were deleted in later reports.

IDMS stores data in areas specified by the application program. Areas are used to improve performance by grouping data accessed together in the same area.

IDMS offers three location modes for storage and retrieval of data within an area. The CALC location mode uses hashing techniques to provide rapid direct storage and retrieval of a record. The DIRECT location mode provides improved performance for critical applications with known and constant access patterns. In the DIRECT location mode, the application program specifies the target page in which the record is stored. The VIA location mode stores a record close to the owner of the occurrence of the member record. Thus VIA improves performance when a record type is accessed through a relationship to an owner record type.

IDMS uses linked lists to maintain record relationships. Three different pointer types are used. The NEXT pointer accesses the next record in the occurrence of the set. It is the default pointer. The PRIOR pointer improves performance when member records are added last to an occurrence of a set. PRIOR also improves performance when an occurrence of a set is entered at other than the first record and the entry record is deleted. The OWNER pointer improves performance when a set is entered through a member record and the owner of that occurrence of the set must be determined.

Performance is affected by the data base administrator's selection of the appropriate page size to match the access pattern of the data. Selection of pointers improves performance. Space management pages improve performance as pages become full and IDMS must search for an empty page in which to place a record.

REVIEW QUESTIONS

B.1 What is an area? What is its purpose?

B.2 How is a page formatted? What purpose does the header serve? The footer?

B.3 Describe the function of the CALC location mode.

B.4 Describe the function of the DIRECT location mode. What are the advantages of using DIRECT? What are the disadvantages?

B.5 Describe the function of the VIA location mode. What are the advantages of using VIA? What are the disadvantages?

B.6 When are NEXT pointers used by themselves?

B.7 When are PRIOR pointers normally used? Why?

B.8 When are OWNER pointers normally used? Why?

B.9 Describe the addition of a class record for SA101-XYZ to the COURSE-CLASS set. (Assume that both NEXT and PRIOR pointers are used.)

B.10 How is a space management page used? What is the advantage of using a space management page? When is it updated? Why?

7

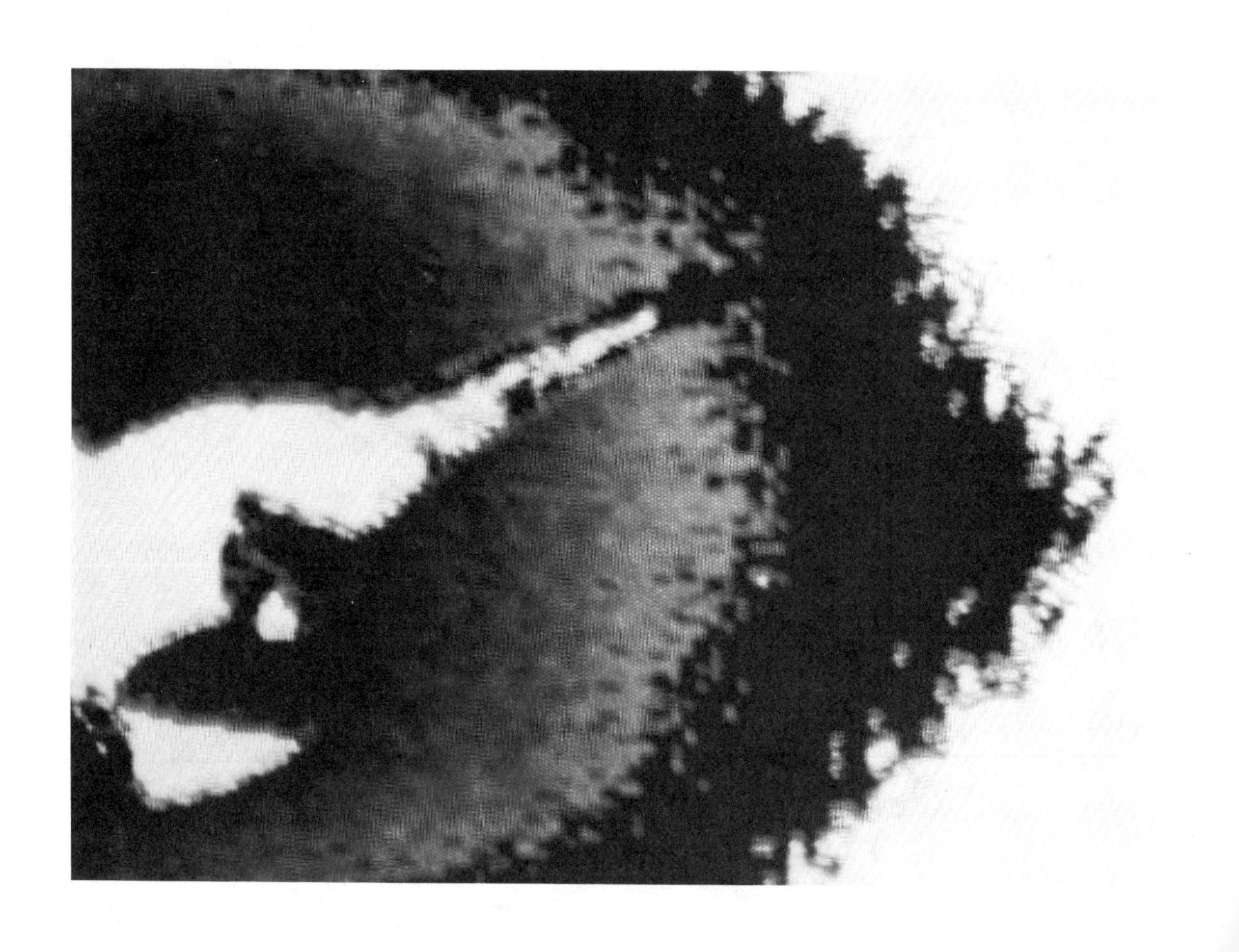

RELATIONAL DATA MODEL

CHAPTER OBJECTIVES

Upon completion of this chapter, you should be able to:

1. Understand the mathematical terminology associated with the relational model and translate it into more simple terms
2. Represent data from the hierarchical and network models using the relational model
3. Name the features of the relational model that contribute to increased data independence and understand their importance
4. Understand the manipulation of relations
5. Explain the functions of the SQL data definition and data manipulation commands

NEW WORDS AND PHRASES

tuple
attribute
domain
degree
relation
view
candidate key
primary key
projection
selection
join

7.1 CHAPTER INTRODUCTION

The relational model represents data as two-dimensional tables. It came into existence because of a need for a tool to make data processing professionals and end users of their services more productive.

The data base models we have previously presented are extremely complex. They require greater expertise than that required by conventional file structures in order to design and navigate the data base. Because the performance of these data bases is highly dependent upon the data base design, many of them have been "over designed" to ensure adequate performance. This complexity has caused a shortage of people with an adequate technical background. In addition, systems using these models require much labor to install. The complexity of these models and the labor needed to install the systems caused a backlog in the requests for data processing services, and users cannot wait for data processing personnel to overcome the backlog of requests for those services. The relational model is a solution to these problems.

Although the software required by the relational model is very complex, mastery of the model's data definition language and a nonprocedural data manipulation language requires far less time and effort than the DDL and DML for either the hierarchical or network models. Also, the design within the relational models is flexible, so that design changes are relatively easy to implement, reducing the need for excessive data base design efforts. Finally, the users are changing, and they now have a higher degree of data processing literacy; the simplicity of the relational model DML allows them to perform their own data manipulation.

The hierarchical and network data structures have been in use in industry since the late 1960s. The theoretical concepts forming the basis for the relational model appeared in the early 1970s, pioneered by E. F. Codd. The relational model is unlike the models we have previously presented, in that it is free of both sequence and path dependencies. The hierarchical and network models require the application programmer to know the physical paths existing between records, and they require a knowledge of the DML in order to navigate the paths. These navigation skills needed for the hierarchical and network data base management systems require additional training, and so there is a shortage of personnel who possess them.

The previous models we have discussed permitted access to data via paths specified in the schema. Since programs depended upon the paths to records within a data base, if the paths to the records changed to accommodate a design for a new system, the programs needed to be changed to account for the change in the paths to the data. The relational model, on the other hand, does not make use of the access paths in its logical structure or its DML.

The hierarchical and network models permit data to be viewed in more than one sequence, and application programs are written to take advantage of the sequence of the data. Naturally, if the sequence of the data is changed, the application programs will not function correctly unless they are modified to account for the new sequence. The relational model, however, does not make use of sequencing in its logical structure or its DML. Data is presented through two-dimensional tabular structures, providing greater data independence than existed in previous models. This increased data independence allows an easier transition to new data relationships, which in turn increases overall productivity.

The relational model is the darling of the academic community, due to its operational simplicity and power which permit users with little training to execute DML commands. However, the power of the relational model initially presented problems in data access performance, causing the model to be largely confined to the research environment through most of the 1970s. However, technology has caught up to the relational model; now, in the 1980s, relational data base management systems are being used in large-scale data processing applications. Indeed, the power, simplicity, and data independence of the network model cause many to believe it is the model of the future.

The relational model is founded on mathematical principles, and much of the early terminology associated with the model was mathematical. The DML for the model uses mathematics as its basis, and relational calculus and relational algebra data manipulation languages have been developed. Thus, a problem exists, for outside of academia, only a small percentage of users have an adequate background to understand the mathematics of the DML.

Fortunately, an understanding of the mathematics involved is not necessary in order to use the model. Instead, the data manipulation operations can be viewed as a series of cutting and pasting operations on the data within a table. Unlike the models previously presented, a user can obtain specific data from the relational model via a nonprocedural language which allows the user to describe the data required, rather than the navigation required. The data base management system then selects the data, based on the description provided by the user rather than by a navigational path through the data base.

Our presentation in this chapter is oriented to business applications of the relational model. Some of the basic terminology of the model will be presented in its mathematical terms for those who will perform further research in the area, but the mathematics is then translated into more familiar terms. Since the familiar terms will be more understandable for most of us, they will be used for the remainder of the chapter.

7.2 RELATIONAL DATA MODEL CONCEPTS

Formal Terminology

As with each of the models we discussed in earlier chapters, the relational model has its own terminology. In this section, an overview of the formal terminology is presented, followed by the terminology in simpler language.

In the relational model, data is viewed in a two-dimensional tabular structure called a **relation**. Figure 7.1 shows a relation with eight occurrences of the data for students at Blue Whale College. The relation is named the STUDENT relation. Each occurrence of the data is called a **tuple** (rhymes with *couple*). The STUDENT relation contains seven attributes, and each of the attributes is named: S-NAME, S-ID, S-ADDRESS, MAJOR, DATE-OF-BIRTH, SEX, and GPA.

Each attribute can take on a specified set of values over a period of time. All of the values the attribute can take on at any point in time are

Attribute Names

Student

S-NAME	S-ID	S-ADDRESS	MAJOR	DATE-OF-BIRTH	SEX	GPA
PLATO	123456789	111 FIRST ST.	PHILOSOPHY	6/26/51	FEMALE	3.4
SHAKESPEARE	789789789	222 SECOND ST.	ENGLISH	2/20/53	FEMALE	3.0
DUNN	987654321	333 THIRD ST.	ENGLISH	10/28/43	FEMALE	3.0
NEWTON	123123123	444 FOURTH ST.	PHYSICS	3/3/47	FEMALE	2.4
WILLIAMS	111111111	123 FIRST ST.	ENGLISH	10/2/54	MALE	3.1
ARCHIMEDES	222222222	100 BROAD ST.	PHYSICS	6/15/66	MALE	3.5
BROWNING	333333333	10 MAIN ST.	ENGLISH	7/25/54	MALE	2.0
LINCOLN	444444444	333 MAIN ST.	POLITICAL SCIENCE	2/9/54	MALE	3.6

Tuples

Attributes

Figure 7.1 Occurrences of data for the STUDENT relation.

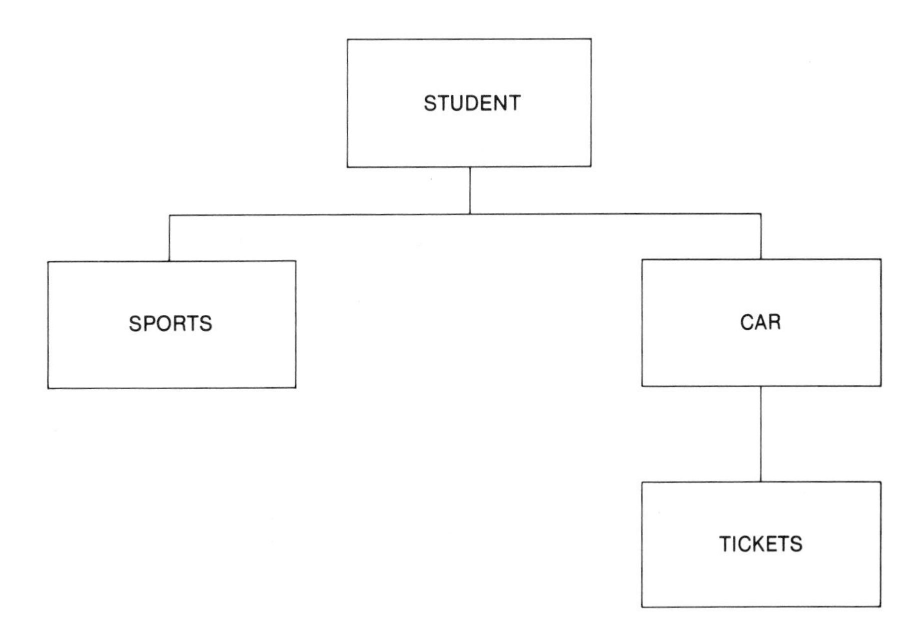

Figure 7.2 One-to-many data relationships in the hierarchical model.

called the **domain** of the attribute. The attribute named SEX can only take on two values—male or female—and so male and female are the domain of the attribute SEX. If AGE were included as an attribute in the STUDENT relation, the domain of age would be the set of numbers from 0 to 120, to represent the life span, in years, of most human beings.

Each attribute in a tuple takes its value from the domain of possible values for that attribute. The second tuple in the STUDENT relation contains the value of Shakespeare for the attribute S-NAME, the value of 789789789 for the attribute S-ID, the value 222 Second Street for the attribute S-ADDRESS, the value English for the attribute MAJOR, the value of 2/20/53 for the attribute DATE-OF-BIRTH, the value of female for the attribute SEX, and the value 3.0 for GPA.

The **degree** of a relation refers to the number of attributes within a relation. In Figure 7.1, the STUDENT relation has eight tuples and seven attributes; therefore, the relation has a degree of 7.

N-ary relations refer to relations with *N*-number of attributes. *N*-tuples refer to tuples within a relation having *N*-columns. For instance, a relation containing only attributes for S-ID and MAJOR is called a binary relation and a 2-tuple.

In previous chapters, data relationships with implied dependencies were depicted with blocks identifying the record (segment) type and lines or arrows indicating the relationships between the record types. For example, Figure 7.2 represents the hierarchical model data relationships at Blue Whale College among the record types for STUDENT, SPORTS, CARs, and TICKETS. The lines connecting these blocks represent one-to-many relationships between STUDENT and CARs, STUDENT and SPORTS, and CARs and TICKETS.

The lines also imply a path to be followed from one record type to another. In contrast, E. F. Codd, the relational model pioneer, has developed a notation that emphasizes the pathlessness of the relational model. In this notation, the relation is named, then the attributes in the relation are named in parentheses. Codd's notation describing the STUDENT relation is:

STUDENT (S-NAME, S-ID, S-ADDRESS, MAJOR, DATE-OF-BIRTH, SEX, GPA)

In this example, STUDENT is the name of the relation, and S-NAME, S-ID, S-ADDRESS, MAJOR, DATE-OF-BIRTH, SEX, and GPA are the attributes in the relation.

Rules

As with each of the models we presented in earlier chapters, rules exist for the relational model, defining the way in which data is stored and manipulated. This section identifies the major rules associated with the relational model.

1. *Each attribute is distinct.* Repeating groups are not allowed. The relational model does not permit two attributes with the same name in the same relation. If a student plays in many sports, only one attribute named SPORTS is permitted in the relation. Later in this chapter, a technique will be presented to handle one-to-many relationships.
2. *Each attribute must be named.* This is a departure from the rules of the hierarchical model, which only required the fields explicitly searched by the data base management system to be named.
3. *Each tuple is unique.* Duplicate tuples are not allowed. And, uniqueness of a tuple is not limited to the tuples currently viewed: Each tuple must be unique for all time. Thus, the data base administrator must determine the attribute, or attributes, within a relation that ensure that the tuple will remain unique over time. Those attributes that uniquely define a tuple are called *candidate keys.* When more than one attribute is needed to develop a candidate key, the attributes are chosen such that no attribute is superfluous in maintaining the uniqueness of the tuple (that is, such that no attribute can be deleted and the remaining attributes in the candidate key still maintain the uniqueness of the tuple).

   For example, in Figure 7.1, one of the candidate keys is S-ID (student identification number). It is assumed that an S-ID is assigned by the college in such a way that no two students will have the same S-ID. Another candidate key is composed of the S-NAME, S-ADDRESS, and DATE-OF-BIRTH fields. It is improbable that two people with the same name and address will have the same birth date, or that two people with the same name and date of birth will have the same address. S-NAME is not chosen as a candidate key by itself, since there is no guarantee that S-NAME will be unique for all periods of time. Nor is the combination of attributes S-NAME and S-ID considered a candidate key, for S-NAME is superfluous: It can be removed from the combination of S-NAME and

STUDENT

S-NAME	SEX	GPA	MAJOR	S-ID	S-ADDRESS	DATE-OF-BIRTH
LINCOLN	MALE	3.6	POLITICAL SCIENCE	444444444	333 MAIN ST.	2/9/54
SHAKESPEARE	FEMALE	3.0	ENGLISH	789789789	222 SECOND ST.	2/20/53
PLATO	FEMALE	3.4	PHILOSOPHY	123456789	111 FIRST ST.	6/26/51
BROWNING	MALE	2.0	ENGLISH	333333333	10 MAIN ST.	7/25/54
DUNN	FEMALE	3.0	ENGLISH	987654321	333 THIRD ST.	10/28/43
ARCHIMEDES	MALE	3.5	PHYSICS	222222222	100 BROAD ST.	6/15/66
NEWTON	FEMALE	2.4	PHYSICS	123123123	444 FOURTH ST.	3/3/47
WILLIAMS	MALE	3.1	ENGLISH	111111111	123 FIRST ST.	10/2/54

Figure 7.3
The STUDENT relation with attributes and tuples in an altered sequence.

S-ID, and S-ID still maintains the uniqueness of the tuple over all time.

From the list of candidate keys, the data base administrator selects one of the candidate keys as the *primary key*. Note that in the example of Codd's notation we presented earlier, the primary key is underlined.

4. *Navigation in the relational model is through the value an attribute takes.* The DML specifies an attribute name and the value of the attribute to satisfy the request from the user. Pointers from one record to another do not exist; therefore, path dependencies do not exist.
5. *Tuples are presented to the user independent of sequence.* Tuples may be presented to the user in any order. Therefore, the user should make no assumptions about the sequence in which tuples are presented.
6. *Attributes are presented in any order.* Although the relations presented in Figure 7.1 and Figure 7.3 have different physical appearances due to a difference in the sequence of tuples and attributes, both relations contain the same data and are functionally equivalent. Therefore, sequence dependencies do not exist in the relational model.
7. *Relations produced as a result of a DML command adhere to all of the rules for relations.* Relations can be manipulated to provide the user different views of the data. The result of the manipulation is a new relation; that is, new relations are produced when relations are manipulated.

Business Terminology

The relational model has its foundation in relational mathematics, as reflected in the terminology we have just presented. This mathematical terminology was in vogue in the 1970s, when the relational model was in its infancy and was used in research environments. The terminology could be expected in that academic environment.

But in the eighties, the relational model has moved into the business world. Few in the business world understand, or even want to understand, the terminology of relational mathematics. The business community is interested in accomplishing a job in the simplest manner possible. Thus there is a current trend of translation of the relational terminology into terminology understood by the layman. For those who are not data processing professionals, relations become *tables,* tuples become *rows,* and attributes become *columns.*

On the other hand, data processing professionals, for their part, adapt the terminology to the background from which they have evolved. A column (attribute) bears a striking resemblance to a building block they know as a field. A row (tuple) resembles a building block they have called a record and a table is similar to a file.

7.3 DECOMPOSITION OF TREE AND NETWORK STRUCTURES INTO TABLES

The relational model allows data to be viewed naturally; that is, artificial constructs are not needed to represent data relationships. In the relational model, the logical data structures presented in the hierarchical and network models can be stored in tables. In Chapter 5, network structures were decomposed into hierarchical structures by duplicating data. In Chapter 6, complex networks were decomposed into simple networks by duplicating data. In this chapter, both hierarchical structures and network structures are decomposed into tables with the duplication of data, to demonstrate how each of these data structures are stored when using the relational model.

To accomplish this, each access path in a hierarchical or network structure is reproduced as a key field in a table. When the data is viewed in tables, the user may have the impression that the data exists in flat files. If so, it would appear that the industry has come full circle and is now back where it started! However, we are dealing with logical data structures. The tabular view of the data has no implications about how the data is stored.

Example G19 illustrates how a hierarchical structure is decomposed into a table.

Example G19
Decomposing a Hierarchical Structure into a Table

The hierarchical path for STUDENT, SPORTS, CARs, and TICKETS at Blue Whale College has been selected from Figure 4.4 and reproduced in Figure 7.2. The data relationship in Figure 7.2 can be decomposed into a table by selecting the primary key for each parent record type in the hierarchical structure and reproducing it in a table containing the data of the record type of its children. Therefore, the SPORTS table can be described as follows:

Figure 7.4
SPORTS relation.

SPORTS

S-ID	SPORTS-NAME	POSITION	DATE
789789789	FOOTBALL	TIGHT END	FALL 83
123456789	SOCCER	GOAL KEEPER	FALL 82
222222222	FOOTBALL	TIGHT END	FALL 83
789789789	BASEBALL	SHORTSTOP	SPRING 84

SPORTS (S-ID, SPORTS–NAME, POSITION, DATE)

Each sports record in the SPORTS table has four fields: S-ID, SPORTS-NAME, POSITION, DATE (see Figure 7.4). The S-ID field is the primary key of the STUDENT record. Thus, in the decomposition the S-ID field has been included in the SPORTS table, because if it were not, duplicate records would occur in the table. In Figure 7.4, the first and third records—containing values of football, tight end, and Fall 83—are not unique if the field for S-ID is omitted. Remember, the relational model prohibits duplicate records, and a mechanism is needed to make each record unique. The mechanism in this example is the inclusion of the S-ID field.

The duplication of the key field is repeated for the CARS table (Figure 7.5) and the TICKETS table (not shown). Each record in the CARS table contains the S-ID field, in addition to the fields we would find in the CARs record in hierarchical and network models.

One of the fields in the CARS table is the LICENSE-NUMBER field, which is the primary key for the CARS table. Both the LICENSE-NUMBER field and the S-ID field from the CARS table are included in the TICKETS table.

Simple networks are represented in the relational model in the same manner as hierarchical structures are represented. Simple networks require the key field from each parent record to be duplicated in the child. Figure 7.5 shows the CARS table with the addition of the INSURANCE-NAME field, which is the primary key of the INSURANCE table. Only the LICENSE, MAKE, and MODEL fields exist in the CARs record in the network model. In the relational model, INSURANCE-NAME exists in two tables, the INSURANCE table and the CARS table. The values in the S-ID and INSURANCE-NAME fields are used to maintain the relationships with the student records and the insurance records.

Complex networks are represented in a similar manner. A table is created containing intersection data for both record types involved in a many-to-many relationship. The table containing intersection data contains, at a minimum, the primary key of each table involved in the many-to-many relationship. In Figure 7.6, a many-to-many relationship exists between students and the courses they take. The intersection data is composed of the data to represent the key field of the STUDENT table and the key field of the COURSE table. The STUDENT-CLASS table contains the S-ID field from the STUDENT table to identify the student taking the course. The STUDENT-CLASS table also contains the COURSE-ID field from the COURSE table to indicate which course is taken by the student. C-SECTION is intersection

CARS

S-ID	LICENSE-NUMBER	MAKE	MODEL	INSURANCE-NAME
123456789	ABC-123	FORD	FUTURA	BIG BUCKS INSURANCE
123456789	ABC-124	DODGE	DART	BIG BUCKS INSURANCE
789789789	BZY-001	CHEVY	CHEVELLE	FLY-BY-NITE INSURANCE
987654321	CAR-054	LINCOLN	MARK V	FLY-BY-NITE INSURANCE
123123123	DUN-008	STUTZ	BEARCAT	BIG BUCKS INSURANCE
444444444	DDN-518	JEEP	CHEROKEE	BIG BUCKS INSURANCE
444444444	DDN-519	CADILLAC	EL DORADO	BIG BUCKS INSURANCE

INSURANCE

INSURANCE-NAME	ADDRESS
BIG BUCKS INSURANCE	100 MAIN ST.
FLY-BY-NITE INSURANCE	200 BROAD ST.

Figure 7.5
INSURANCE and CARS relations.

data to represent the specific class section in which the student is enrolled.

Thus we see that hierarchical structures, simple network structures, and complex network structures can be represented in the relational model. Each record type from these structures is represented as a table. Record types occurring as children in the other models have the primary key of the parent record type duplicated in the table in which they occur. If multiple levels of relationships exist, the new key of each parent record type is reproduced in its child. This process repeats itself to the lowest level of the structure. This does not imply that there is a multi-level structure in the relational model. Instead, it represents the natural relationships of the data.

The reproduced keys serve two purposes. First, in tables such as SPORTS, the duplicated key ensures the uniqueness of the records within the table. The uniqueness would not occur without the duplicated key.

However, in some tables, such as the CARS table, a field like the LICENSE-NO field ensures uniqueness of all records for all time. The duplicated key is not necessary for uniqueness in the tables of this nature. The second purpose of the duplicated key is to establish a method to relate two tables.

Figure 7.6
Intersection data in the STUDENT-CLASS relation.

STUDENT-CLASS

S-ID	COURSE-ID	C-SECTION
123456789	SA101	AXY
123456789	BA202	ABY
789789789	SA101	ABF
789789789	BA202	EDA
789789789	DP209	EBA
789789789	DP101	BFF
111111111	DP209	EBA
111111111	AC101	BBA
111111111	EC101	CDX
333333333	DP209	EBA

COURSE

COURSE-ID	DESCRIPTION
DP209	DATA BASE MANAGEMENT
SA101	SANDBOX I
BA201	BASKETWEAVING
AC101	ACCOUNTING I
EC101	ECONOMICS I

In the previous models we presented, pointers (paths) existed to provide this relationship. Instead of using pointers, the relational model uses the value of fields to establish the data relationships between tables.

In the relational model, tables are manipulated through operations that resemble cutting and pasting operations. Example G20 illustrates the operation of projection, selection, and the join.

Example G20
Projection, Selection, and the Join

In the system presented in Chapter 4 to generate mailing labels for course catalogs, only the S-ID field and S-ADDRESS field were necessary to generate the mailing labels. In the relational model, the number of fields presented to the user can be restricted through the **projection** operation. Projection presents only the named fields of a table and their contents to the user. In response to the question, "What are the names and addresses of the students actively attending college?" The STUDENT table can be projected on the S-NAME and S-ADDRESS fields to provide the MAILING-LABEL relation in Figure 7.7. The projection simulates cutting out the S-ID field and the S-ADDRESS field from the STUDENT table and pasting them together in the

Figure 7.7
Projection of name and address to provide mailing labels.

MAILING-LABEL

S-NAME	S-ADDRESS
PLATO	111 FIRST ST.
SHAKESPEARE	222 SECOND ST.
DUNN	333 THIRD ST.
NEWTON	444 FOURTH ST.
WILLIAMS	123 FIRST ST.
ARCHIMEDES	100 BROAD ST.
BROWNING	10 MAIN ST.
LINCOLN	333 MAIN ST.

ENGLISH-MAJORS

S-NAME	S-ID	S-ADDRESS	MAJOR	DATE-OF-BIRTH	SEX	GPA
SHAKESPEARE	789789789	222 SECOND ST.	ENGLISH	2/20/53	FEMALE	3.0
DUNN	987654321	333 THIRD ST.	ENGLISH	10/28/43	FEMALE	3.0
WILLIAMS	111111111	123 FIRST ST.	ENGLISH	10/2/54	MALE	3.1
BROWNING	333333333	10 MAIN ST.	ENGLISH	7/25/54	MALE	2.0

Figure 7.8
Table returned in the selection of students majoring in English.

MAILING-LABEL table. Remember, the manipulation of a table always results in a new table.

The number of records from a table presented to a user can also be reduced through the **selection** operation, which allows records with specified values in specified fields to be presented to the user. In response to the question, "Who are the students majoring in English?" the records for students who have a value of English in the field named MAJOR can be selected from the STUDENT table. Figure 7.8 shows the table that results from the selection process. This gives the visual impression that the records for Shakespeare, Dunn, Williams, and Browning have been cut out of the STUDENT relation and pasted in the ENGLISH-MAJORS table.

The selection and projection operations can be combined into one operation. To answer the question, "What are the names of the students who are majoring in philosophy?" both operations are needed. Only the S-NAME field is required; no other fields are necessary. The S-NAME field is projected on the STUDENT table. Only the names of the students who are majoring in philosophy are selected. Figure 7.9 shows the results of the combined operations. Only the S-NAME field is shown. The only student in the STUDENT table majoring in philosophy is Plato.

Through the **join** operation, two tables can be combined to allow the user to obtain the desired data. To answer the question, "What sports does each student play?" data must be obtained from both the STUDENT table and the SPORTS table. Fields must exist in each table which have comparable domains—it must be reasonable to compare the values in each field. It is not reasonable to compare values in a field for S-ID and LICENSE-NO, for it is unlikely a match

Figure 7.9
Table generated to answer the question, "What are the names of the students majoring in philosophy?"

PHILOSOPHY-MAJORS

S-NAME
PLATO

Figure 7.10
Table generated in response to the question, "What sports does each student play?"

S-ID	S-NAME	SPORTS-NAME
789789789	SHAKESPEARE	FOOTBALL
789789789	SHAKESPEARE	BASEBALL
123456789	PLATO	SOCCER
222222222	ARCHIMEDES	FOOTBALL

would occur, and if a match did occur, the result would have no meaning. Since S-ID exists in the STUDENT table and is duplicated in the SPORTS table, these tables can be combined to provide the desired data. The STUDENT and SPORTS tables are combined based on matching values in the S-ID field. This combining of tables based on the values in columns which have comparable domains is termed a *join.* The join can be used in combination with a projection on S-NAME and SPORTS-NAME to provide the table in Figure 7.10, answering the question.

7.4 SQL

SQL is the data manipulation language for an IBM commercial implementation of the relational data base model. It has evolved over a number of years. SQL has commands to perform several different types of functions. This section presents an overview of some of the data definition, data manipulation, and security commands.

Data definition commands define the environment in which SQL operates, creating tables, views, and indexes and adding columns to existing tables. The data manipulation commands perform data retrieval and maintenance. Security commands define the privileges of each user.

Data Definition Commands

As with other models, the first operation to be performed is data definition. Data definition in SQL is performed through CREATE TABLE and ALTER TABLE commands.

The CREATE TABLE command provides a name for the table, defines the field names used, and describes the physical attributes of the data in the fields. The following command shows a sample data definition for the STUDENT table:

```
CREATE TABLE STUDENT
    (S-NAME             CHAR(30),
    S-ID                SMALLINT,
    S-ADDRESS           CHAR(30),
    MAJOR               CHAR(20),
    DATE-OF-BIRTH       CHAR(8),
    SEX                 CHAR(6)
    GPA                 DECIMAL(2))
```

The CREATE TABLE command above names the STUDENT table as the table to be created. Subsequent lines define each of the column names in the table: S-NAME, S-ID, S-ADDRESS, MAJOR, DATE-OF-BIRTH, SEX, and GPA. The names of the columns are followed by the physical description of the data. S-NAME is composed of 30 alphabetic characters. S-ID is a small integer—a binary value occupying 16 bits of storage. SQL permits five other data types: INTEGER, DECIMAL, FLOAT, VARCHAR, and LONG VARCHAR. These data types are similar to the SMALLINT and CHAR commands in that they operate on numeric and character data, but they differ in the specification of the length of the data.

This definition establishes the table but does not place any data in the table. Data is placed in the table through the DML with an INSERT command. (The format and use of the DML for SQL are presented later in this section.)

SQL is very flexible in its operation. Through an ALTER command, a column may be added to a table at any time. Immediately after the command is issued, the additional column is available for use but does not contain any data. Example G21 illustrates use of the ALTER command.

Example G21 The ALTER Command

After the SPORTS table is created and in operation, a new system is installed at Blue Whale College to capture the date of each athlete's last physical. The format of the command to add a column to the existing table to store this data is:

```
ALTER TABLE SPORTS
    ADD PHYSICAL CHAR(8)
```

SPORTS names the table to be modified. PHYSICAL is the name of the column to be added. It is character data and occupies eight positions. In Figure 7.11, PHYSICAL is added to the SPORTS table but does not contain any data. Each record has a null value, indicated by a question mark. As members of the sports teams present confirmation of their physicals, the data is recorded in the PHYSICAL column using SQL.

SPORTS

S-ID	SPORTS-NAME	POSITION	DATE	PHYSICAL
789789789	FOOTBALL	TIGHT END	FALL 83	?
123456789	SOCCER	GOAL KEEPER	FALL 82	?
222222222	FOOTBALL	TIGHT END	FALL 83	?
789789789	BASEBALL	SHORTSTOP	SPRING 84	?

Figure 7.11 Addition of the PHYSICAL column to the SPORTS table.

Data Manipulation Commands

SQL uses English-like commands to manipulate data within tables. Consistent with the transition from the academic to the business environment, the documentation uses the layman's terminology of tables, columns, and rows. Each table is identified by name. Each column is labelled by a column name. The SQL commands provide for query operations (retrieving data to answer questions) and data manipulation (for inserting, deleting, or updating data).

The query commands permit the user to define the data needed, the table or view in which the data is stored, and qualifications that are to be placed on the data retrieved. The user need not be aware of whether the data accessed is through a view or through a table, for the operations performed by the user are the same regardless of the source of the data. The tables presented in Figures 7.1, 7.4, and 7.6 are the source tables to demonstrate the use of the SQL query language. The format of the query command is:

```
SELECT . . . (data)
FROM . . . (table)
WHERE . . . (qualifications are placed on the data
   retrieved)
```

The SELECT clause identifies the column name(s) that contain the data the user desires. The FROM clause identifies the tables in which the column resides. The WHERE clause identifies specific conditions the data must meet to satisfy the request.

The query command can be viewed as a statement describing the data—a statement that answers a question. To properly format a query statement, the user must know the column names in the table, the table name, and the values in the fields. SQL allows the user to begin with a primitive query and enhance it as more is learned about the data being examined. In our examples, the following primitive query can be used to gain additional information about the table containing the desired data:

```
SELECT *
    FROM STUDENT
```

The * following SELECT indicates that the user desires all columns in the table. FROM STUDENT indicates that the columns are to be obtained from the STUDENT relation. This form of the query can be used to serve one of two objectives. First, the user may actually need the data in all columns in the STUDENT table. Then, the * is a shorthand technique to reduce the effort needed to request all columns in a table be returned. Second, the user may not be aware, or may not remember, the names of the columns in the STUDENT table.

The result of issuing this command is the table presented back in Figure 7.1. After this result is obtained, the user can issue additional commands to qualify the data returned. For example, if the user wishes to answer the question, "What are the names and address of the students?" the following query is issued:

```
SELECT S-NAME S-ADDRESS
    FROM STUDENTS
```

S-NAME and S-ADDRESS following the SELECT statement define the columns to be returned. The result of this query is the table in Figure 7.7.

The user may further qualify the query by placing additional restrictions on the data returned. To answer the question, "Who are the students majoring in English?" the following query is entered:

```
SELECT *
    FROM STUDENTS
    WHERE MAJOR = 'ENGLISH'
```

This query is similar to the previous one. The WHERE clause restricts the data to be returned. Only the students who have the value ENGLISH in the column named MAJOR are presented to the user. The result of this query is shown in Figure 7.8.

Although general principles of the relational model do not permit duplicate rows, SQL is more flexible: SQL permits the user to determine whether or not duplicates are allowed. If the user wishes to obtain a list of sports played at a college, the response to the inquiry should contain one row per sport. If the user wishes to ensure that rows are not duplicated, the UNIQUE parameter of the SELECT clause may be used as follows:

```
SELECT UNIQUE SPORTS-NAME
    FROM SPORTS
```

Figure 7.12
Table generated in response to a "SELECT UNIQUE SPORTS-NAME . . ." inquiry.

SPORTS

SPORTS-NAME
FOOTBALL
SOCCER
BASEBALL

The preceding command will present a table containing a list of the SPORTS-NAMEs from the SPORTS table. If duplicate rows exist, only one of the duplicate entries is presented to the user (see Figure 7.12). In Figure 7.4, two rows contain the SPORTS-NAME of football. The UNIQUE parameter removes duplicate entries such as football from the table presented to the user.

The qualifications on the data returned are not limited to one column. Boolean operators such as AND or OR can be used in the WHERE clause to impose multiple conditions on the data to be retrieved. To answer the question, "What are the names and addresses of female students majoring in English?" the following command uses the Boolean AND operator to further limit the data presented:

```
SELECT S-NAME S-ADDRESS
    FROM STUDENTS
    WHERE MAJOR = 'ENGLISH'
        AND SEX = 'FEMALE'
```

The data returned must meet two conditions: the value of the field named MAJOR must be English, and the value of the field named SEX must be female. The response to this query is shown in Figure 7.13.

The user may not be interested in the actual data but may be interested in quantitative information about the data instead. SQL has several built-in functions to provide this type of information, including parameters to determine the number of rows having a specified value, to determine the minimum value of a column, to determine the maximum value of a column, and to determine the sum of the column. A user performing classroom space allocation, for example, would likely be more interested in the number of students than in their names and addresses. The following command provides this information.

Figure 7.13
Table generated in response to the query "What are the names and addresses of the female students majoring in English?"

FEMALE-ENGLISH-MAJORS

S-NAME	S-ADDRESS
SHAKESPEARE	222 SECOND ST.
DUNN	333 THIRD ST.

Figure 7.14
Table generated in response to a query for the name and courses taken by S-ID of 111111111.

COURSES-TAKEN

S-NAME	COURSE-ID
WILLIAMS	DP209
WILLIAMS	AC101
WILLIAMS	EC101

```
SELECT COUNT (*)
    FROM STUDENT
    WHERE MAJOR = 'ENGLISH'
```

This differs from previous queries in that SQL now tabulates the number of rows in the table which satisfy the specified criteria. This is the operation requested by the COUNT(*) operation. For the STUDENT table, four rows match the specified criteria. This result is returned to the user. If it were necessary to determine the total number of students in all majors, the WHERE clause can be omitted. COUNT can be replaced by either MIN, MAX, AVERAGE, or SUM to receive simple descriptive information about the data.

The data needed to satisfy a request may not reside in one table, but in two or more tables. To answer the question, "What courses are taken by the student with a student ID of '111111111' and what is the student's name?" data must be extracted from both the STUDENT and STUDENT-CLASS tables. The name of the student whose S-ID = 111111111 is selected from the STUDENT table. The COURSE-ID from the STUDENT-CLASS table is selected for all rows that have a value of 111111111 in S-ID. The operation performed is a join with selection and projection. The SQL command to determine the answer to the question is:

```
SELECT S-NAME, COURSE-ID
    FROM STUDENT, STUDENT-CLASS
    WHERE S-ID = '111111111'
```

S-NAME and COURSE-ID are the projected columns taken from a join of the STUDENT and STUDENT-CLASS tables. Only the rows for student ID 111111111 are selected. The result of the query is shown in Figure 7.14. Williams is the name of the student having a student ID of 111111111. Williams is taking three courses having COURSE-IDs of DP209, AC101, and EC101.

SQL also can sequence the rows of a table as they are returned to the user. To provide a class roster for course DP209, the following command is issued:

```
SELECT COURSE-ID, S-NAME
    FROM STUDENT, STUDENT-CLASS
```

Figure 7.15
Table generated in response to a request for a class roster in sequence by S-NAME.

CLASS-ROSTER

COURSE-ID	S-NAME
DP209	BROWNING
DP209	SHAKESPEARE
DP209	WILLIAMS

```
WHERE COURSE-ID = 'DP209'
    AND C-SECTION = 'EBA'
ORDERED BY S-NAME
```

The SELECT clause creates a table containing a student's name and course ID number in a table. The FROM clause specifies that the data is extracted from the STUDENT and STUDENT-CLASS tables. The WHERE clause limits the data returned to the students taking course DP209, section EBA. The table is placed in alphabetic sequence (ORDERED BY S-NAME) before it is presented to the user (see Figure 7.15).

Since in the relational model the result of each operation performed on a table results in a table, the result of one operation can be input into the next. This allows operations to be nested within a single query when a subselect operation is performed and the resulting table is operated upon by another select.

For instance, let's say that a list of all students in the top one-half of their class is needed. To determine the students who have a grade point average (GPA) greater than the average for the entire student body, the following query is issued:

```
SELECT S-NAME GPA
    FROM STUDENT
    WHERE GPA >
        (SELECT AVG(GPA)
            FROM STUDENT)
```

In this query, two separate operations are performed on the same table, although the operations could be performed on separate tables. First, the GPA average for all students in the STUDENT table is calculated through the built-in average (AVG) function, as a result of the subselect in the WHERE clause. This calculation, when performed on the STUDENT relation in Figure 7.3, results in a GPA of 3.0. Second, after the subselect is evaluated, the query proceeds *as if* the following query were issued:

S-NAME	GPA
LINCOLN	3.6
PLATO	3.4
ARCHIMEDES	3.5
WILLIAMS	3.1

Figure 7.16
Table generated in response to a query to list students who have an above-average GPA.

```
SELECT S-NAME GPA
    FROM STUDENT
    WHERE GPA > 3.0
```

The execution of this query results in the table in Figure 7.16.

Complex queries can be generated through the use of multiple subselects. There is no limit to the number of subselects which may be used in a query.

SQL also permits the comparison of two rows in the same table. The power of the language is demonstrated in the following example.

A request is made to compare English majors to determine how they compare against each other. Since they exist in the same table, they are extracted from the table and placed in a virtual table to permit comparison. Since the same column names exist in each virtual table, the column names are qualified to specify which virtual table and which column is used. The comparison is demonstrated through the following command:

```
SELECT VT1.S-NAME, VT1.GPA,
    VT2.S-NAME, VT2.GPA
FROM STUDENT VT1, STUDENT VT2
WHERE (VT1.MAJOR = 'ENGLISH'
    AND VT1.SEX = 'MALE')
    AND (VT2.MAJOR = VT1.MAJOR
    AND NOT VT2.SEX = 'MALE')
```

In this example, the STUDENT table was joined to itself by repeating the STUDENT table name in the FROM clause, creating two virtual tables, VT1 and VT2. SELECT indicates that virtual table one (VT1) is to contain S-NAME and GPA, and virtual table two (VT2) is also to contain S-NAME and GPA. The conditions to be met for storage in VT1 are for rows which have a value of English in MAJOR to have a value of male in SEX. VT2 contains rows that have the same value for MAJOR as in VT1 and do not have a value of male in SEX. Since the same column names exist in both tables, each column name is prefixed with the name of the table in which it resides, VT1 or VT2. This generates the table in Figure 7.17.

This provides the same results as if SQL compared one row in VT1 with all rows in VT2. Any row in VT2, meeting the specified conditions, is placed in the resulting table. This process is repeated for all rows in VT1. In Figure 7.17, Browning satisfies the conditions for VT1. Both Shakespeare and Dunn in VT2 have the same value in MAJOR as does Browning and do not have a value of male in SEX. SQL repeats the process for each entry in VT1.

After a table is CREATEd, data is placed in the table with the INSERT

Figure 7.17
Results of comparing entries in the same table through the creation of virtual tables.

S-NAME	GPA	S-NAME	GPA
BROWNING	2.0	SHAKESPEARE	3.0
BROWNING	2.0	DUNN	3.0
WILLIAMS	3.1	SHAKESPEARE	3.0
WILLIAMS	3.1	DUNN	3.0

VT1 VT2

command. The INSERT command places a row of data in a table with one execution of the command. The INSERT command names the table to be updated and the values to be placed in each column. The format of the INSERT command is:

```
INSERT INTO STUDENT
    VALUES ('WASHINGTON',000000001,
        '1600 PENNSYLVANIA AVE.',
        'POLITICAL SCIENCE','2/12/59','FEMALE',3.0)
```

STUDENT is the name of the table to which the row is added. The data following the VALUE clause is positional. The data prior to the first comma is placed in the first column of the table. The data between the first and second commas is placed in the second column, and so on. Figure 7.18 shows the table after execution of the INSERT command.

Removing rows from a table is performed by the DELETE command. The DELETE command specifies the table to be updated and the values that identify the rows to be deleted. When a student drops a course, the format of the DELETE command is:

```
DELETE FROM STUDENT-CLASS
    WHERE S-ID = '123456789'
    AND COURSE-ID = 'SA101'
```

The FROM clause specifies that the STUDENT-CLASS table is the table of interest. The row identified by S-ID of 123456789 and COURSE-ID of SA101 is deleted. In this command, only one row of the STUDENT-CLASS table is deleted. However, one execution of the DELETE command can delete multiple rows of a table. For example, if the student with an S-ID of 789789789 drops out of school, the entries for all classes taken by the student are deleted with the following command:

```
DELETE FROM STUDENT-CLASS
    WHERE S-ID = '789789789'
```

STUDENT

S-NAME	S-ID	S-ADDRESS	MAJOR	DATE-OF-BIRTH	SEX	GPA
PLATO	123456789	111 FIRST ST.	PHILOSOPHY	6/26/51	FEMALE	3.4
SHAKESPEARE	789789789	222 SECOND ST.	ENGLISH	2/20/53	FEMALE	3.0
DUNN	987654321	333 THIRD ST.	ENGLISH	10/28/43	FEMALE	3.0
NEWTON	123123123	444 FOURTH ST.	PHYSICS	3/3/47	FEMALE	2.4
WILLIAMS	111111111	123 FIRST ST.	ENGLISH	10/2/54	MALE	3.1
ARCHIMEDES	222222222	100 BROAD ST.	PHYSICS	6/15/66	MALE	3.5
BROWNING	333333333	10 MAIN ST.	ENGLISH	7/25/54	MALE	2.0
LINCOLN	444444444	333 MAIN ST.	POLITICAL SCIENCE	2/9/54	MALE	3.6
WASHINGTON	000000001	1600 PENNSYLVANIA AVE.	POLITICAL SCIENCE	2/12/59	FEMALE	3.0

Figure 7.18 STUDENT table after the insertion of WASHINGTON.

S-ID identifies four rows in the STUDENT-CLASS table, and all four rows are deleted with this DELETE command. Figure 7.19 shows the STUDENT-CLASS table after the DELETE command is issued.

The UPDATE command changes data in a table. The UPDATE command, like the DELETE command, may affect more than one row in a table. Let's say that BASKETWEAVING (BA202) has been established as an upper-level course and the course descriptor changed to BA502. The format of the UPDATE command to implement this change is:

```
UPDATE STUDENT-CLASS SET COURSE-ID = 'BA502'
    WHERE COURSE-ID = 'BA202'
```

STUDENT-CLASS is the name of the table to be updated. The WHERE clause indicates that rows that have a value of BA202 in the COURSE-ID column are to be changed. The SET COURSE-ID clause of the UPDATE command identifies the column to be updated and the value to be placed in the column. (Although the columns named in the SET clause of the UPDATE command and the WHERE clause are the same in this example, they need not be.) This descriptor, BA202, occurs twice in Figure 7.6. The previous UPDATE command replaces each occurrence of BA202 with BA502 (see Figure 7.20).

Security Commands

The security definition in SQL is provided through the GRANT and REVOKE commands.

The GRANT command defines the privileges of users. The user may have the privilege of using one or more of the SQL DML commands: SELECT, INSERT, DELETE, and UPDATE. The syntax of the GRANT command is, for example:

Figure 7.19.
STUDENT-CLASS table after the deletion of entries for S-ID of 789789789.

STUDENT-CLASS

S-ID	COURSE-ID	C-SECTION
123456789	SA101	AXY
123456789	BA202	ABY
111111111	DP209	EBA
111111111	AC101	BBA
111111111	EC101	CDX
333333333	DP209	EBA

```
GRANT SELECT, INSERT ON STUDENT TO ADVISOR
```

This command permits the privileges of inquiring (SELECT) and adding (INSERT) new rows in the STUDENT table to a user named ADVISOR. Use of any combination or all of the DML commands may be authorized, in addition to privileges to alter either the table or its performance characteristics.

The privileges provided by the GRANT command can be reversed at any time through the REVOKE command. The format of the REVOKE command is, for example:

```
REVOKE INSERT ON STUDENT FROM ADVISOR
```

This command removes the privilege of INSERT from the user named ADVISOR. Based on the previous GRANT command, ADVISOR retains the use of the SELECT command after the REVOKE command is issued.

Additional Features

SQL provides an additional data definition command, the CREATE VIEW command, to provide an alternate view of data. A view is a logical table derived from one or more tables. A view may be as small as one column and selected rows from a table or may be as large as a table created from the rows and columns of two or more tables. The view can be used to simplify the appearance of the table to facilitate the user's work, or it can be used to restrict a user's access to certain data.

The data base administrator determines the data needed by a user to perform the business of the enterprise and provides access to the data through a command such as the following:

```
CREATE VIEW POLITICIAN
    AS
    SELECT S-NAME S-ADDRESS
    FROM STUDENT
    WHERE MAJOR = 'POLITICAL SCIENCE'
```

Figure 7.20. STUDENT-CLASS table after the course descriptor is changed to BA502.

STUDENT-CLASS

S-ID	COURSE-ID	C-SECTION
123456789	SA101	AXY
123456789	BA502	ABY
789789789	SA101	ABF
789789789	BA502	EDA
789789789	DP209	EBA
789789789	DP101	BFF
111111111	DP209	EBA
111111111	AC101	BBA
111111111	EC101	CDX
333333333	DP209	EBA

The CREATE VIEW clause creates a view of the STUDENT table which contains only rows of students who major in political science. The table, named POLITICIAN, contains only the columns containing S-NAME and S-ADDRESS. SQL allows duplicate rows in a table unless otherwise specified. The user of the table for POLITICIAN may perform the same inquiries and updates against the view as would be permitted against the STUDENT table if given the appropriate privileges. The view named POLITICIAN restricts the rows and columns of the STUDENT table made available to the user: Only S-NAME and S-ADDRESS columns are available, and only the rows having political science as the value in the column named MAJOR may be accessed.

SQL commands may be entered interactively from an individual working at a cathode ray tube (CRT) or may be issued from an application program. Regardless of the source of the command, the format of the command does not change. SQL commands are different from the DML commands we have previously presented in that the previous ones operated on one record in a data base at a time. SQL, on the other hand, operates on all the rows (records) that satisfy the selection criteria. Again, the language is powerful. However, third-generation languages do not handle multiple records from tables, so SQL provides a piped facility which allows an application program to process one record at a time through a feature called a *cursor*. As we have demonstrated in our discussion of the DML, many rows (records) may be retrieved, updated, or deleted with just one SQL command.

If authorized by a GRANT command, the user may create indexes on columns in a table. An index may be created or deleted at any time. The purpose of the index is to improve performance when retrieving data. However, additional time is required to INSERT or DELETE rows, due to the manipulation required to create the index. Also, additional time may be required to perform an UPDATE if the column being updated is indexed. (This extra consumption of time is a departure from the theoretical time-saving basis for the relational model, but it is a necessary consideration in the application of the theory in a real-world production environment.)

An index may be created or removed at any time. Unlike with the hierarchical and network models, with the relational model it is unnecessary to remove the data base from production use while the index is created. The command to create an index on student ID is:

```
CREATE INDEX SIDINDEX
    ON STUDENT
    (S-ID)
```

SIDINDEX is the name of the index created. STUDENT is the name of the table. S-ID is the name of the field on which the index is created. One or more fields may be used to create the index, which becomes available after the execution of the CREATE INDEX command. The user never references the index in the SQL data manipulation commands. SQL uses the index as necessary to locate data. An index may be removed at any time with the DROP INDEX command:

```
DROP INDEX SIDINDEX
```

This command removes the index on S-ID from the STUDENT table.

With the network and hierarchical models, the path the data base management system follows between related records has a direct impact upon performance. Since SQL has no user-specified paths between related records, unless an index is created, there are no physical paths to follow to obtain data. SQL performs query optimization algorithms to determine the technique that offers the best performance when accessing data. Although the user may create an index to improve performance, there is no guarantee that SQL will use the index to access data. If SQL, through its query optimization algorithm, determines that a more suitable method of access is available to obtain the requested data, it uses the best technique available, whether or not it is the technique specified by the user.

7.5 DATA MODEL COMPARISON

The features of the three major data models are summarized in Figure 7.21. A more detailed explanation follows in this section.

Representative System

The most widely used implementation of the hierarchical data model is DL/I, marketed by IBM. IDMS, marketed by Cullinet, is based on the 1971 DBTG report and represents the network data model. SQL, the data manipulation language for DATABASE 2 (DB2), marketed by IBM, is representative of the relational data model.

	HIERARCHICAL	NETWORK	RELATIONAL
Representative system	DL/I (IBM)	IDMS (Cullinet)	SQL—the DML for IBM's DATABASE 2
Data building blocks	Field Segment Physical data base	Data item Record Set	Attribute (column) Tuple (row) Relation (table)
Representation of logical data structures			
—Trees	Directly	Decomposition into sets	Decomposition into tables
—Simple networks	Unidirectional logical relationship	Decomposition into sets	Decomposition into tables
—Complex networks	Bidirectional logical relationship	Decomposition into sets using intersection data	Decomposition into tables using intersection data
Data independence			
—Path	No	No	Yes
—Sequence	No	No	Yes
DML commands			
—Retrieval	GU, GHU, GN, GHN, GNP, GHNP	FIND, GET	SELECT
—Data alteration	REPL	MODIFY	UPDATE
—Data addition	ISRT	STORE	INSERT
—Data deletion	DLET	ERASE	DELETE
—Miscellaneous		READY, FINISH CONNECT, DISCONNECT	
Means of data base navigation	Through hierarchical path	Through sets	Through the value of the attributes
Navigator	Experienced, trained programmer	Experienced, trained programmer	End user
Performance	High—with well-defined access paths Low—with unstructured access paths	High—with well-defined access paths Low—with unstructured access paths	High—with unstructured access paths Low (in comparison to hierarchical and network data models)—with well-defined access paths
Additional pointers available to improve performance	Yes—retrieval	Yes—retrieval	Yes—but SQL may choose not to use them
Security	Defined in subschema	Defined in subschema	Defined in subschema—but may be modified at any time including during on-line execution
Security officer	DBA or equivalent	DBA or equivalent	DBA or equivalent—may be delegated
Responsibility for adding data to the data base	Data base management system—governed by INSERT, REPLACE, DELETE rules	Data base management system or application program—governed by insertion status	Data base management system
Modification of the data structure	Redefine structure, reload new structure	Redefine structure, reload new structure	Restructure at any time, including operation in an on-line environment

Figure 7.21 Framework for the evaluation of data models.

Data Building Blocks

The smallest unit of data defined in DL/I is a field, which is comparable to a data item in the DBTG model and a column in the relational data model.

The unit of data transferred to an application program is a segment in DL/I and a record in the DBTG model. The relational model offers two different units of data transfer: (1) Application programs, written in third-generation programming languages, currently offer no means for a unit of data transfer of multiple records; therefore, SQL operates in piped mode, which permits the transfer of one row of data at a time through a cursor. (2) When data is operated upon through an on-line terminal in SQL, the unit of data transfer is a table.

The next larger data building block contains data about a subject and is called a physical data base in DL/I, a set in the network model, and a relation or table in the relational data model.

Representation of Logical Data Structures

DL/I represents tree structures directly. Tree structures cannot be represented directly in the network model; instead, they are decomposed into two-level structures called sets. The network model represents an N-level tree structure by decomposing it into $N-1$ sets. The relational model also cannot represent tree structures directly; instead, each segment type in a tree structure is represented as a table. The tables which represent dependent segments include the key of the parent segment. The reproduced keys permit the unique identification of each row and contain values which permit the relationship between two different tables to be established.

Simple networks are not permitted in DL/I. Data is represented as if it were duplicated. However, a unidirectional logical relationship implemented through logical pointers eliminates redundant data. The application program views the simple network as a tree structure. In the network model, simple networks are represented in the same manner as tree structures. Each parent-child relationship is represented as a set. In the relational model, each record type is represented in a table. The key of each parent record type is duplicated in the table that represents the child record type.

DL/I cannot represent complex networks directly; rather, complex networks are represented with an extension of the technique used for simple networks: reproducing data in two different segments in a tree structure, then using logical pointers to eliminate redundant data. Representation of a complex network is called a bidirectional logical relationship. The application program still views the resulting structure as a tree structure. The network model also cannot represent complex networks directly. Instead, a record type is created which contains intersection data for the records involved in the many-to-many relationship. The intersection record is a member in each of two sets in which the related records are owners. The relational model represents complex networks in much the same manner as the network model. A table is created which contains intersection data, including the primary key of each of the record types in the many-to-many relationship. Each of the records in the complex network is stored in its own table, and the values of the reproduced keys in the table containing intersection data relate them.

Data Independence

DL/I makes parameters available in the DBD to allow the logical sequencing of segments and permit multiple secondary indexes to be created for additional sequencing. While this provides great flexibility to the application program, it does cause sequence dependencies. DL/I also has path dependencies, since the correct path must be traversed to obtain the desired segments.

IDMS, like DL/I, provides parameters for the logical sequencing of records and requires a knowledge of the paths to be traversed to obtain the desired record. It is therefore subject to the same sequence and path dependencies.

SQL maintains relationships between tables through the values of the stored data; pointers are not used. Therefore, SQL is free of path dependencies. SQL is also free of any sequence dependencies, since one of the basic rules of the relational data model is that columns and rows may be presented in any sequence.

DML Commands

DL/I has six different commands, each with a different function to make data available to the application program: GU, GN, GNP, GHU, GHN, and GHNP. The network model has one command, GET, to make data available to the application program, but it must be preceded by a FIND command which locates the data. IDMS reduces the number of interactions between the application program and itself by offering an OBTAIN command, which combines the functions of the FIND and the GET commands. SQL has only the SELECT command for data retrieval.

Each of the sample data base management systems has only one command to modify existing data in the data base: REPL in DL/I, MODIFY in IDMS, and UPDATE in SQL.

One command is available in each system to add new data to the data base: ISRT in DL/I, STORE in IDMS, and INSERT in SQL.

Each system also has only one DML command to remove existing data from a data base: DLET in DL/I, ERASE in IDMS, and DELETE in SQL.

IDMS has four additional DML commands. The CONNECT command causes a record existing in the data base to become a member of a set when insertion is manual. CONNECT cannot be used when insertion is automatic. The DISCONNECT command causes a record to be removed from an occurrence of a set without removing it from the data base. DISCONNECT can be used when retention is optional, but cannot be used with any other retention status. The program notifies IDMS that it will access a data base through the READY command, and that no further accesses will occur through a FINISH command.

Means of Navigation

Navigation of hierarchical structures is through the traversal of the tree structure. The navigator must know the current location in the data base and the direction of the desired segment and may have to traverse many unwanted segments to obtain the desired segment.

Navigation in the network model is through the traversal of sets. Travel in a complex network structure is especially descriptive of the navigation process, for the navigator must follow the path from the owner to a member record containing intersection data in one set type, then to the owner of the same member record in another set type.

Since paths through the tables do not exist in the relational model, navigation as such is not performed. Desired records are obtained based on the value of the attributes within relations. It is not necessary to direct the relational data base management system in how to find the data, but only in what data is desired.

Navigator

Since data is obtained through predefined paths in the hierarchical model and the navigator must know both the current location and the final destination, the navigator is an application programmer who has had a high degree of training and experience to hone navigational skills.

IDMS also uses predefined paths through occurrences of record types to obtain the desired data. Once again, the navigator requires a high degree of education and training.

Since navigation is not performed in the relational model, there is no need for a highly trained programmer. Commands like those of SQL specify what is to be accomplished, not how to do it, and so end users (with a little training) perform data manipulation themselves.

Performance

With a well-designed data base, a well-defined access path, and a proficient navigator, DL/I can be tuned to provide rapid response. The specific paths through the data base defined by the pointers permit rapid retrieval of the desired data.

IDMS, because of direct access paths to the data, can also be tuned to provide a very responsive system when used with specific access paths. However, neither IDMS nor DL/I is well-suited to an unstructured environment where data relationships can be changed while the user is accessing the data base.

The relational model, as illustrated by SQL, has greater memory requirements and requires more resources than either DL/I or IDMS. But, SQL is not as responsive as either DL/I or IDMS and may require more secondary storage space to store data, unless DL/I or IDMS use many pointers to store the data. SQL is powerful. It performs operations on many records in a single query, whereas DL/I and IDMS operate on one record or segment at a time and may require many commands to perform the work accomplished by one SQL command.

Additional Pointers Available to Improve Performance

Both DL/I and IDMS have default pointers. Both also have optional pointers to improve performance. While these optional pointers do improve performance in data retrieval operations, performance is often reduced by them during operations which add or delete records or update fields on which the additional pointers exist, because of the pointer maintenance required.

SQL permits the creation of indexes by the user to improve retrieval performance. Performance is reduced during the creation of the index and during the maintenance of a table on which indexes have been created.

SQL is different from DL/I and IDMS in the use of indexes. DL/I and IDMS observe the path specified by the navigator in the DML command and follow the paths created by the indexes when requested to do so. SQL, on the other hand, analyzes each query and the indexes available. SQL may use the index if analysis determines it will improve performance, but it is not bound to do so and may reject it if analysis determines that it will degrade performance.

Security

In all three systems, security is defined through the subschema. With DL/I and IDMS, the subschema definition is translated before the execution of the application program and stored for use during execution. SQL differs from the other two in that the subschema definition may be modified at any time, even during on-line execution.

Security Officer

All three systems provide the highest degree of security when controlled by the data base administrator or by the security officer of the enterprise. However, it is sometimes difficult to determine which users have a legitimate need to access data.

SQL offers an additional option to the security officer: to delegate access to the data base. SQL may permit the user to in turn grant access to other users. This enables a responsible user to grant access to the individuals who have a legitimate need to access and update the data base.

Responsibility for Adding Data to the Data Base

The DL/I and SQL data base models have the responsibility to add data to the data base, based on schema and subschema definitions, when requested to do so by the programmer or the end user.

IDMS has the same responsibility. However, when a record is added, it may or may not become a member of a set. This responsibility is defined in the schema. When the same record type participates in more than one set type, IDMS may be responsible for connecting it in one set type and the application program responsible for connecting it in another set type.

Modification of the Data Structure

Since both DL/I and IDMS have fixed paths to segments and records, modification of the data structure requires a working copy of the data base(s) to be made, the new data structure to be defined, and the data base to be recreated in the new structure from the working copy. While the restructuring is occurring, programs may not access or modify the existing data and retain data integrity.

Since SQL does not have path dependencies, the data structure may be modified at any time. New columns may be added or new tables created while the system is executing. There is no need for the user to perform the copying of data as is done in DL/I and IDMS; data base definitions take effect immediately. This is advantageous when new systems are developed, for it permits a prototype of the new system to be developed and modified during development. Because of this flexibility, design errors are easily corrected and the impact of design changes is reduced.

7.6 SUMMARY

The theoretical concepts of the relational model were pioneered by E. F. Codd in the early 1970s. The relational model is based on relational mathematics and uses mathematical terms to describe simple concepts such as *relation* (for table), *tuple* (for record), and *attribute* (for field). The power of the relational model caused performance problems in its early implementations. The relational model had to wait on technology to catch up to the theory before it could be successfully implemented in a production environment.

As with other models, it is governed by its own set of rules. Each field is atomic; it cannot be further subdivided. Repeating groups are not allowed. Each record is uniquely defined by one or more candidate keys. One of the candidate keys is chosen by the data base administrator as the primary key. The sequence in which records and fields are presented to the user is immaterial. Since records are presented unsequenced to the user, and since paths are not used in the logical views or the DML, the relational model has a higher degree of data independence than the hierarchical or network data models. Hierarchical and network structures are represented in the relational model by reproducing the key of the parent record in the table containing data for the child. Duplication of key fields is propagated through each level of the hierarchy. The duplicated fields ensure uniqueness of each record, and the value of the field is the connecting link for relationships with other tables.

The relational model can be manipulated by what can be thought of as a series of cutting and pasting operations. A *projection* on a table (relation) limits the number of fields (attributes) seen by a user. A *selection* on a table reduces the number of records presented to a user. Projection and selection can be performed in the same operation, to reduce the number of records and fields presented to a user. A *join* of tables provides a new table containing fields from two or more tables.

SQL is the data manipulation language for an IBM commercial implementation of the relational model. In SQL, data definition is through a CREATE TABLE command. Columns can be added to a table at any time through an ALTER TABLE command. After the CREATE TABLE or ALTER TABLE command is issued, the INSERT command is used to enter data in the table. The

SELECT command satisfies queries against one or more tables. The SELECT command allows duplicate rows within a table—rows that can, optionally, be removed using the UNIQUE parameter. Data presented in the table is normally unordered but may, optionally, be sequenced using the ORDERED BY parameter. The UPDATE command changes specified fields within a table. The DELETE command removes rows from a table.

SQL is unlike previous DMLs in that it operates on multiple rows of a table in the execution of one command; the DMLs of the hierarchical and network models require one command for each record changed.

REVIEW QUESTIONS

7.1 Define the following relational terms:
a. Relation
b. Tuple
c. Attribute
d. Domain
e. Candidate key
f. Primary key

7.2 Represent the following hierarchical structure in a relational structure, using Codd's notation.

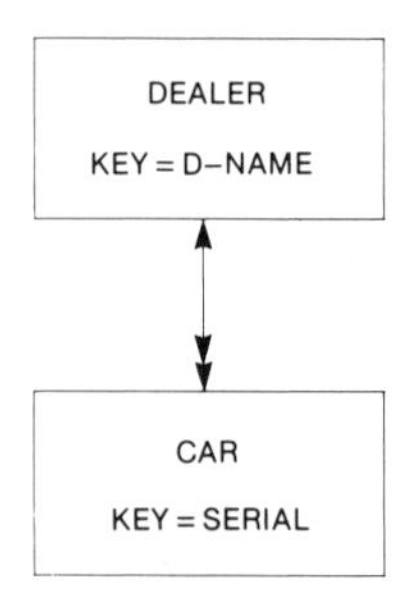

7.3 Represent the following simple network in a relational structure, using Codd's notation.

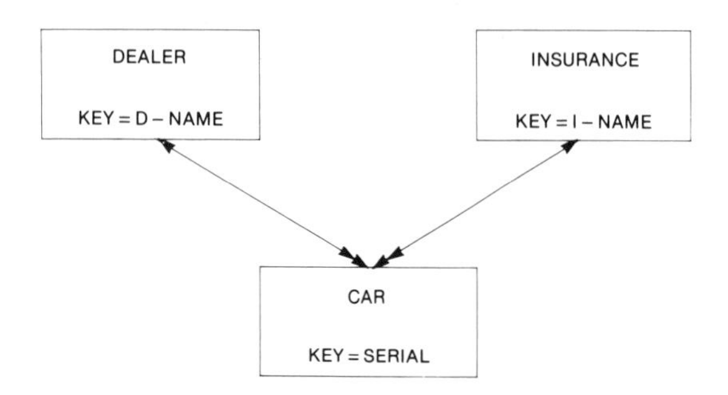

7.4 Represent the following complex network in a relational structure, using Codd's notation.

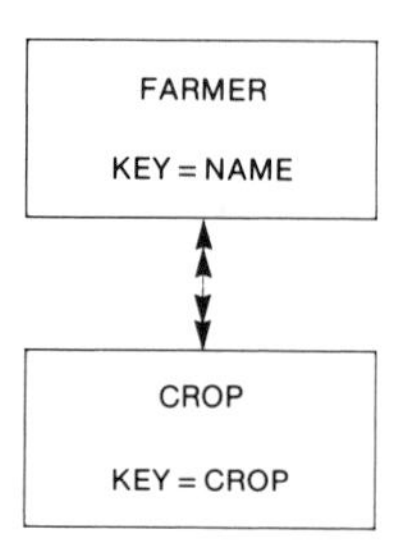

7.5 What effect does use of mathematical terminology have on business data processing users?

7.6 What benefit is obtained by eliminating path and sequence dependencies?

7.7 What is the disadvantage of eliminating path and sequence dependencies?

7.8 How does the relational model eliminate path and sequence dependencies?

7.9 What features does SQL include which are contrary to the theoretical basis for the relational model?

7.10 What procedure is used to represent hierarchical and network relationships in the relational model?

7.11 What effect does a projection have on the view of a table?

7.12 What effect does selection have on the view of a table?

7.13 What effect does a join have on the view of a table?

7.14 With regard to the example in this chapter, write the SQL command to return a table listing the names of the courses offered.

7.15 With regard to the example in this chapter, write the SQL command to add 4/15 as the date of the physical for 789789789 so that the student is eligible to play lacrosse.

7.16 With regard to the example in this chapter, write the SQL command to delete all the classes taken by a student with a student ID of 111111111 after the student withdraws from college.

7.17 With regard to the example in this chapter, write the SQL command to change the course ID BA201 to BA300.

7.18 Write the SQL command to allow the registrar to create and remove entries from the STUDENT-CLASS table.

7.19 Write the SQL command to change the authority of the registrar provided by the previous command so that the registrar may only create entries in the table.

7.20 What SQL command improves inquiry performance?

7.21 What effect does the command from the previous question have on performance for SQL data manipulation commands?

8

DATA BASE DESIGN

CHAPTER OBJECTIVES

Upon completion of this chapter, you should be able to:

1. Describe the three levels of data base design
2. Define the terminology associated with conceptual design
3. Describe the transformation of the conceptual design into a logical data base design
4. List and explain the factors to be considered in physical data base design

NEW WORDS AND PHRASES

entity
entity-relationship model
conceptual schema
semantic synonyms
semantic homonyms
aggregation
generalization
logical data base design
horizontal partitioning
vertical partitioning
central data base
replicated data base
functional dependency
transitive dependency
normal forms
loading factor

8.1 CHAPTER INTRODUCTION

Data base management systems came into vogue in the 1970s. Since one of the main features of data base management systems is their ability to create data relationships using both new and existing data relationships, they at first provided a false sense of security to the unwary. As new systems were developed in a company, especially in diverse areas, each system had its own data base. After installing many of these systems, problems developed in interfacing the many data bases—the same shortcoming as with conventional file systems. Indeed, in some aspects, things were worse off than before, due to the effort needed to restructure the data bases to integrate them.

After more than a decade of general use, data base design remains more an art than a science. A number of approaches have been suggested, but no one methodology dominates. However, data base design must be based on practical considerations that are a part of any data processing endeavor. To create an adequate design, a thorough knowledge of the enterprise's business, its use of the data, and the data base management system itself is necessary.

Data base management systems are being used on everything from personal computers to large-scale mainframes, and for all these it is important to plan the design and implementation of the data base. The planning must be long-range to minimize conflicts as future systems are installed, and the planning must be done at three levels:

1. The *strategic plan* involves the top decision makers in the corporation—the executives. The strategic plan defines, in a general way, the data needed to support the business of the enterprise. This level of planning involves grouping data that should be accessed together, considering the geography of the storage system, and considering how data is used.
2. *Tactical planning* is performed by the Data Processing Department in conjunction with the business's executives. The tactical plan includes the logical data base design, including the analysis of anomalies which may occur due to improper planning for future requirements, and determination of which systems have the highest return on investment and also satisfy the data needs of the enterprise.

   Anomalies can occur if the design is not properly planned. Traditionally, anomalies are identified in the development of the relational data base model through the presentation of normal forms. However, anomalies can also occur in other data models. They must be considered in the design of all data base systems.
3. The third level of planning is the *operational plan,* the planning that in the past has traditionally been identified as data base design. This level of planning optimizes the way the logical data base design is mapped onto secondary storage.

The subject of data base design is so complex that a complete treatment would require a book of its own. Although there are some who tout data base design as a science, in its present stage of development, it might be best described as an art form based upon a scientific methodology. The number of techniques available are almost as plentiful as the number of self-professed experts in the field! Thus, this chapter does not provide an exhaustive coverage of these methods. Instead, it is a sampler of those methods which have the best opportunity to be incorporated into the science of data base design in the future, and it provides an overview of the processes performed in the strategic, tactical, and operational planning levels.

8.2 CONCEPTUAL DATA MODEL

An enterprise's conceptual data model attempts to ensure that both the Data Processing Department and management know the subjects about which they wish to capture data. Since high-level managers are the primary participants, a conscious effort is made to minimize the amount of time needed in its development. By design (!), the conceptual model is a coarse description of the subjects about which data is captured and the relationship between the subjects. In this section, we will discuss the background which leads to this approach, the terminology of the conceptual design, and some of the tools to document these data relationships. We will also present an overview of the ways in which data bases can be distributed.

Background

In the past, the enterprise determined which function of the business could most benefit from automation. The project with the highest return on investment was selected for development. An analysis of the function was performed, and the data elements to support the system were determined. The scope of the project was limited so that a functional system could be implemented within a reasonable time frame. The limited scope of this bottom-up design guaranteed that data would not be integrated. However, bottom-up design offered relatively fast results and a short-term payback period.

With the advent of data base management systems, there was talk of *management information systems* which offered the promise that data would be integrated so that more than just operational functions could be satisfied. They promised that all personnel within the enterprise could take advantage of the data collected by the foundation systems.

However, due to the many fragmented systems being installed, management realized that they were no closer to an integrated data base than they had been in the past. The Data Processing Department had continued developing data base systems in the same manner that they had developed systems using conventional files. They were building the foundations of management information systems over and over again! Many foundations came into existence that were never built upon (see Figure 8.1). Instead of building an integrated data base, they had continued to build individual systems. Data was not integrated; it was duplicated in several places. This is typical of systems developed by bottom-up design.

After failing to provide the long-promised integrated data, a new solution to the problem was attempted: top-down design. It was felt that if the total information needs of the enterprise could be determined, systems could be designed to deliver integrated data bases. Individuals were assigned to define every data element used in the business of the enterprise. But long periods of time are needed to perform such a massive task. The effort tended to drag on, sometimes for years, and management lost interest. Top-down design, by its very nature, forces data to be integrated; however, top-down design requires such an extended time, business conditions may change before the design is completed. Example H1 demonstrates.

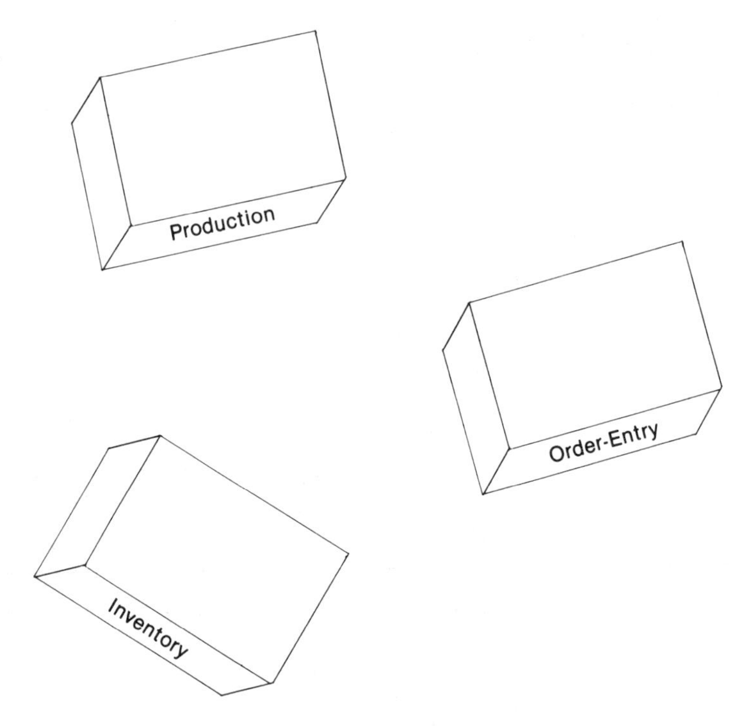

Figure 8.1
Bottom-up design: Many foundation systems, no data integration.

Example H1
Top-Down Design at Black Goo Petroleum

Black Goo Petroleum started a top-down design of their business processes in 1978. Emphasis was placed on full-service gas stations and the inventory of auto parts to stock them.

The design was not completed at the time the oil shortage occurred in 1979. Business conditions changed, and the new emphasis was on "gas and go" stations. The top-down design effort required so much time, the business had changed before the design was complete.

Current Processes

Current efforts in data base design are divided into three separate steps: development of the conceptual schema, development of the logical data base design, and physical data base design. This division is designed to overcome the problems with previous attempts at data base design.

1. The first step is the development of the **conceptual schema**. The conceptual schema is a global (incorporating the data relationships of the entire business) high-level design which, independent of any data base model, describes the data and the data relationships needed to perform the business of the enterprise. To keep management's interest and to remain current with business conditions, the conceptual schema is usually completed in a period of months. The design performed at this level is very coarse, intended to be completed in a short time and to show groupings of data so data will be integrated when new systems are developed.

2. The second step is the development of the *logical data base design.* In the logical data base design, the conceptual schema is mapped into structures supported by a specific data base management system. It is at this level that the design is refined. Specific data elements are defined and grouped into records.
3. The third and final phase of data base design is *physical data base design.* In physical data base design, the logical data base design is mapped into an efficient physical structure.

A data base design that adequately integrates data and also provides a reasonable business framework demands a balance between the extremes of top-down and bottom-up design. IBM has developed one such methodology for balanced data base design—the Business Systems Plan. The emphasis in this methodology is on top-down design of an information architecture and bottom-up development of those projects which first serve the greatest needs of the enterprise. Top-down design is a necessity to ensure that integrated data structures are developed. Bottom-up development provides rapid paybacks of the investment and relatively fast implementation of information systems to support the enterprise's immediate needs.

Terminology Used in the Development of Conceptual Schema

While still an art, data base design has become more scientific over the years due to academic interest in developing a more precise methodology. Academic interaction has created terminology similar to that used in the relational model. This terminology is highly abstract. The terms used are *entity, attribute, value,* and *relation.*

An **entity** is something humans are interested in and therefore record data about. An entity can be tangible—persons, places, or things. Examples of tangible entities are employees and product orders. An entity also can be intangible, such as interest rates or daily temperature readings.

An attribute is a characteristic of an entity. Each entity has a certain number of attributes about which data is recorded. An attribute may be a student identification number, an address, or the color of a part in inventory.

Each attribute can take on a value, which provides information about the entity. Examples of values of attributes are 123456789 for student identification number, 612 Boxelder Drive for address, or blue for the color of a part in inventory. The definitions of attributes and values are consistent with the definitions in the relational model.

Entities may form relations with each other. A relation is a nondirectional association between two entities. A conceptual design identifies the entities and relationships which support the business processes.

The design of a conceptual schema begins by gaining the commitment and involvement of top management in determining what data is needed to support the business of the enterprise. The conceptual schema must be completed in a relatively short time or management will lose interest. A conceptual design team is formed. Since people from the business side of the enterprise usually understand the business processes better than do

Figure 8.2 Entity relationship between a dentist and patients.

members of the Data Processing Department, they should be well represented on the team. The team is sent into the business areas of the enterprise to interview managers and determine the data required to operate the enterprise. The interviews are performed at the managerial level of the business instead of the operational level, and thus the data obtained is highly abstract. But this is consistent with the terminology of the conceptual schema. After the team collects the data, it meets to review and organize it.

Entity-Relationship Model

One of the techniques to organize the findings of this data collection effort is the **entity-relationship model**, which describes entities and their relations to other entities. It has a number of variations; we will present one common method.

Each entity is given a short descriptive name and placed in a rectangular box. The relationship between two entities is indicated by a diamond-shaped symbol and a description of the relationship. The relationship between a dentist and patients is shown in Figure 8.2. The degree of association of an entity is also specified, in the same manner presented in the chapters on data models: one-to-one, one-to-many, or many-to-many. The association of one (1) or many (M) is expressed outside the box representing an entity. In Figure 8.2, one dentist has many patients.

Example I1 and Figure 8.3 illustrate a more complex entity-relationship model.

Example I1 Entity-Relationship Model for Happy Home Appliances

The entity-relationship model is used to refine relationships of collected data. In Figure 8.3, an entity-relationship model describes the business processes of a retail appliance chain, Happy Home Appliances. In this figure, an entity named CUSTOMER has a relationship, PLACES, with another entity named ORDER. The degree of association is one customer to many orders. The figure presents a few of the entities and relationships in the order entry and shipping processes.

Happy Home Appliances is a small company. A large installation may have hundreds of entities and relationships to perform all of the business activities of the enterprise.

Since data about the entities of a business is obtained through interviewing, and since the terminology of the business function is not always precise, the designers must make a special effort to understand the processes performed and to document the processes precisely. The entity-relationship model is a tool to ensure that the data is complete and all redundancies and semantic differences are removed. During the review process

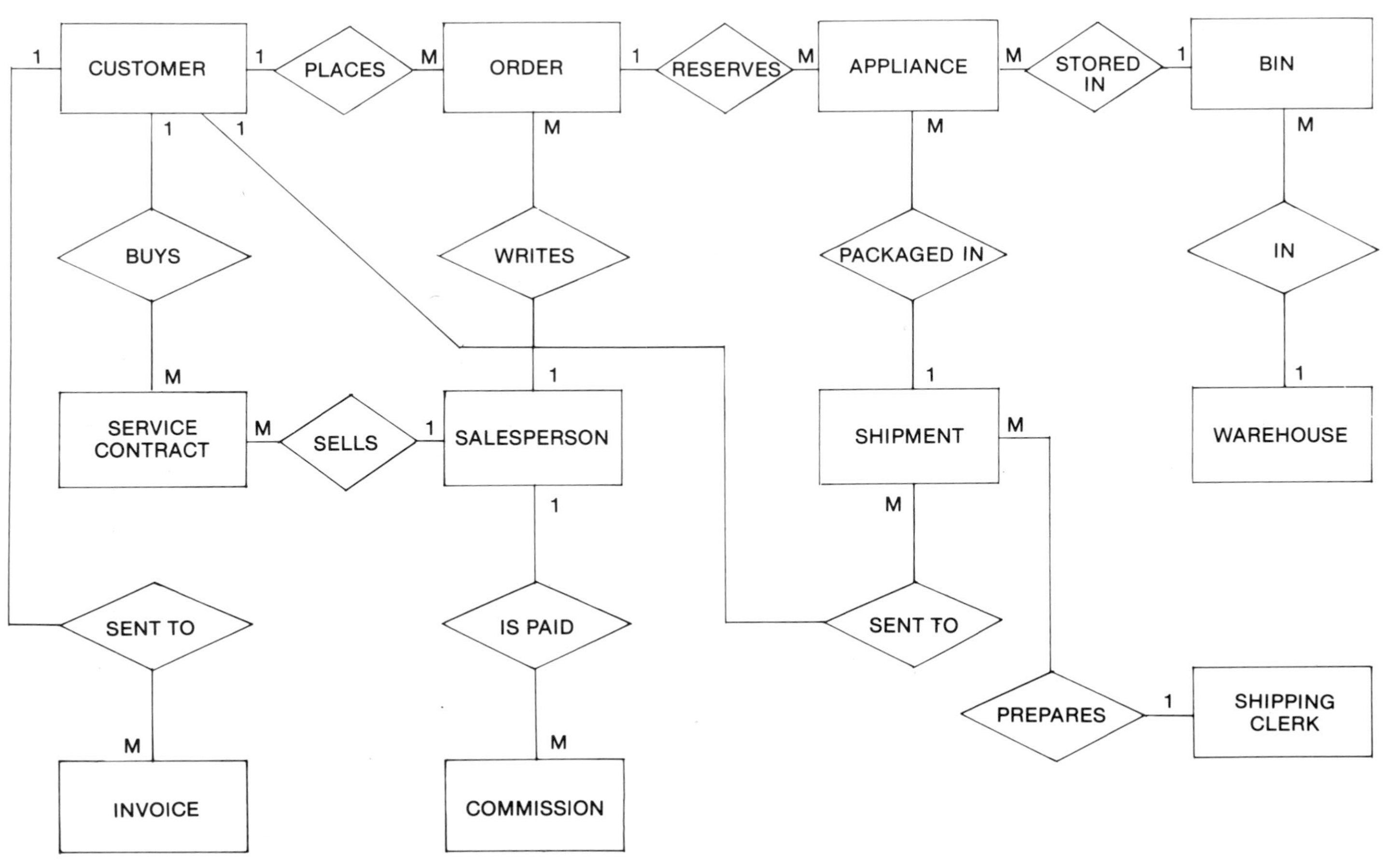

Figure 8.3 Entity-relationship model showing order entry and shipping relationships.

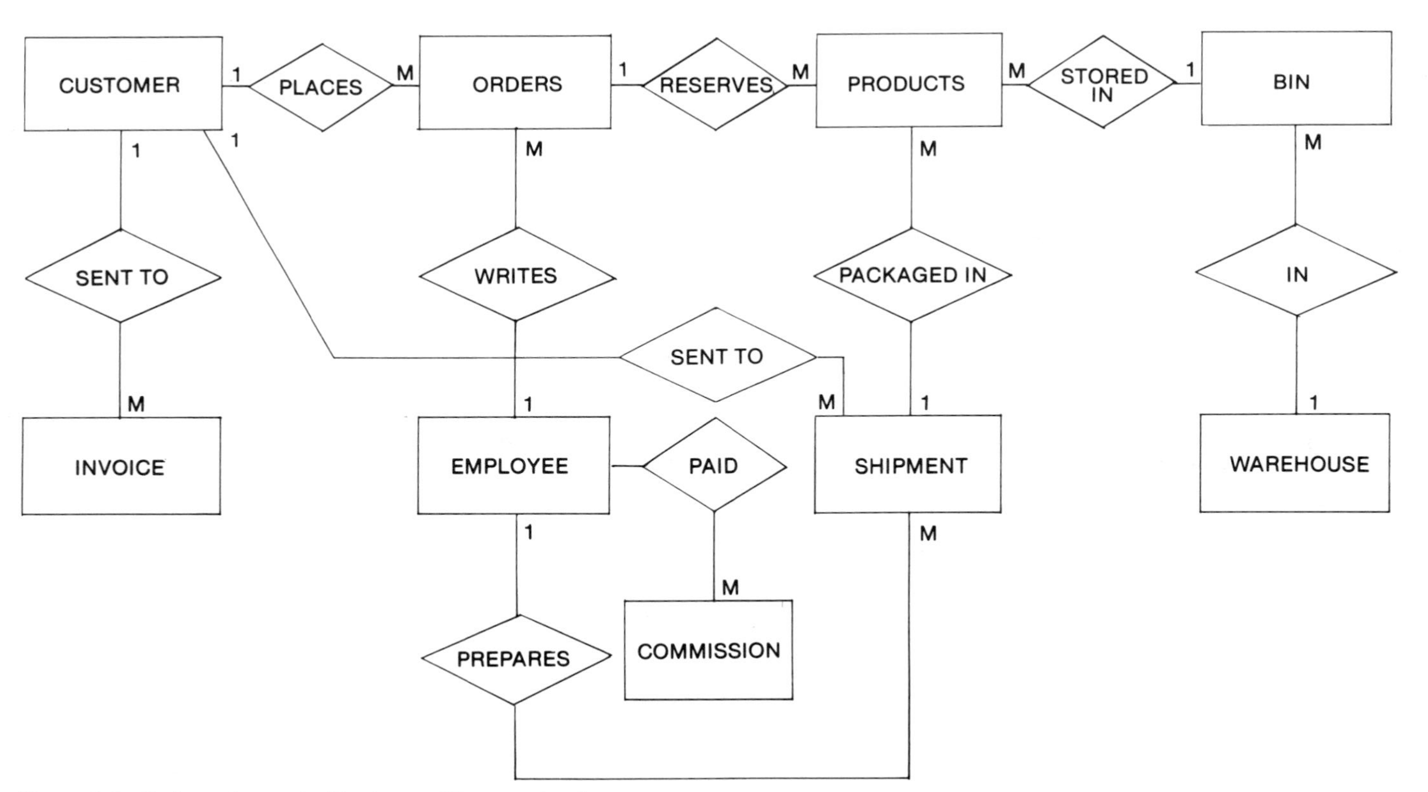

Figure 8.4 Order entry and shipping entities—revised.

by the conceptual design team, the entities are consolidated through identification, generalization, and aggregation of entities.

Identification is the process of identifying semantic synonyms and homonyms. **Semantic synonyms** occur when one entity is referred to by different names. **Semantic homonyms** occur when two different entities are referred to by the same name. As information is collected by the team, the people being interviewed may identify the same entity by two different names or may identify two different entities by the same name. In the review process, these are noted and each is defined. In Figure 8.3, entities for salesperson and shipping clerk are shown. These are synonyms for an employee. As the design is refined, the entity EMPLOYEE is substituted for salesperson and shipping clerk (see Figure 8.4).

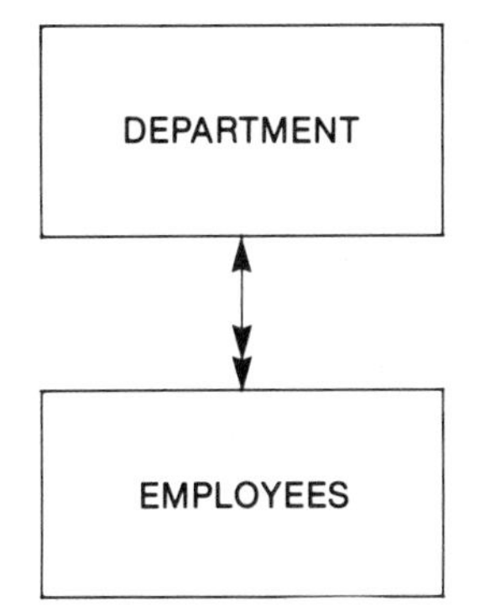

Figure 8.5
Entity chart showing one-to-many association between department and employees.

Generalization is the grouping of like objects. "Dogs" is a generalization of poodles, German shepherds, and Labrador retrievers. In Figure 8.3, appliance and service contract represent two objects sold by the business. They can be generalized into an entity named PRODUCTS (see Figure 8.4). **Aggregation** is the use of a higher-level element to identify an association between two lower-level elements. Automobile engine is an aggregation of block, pistons, manifold, and carburator.

Example I2 illustrates identification and generalization at Happy Home Appliances.

Example I2
Identification and Generalization at Happy Home Appliances

As a result of a review process, the entity-relationship model for Happy Home Appliances is redrawn showing the entities with all semantic inconsistencies resolved (Figure 8.4). By the identification and generalization of entities as previously described, the new entity-relationship model provides a clearer picture of the entities required to support the enterprise. The revised model depicts the processes occurring repeatedly throughout the enterprise.

Entity Charts

Entity charts are another way to organize data for the conceptual schema. They are similar to the entity-relationship model, but the relation between entities is directed and is shown by lines and arrows. A line with a single arrowhead represents a one relationship. A line with a double-headed arrow represents a many relationship. Figure 8.5 shows a one-to-many relationship between a department and the employees in the department. You will recognize entity charts from previous chapters, where they depicted data relationships.

Figure 8.6 is an entity chart depicting the Happy Home Appliances entities and relationships that were shown in Figure 8.4. The relationships between the entities are removed, and the degree of association between the entities is shown. Even though this chart is very simple, showing only the entities needed for illustrative purposes, the proper clustering of entities is not immediately discernible.

An iterative technique for creating structured entity charts has been pro-

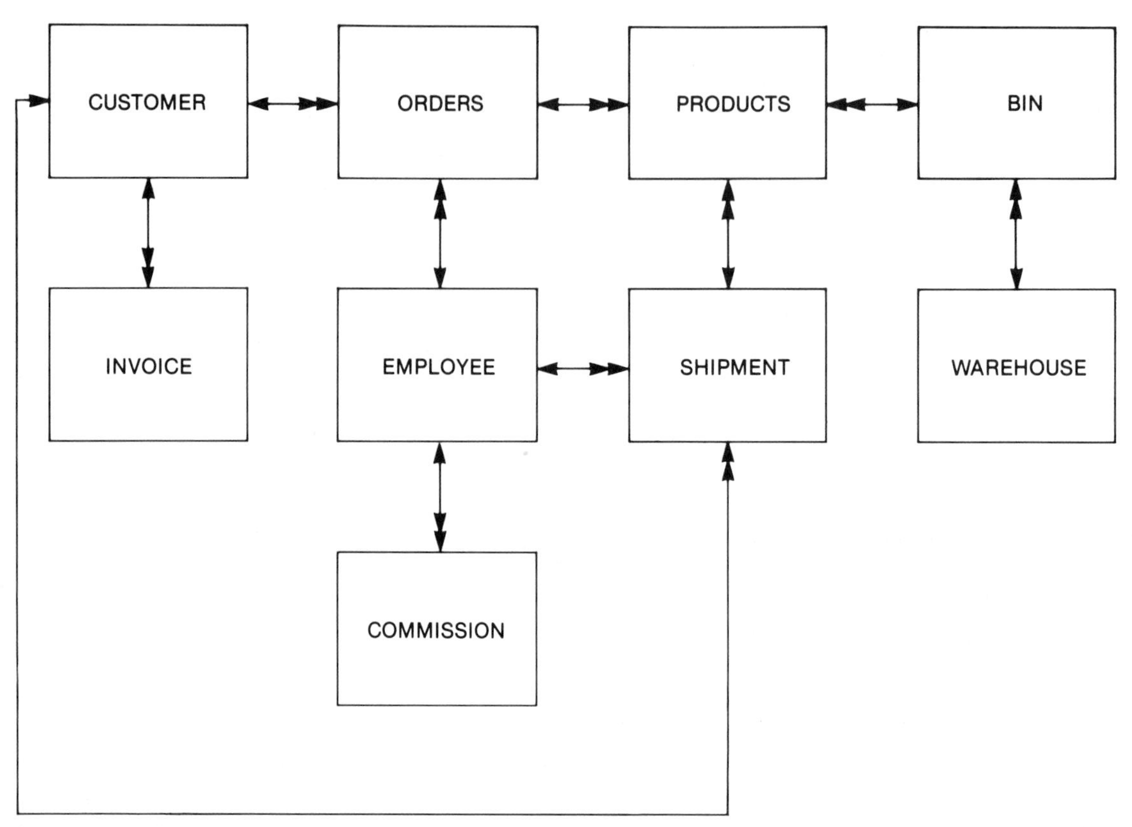

Figure 8.6
Entity chart showing associations between order entry and shipping entities.

posed by James Martin (*Strategic Data-Planning Methodologies,* Prentice-Hall, 1982). His technique facilitates the clustering of entities, as we shall now describe.

Martin's structured entity charts are drawn horizontally instead of vertically. The first step in developing a structured entity chart is to identify the depth of each entity on the entity chart. Each entity having no single-headed arrows leaving it is a root entity and is labelled with a 1. Depth 2 entities are those which have a single-headed arrow pointing to a depth 1 entity. Depth 3 entities have a single-headed arrow pointing to a depth 2 entity, but no single-headed arrow pointing to a depth 1 entity. This process is repeated until the depths of all entities have been identified.

To summarize, an entity satisfies the criteria for a level when it has a single-headed arrow pointing to the next higher-level entity, but no single-headed arrow pointing to a lower-level entity.

Next the entity charts are structured based on the depth of each entity. Depth 1 entities are drawn near the left of the page. Each lower-depth entity is offset one increment to the right for each level of depth and is clustered with the next higher-level entity to which it points. Then, arrows depicting the associations between entities are drawn. Some entities may present a

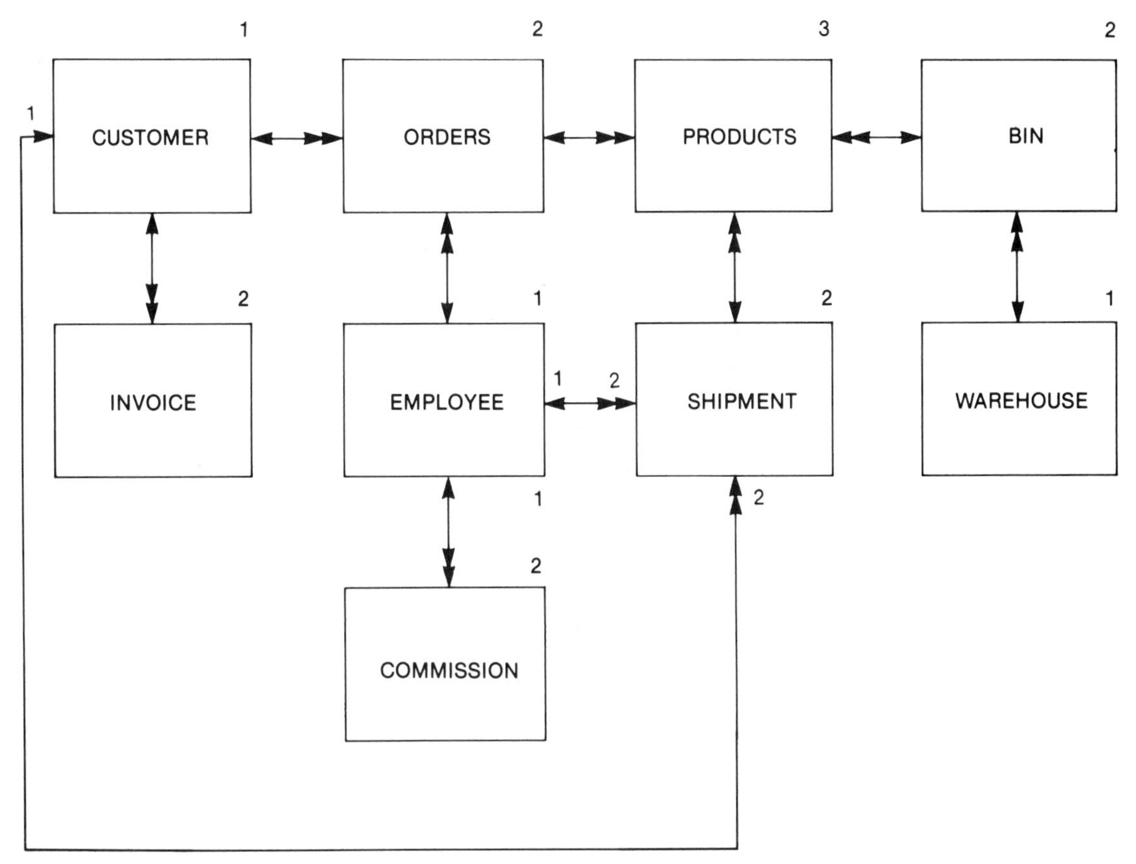

Figure 8.7
Entity chart showing depth of entities.

choice of parents. When choosing a parent, the entity should be clustered with the parent with which it has the strongest association—that is, the one with which it is most frequently accessed.

Example I3 describes the use of a structured entity chart for Happy Home Appliances.

Example I3
Structured Entity Chart for Happy Home Appliances

At Happy Home Appliances, the entities CUSTOMER, EMPLOYEE, and WAREHOUSE are root entities and have a depth of 1; each has no single-headed arrow leaving it. INVOICE, ORDERS, COMMISSION, SHIPMENT, and BIN are depth 2 entities. Each of these entities has a single-headed arrow pointing to a depth 1 entity. PRODUCTS is the only depth 3 entity, having a single-headed arrow pointing to a depth 2 entity. Figure 8.7 illustrates the depth of each entity in Figure 8.6.

Figure 8.8 illustrates the use of a structure chart for Happy Home Appliances. The depth 1 entities (CUSTOMER, WAREHOUSE, and EMPLOYEE) are drawn near the left of the page. The depth 2 entities are drawn

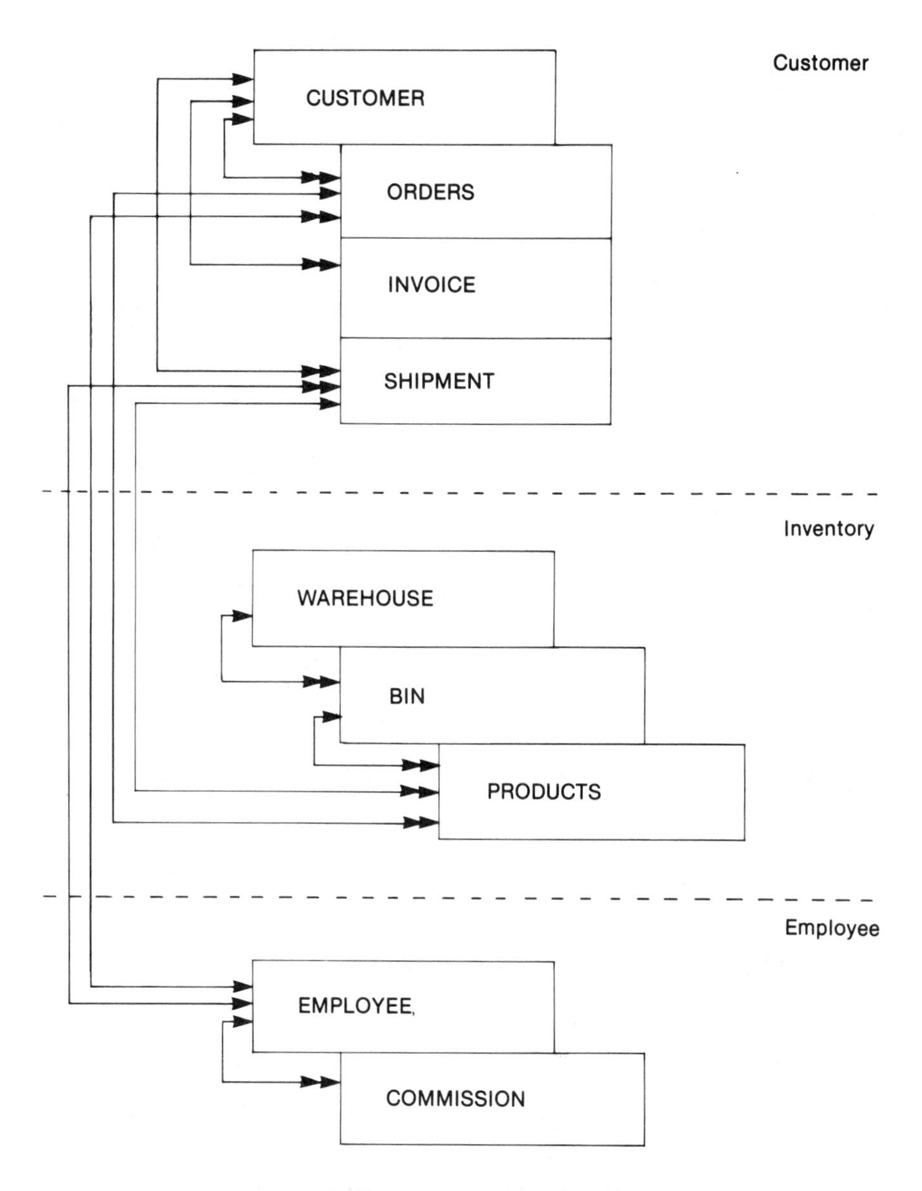

Figure 8.8
Structured entity chart divided into subject data bases.

one increment to the right of the depth 1 entities. For instance, ORDERS, INVOICEs, and SHIPMENTS are below and to the right of CUSTOMER. The entity PRODUCTS has its choice of parents. At Happy Home Appliances, PRODUCTS is most frequently accessed with BIN and therefore is drawn in the same cluster.

Figure 8.8 has three clusters: CUSTOMER, INVENTORY, and EMPLOYEE. Martin calls these clusters *subject data bases.* Each one is a group of data concerning a business function. Subject data bases integrate data for multiple data processing applications.

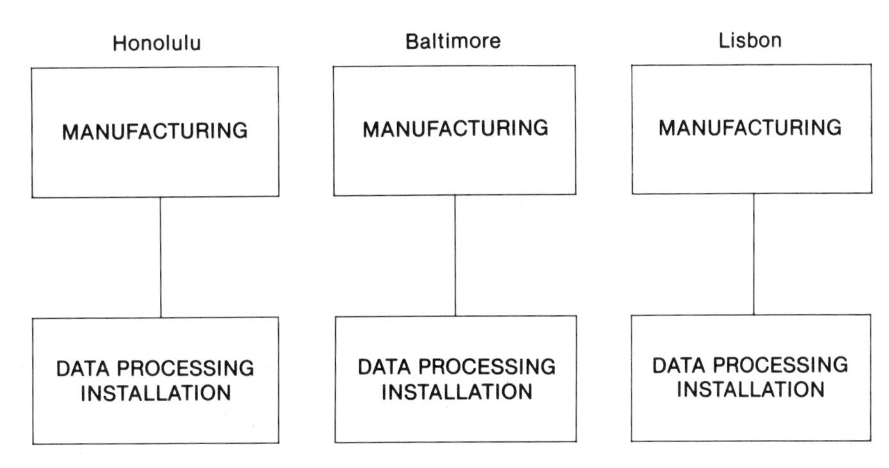

Figure 8.9 Manufacturing and data processing installations for International Gismos and International Widgets.

Distributed Data Bases

During the development of the conceptual schema, the design team must, in addition to defining and clustering entities, determine the location in which the entities are stored. If the enterprise operates one installation using one CPU for its production system, the question of location is settled. However, if the enterprise operates more than one production CPU, regardless of their geographic location the possible use of distributed data bases must be investigated. The decisions surrounding the use of the data in the data base depend upon availability requirements, volume of access and update, response time requirements, and financial considerations.

Examples F2 and F3 show how distributed data bases are developed and how their use can be affected by things other than data relationships, such as company policy.

Example F2 Horizontal Partitioning at International Gismos and International Widgets

International Gismos and International Widgets both have home offices in Baltimore and sales offices in Honolulu and Lisbon (see Figure 8.9). Each enterprise has a data processing installation and a manufacturing plant in each of these three locations. Each enterprise has a sales force concentrated in each of these three geographic areas. Salespeople place their orders at the closest office. As a company policy, when a salesperson takes an order, he or she must provide the customer a ship-by date for the entire order—based upon availability of stock—before the order entry process is completed. Salespeople, regardless of geographic location, accept orders for the entire product line.

The two enterprises differ in the composition of their manufacturing plants and their order entry procedures. At International Gismos, each plant manufactures and stocks every

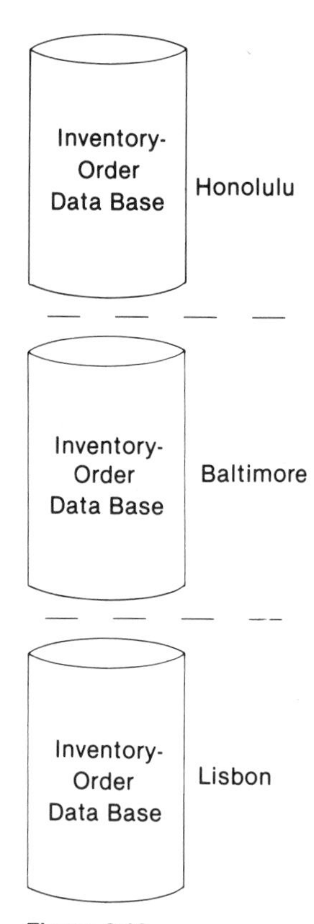

Figure 8.10
Horizontal partitioning of data with the data from the Inventory-Order Data Base stored in the location which uses the data.

product in the product line. At International Widgets, each plant makes a different product in the product line; the products manufactured by two plants may overlap, but no single plant manufactures the entire product line. At International Gismos, by company policy, an entire order is always shipped from one location. At International Widgets, by company policy, the order is shipped from the minimum number of locations which can satisfy the entire order.

At International Gismos, the Inventory-Order Data Base is geographically dispersed and has been **horizontally partitioned** such that the programs and data needed to satisfy a salesperson's request exist at each location (see Figure 8.10). The schema for the data base is the same at all three installations, but only the data needed to support an installation is stored at that installation. For example, the data needed to support the Baltimore installation exists only at the Baltimore location.

Horizontal partitioning of the data base provides several advantages in this example. Data is stored in the location where it is used, allowing fast access and update of the Inventory-Order Data Base. Since the volume of order and inventory updates is divided among three systems, the load placed on each CPU is relatively small. By distributing the volume of processing across three installations, response time is improved. Data is stored once, thus using the minimum amount of secondary storage space. And if a failure occurs at one location, the other installations continue to operate.

On the other hand, occasions exist when all data is used by another location such as in determining overall corporate performance. Since all of the data must be analyzed in this process, each location must transmit the data to the central location, incurring a communication cost. Now, if the hardware or software which supports the data base management system fails at one installation, overall corporate performance cannot be determined until the failure has been recovered.

Another type of partitioning of data bases may be used, as illustrated in Example F3.

Example F3
Vertical Partitioning, the Central Data Base, and the Replicated Data Base

Data bases may be **vertically partitioned** by function. At International Gismos, all employees, regardless of work location, are paid by the home office. While the Inventory-Order Data Bases exist at each location, the Payroll Data Base exists only at the home office. The Inventory-Order Data Bases and the Payroll Data Base are vertically partitioned, due to the data access requirements (see Figure 8.11). This is another mechanism to store data where it is used. Vertical partitioning has the same advantages of horizontal partitioning.

International Widgets must face a similar decision about where to store its Inventory-Order Data Base. Partitioned data bases are undesirable, since the International Widgets user

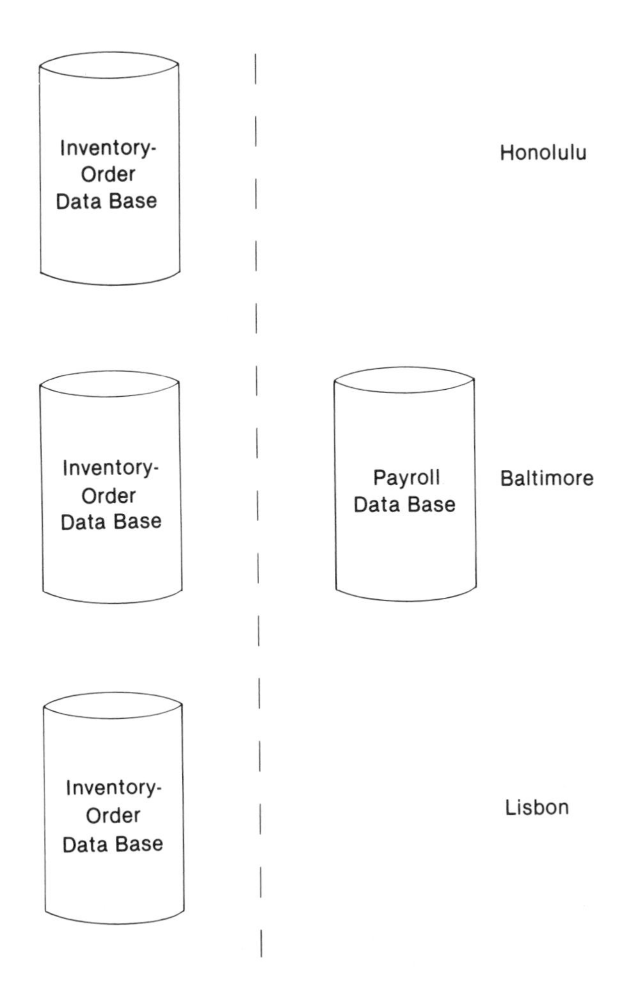

Figure 8.11
Vertical partitioning of the Inventory-Order and Payroll Data Bases.

must access multiple data bases to determine the availability of stock for an entire order.

International Widgets has some other alternatives. The simplest alternative is to store all of the data in a **central data base** (see Figure 8.12). In a central data base, all data is stored in one location. This approach has several advantages. The central data base requires only enough secondary storage to hold one copy of the data base. A transaction need only access the data in one location to satisfy an order. All of the data is available to the user and is current. Also, the coordination required to update data in multiple locations is not required.

But this approach has its disadvantages, too. First, overall availability may be reduced; if a failure occurs, all users are affected. Second, the communications costs are higher than with partitioned data bases, since every transaction must access the central data base. Finally, the high volume of transactions may cause response-time problems, since all transactions are executing on one CPU instead of being dispersed across three locations.

International Widgets has another alternative: a **replicated data base.** In a replicated data base, the data from the central data base can be duplica-

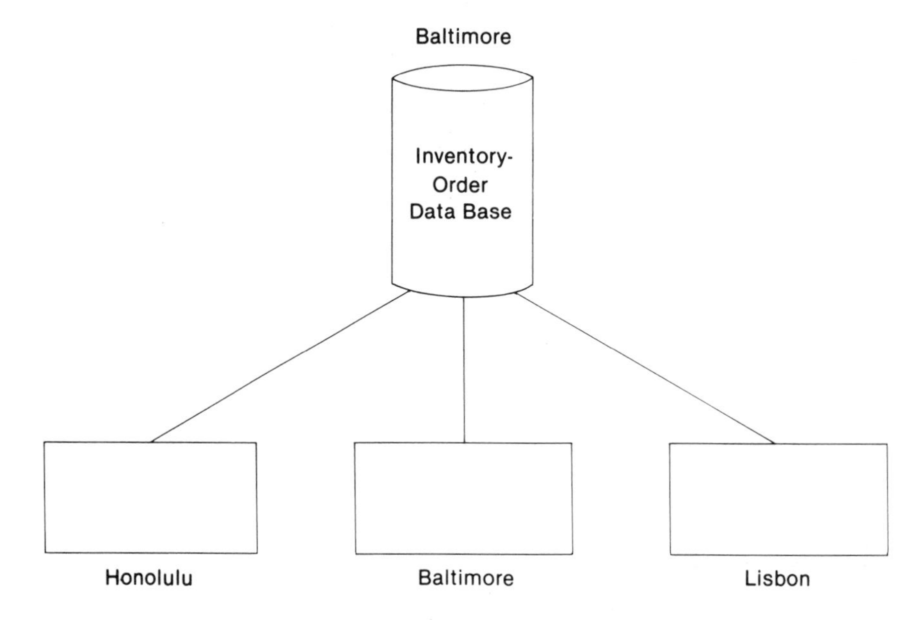

Figure 8.12 International Widgets' use of a central Inventory-Order Data Base.

ted and sent to all locations. Every transaction entered must update all copies of the data base (see Figure 8.13). This provides the benefits obtained with the central version: All users have access to all data at one location, and when an inquiry is made against the data base, only the data base at one location need be examined. The replicated data base has additional advantages over the central version. It provides the highest overall availability, for if a failure occurs at one location, processing continues at the other locations. Even if the data base at one location is destroyed, an up-to-date copy can be retrieved from another location.

A major disadvantage of replicated data bases is the synchronization required to ensure that all copies contain the same data. When a change is made to data at one location, the same change must be made to data at all locations. The second major disadvantage is the amount of secondary storage required for duplicate copies of the data base.

In Examples F2 and F3, two companies with similar data relationships use different methods of distributing data bases, depending on company policies which affect the way the data is used within the enterprise. Although in the examples data is stored in different geographic locations, this is not a requirement. If an installation has such a large processing load that more than one CPU is used for processing, the same considerations for distributed data bases apply even if the CPUs are at one site. The design team's choice among alternatives depends upon the data requirements of the user, the volume of transactions to be supported, the availability requirements for the data, and the monetary expenditure the enterprise is willing to make to support the user's requirements.

When the conceptual design team's analysis of the interviews is complete, a meeting is held with top management. A description of the data

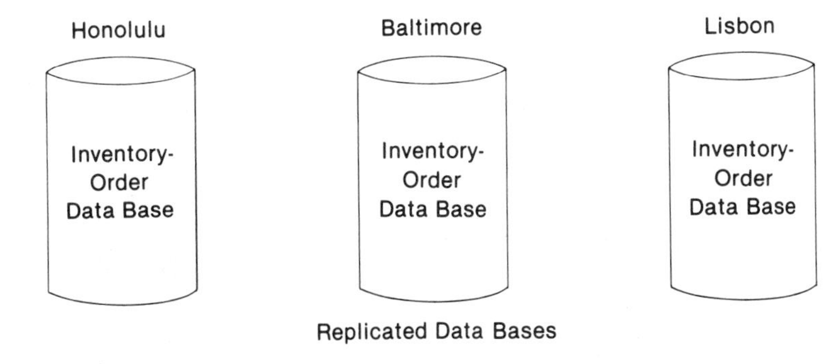

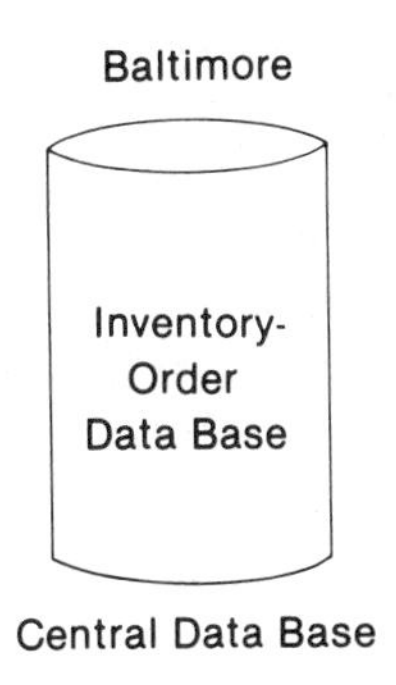

Figure 8.13 International Widgets' choices of a central data base or replicated data bases.

required to support the business is presented using pedagogical aids such as the entity-relationship model or the entity charts. Any discrepancies between the interviewers' findings and management's perception of the data relationships is resolved. When this process is complete, the conceptual schema for the enterprise is complete. However, this document should not be "cast in concrete." This is a working document which is reviewed periodically to ensure that it remains in tune with the business.

To summarize: The conceptual schema provides a general description of the way in which data is used within an enterprise and is developed in a relatively short time. It is a strategic plan which identifies the entities used and their relationships to each other. The conceptual schema also includes a plan for distributed data bases if they are needed.

8.3 LOGICAL DATA BASE DESIGN

The step in which the conceptual design is mapped into a specific data base management system has been described by many different terms. Here we have chosen to use the term *logical data base design,* to be consistent with the separation of logical and physical data structures described in Chapters

4 through 7. In this section, we will discuss the use of an affinity matrix to map entities into logical records, the normalization of data, and an implementation plan.

As we have seen, the conceptual schema identifies the entities required to support the business of the enterprise and their relationships to each other. The conceptual schema is independent of any specific data base management system. In **logical data base** design, the conceptual schema is transformed into a data base design which will function on a specific data base management system. The logical design provides a foundation to generate the schema, the subschema, and the physical data base design specifications. The logical data base design is a refinement of the coarse design provided by the conceptual schema. This does not imply that the conceptual design is not accurate, but it does mean that additional details must be ascertained about entities needed to support the enterprise.

The logical data base design may be created by individuals other than those who created the design of the conceptual schema. In that case, a method is needed to transfer the knowledge obtained by the first group to the second group. Indeed, formal documentation must be prepared as an educational tool whenever a new individual is added to the effort. One such documentation tool is the previously presented entity-relationship model. A second tool is the *data dictionary*. Definitions of entities identified during the development of the conceptual schema are placed in the data dictionary. The data is updated regularly during the life of the data base.

Data Dictionary

The data dictionary is sometimes called a data dictionary/directory. As we saw in Chapter 6, a data dictionary is somewhat like an English language dictionary. Within a data base environment, it is used as an automated means to define entities, attributes, and relationships during conceptual design. As the design progresses, the data dictionary is used to define records, the location of the data base(s) in which each record occurs, the means by which the value of the attribute is obtained, and the programs which access the record.

The data dictionary performs several additional functions. First, it provides an automated means to store, update, and retrieve information about the data used by the enterprise. This is of prime importance in the design of new applications. It also provides an automated means of examining the data bases affected when new applications are installed which cause new attributes to be added to existing data bases. It also identifies which programs need to be modified if a business activity causes the length of an attribute to be modified, such as the case of the change from a five-digit zip code to a nine-digit zip code.

Second, if standards for its use are properly controlled by the data base administrator, it provides an automated means of documentation. However, if it is not properly managed, it does not provide this function. Worse, it can lead to data redundancy and inefficient data base design.

Third, some data dictionaries generate the schema and subschema def-

NAME	LENGTH MIN.	LENGTH MAX.	TYPE	WHERE USED	ALLOWABLE VALUES	SEQUENCE FIELD
STUDENT-ID	9	9	NUMERIC	STUDENT-CLASS	0-999999999	YES
DESCRIPTION—A NUMBER WHICH UNIQUELY IDENTIFIES EACH STUDENT						
DERIVATION—THIS NUMBER IS THE SAME AS THE STUDENT'S SOCIAL SECURITY NUMBER. IT IS OBTAINED FROM THE SOCIAL SECURITY NUMBER ON THE COURSE REGISTRATION FORM.						

Figure 8.14
Sample data dictionary output.

initions for the data base management system, reducing the work of the data base administrator in installing a new system.

Fourth, some data dictionaries permit modifications which aid in the operation of the data base management system (see Chapter 9).

Finally, data dictionaries may be accessed directly by the user to determine the names used to identify data. Use of the data dictionary in this manner allows the user to write some of his or her own programs (see Chapter 11).

Figure 8.14 is a data dictionary output describing an attribute named STUDENT-ID. (This is a composite of the output from several commercially available data dictionaries.) The attribute is named and the minimum and maximum length, the type of data, the allowable values, and whether or not the attribute is an identifying attribute (that is, a sequence field) are shown. The output also includes the names of the records where the attribute is used, a description of the attribute, and the means by which the attribute takes on a value (derivation). If the attribute is computed from other attributes, the computation is expressed in the derivation. If the designer needs more information, data dictionary entries for other attributes used in the computation may be examined. If the attribute was retrieved as part of the design process, the names of the records where the attribute is used may be examined to provide structural information.

Mapping Entities Into Records

The initial step in logical data base design is to cluster the entities of subject data bases identified in the conceptual schema into records in a logical data base. Several different mappings are possible. There may be a one-to-one mapping between an entity and a record. Or, an entity may be subdivided and mapped into multiple records. Or, two or more entities may be combined and mapped into one record. Mapping is determined by the frequency of reference between entities, security requirements, and the ability to support new applications in the future with little, if any, redesign effort.

In logical data base design, further analysis is performed to determine the attributes associated with each entity. Attributes which identify entities must be determined, since they will be the keys of the records in the logical data base. Attributes which do not identify entities are clustered into records.

Generally speaking, if two attributes are always referenced together, they should be stored in the same record. If two attributes are never referenced together, they should not be stored in the same record. However,

Figure 8.15
Affinity matrix.

	A1	A2	A3	A4	A5	A6
A1	—	.00	.91	.15	.00	.00
A2	.00	—	.23	.00	.35	.10
A3	.91	.23	—	.00	.00	.00
A4	.15	.00	.00	—	.05	.29
A5	.00	.35	.00	.05	—	.88
A6	.00	.10	.00	.29	.88	—

the world of data processing is never that black and white; it exists in shades of gray.

One analytic aid used to map attributes into records is the *affinity matrix*. The affinity matrix is developed from data gathered during the development of the conceptual schema. The affinity matrix contains one row and one column for each attribute defined for the enterprise. Each activity performed by the enterprise is evaluated. If an attribute participates in that activity, the cell corresponding to that attribute is incremented. In Figure 8.15, the creation of an invoice (A2) uses attributes A5 and A6. The cells for attributes A5 and A6 at row two are incremented by one. The cell for attributes A2 and A6 at row five (A5) are also incremented by one, and so on.

If the business activity were the generation of a picking list, attributes necessary to create the list are customer name, customer address, method of shipment, method of packaging, part number, part description, quantity, and inventory location. The cells in the matrix corresponding to each of these attributes are incremented by one. This designates that these attributes are used together.

For each business activity, the attributes to complete the activity are identified. Each attribute is represented by one row and one column in the matrix. For each activity, the cell which represents the interaction of a row and column is incremented by one each time two attributes are used together.

When all activities are analyzed in this manner, each cell is represented as a percentage or a number between zero and one to indicate the relative number of times one attribute is referenced with another. In Figure 8.15, attribute A3 is referenced .91 times for each time attribute A1 is referenced.

Figure 8.15 is a small matrix. Hundreds of attributes may be required to support the activities of a large, diverse enterprise. Instead of the designer using a heuristic approach to attribute grouping, the affinity matrix allows for automated processing to determine attribute mapping.

It is rare for two attributes to always be used together (that is, to have an index of 1.00). The designer establishes the threshold at which attributes are grouped together and an automated analysis is performed. For example, if the threshold for grouping was established as .90, attributes A1 and A3 would be combined and placed in one record.

EMPNO	EMPNAME	EMPADDRESS	NUMBER OF DEDUCTIONS	HOSPITALIZATION	PAY RATE	FICA	YTD WAGES	FEDERAL WITHHOLDING	STATE WITHHOLDING	CHARITY	MISC

Figure 8.16
Attributes contained in an employee record.

The automated mapping of attributes is not followed blindly by the designer. Rather, the threshold at which attributes are mapped together is varied to provide several alternate mappings. The designer reviews each mapping to determine which one provides the best grouping for the needs of the installation. For example, if the threshold for grouping attributes is set at .85, not only are attributes A1 and A3 combined into the same record, but attributes A5 and A6 are also combined. Thus, the designer must be aware of the use of the attributes to determine which grouping provides the best results.

After the initial mappings are performed, the data base designer reviews the records to ensure that they satisfy the security requirements of the specific data base management system. Some data base management systems establish security at the record level. In this case, if two attributes have different security requirements, they may be split into two separate records so that each record may be defined with appropriate restrictions.

Example F4 illustrates the division of records to improve security.

Example F4
Improved Security at International Gismos

Figure 8.16 depicts the attributes mapped into the employee record for International Gismos. The enterprise carefully guards its salary structure to prevent jealousy between employees. While information about the employee name, address, and hospitalization can be updated by anyone in the Payroll Department, salary information can only be viewed and updated by the Payroll Department's manager.

The attributes in the employee record can be divided into two record types (see Figure 8.17). The base employee information is placed in one record type. The security definition permits all members of the Payroll Department to access and update this record type. The confidential employee information is placed in a separate record type. Security is defined such that the confidential employee information can be accessed and updated only by the Payroll Department manager.

Normal Forms

As entities are mapped to records in the logical data base design, the designer must ensure that the design will satisfy the test of time. The records developed must support not only systems currently under development, but also systems to be developed in the future whose requirements are not completely known at the time of the logical data base design.

Codd identified certain anomalies which occur using the relational model. Anomalies are unexpected results during data base maintenance. *Deletion anomalies* are experienced when a value for one attribute about which we wish to keep is unexpectedly removed when a value for another attribute

BASE EMPLOYEE RECORD

EMPNO	EMPNAME	EMPADDRESS	NUMBER OF DEDUCTIONS	HOSPITALIZATION	MISC	CHARITY

CONFIDENTIAL EMPLOYEE RECORD

EMPNO	PAY RATE	FICA	FEDERAL WITHHOLDING	STATE WITHHOLDING	YTD WAGES

Figure 8.17 Employee record divided to permit separate levels of security.

is deleted. *Insertion anomalies* are experienced when we attempt to store a value for one attribute but cannot because the value of another attribute is unknown.

These anomalies do not occur as a result of problems with the relational model but come about due to the ever-changing nature of a data base. Data bases are designed to contain attributes for specific applications as applications are developed. New attributes are added as a result of adding new systems which require new data relationships. This is precisely the environment Codd was addressing when he demonstrated the anomalies that occur with certain attribute groupings in a relation. The anomalies are not restricted to relational data bases; they can occur with any data model. If the anomalies are understood, today's data bases can be designed such that redesign to add future systems will be minimized or eliminated. Thus, the process of *normalization* provides stability of data structures over time.

Codd identified anomalies of data relationships in three normal forms. Actually, other normal forms exist, but Codd's three forms are the ones most likely to be encountered.

Data is placed in a higher normal form by placing certain restrictions on the way in which attributes are grouped within records. Thus, data stored in the second normal form is a subset of data stored in the first normal form, and data stored in the third normal form is a subset of the data stored in the second normal form (see Figure 8.18). The normal form in which the data is stored identifies certain anomalies which may occur. Example F5 illustrates anomalies of the first normal form.

Example F5 Anomalies of the First Normal Form

Figure 8.19 depicts the employee relation for International Gismos. The employee relation maintains information about each employee and the department in which the employee works. The primary key of this relation is employee number, department number, and job worked. A cursory examination of this figure reveals that the relation adheres to the rules established for a relation in Chapter 7: It has no repeating attributes and no duplicate tuples, each attribute is named, and the primary key field is not null. Because this relation adheres to the rules for storing data in relations, it is said to be in the first normal form.

Let's examine the insertion and

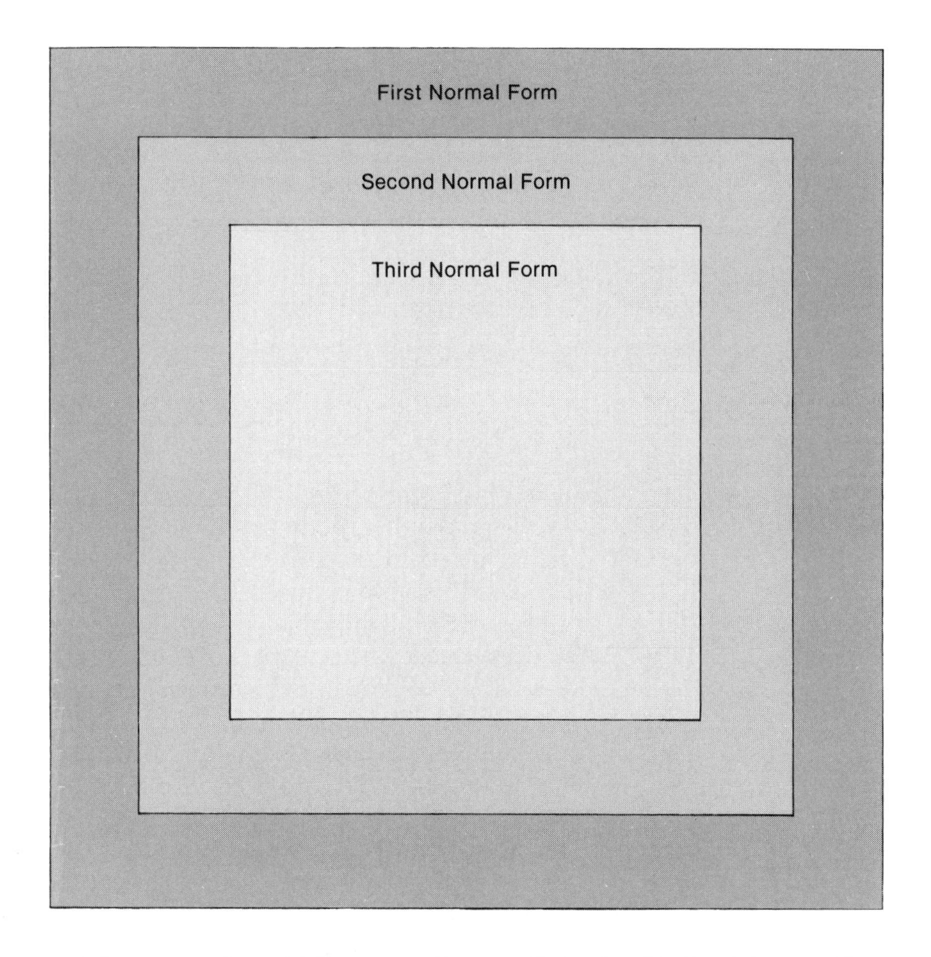

Figure 8.18 Increasing the level of normalization through subsetting.

deletion anomalies which occur with relations in the first normal form. Using the relation in Figure 8.19 as an example, if an employee is hired, data cannot be stored for the employee until he has worked his first job, since the value of DEPTNO, which is one of the attributes of the composite primary key, is unknown. If a new job is created, data about the job cannot be entered until someone works in that position, since EMPNO, which is also one of the attributes of the composite primary key, is unknown. These are all insertion anomalies.

Data stored in the first normal form also has deletion anomalies. If the last employee in a department is deleted, information about the department is also removed. If a department is affected by seasonal variations in employment (for example, at a ski resort), information about the department is lost. In Figure 8.19, if the employee Donaldson is deleted, not only is the data for the employee removed, but the data for the Accounting Department is also lost. These anomalies occur because data is stored in the first normal form.

These anomalies may be explained by **functional dependencies**, which occur when data is stored in the first normal form. Functional dependencies

JOB	EMPNAME	EMP-ADDRESS	EMPNO	DEPTNO	DEPTNAME	DEPTHEAD
MECHANIC	DOAKS	111 FIRST ST.	123	001	MECHANICAL	WATT
HELPER	SPITTLE	222 SECOND ST.	786	001	MECHANICAL	WATT
ELECTRICIAN	MURPHY	100 MAIN ST.	666	002	ELECTRICAL	FRANKLIN
FOREMAN	SCHWARTZ	300 BROAD ST.	777	100	PRODUCTION	GARFIELD
CLERK	DONALDSON	333 THIRD ST.	999	007	ACCOUNTING	KANE
HELPER	DOAKS	111 FIRST ST.	123	001	MECHANICAL	WATT
CLERK	SPITTLE	222 SECOND ST.	786	001	MECHANICAL	WATT
CLERK	DOAKS	111 FIRST ST.	123	001	MECHANICAL	WATT

Figure 8.19 Employee relation stored in the first normal form.

have their basis in mathematics, but they can be more simply viewed as a positive response to the question, "If the value for an attribute, *X*, is known, can the value of another specified attribute, *Y*, be determined?" If the answer is yes, then *Y* is said to be functionally dependent on *X*.

In Figure 8.19, if the value of EMPNO is known, the value of EMPNAME can be determined. When the value of EMPNO is 123, the value of EMPNAME is Doaks. Thus, EMPNAME is functionally dependent on EMPNO—that is, the value of EMPNO determines the value of EMPNAME. Likewise, EMP-ADDRESS is functionally dependent upon EMPNO: When the value of EMPNO is known, the value of EMP-ADDRESS can be determined. DEPTNAME is functionally dependent on DEPTNO: When the value of DEPTNO is known, the value of DEPTNAME can be determined.

The last definitions needed to understand the anomalies of the first normal form are those of prime and non-prime attributes. Simply stated, a *prime attribute* is an attribute which is part of the primary key of a relation. A *non-prime attribute* is an attribute that is not a part of the primary key of a relation.

The anomalies of the first normal form occur because functional dependencies exist that are not based on the full key of the relation. For example, the attributes EMPNAME and EMP-ADDRESS in Figure 8.19 depend on only part of the key EMPNO. The attributes DEPTNAME and DEPTHEAD depend upon only part of the key DEPTNO. These anomalies can be corrected by altering the way in which attributes are stored in a relation. This is accomplished by storing the data in the second normal form. All relations in the second normal form are also in the first normal form, but all non-prime attributes in the second normal form are fully functionally dependent—that is, all non-prime attributes depend on all of the key, not just a part of the key.

The data in the relation presented in Figure 8.19 is regrouped in Figure 8.20 to satisfy the rules of the second normal form. In Figure 8.20, three relations have been created to store the department-employee data. They are:

EMPLOYEE

EMPNAME	*EMP-ADDRESS*	*EMPNO*
DOAKS	111 FIRST ST.	123
SPITTLE	222 SECOND ST.	786
MURPHY	100 MAIN ST.	666
SCHWARTZ	300 BROAD ST.	777
DONALDSON	333 THIRD ST.	999

JOB WORKED

DEPTNO	*EMPNO*	*JOB*
001	123	MECHANIC
001	786	HELPER
002	666	ELECTRICIAN
100	777	PRODUCTION
007	999	CLERK
001	123	HELPER
001	786	CLERK
001	123	CLERK

DEPARTMENT

DEPTNO	*DEPTNAME*	*DEPTHEAD*
001	MECHANICAL	WATT
002	ELECTRICAL	FRANKLIN
100	PRODUCTION	GARFIELD
007	ACCOUNTING	KANE

Figure 8.20
Department and employee data stored in the second normal form.

EMPLOYEE (EMPNAME, EMP-ADDRESS, <u>EMPNO</u>)

JOB-WORKED (<u>DEPTNO</u>, <u>EMPNO</u>, <u>JOB</u>)

DEPT (<u>DEPTNO</u>, DEPTNAME, DEPTHEAD)

No data or data relationships are lost in this transformation. The original relation can be obtained by a join in the relational model, by following owner-member paths in the network model, and by following parent-child paths in the hierarchical model.

Data stored in the second normal form removes the anomalies existing in the first normal form. All non-prime attributes are fully functionally dependent on all of the primary key. For example, in Figure 8.20, all non-prime attributes depend upon all of the primary key. EMPNAME and EMP-ADDRESS depend upon EMPNO. DEPTNAME and DEPTHEAD depend upon DEPTNO. The JOBS-WORKED relation has no non-prime attributes; all of the attributes are part of the key.

Example F6 shows anomalies which occur with data stored in the second normal form.

Example F6
Anomalies of the Second Normal Form

In Figure 8.20, all non-prime attributes of the DEPARTMENT relation are fully functionally dependent upon all of the primary key. The DEPARTMENT relation contains a dependency that does not involve the key. DEPTNO determines the value of DEPTNAME and DEPTNAME determines the value of DEPTHEAD, but DEPTHEAD does not determine the value of DEPTNO. (Remember, the statement must be true at any point in time, and there is no guar-

EMPLOYEE

EMPNAME	*EMP-ADDRESS*	*EMPNO*
DOAKS	111 FIRST ST.	123
SPITTLE	222 SECOND ST.	786
MURPHY	100 MAIN ST.	666
SCHWARTZ	300 BROAD ST.	777
DONALDSON	333 THIRD ST.	999

JOB-WORKED

DEPTNO	*EMPNO*	*JOB*
001	123	MECHANIC
001	786	HELPER
002	666	ELECTRICIAN
100	777	PRODUCTION
007	999	CLERK
001	123	HELPER
001	786	CLERK
001	123	CLERK

DEPARTMENT

DEPTNO	*DEPTNAME*
001	MECHANICAL
002	ELECTRICAL
100	PRODUCTION
007	ACCOUNTING

MANAGER

DEPTNO	*DEPTHEAD*
001	WATT
002	FRANKLIN
100	GARFIELD
007	KANE

Figure 8.21
Department and manager data stored in the third normal form.

antee that two John Smiths will not be heads of two separate departments.) Therefore, DEPTNO indirectly determines the value of DEPTHEAD—a dependency exists which does not involve the key field. Dependencies not involving the key field are called **transitive dependencies.**

Relations in the second normal form experience insertion and deletion anomalies. For example, if a department is phased out of operation and deleted from the relation, not only is the DEPTNO and DEPTNAME removed from the relation, but the name of the DEPTHEAD is also removed. Thus, more information is removed from the relation than is desired. Or, if an individual is named the head of a new department, information about the DEPTHEAD cannot be recorded until the DEPTNO is determined and added to the relation.

Anomalies of the second normal form can be eliminated by placing the relation in the third normal form. All relations in the third normal form are also in the second normal form, but the third normal form does not contain any transitive dependencies. Figure 8.21 shows the division of the DEPARTMENT relation into two relations in the third normal form, DEPARTMENT and MANAGER. Every attribute in each relation is fully functionally dependent on the entire key, and all transitive dependencies have been eliminated.

The purpose of normalization is to design data structures in such a manner as to eliminate the need to redesign them when new applications are added. By storing data in the third normal form, structures designed today can be integrated with new applications in the future with little, if any, redesign effort.

Implementation Plan

After logical data base design is complete, the enterprise must develop a tactical plan for the development of integrated data bases. The current status of the enterprise is assessed to determine what data already exists in conventional files and what data is stored in existing data bases. The critical business problems confronting the enterprise are identified, as are the application development projects which are scheduled to be implemented. The management of the enterprise and the data processing department jointly make tactical decisions to schedule the development of projects which will satisfy the critical business problems of the enterprise. Once these critical applications are identified, their data requirements are re-examined. If an application uses data created by another application with a lower priority, the portion of the lower priority application which creates the data will be scheduled for installation, to ensure data integration between the two applications (see Chapter 10).

8.4 PHYSICAL DATA BASE DESIGN

When the logical data base design is complete, the data base design is further refined through physical data base design in which logical structures are mapped onto an efficient secondary storage structure. The objective of the physical design is to store data in such a manner that it can be retrieved and updated in as short a time as possible. This generally means that data is stored such that it can be retrieved and updated with the fewest I/O operations.

In physical data base design, each data base is analyzed with respect to all access patterns of all users to develop a satisfactory storage structure. The physical structure may be tuned to provide maximum performance by clustering, partitioning, selecting the correct access method, selecting a good randomizing algorithm for direct files, developing an efficient loading factor (free space), blocking, use of secondary access paths (keys), pointer options, and determining the reorganization frequency.

Often, little information originally exists about actual user data access patterns. The information is derived from analyses performed in development of the conceptual schema and the logical data base design. The data access patterns are estimated, based on frequency of access by manual methods or counts of accesses to conventional files.

After the data base is implemented, a number of factors may cause access patterns to change. Thus, whatever physical design is implemented must be continually monitored to determine actual usage patterns, and the physical structure is then adjusted to conform to reality (see Chapter 10). Note that the emphasis here is on a physical restructuring to improve performance; this should not affect the logical data base design. Also, physical

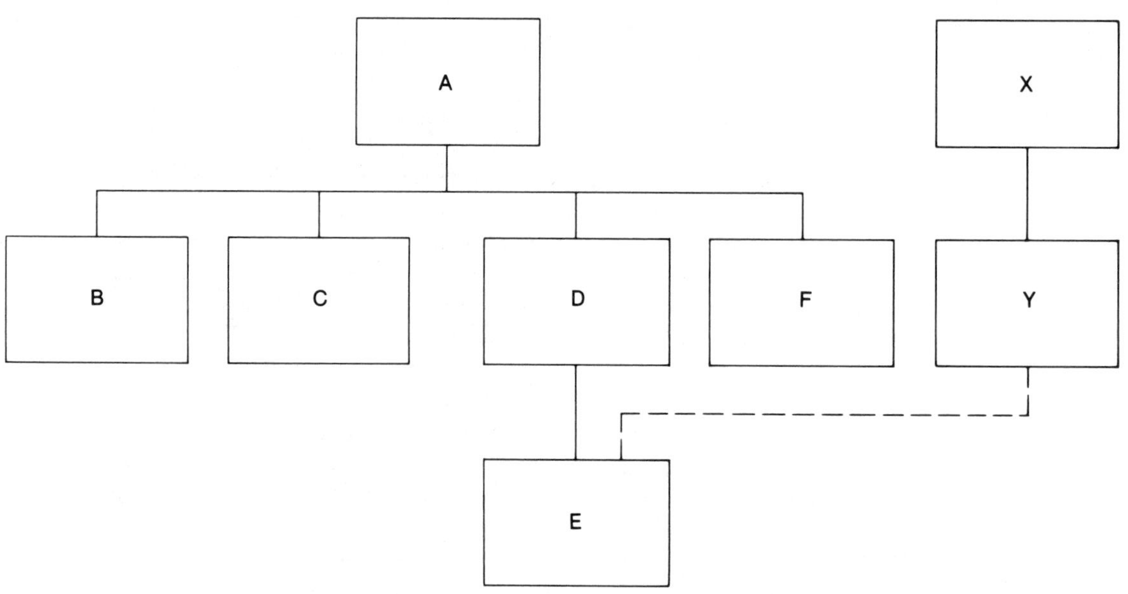

Figure 8.22 Data relationships developed in logical data base design.

changes should not affect application programs unless the data base management system used has a low degree of data independence.

Clustering

One of the first steps in physical design is to cluster records which are used together. Figure 8.22 illustrates a logical data base structure that is an accumulation of logical views of the data. (Although represented here as a hierarchical structure, it could be decomposed into a network structure using techniques described in Chapter 6.) Figure 8.23 shows information about record relationships captured during the logical data base design. Following each record is the relative frequency of reference—for example, Record B is referenced .30 times for each time Record A is referenced. The chart shows the time period in which the records are referenced (access frequency), the number of records added and deleted over a week, the number of records in the data base (frequency) at the time it is initially loaded, the length of each record, and the access patterns of the records.

Figure 8.24 shows how clustering of records (which is an extension of the clustering of attributes) is performed using the affinity matrix during logical design. By reviewing the frequency of reference (Figure 8.23), records accessed together are determined. Record C is accessed .75 times each time Record A is referenced. Record F has the same frequency of reference. From Chapter 2, you know that records accessed together should be stored together. Figure 8.24 shows the structure after records are regrouped by frequency of reference.

This reorganization does not affect the data relationships, but in combination with the block size, it does decrease the number of I/O operations required to retrieve the data. In DL/I, records are clustered by moving them

RECORD	RELATIVE FREQUENCY OF REFERENCE	ACCESS FREQUENCY	ADDITIONS	DELETIONS	FREQUENCY	LENGTH	ACCESS PATTERN
A	1.00	DAILY	1,000	1,900	200,000	425	DIRECT
B	.30	WEEKDAYS	0	0	2,000	500	SEQUENTIAL
C	.75	MONTH END	40,000	15,000	400,000	120	DIRECT
D	.40	DAILY	500	400	75,000	300	SEQUENTIAL
E	.10	DAILY	2,100	1,500	33,000	175	DIRECT
F	.75	WEEKDAYS	25,000	20,000	100,000	350	DIRECT

Figure 8.23 Logical record characteristics and relationships.

to the left and toward the top of the hierarchical structure. In IDMS, records are clustered by using the location mode of VIA to store member records. Clustering of records in combination with the correct block size permits multiple records accessed together to be retrieved in one I/O operation.

Partitioning

Just as clustering of records improves performance of records accessed together, partitioning improves performance by isolating records which have different characteristics from other records. Let's say that in reviewing the time periods in which records are referenced, we find that most records are referenced almost continuously throughout the month. However, while Record C has a high frequency of reference when used, it is only referenced during month-end processing. Thus, for the balance of the time, occurrences of Record C are traversed to access other records, slowing their retrieval. Even though optional pointers may be used to bypass access to this record when accessing others, Record C still occupies space within the file which must be traversed when accessing the desired record. Record C can be partitioned such that it can be accessed when needed, yet be segregated to permit fast access to other records during the times when Record C is not needed. (This partitioning is not related to the partitioning of distributed data bases. Partitioning, as used here, refers to the splitting of one data base into separate files to improve performance, whereas the partitioning of distributed data bases refers to the division of data bases across multiple CPUs.)

DL/I permits occurrences of Record C to be placed in a file separate from the other records in the structure. In DL/I, this separation is called a *secondary data set group*. IDMS offers a similar facility through its use of AREAS. With Record C partitioned from the remainder of the structure, it is not retrieved in conjunction with Record A (see Figure 8.25). The data base management system must perform a separate I/O operation to the data set containing Record C for month-end processing. The balance of the time, access to other records is improved since Record C is not traversed to access them. During month-end processing, if the file containing Record C is placed on the same disk drive as the balance of the records, performance is de-

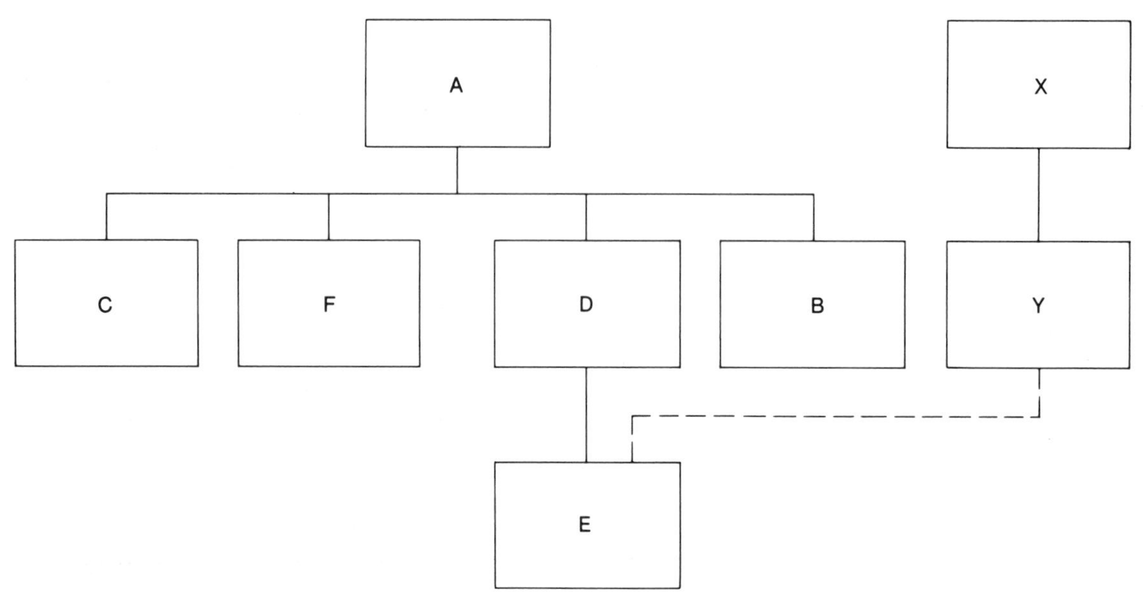

Figure 8.24
Clustering of records to improve performance.

graded, due to the seek time required to traverse the data base. If the file containing Record C is placed on a separate disk drive, performance is improved, since I/O operations do not contend for the same access mechanism.

In the preceding example, partitioning was used to segregate records by access in different time periods. Partitioning is used to segregate records which are different from others. Partitioning may be performed due to differences in frequency of access, differences in block size, or differences in frequency of deletion.

Selection of Access Methods

Choice of the correct access method is important for optimum performance of the data base. From the data obtained during logical data base design, the access patterns to the data base are established. The data base designer must determine whether the access patterns are primarily sequential or primarily direct. The access method is chosen accordingly. In Figure 8.23, records within the same data base are accessed both sequentially and directly. This is not unusual. It occurs because entities for business processes are clustered. Each activity in a business process may have different access requirements.

DL/I offers four access methods from which to choose. IDMS offers facilities for both sequential and direct processing. If records in all levels of the data base are accessed directly in DL/I, one of the direct access methods (HDAM or HIDAM) is chosen. If the processing is primarily sequential, one of the sequential access methods (HSAM or HISAM) is chosen. Figure 8.23 shows direct access to some segments (records) below the root. In DL/I, one of the direct access methods is chosen to support this access pattern

Figure 8.25 Partitioning of records to improve performance.

even though some sequential processing is performed. Remember, segments, except roots stored using HDAM, can be accessed sequentially via pointers even though a direct access method is chosen. In IDMS, if a record is accessed directly, the CALC location mode is chosen. If the processing of the member records is sequential through the path of the owner record type, the VIA location mode is chosen. IDMS provides a finer degree of control, since this structure is decomposed into a number of sets. In IDMS, a VIA location mode would be chosen for member Records B and D (which are accessed sequentially), and a CALC location mode would be chosen for Records A, C , E, and F, which are obtained directly.

Randomizing Algorithm

If a direct access method is chosen, a randomizing algorithm must be selected. Each data base may have a different randomizing algorithm, although, quite often, a general-purpose randomizing algorithm may prove satisfactory for use with many data bases. Automated tools exist to determine the effectiveness of several randoming algorithms using the keys of the records in the data base. The algorithm which provides a minimum number of synonyms and distributes records evenly across secondary storage is selected for use.

Loading Factor

It is unusual for a data base to remain the same size. They tend to increase and contract. Performance is improved when adding new records if, when the data base is initially loaded, sufficient space is reserved to add new records adjacent to the records with which they are referenced. The amount of space reserved for future additions to the data base is called the **loading factor** or packing density.

In IDMS, free space is reserved indirectly. The data base administrator determines the typical number of member records accessed via the owner record and then calculates the amount of space required for the owner and member records and their prefixes plus IDMS overhead. The amount of free space is added to this number. The result is specified as the page size in the DMCL.

In DL/I, the data base administrator determines the typical number of segments which will be added per parent segment. The number of segments is multiplied by the segment length to determine the number of characters to be reserved. This is converted to a percentage of a block. The data base administrator specifies the percentage of space to be reserved in the DBD.

There is a trade-off. If too much free space is specified, secondary storage is used inefficiently. Also, the data base is dispersed over a larger area and performance may degrade because of the "dead space" traversed to access the desired data. If too little free space is specified, performance is slowed while the data base management system searches for a location to store the new record. In an extreme case, applications may cease to function if there is no free space in which to add a record.

The amount of free space is dependent upon the number of occurrences of records added between data base reorganizations. If the number of occurrences of records is evenly distributed, sufficient free space should be allowed for all records added between reorganizations. If occurrences of records to be added are concentrated, embedded free space only wastes space in secondary storage and in extreme cases may degrade performance.

Analysis of the loading factor must be performed in conjunction with an analysis of the records deleted from the data base. In Figure 8.24, if occurrences of Record F are deleted from the same parent record occurrences in which new occurrences of Record F are added, the loading factor should account for the net addition of 5000 records: 25,000 additions minus 20,000 deletions. If occurrences of Record F are deleted from different parent record occurrences than those in which Record F is added, to improve performance the loading factor should account for the addition of 25,000 records.

Block Size

Selection of the correct block size is important to performance. If the block size is too large, records unnecessary to satisfy the current request are brought into storage, thereby extending the time required to retrieve data. If the block size is too small, additional I/O operations are needed to satisfy the request. As we saw in Chapter 2, selection of the incorrect block size can waste space in secondary storage. When establishing the block size, the loading factor is included in the block size estimate.

Since Record C is in a separate data set group or area and is accessed directly, the block size can be set at 120. This provides optimum performance but wastes space in secondary storage, since fewer records can be placed on a track. If the block size is increased, performance is degraded somewhat, but use of secondary storage is improved. The designer must determine which is more important. Most often, a compromise is reached between performance and efficient use of secondary storage.

The objective for selection of block size is the same for hierarchical and network structures, but the value chosen is different due to the manner in which each operates. In IDMS, the blocking factor, specified through the page size, should be large enough to hold the owner and member records which are accessed via the owner record. Since the number of member

Figure 8.26
Use of a secondary index to improve access performance.

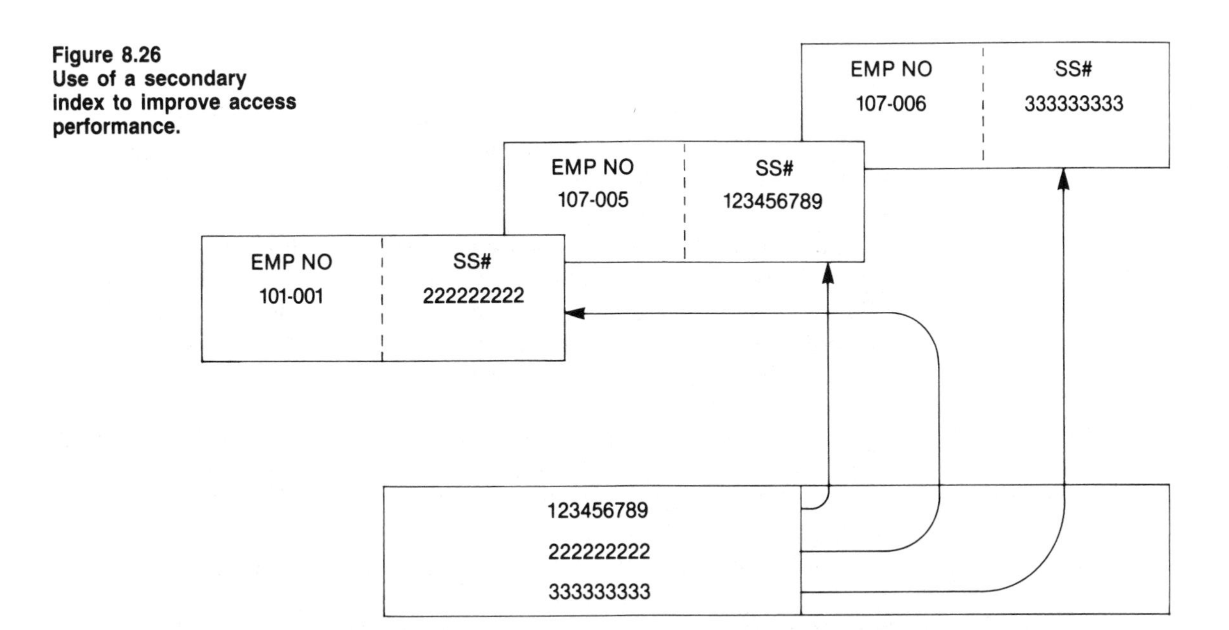

record occurrences may vary from one owner record occurrence to the next, this is another situation in which the block size chosen is a compromise between performance and wasted space in secondary storage. If a record is obtained with a CALC location mode and no other occurrences of records are retrieved, for optimum performance the block size should be just large enough to hold the desired record and its prefix.

DL/I permits records to be placed in a number of files through secondary data set groups, data files, and indices. The designer may specify a different block size for each of these files. As in IDMS, the block size reflects the primary access patterns of the user.

Secondary Keys

Some applications require records be accessed in sequences other than the sequence in which they are stored. If the alternate sequence occurs with a sufficiently high frequency, secondary keys may be added to improve performance. Secondary keys improve access performance but degrade performance during addition, deletion, and modification, when the modification is to the field indexed.

In Figure 8.26, employee data is stored in sequence by employee number. For all accesses of the employee for activities within the company, employee number is the primary key. However, the enterprise has reporting requirements to local, state, and federal governments. To satisfy these requirements, the employee record is accessed via social security number. If accesses by social security number do not occur frequently and do not require an immediate response, every employee record can be read from the data base and sorted, if necessary, to satisfy reporting requirements. If the accesses are frequent and demand a short response, then a secondary key, implemented through an inverted file, is established. Although there is no practical limit on the number of secondary keys which may be established for a record, they should be used judiciously due to the maintenance requirements of the inverted file whenever a record is added or deleted, or when the indexed attribute is modified.

Pointer Options

Performance may be improved with the correct specification of pointer options in DL/I and IDMS. The following is a small sample of the additional pointers available to the designer to improve performance. In Figure 8.23, occurrences of Record F are frequently added to the data base and are maintained in chronological order. Performance is slowed if all occurrences of Record F are retrieved each time a new occurrence is added. Performance is improved if a pointer is added to point to the last occurrence of Record F. DL/I permits the specification of a PHYSICAL CHILD LAST pointer to accomplish this task. IDMS permits the specification of POINTER IS PRIOR.

If a record is obtained for deletion through more than one path, delete performance is improved by the use of backward pointers in the path the record is not obtained from. In DL/I, this is accomplished through a TWIN BACKWARD pointer. In IDMS, this is accomplished through POINTER IS PRIOR. If Record E is accessed through Record Y for deletion, and if forward pointers are used, all occurrences of Record E must be searched to update the pointers to cause deletion of that occurrence. If the backward pointers option is chosen, only records associated with a specific occurrence of Record E need be accessed to perform deletion.

Once again, inclusion of these pointers is not followed blindly. The pointers should be used if a significant number of I/O operations is required to accomplish the deletion. If all records and prefixes necessary to perform the deletion are brought into storage in one I/O operation through the use of clustering and blocking, these pointers are not necessary. The purpose of including additional pointers is to reduce the number of I/O operations needed to accomplish a specific task.

Reorganization

Since data bases do not remain the same, performance is improved if they are reorganized periodically. Any data base which uses an indexed sequential organization and has a high frequency of insertions or deletions should be reorganized periodically to ensure satisfactory performance. (Reorganization may improve the performance of direct files. However, an important and sometimes overlooked point is that activity against the file must be analyzed to determine whether or not a direct file will benefit from reorganization.)

The period in which a data base is reorganized should be established in conjunction with the development of the loading factor. The period depends upon the amount of secondary storage available for use as free space, the distribution of record insertions or deletions across the data base, the amount of response degradation the user will tolerate, and—last but not least—the maximum unavailability of the data base the user can tolerate. As part of the specifications of a new application, the user specifies the response time needed to satisfactorily perform an activity. The number of I/O operations needed to access a specific record makes a significant contribution to response time. With the knowledge of the insertion activity, the designer can calculate the number of I/O operations needed to access a record after a specified amount of insertion activity has occurred. This can be converted to a *minimum* response time. The period in which reorganization is performed should allow a comfortable margin between this calculated minimum and the maximum allowable response time specified by the user. Since the data base is unavailable to the user during reorganization, the designer should schedule the reorganization at a time when the data base is not needed by the user, or at least at a time which will not significantly hinder the user's work.

Thus we see that modern data base management systems offer the designer a number of options for the physical storage of data to improve performance. The data base designer cannot investigate options individually, for the options selected will interact with each other. Thus the data base designer must understand not only each option but also its effect on other options.

8.5 SUMMARY

In early implementations of data base management systems, Data Processing Departments continued to design data base applications using the methods they had used with conventional files. This approach failed to integrate data for higher-level uses. The current approach is to design top-down by developing a conceptual model using tools such as the entity-relationship model.

The conceptual schema is a coarse design that is refined during logical and physical data base design. Entities which are associated with business processes, such as purchasing or receiving, are identified during design of the conceptual schema. The conceptual schema is developed within months, enlisting the aid of top management. Development of the conceptual schema is an iterative process to remove semantic discrepancies and to document the use of data within the enterprise.

After the entities have been established, the location in which data is stored is determined. Data may be partitioned so that it is stored in the location where it is used, centralized in one location, or replicated in some or all locations. Each of these techniques have advantages and disadvantages. The final configuration depends upon the use of data within the enterprise, availability requirements, and the cost management is willing to pay for implementation.

The conceptual schema describes the data relationships of the enterprise independent of any data base management system, but logical data base design then maps the conceptual schema into a logical design for a specific data model. The data dictionary is used in logical data base design and through the life of a data base management system as an automated tool for documenting data definitions, data location, and data manipulation.

During logical data base design, business processes are broken down into activities, and the attributes which support an activity are identified. Attributes are mapped into records based on their affinity for other attributes. The affinity matrix is one of the automated tools used as an aid to mapping.

As part of the logical data base design, security requirements must be determined. Records may be divided for data base management systems that only have security to the record level.

Certain anomalies may occur, depending on the clustering of attributes. Through normalization, a specific unit of data is stored by itself and only one time. The degree of normalization of data controls its sensitivity to anomalies. When data structures are stored using a higher normal form, they are relatively free from insertion and deletion anomalies when new systems are installed.

Logical data base design develops the specifications for physical data base design. Physical data base design maps the logical data base structure onto efficient secondary storage structures. Records are clustered in much the same manner that is used to cluster entities during the logical data base design. Records are partitioned into separate files if they are dissimilar in usage. A choice is made between sequential or direct access methods, based on the most frequent access patterns. Loading factors are determined to allow for the addition of new records. A block size is chosen consistent with the access method. Optional pointers are specified when their use improves overall performance. Secondary access paths are identified and pointers or indices created. Data base reorganization is scheduled, based on the loading factor, record insertions and deletions, the degradation of response the user will tolerate, and the maximum unavailability permitted.

REVIEW QUESTIONS

8.1 What is the difference between horizontal and vertical partitioning of data?

8.2 Why do anomalies occur when data is stored in the first normal form?

8.3 Why do anomalies occur when data is stored in the second normal form?

8.4 What is the difference between a central data base and a replicated data base?

8.5 Why were early data base design efforts unsuccessful?

8.6 How does the conceptual schema differ from the logical data base design?

8.7 How does the logical data base design differ from the physical data base design?

8.8 What is the major advantage of top-down design?

8.9 What is the major disadvantage of top-down design?

8.10 What is the major advantage of bottom-up development?

8.11 Under what conditions is a distributed data base design created?

8.12 Define functional dependency.

8.13 Define transitive dependency.

8.14 What is a data dictionary?

8.15 How does clustering affect logical data base design? How does it affect physical data base design?

8.16 What effect does partitioning have on physical data base design?

8.17 What is the purpose of establishing the loading factor in physical data base design?

8.18 How do pointer options affect physical data base design?

8.19 What is the purpose of secondary keys?

8.20 What factors must be considered when determining the period in which data base reorganizations are performed?

DATA BASE IN THE WORKPLACE

How to Succeed in Data Processing

When D. L. Brown, Vice-President of Data Processing at Acme Widgets, accepted his position, he recognized that the image of the department was badly tarnished. In the past, systems had been developed vertically from the bottom up. Systems within one area were completed before moving to the next area. This resulted in a number of problems.

First, systems required extensive time to be developed. Sometimes, implementation took so long that portions of the system were obsolete almost before they were installed. Second, as a result of attempting to design a system from the cradle to the grave, the final implementation dates were difficult to predict and often were missed. Third, development costs were as difficult to predict as implementation dates, and most projects exceeded their budgets. Fourth, since systems were developed one at a time, data could not easily be shared between systems. Fifth, and most important, the systems installed were not tied to the direction of the business. While systems which provided the greatest return on investment were the ones selected for development, they were not necessarily developed for the products which were most essential to the survival of the company.

As a result of all these problems, the Data Processing Department had little credibility within the business. Brown realized that the image had to be changed if both he and the department were to be successful. He vowed that the Data Processing Department would be run as a business within a business. The resulting story is a classic case of a methodology for the successful operation of a Data Processing Department.

Brown wanted to affect the bottom line: the profitability of Acme. He realized that the Data Processing Department had to be in tune with the needs of the business. He enlisted the aid of IBM to perform a Business Systems Plan. In this structured process, he met with other Acme vice-presidents to identify the products with the greatest impact on Acme's profitability. The data needs of each process were documented in a manner similar to an entity-relationship model. The data requirements of each business process were identified to ensure that systems would be able to share data when they were developed. In conjunction with the other vice-presidents, Brown identified data processing plans which would have a positive effect on Acme's lifeline products. A data architecture was developed which showed which business processes created data and which processes updated or used the data.

Thus, for the first time, a business approach was developed for Acme's data processing needs. Top management had identified critical products, data relationships, and an implementation sequence for new data processing systems which supported the business plan.

To support the new development approach, new philosophies were established for the development of systems. First, all new development was subdivided into manageable pieces. The maximum duration of any project was two years. Second, new development was horizontal instead of vertical. For instance, when an inventory system was installed for one product, a member of the development team was assigned as a member of the development team for an inventory system for a different product. Even though each product had different requirements, there were many similarities between inventory systems, and an attempt was made to use as much as possible of the existing programs from the first inventory system in the second inventory system. Third, work proceeded under the 80/20 rule: 80 percent of the benefit was achieved with 20 percent of the effort.

Although several years were needed to fully implement this plan, the image of the Data Processing Department now shines brightly. They have achieved credibility. New projects consistently meet projected target dates and costs. As another benefit of this approach, the life of new systems is extended because they can be more easily altered to meet changing business needs. Maintenance costs are reduced, since the systems are flexible and easier to maintain. Operational costs are reduced because the same basic system can be run in many different locations. Finally, segments of systems can be developed out of sequence; that is, by having an overall development plan, segments of systems can be added without redesigning segments of systems that were installed earlier, out of sequence.

The Acme Data Processing Department now captures data in a finite number of ways in an operational or subject data base. It also acts as a consultant to the user, to educate him or her in the use of data as a corporate resource. The user has now been given the tools to manipulate the data in an infinite number of ways through the Information Center. (Information Centers will be discussed in Chapter 11.)

Could this new approach to data processing development be attained without data base management systems? Brown feels that the major reasons for the success were the planning of data processing activities in tune with Acme's business objectives and the early identification of data relationships. However, without data base management systems, horizontal development could not have been carried out cost effectively, for the addition of new subsystems would incur large costs in the redesign of existing systems. The ease with which record types are added to data bases allows some systems to be developed which would be prohibitively expensive using conventional files. Thus, long-range planning and the use of data base management systems go hand-in-hand.

9

THE ON-LINE ENVIRONMENT

CHAPTER OBJECTIVES

Upon completion of this chapter, you should be able to:

1. Explain the techniques used to secure data in an on-line environment
2. Explain how data integrity is affected by concurrent processing in an uncontrolled environment
3. Explain how locking resources solves the data integrity problems of concurrent processing
4. State the problems caused by locking resources and explain the resolution to the problems
5. Explain how back-up and journaling are used in disaster recovery
6. State why rapid response time is important in an on-line environment
7. Explain how the data dictionary can be extended to aid in the on-line operation of a data base management system

NEW WORDS AND PHRASES

data encryption
response time
rollback
lock-out
deadly embrace
deadlock
data base back-up
journal

9.1 CHAPTER INTRODUCTION

Each year, the quantity of data stored on-line increases dramatically. Increases of 30 to 50 percent per year were seen in the early 1980s. Acquisition and maintenance of data in an on-line environment creates new potential problems that demand solutions.

For example, many users have terminals at their work stations that are used to access data from an on-line data base. They depend upon rapid access to correct information in order to make business decisions for the enterprise.

Also, when an enterprise allows on-line access to data, physical security of the data center no longer adequately protects the data. Additional measures must be taken to ensure that only authorized users can obtain data.

And it is not rare for thousands of terminals to be attached to a computer using a data base management system. With this great demand, it is inevitable that two users will concurrently request the same record to be updated. If this is permitted, one user's update will be lost. With conventional file processing, the traditional solution was to use controls built into the operating system to permit only one user to update a file at a time. In an on-line environment, the data base management system must control concurrent processing to ensure data integrity.

Another problem created by on-line systems is the increased effect of system failure. Batch processing of conventional files provided an orderly, well-documented flow of processing. The computer operator had standard operating procedures which described the sequence of jobs that processed a file. If a failure occurred, the number of people affected was small in comparison to those affected by failure of an on-line data base management system. With thousands of terminals updating an on-line data base, a failure of a terminal, the data communications hardware, the operating system software, the data base management system software, or an application program can make part or all of the data base management system unavailable to one or more users until corrective action is taken. Since updates in an on-line environment take little time (seconds) and are frequent (thousands per hour), the computer operator is not aware which programs access or update the data bases. Thus, human control disappears in an on-line environment, and tools must be set in place to minimize the time required to recover from catastrophic failures.

In an environment as complex as an on-line data base management system, the computer operator must have documentation about each user's interaction with the system. This enables the computer operator to service the user when problems occur. The data base management system can provide information about the use and access of the data base to the operator when problems occur.

On-line Environment

Figure 9.1 represents the large-scale data base management system that will be used in the examples in this chapter. All nonessential hardware and software have been omitted for clarity.

The operating system software controls the execution of all other programs in storage. The data communication software is responsible for receiving a request from a terminal and forwarding the request to the program which will process the request. Some data base management systems include communications software. In that arrangement, the communications software forwards the request to the data base management system, which in turn passes the request to the application program. Other data commu-

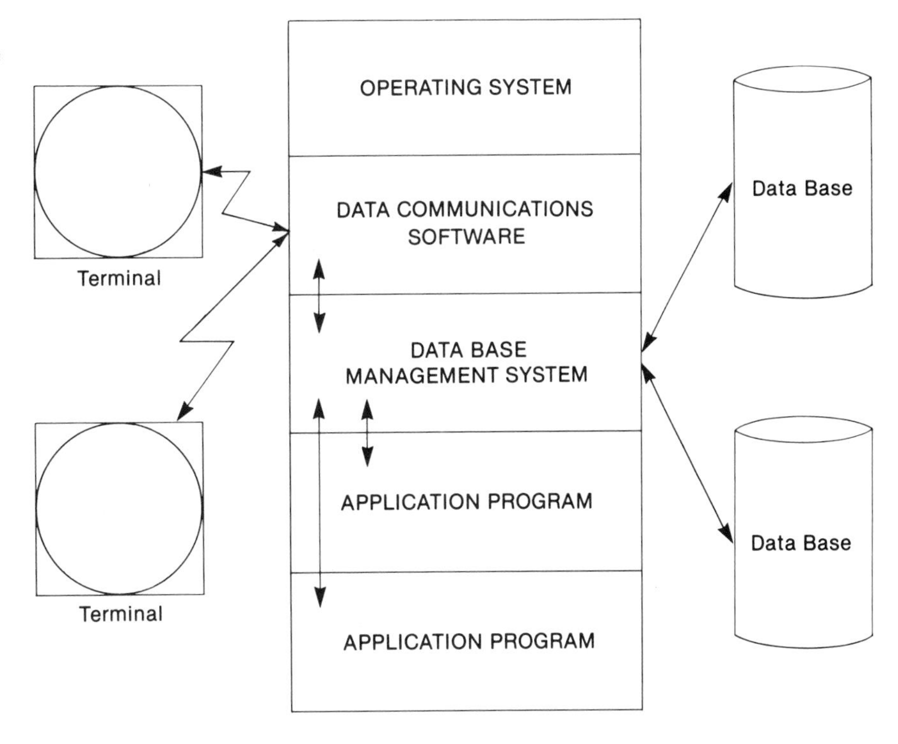

Figure 9.1 Schematic of an on-line data base management system.

nication software forwards the request directly to the application program. It does not matter which method is used, since the application program inevitably receives the request.

After interpreting the request, the application program requests data from the data base management system. The data base management system provides the data to the application program. The interaction between the application program and the data base management system may require several iterations before the program has the data to satisfy the user's request. When the program has formulated a response, the application program sends it to the data communications software, which in turn forwards it to the correct terminal.

In Figure 9.1, only two terminals are shown, and only the minimum number of programs needed for illustration of the on-line environment have been included. However, as we stated earlier, it is not unusual for thousands of terminals to be connected and active, and many programs may be active.

9.2 SECURITY

When the data of the enterprise is accessed from outside the computer room, additional security measures must be employed to ensure that only authorized personnel retrieve and update data. What additional security measures are used depends upon the value of the data. Several techniques are used, ranging from very simple to very complex. The security measures may include additional hardware to prevent access to the data, or additional software, or both.

Each installation must determine the value of its data. Then, an evaluation is made of the cost if an unauthorized user views the data. Finally, an evaluation is made of the cost of alteration or destruction of the data. The type and quantity of protection is based upon the cost determined by these studies. It is frivolous for a company to spend more protecting the data than the data is worth.

Let's take a look at the security measures that may be used.

First, almost all on-line systems require each user to identify himself or herself when accessing the system from a remote terminal. The first interaction between the user and the system is a request for the user to identify himself or herself via a user identification number and a password. The user identification number is a string of characters known to the user and previously registered with the computer. It is usually visible to the user while it is keyed in. When the user enters the password, one of many techniques is used to make the password invisible (in case someone is looking over the user's shoulder while the password is keyed in).

Second, after the user has properly identified himself or herself, data encryption can be required. **Data encryption** is the transmission or storing of data in code instead of its normal format. When data encryption is used over communication lines, the data is translated (encrypted) before it is sent. It is decrypted when it is received at the terminal. Special hardware is needed at the terminal to perform the decryption. Data encryption prevents unauthorized users from "listening" to communications to gain access to data, for the user must know the code before the data becomes meaningful. Data can also be encrypted before it is placed in secondary storage. If this is the case, it must be decrypted before it can be used by an application program. This prevents unauthorized users from viewing the data in secondary storage.

Third, as we presented in Chapter 4, the subschema is another tool to secure data. The subschema restricts a program to predefined views of data relationships and also limits the program to specific types of access to the data. This restricts the amount of data a user is permitted to access and update.

Fourth, the type of request made from a given terminal can be restricted. For instance, a terminal in a payroll office may be used to determine an individual's address. However, a request to update an employee's pay rate from the same terminal can be rejected. This type of request will only be honored if it is entered (by an individual with the appropriate user identification number) from a terminal in the office of the payroll manager.

Fifth, some data centers may have such stringent security requirements that the previous measures may not satisfy their needs. Additional software may be purchased from vendors, or the installation may write its own programs to add another layer of security between the user and the data. Relatively few installations have identified these requirements to date. However, as chief information officers learn the value of data to their enterprises, the number of installations using this additional software protection is increasing.

In summary, each installation has its own security requirements. The techniques we have described may be used individually or in combination to fulfill the installation's needs.

9.3 CONCURRENT PROCESSING

When performing batch updates of data, the operating system determines which task "owns" the file. In an on-line environment, however, the data base management system "owns" the data bases. Thus, the operating system controls that protect conventional files are inoperative, and certain anomalies can occur during concurrent processing. In the following examples, the on-line environment of Figure 9.1 is in effect. The programs and the data base management system are the salient points of the examples.

Concurrent Access

Example J1 illustrates concurrent access problems at Apex Doodads.

Example J1 Concurrent Access Problems at Apex Doodads (Two Concurrent Updates)

At Apex Doodads, the Order Entry Program requests the data base management system to obtain a record for 1-inch doodads. The record is placed in the USER-WORK-AREA for the Order Entry Program.

The Order Entry Program updates the USER-WORK-AREA for an order of 700 1-inch doodads committed to be sold to International Gismos (see Figure 9.2). However, the Order Entry Program loses control before it can request the data base management system to update the data base. The Production Program gains control and requests the data base management system to obtain the record for 1-inch doodads.

The Production Program updates the quantity on hand each time a crate of doodads is produced. It makes a significant difference which of the two programs completes last. If the Production Program completes first, the record for 1-inch doodads indicates that 3000 1-inch doodads are in stock, and 700 are committed to be sold. However, when the Order Entry Program completes, it replaces the record for 1-inch doodads on the data base with the record in the USER-WORK-AREA. This indicates 2000 1-inch doodads in inventory and 1400 committed to be sold. If the Order Entry Program completes first, the opposite situation occurs.

In Example J1, one of these programs does not achieve its purpose. In this situation, the result of an update depends on chance, and the final effect of the two concurrent updates is variable. You would expect the Order Entry Program to finish first half of the time and the Production Program to finish

Figure 9.2
Concurrent update of the record for 1″ doodads.

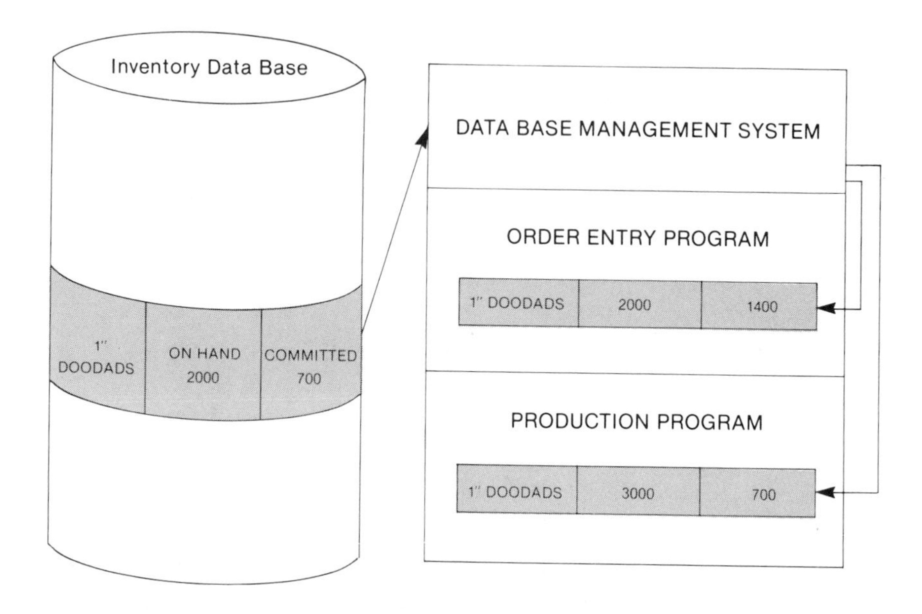

first half of the time. Obviously, this is not what was intended by the user who made the updates to the data base.

The problem caused by concurrent access does not disappear when only one program concurrently accessing a data base updates it. Example J2 illustrates.

Example J2
Concurrent Access Problems at Apex Doodads (Read and Concurrent Update)

Back again at Apex Doodads a Production Program requests the data base management system to provide the record for 1-inch doodads. The manufacturing department is setting production records! It has just manufactured 2000 1-inch doodads (see Figure 9.3).

The Production Program updates the record and presents it to the data base management system. The Production Program has more updates to perform. This is the first of 20 records to be updated during this execution of the program. However, it loses control and the Incentive Analysis Program gains control.

The Incentive Analysis Program is a report program that reads the data base to determine the number of doodads manufactured on each shift. The Incentive Analysis Program requests the data base management system to retrieve records from the data base sequentially. This information is gathered to provide additional compensation to those workers who expend extra effort in the performance of their jobs. The Incentive Analysis Program eventually obtains the record for 1-inch doodads. It updates the shift production totals with the 2000 doodads manufactured. The Incentive Analysis Program loses control and the Production Program regains control and continues execution.

However, the Production Program abnormally terminates. If the data base

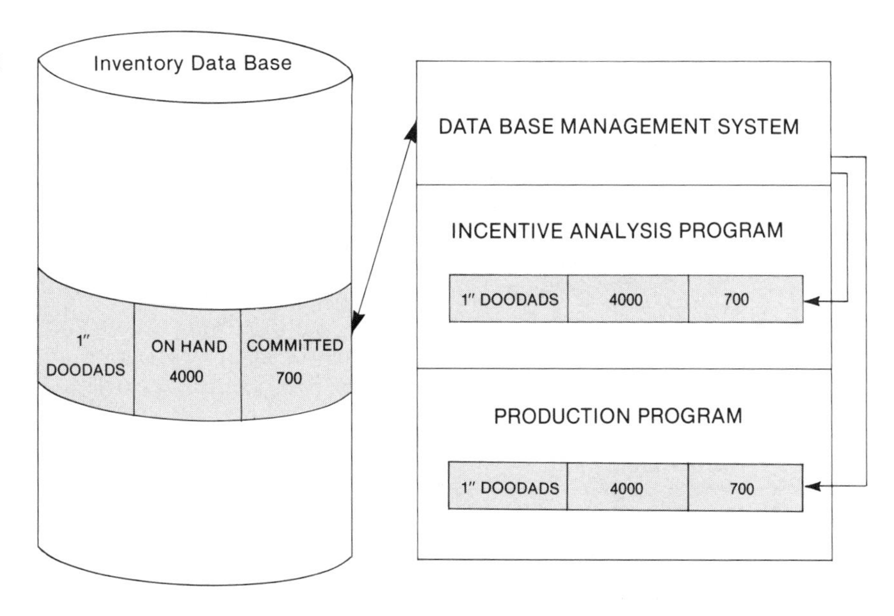

Figure 9.3
Concurrent access and rollback of the record for 1″ doodads.

remains in its current state, the next time the Production Program executes it will again increase the amount of 1-inch doodads in inventory by 2000, twice the amount actually produced. The results of the Production Program's execution must be reversed. The process of reversing the updates to the data base made during the execution of a program is called **rollback.**

The changes made by the Production Program must be rolled back to the point when the Production Program committed to its changes—in this example, when the Production Program began execution. When the rollback occurs, the record appears as it did before the Production Program updated it. Therefore, the Incentive Analysis Program has a copy of a record (the updated record for 1-inch doodads) that does not logically exist.

This is another situation in which the intent of the user causing the update has not been carried out. Once again, the result of the update depends upon chance. Obviously, anomalies may occur when one program updates a record while other programs are permitted access to the same record.

Clearly, these situations are undesirable. Thus, when a program updates a record, no other program can be allowed to concurrently access the same record. This is accomplished by lock-out. **Lock-out** allows a program to maintain exclusive ownership of a record until all of the records that are part of the update have been processed and the program is committed to the updates. Thus, lock-out solves the problem in Example J1. The data base management system locks out the record for 1-inch doodads after it is retrieved by the Order Entry Program. When the Production Program requests the record, it must wait until the Order Entry Program has committed to its update before the Production Program is permitted access to the record.

Then, any update made by the Order Entry Program will be reflected in the record retrieved by the Production Program. The problem in Example J2 is also solved, since the data base management system does not present the record to the Incentive Analysis Program until the rollback for the Production Program has completed. Lock-out prevents a program from obtaining records that have uncommitted changes applied.

However, lock-out creates a new problem. It has the potential to increase response time for programs waiting on the locked record. These programs (and the users sitting at the terminals who caused the programs to be initiated) must wait until the owner of a record releases ownership.

Another problem may be created. Programs may encounter a condition in which they wait forever to obtain a record, as in Example K1.

Example K1 Deadlock at Lotsofhype Advertising

The Lotsofhype Advertising Agency maintains Product and Payroll Data Bases to support their business. The Product Data Base contains data about the products promoted by Lotsofhype. The Payroll Data Base contains payroll data. The Ratings Program updates each of the products with the latest consumer rating of the product. In addition, the Ratings Program compensates the writers of commercials based on the rating evaluation. The Payroll Program creates the paychecks for the writers. A bonus is given if the writer has contributed to commercials with two products in the top 20 on the rating scale.

During one update, the Ratings Program requests the record for Raisons D'Etre (a new snack food made from dried grapes). The data base management system extends exclusive ownership of this record to the Ratings Program (see Figure 9.4). This locks out the record from access by any other program. The Ratings Program loses control.

The Payroll Program retrieves the payroll record for Hugh Hardsell, a promising writer. The record for Hugh Hardsell is locked out from access by any other program. Hugh Hardsell was one of the writers for the Raisons D'Etre commercial. The Payroll Program requests the Product Record for Raisons D'Etre, to determine its position on the rating scale. Since this record is owned by the Ratings Program, the Payroll Program must wait until the Ratings Program commits to its update of the record. The Payroll Program cannot perform any other work until this record is available, so it gives up control.

The Ratings Program regains control. The Ratings Program requests the record for Hugh Hardsell. Since this record is owned by the Payroll Program, the Ratings Program must wait until the Payroll Program commits to its update of the record.

As you see, both programs wait for the other to complete, an event that can never happen! This situation is called a **deadly embrace** or a **deadlock.**

The data base management system must recognize when deadlock occurs and must have a mechanism for resolving the deadlock. DL/I, for instance, breaks the deadlock by abnormally terminating one of the programs and rolling back its updates. It allows the second program in the deadlock

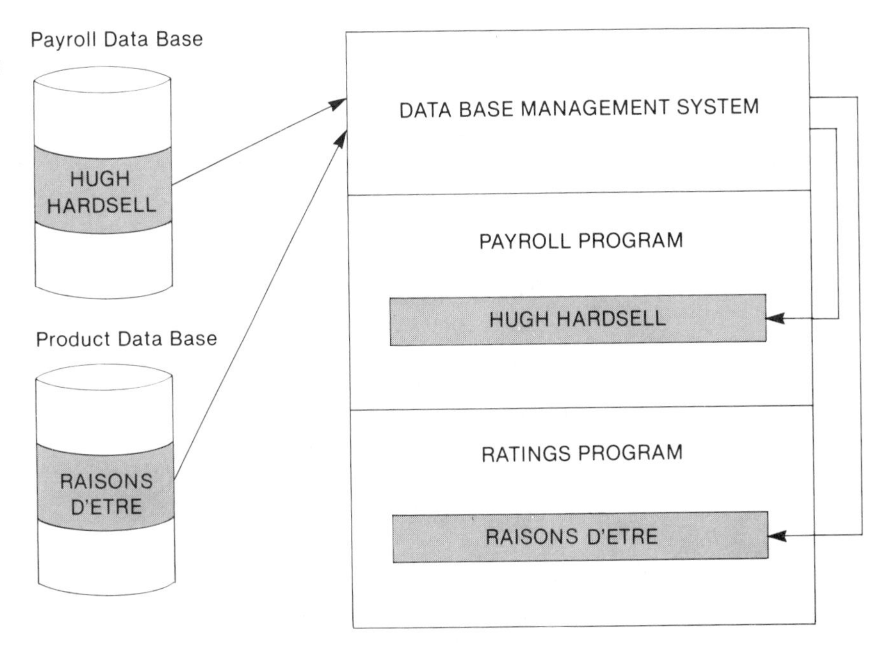

Figure 9.4
Deadlock. Each program requests a record, then each program requests the record owned by the other program.

to complete and then allows the abnormally terminated program to begin execution again. IDMS rolls back all of the changes made since the last commit point, releases ownership of all records, issues an error status code to the application program, and allows the application program to perform the necessary restart sequence.

Waiting for programs to release owned records and recognizing and correcting deadlock situations are expensive in terms of the time a user must wait for a response and the number of instructions in the data base management system needed to perform these functions. This is one of the trade-offs in data processing. The extra time and effort is part of the price paid for data integrity in the data base.

9.4 DISASTER RECOVERY

In an on-line environment, the availability of a data base to the user is governed by the availability of the links in the chain of hardware and software. As Figure 9.1 shows, the chain can be lengthy. If any of the links malfunction, one or more users will not be able to access the data base. If a major link becomes unavailable, the entire data base management system becomes temporarily unavailable. The links in the chain that have a direct effect on the data bases are the application program, the data base management system, and the operating system.

In an on-line environment, thousands of requests to access and update data bases enter the system from remote terminals each hour. In the event of a failure of any kind, the data bases must be reconstructed. A means must be available to provide a base line to begin the recovery of the data base, and to determine the data that is changed on the data base.

Recovery Tools

Two separate tools are required to recreate a damaged data base: a data base back-up and a journal. The first tool is a copy of all the data bases at a known point in time—a **data base back-up**. The data base back-up serves a function similar to a back-up of conventional files. If a data base is damaged, the back-up copy of the data base is a starting point to return the data base to its state immediately before the failure.

The second tool is a **journal**, a record of every significant event occurring while the data base management system is functioning. It includes an indication of each program executed, every change made to a data base, and every time a program commits to a change.

In case of a disaster, the journal and the data base back-up are used to recreate the data base as it existed immediately prior to the failure.

Component Failure and Recovery

Example J3 illustrates processing by several programs at Apex Doodads prior to a failure and the recovery after a failure.

Example J3
Failure and Recovery at Apex Doodads

At midnight, a back-up copy of the Inventory Data Base is made. Immediately after, work is performed by the Order Entry Program, the Inventory Analysis Program, and the Production Program. All three are initiated by users at remote terminals, so the computer operator is unaware that this work is being performed.

The Order Entry Program updates inventory items to show what portion of the inventory is committed to be sold to a customer. The Inventory Analysis Program compares the amount in inventory for each item against the committed-to-be-sold amount. If the uncommitted amount is low, the record is flagged and an order is generated to produce more of the item. The Production Program increases the inventory quantity of each item as it is produced and turns off the flag set by the Inventory Analysis Program.

Figure 9.5 shows the status of the data base before any changes are made. A data base back-up is made at this point. The Order Entry Program begins execution after the data base back-up has completed, and the data base management system writes Record 1 to the journal to record this event (see Figure 9.6). As the record for 1-inch doodads is retrieved for the Order Entry Program by the data base management system, the data base management system writes Record 2 to the journal. Record 2 is an image of the record for 1-inch doodads as it existed on the Inventory Data Base before it is presented to the Order Entry Program to be updated. The Order Entry Program updates the record, showing an additional 1000 doodads committed to be sold. The data base management system writes a copy of the changed record (Record 3) to the journal before the record is updated in the data base. When the Order Entry Program terminates, the data base management system writes Record 4 to the journal,

Figure 9.5
Data base back-up—before changes are applied.

	IN STOCK	COMMITTED	REORDER
1″ DOODADS	10,000	8,000	NO
7″ DOODADS	15,000	15,000	NO
10″ DOODADS	5,500	9,000	NO

indicating the normal completion of the program.

Now, the Inventory Analysis Program begins execution, and the data base management system writes Record 5 to the journal to record this event. As the data base management system retrieves the record for 1-inch doodads for the Inventory Analysis Program, it writes an image of this record (Record 6) to the journal. The Inventory Analysis Program flags the record for 1-inch doodads, denoting that additional production is needed. A copy of the changed record is written to the journal (Record 7). Records 8 and 9 are written to the journal as this process is repeated for 7-inch doodads. The Inventory Analysis Program has not completed processing but loses control due to the vagaries of a multiprogramming environment.

Next, the Production Program begins execution, and Record 10 is written to the journal to record this event. As the data base management system retrieves the record for 10-inch doodads, it writes an image of the record (Record 11) to the journal. The Production Program increases the number of 10-inch doodads in inventory by 5000. Then the record is written to the journal (Record 12). The Production Program terminates, and Record 13 is written to the journal to record this event.

The Inventory Analysis Program again gains control. It retrieves the record for 10-inch doodads. The Inventory Analysis Program updates the record for 10-inch doodads, causing Records 14 and 15 to be written to the journal (see Figure 9.6). (Note that records are written to the journal for each program initiation and program termination, and before and after copies of each record changed. If a record is accessed but not changed, no entries are made in the journal.)

Figure 9.7 depicts the updated data base. In our following discussion, we begin the recovery process with the data bases in the state shown in this figure.

Four types of problems may affect data base integrity in an on-line environment:

1. The user or the program may enter incorrect data.
2. A program may abnormally terminate.
3. The data base management system or the operating system may abnormally terminate (crash).
4. Physical damage of a data base on secondary storage may occur.

If any of these four problems occurs, data integrity may be affected. Therefore, each problem deserves attention.

Let's examine problem 1, the user or application program entering in-

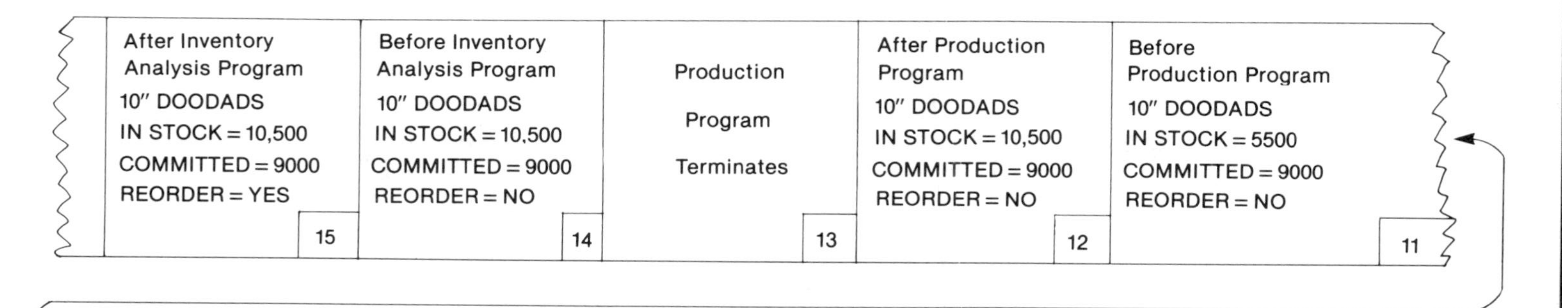

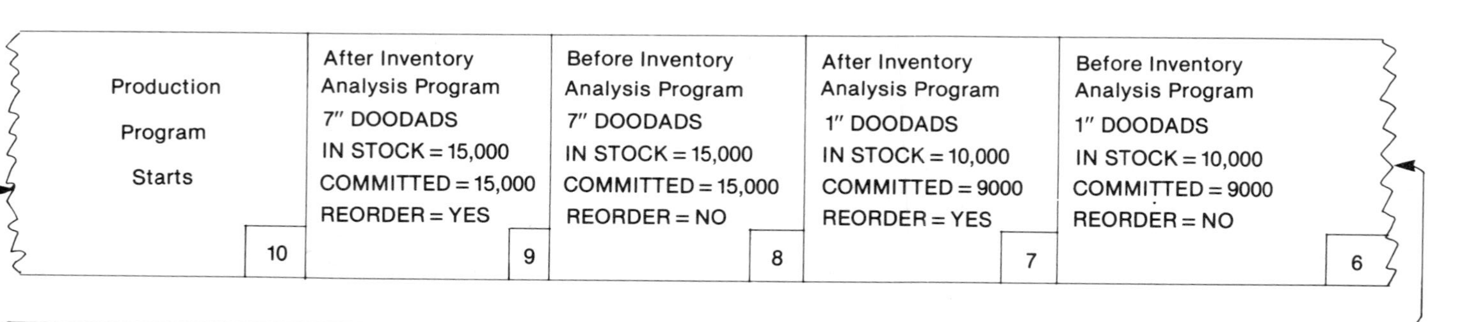

Figure 9.6 **Journal of events occurring during the operation of the data base management system.**

Figure 9.7
Status of the Doodad Data Base at the time of failure.

	IN STOCK	COMMITTED	REORDER
1″ DOODADS	10,000	9,000	YES
7″ DOODADS	15,000	15,000	YES
10″ DOODADS	10,500	9,000	YES

correct data. This is difficult if not impossible to correct. First, the data base management system has no method of knowing the data is incorrect. Therefore, it is processed as if it were valid data. Second, while the journal can be used to recreate the original data, this does not solve the problem, for other users may have viewed the data and changed the data base based on the incorrect data. In Example J3, if the Order Entry Program erroneously updated the record for 1-inch doodads by overstating the number of doodads committed to orders, the Inventory Analysis Program's decision to order production to ensure a satisfactory number of uncommitted doodads is incorrect. The journal can restore the original data, but it cannot reproduce the decision-making process of the Inventory Analysis Program. To correct the data, every user of the data must be interviewed and corrective action taken based on the revised data. This would not be too difficult in this example, but it would be nearly impossible in systems where 100,000 transactions may have been processed in this time frame.

Now let's look at the next problem—a program abnormally terminates. If the Inventory Analysis Program in Example J3 abnormally terminates, the changes it made to the data base must be reversed or rolled back. This is accomplished by reading the journal backward, searching for the copies of the records as they existed before they were changed by the Inventory Analysis Program. Record 14 contains the copy of the record for 10-inch doodads that existed before the record was updated by the Inventory Analysis Program. The data base management system replaces the record for 10-inch doodads on the data base with Record 14 (see Figure 9.8). The data base management system continues processing the tape backward. It replaces the record for 7-inch and 1-inch doodads on the data base with Records 8 and 6 from the journal (see Figure 9.8). When the data base management system reads Record 5 on the journal, replacement of the records changed by the Inventory Analysis Program is complete. However, the record for 10-inch doodads on the data base still reflects the updates made by the Production

Figure 9.8
Status of the Doodad Data Base after rollback of the changes made by the Inventory Analysis Program.

	IN STOCK	COMMITTED	REORDER
1″ DOODADS	10,000	9,000	NO
7″ DOODADS	15,000	15,000	NO
10″ DOODADS	10,500	9,000	NO

Program. The same is true for the record for 1-inch doodads updated by the Order Entry Program. Only the changes made by the Inventory Analysis Program were reversed. The rollback procedure does not destroy any updates made by programs that committed to the updates. With this type of processing, only the changes made to the data base by the failing program are reversed. Any changes made by and committed to by other programs remain in effect.

Next we shall illustrate the third problem—when the data base management system or operating system abnormally terminates. Both of these failures have the same effect on the data base management system: It cannot come to a normal termination. The resolution to this problem is similar to the resolution to the previous problem. When restarted, the data base management system treats the application programs as if they have abnormally terminated. After the operating system and the data base management system are functioning, the data base management begins the recovery process. The actions taken for recovery of the Inventory Analysis Program in the preceding problem are repeated. First, the journal is positioned at the last record written before the failure and the journal is processed backward. The data base management system searches the journal for programs having a record indicating that they have started but not having a record indicating that they have ended. The absence of a record denoting the termination of a program indicates to the data base management system that the program was active when the data base management system (or operating system) abnormally terminated. For each active program, the data base management system finds the copy of each data base record as it existed before the program started. It places this copy of the record on the data base. In Example J3, the Inventory Analysis Program is the only program active. The data base management system rolls back all of the records changed, just as in the previous problem. After the rollback is complete, the Inventory Analysis Program and any other programs not completed are rescheduled, and they process the data from the point at which they last committed to changes to the data base.

Finally, let's look at the fourth problem—when there is physical damage to the secondary storage media containing the data base. This process is not automatically performed by the data base management system. Rather, the computer operator notifies the data base administrator of the problem. The data base administrator establishes recovery procedures to be followed. The first step is to restore the last back-up copy of the data base to a new secondary storage area. Then all of the journals written since the last back-up copy of the data base was taken are gathered. Utility programs distributed with the data base management system process the journals in chronological sequence. As each before-after record pair is encountered on the journal, the after-image replaces the corresponding record on the data base. In Example J3, Records 2 and 3 are the first pair of change records encountered. Record 3 (the record as updated by the Order Entry Program) replaces the record for 1-inch doodads on the data base (see Figure 9.9). This process

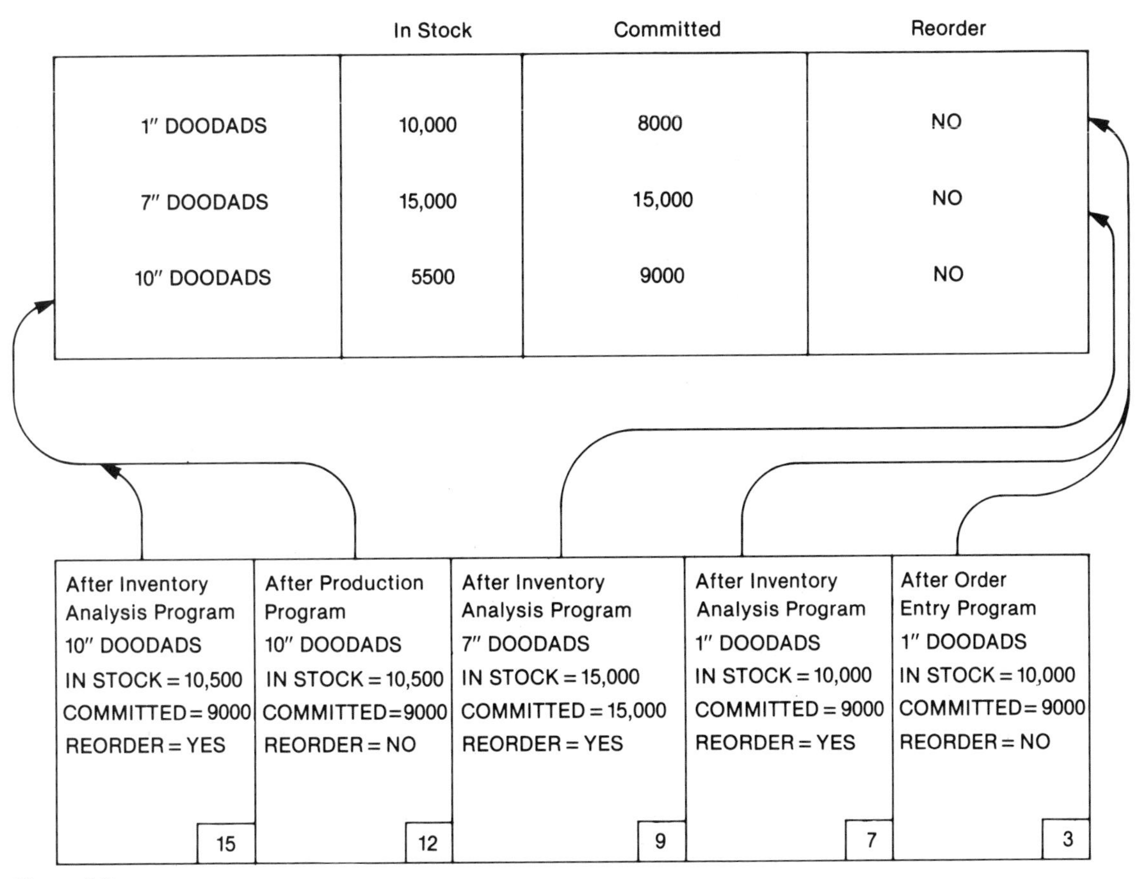

Figure 9.9
Applying "after" images from the journal to a data base created from a data base back-up.

is repeated for the remainder of the change records on the journal. Each changed image is rewritten to the data base until the data base is in the state when the damage occurred. The updates for all programs are reflected on the data base.

These examples do not reflect the actual processing performed when data base recovery is performed. They represent the functional manipulation which must take place to ensure data integrity, but the processing as described is too slow for an on-line environment. In an actual on-line environment, special processes—variations of the ones we have presented—would speed the recovery. The processes just described appear to be very involved. They are! A great deal of effort is necessary to ensure data integrity under catastrophic conditions. This is yet another trade-off in data processing. The programs to perform the functions we have described add to the complexity of the data base management system, to the computer resources needed to support a data base management system, and to the length of time needed to satisfy a request from a user. However, the additional programs provide the benefit of increased data integrity.

9.5 OPERATING IN AN ON-LINE ENVIRONMENT

Two different groups of individuals are involved in the on-line operation of a data base management system: the users and the computer operators. Each has a different perspective on the operation. The user uses the data base management system as a tool to perform the work of the enterprise. The computer operator services the user when the user encounters an unusual condition.

Users

On-line users inquire against data bases to receive information to make business decisions, and they update data bases to provide information to others to make business decisions. They need a short response time when interacting with the data base. **Response time** is loosely defined as the elapsed time from the point a user issues a request at the terminal until a response is received from the data base management system.

There are two distinct categories of on-line users. The first category is users who use the data base management system to perform the operational and supervisory functions of the enterprise—functions such as order entry, inventory control, and production recording. They deal with the detail data concerning the mechanics of the business. One example of this type of function is depicted in Example A6. The second category of users is members of middle and upper management, who use the data base management system as a tool to help make the tactical and strategic decisions of the business. This function is described in Chapter 11.

Example A6
Operational Users at Acme Widgets

Acme Widgets provides portable terminals to its salespeople. When a salesperson visits a customer, the salesperson connects the portable terminal to the host computer via telephone lines. For each item the customer desires, the salesperson enters the order through the terminal. During processing of the order, several data base records are accessed and updated (see Figure 9.10):

—The description and quantity of the ordered item is checked to ensure that the description is valid and that the quantity is reasonable.

—The Inventory Data Base is checked to ensure that there is a sufficient quantity of uncommitted items available to be shipped to meet the customer's request.

—If the inventory is available, the record for the inventory item is updated to reflect the additional quantity committed. If the item is not in inventory, the Production Data Base is accessed to determine the next production date for the item.

—The line item is extended to determine the cost.

—The Customer Data Base is accessed to ensure that the customer has sufficient credit to pay for the item.

—The Order Data Base is updated with customer and inventory data.

—Finally, the response is returned to the salesperson.

During the course of this processing, many data bases were accessed to provide a response, many salespeople in other customers' offices were

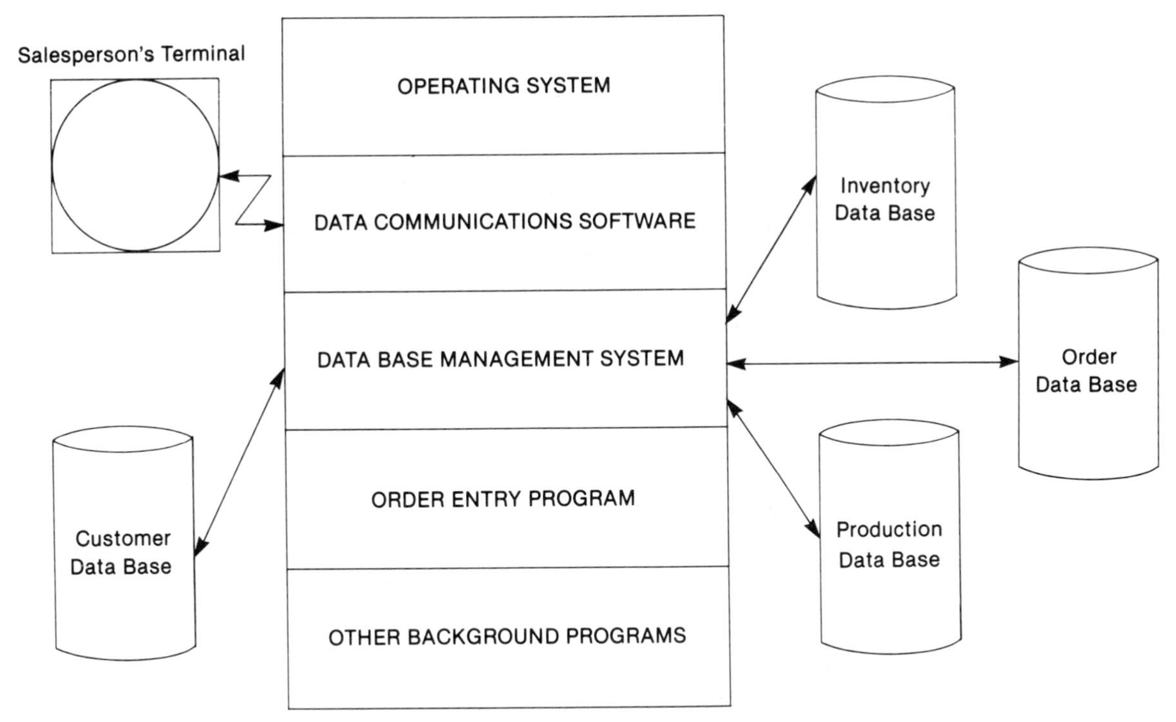

Figure 9.10 Schematic of processing for an order entry transaction. performing similar work, and hundreds of other users made requests specific to their jobs. Yet, the response time for this request is normally measured in seconds. The salesperson and the customer cannot complete their interaction until a response is received from the data base management system; thus, long delays for responses cannot be tolerated.

Typically, the user expects a response to an inquiry in a matter of seconds. In these situations, 10 seconds is a very long time. While users are waiting for a response, they are idle. Ten seconds of idle time for one user waiting for a response is insignificant. However, when the idle time is multiplied by thousands of requests per terminal, for thousands of terminals over 250 working days a year, this amounts to a significant amount of unproductive time for the corporation during a year. In some cases, when response time is extremely bad, the enterprise may have to work people overtime or may need to hire additional personnel, with the corresponding increase in floor space to house them. Thus, poor response time can have a significant impact on both the personnel and the overall productivity of the corporation. Response times of one to five seconds are typical of an effective on-line environment.

Computer Operators

The operation of an on-line data base management system is quite complex. As we indicated earlier in this chapter, the computer operator cannot determine which user is using the system at any given time, for large operations have thousands of users accessing hundreds of data bases. At certain times, maintenance must be performed on the data base management system, the application programs, and the data bases. Maintenance takes several forms.

The most common maintenance is to create back-up copies of the data base. The users must be prevented from modifying the data base while the back-up is being created.

Second, with data bases using an ISAM-based physical storage structure, the ISAM structures must occasionally be reorganized to provide satisfactory performance.

Third, the programs which access the data base change to meet the changing needs of the business environment. When major subsystems are implemented, the data base must be changed to reflect new data relationships.

Finally, no matter what precautions are taken, the laws of Murphy and Schwartz will apply. Murphy has two laws: (1) Anything that can go wrong will go wrong; (2) It will happen at the worst possible time. Schwartz's law states: Murphy is an optimist!

A data base can provide the computer operator with information about the environment in which the data base management system is operating. Thus, the computer operator can use the data base to gain information about procedures to be taken when maintenance is being performed or when a program or data base becomes unavailable to the user. The data base must contain information about the data bases, the programs, the terminals executing the programs, and the programmers to be called when a program abnormally terminates.

The data dictionary for the installation already contains data about the data bases and the programs to aid the data base administration function. The data dictionary can be extended with additional information to satisfy the needs of the computer operator, without creating redundant data. Thus, the data dictionary becomes the data base used by the computer operator when processing problems occur.

Although computer operators do not attempt to correct problems, they must notify the data base administrator or the application programmer when a problem is detected. Computer operators must also notify the users of the problem and give them an estimate of the time needed to resolve the problem.

When a back-up copy of a data base is made, or when a data base is being reorganized, certain users are unable to complete their interactions with the data base. If the user is new or the back-up copy or the reorganization of the data base executes during a time period other than that scheduled, the user may call the data center to determine why his or her requests are not satisfied. The computer operator inquires against the data dictionary to determine which terminal the user is accessing. The operator then makes another inquiry to determine whether or not the terminal has access to one

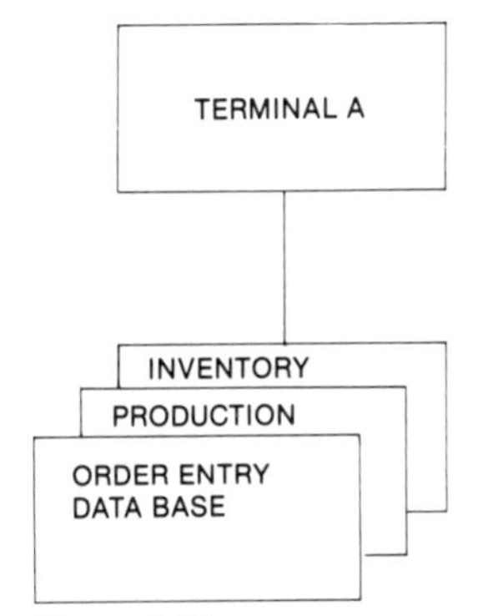

Figure 9.11
Use of the data dictionary to determine which data bases are accessed by Terminal A.

of the data bases being backed up or reorganized (see Figure 9.11). If the user's terminal accesses a data base currently being maintained, the operator notifies the user that data base maintenance is in process and tells him or her the time the data base will again be available. If the back-up or reorganization of the data base is not being performed, the operator continues the investigation to determine the cause of the problem.

A program may abnormally terminate due to a latent bug in the program. When this occurs, the program cannot be executed until corrective action is taken. The computer operator must begin a chain of events to get the program fixed. First, the operator requests the name of the programmer responsible for the failing program from the data dictionary and then notifies the programmer of the problem. Second, the operator determines which users are authorized to execute the failing program. The operator notifies the users of the problem and the corrective action being taken. Since few users understand the internal operation of a data base management system, this advance notification reduces undue worry by a user when a request does not normally complete.

Thus we see the viability of using a data base under the control of the data base management system as a tool to provide data about the operation of the data base management system itself.

9.6 SUMMARY

The on-line environment for a data base management system allows users outside the data center to access data bases. Thus the physical security of the data center is no longer adequate, and additional security measures must be implemented:

1. Terminal security restricts usage to those with proper identification.
2. Data can be encrypted before it is stored or transmitted.
3. The subschema controls the access and updates of data bases.
4. The type of request can be restricted by the location of the terminal.
5. Additional software can be written or purchased to enhance the security of installations with greater-than-normal needs.

The operating system has the controls to prevent concurrent updates to a file. However, the data base management system owns all of the data bases in an on-line environment. Therefore, it must institute controls similar to those existing in the operating system. If the environment is not controlled, two programs can concurrently update the same data base record and one of the updates will be lost. If a program abnormally terminates in an uncontrolled environment, another program may be operating with data that does not logically exist. Lock-out prevents the preceding problems from occurring. However, it may cause additional problems. Lock-out may cause a deadlock situation in which two programs each wait for a record owned by the other program. Since each program is waiting for a record owned by the other, neither will complete. The data base management system must detect deadlock and take corrective action. The controls may also lead to an increase in response time to the user. This is a price paid to ensure data integrity.

Data base management systems must be able to handle catastrophic conditions: failure of the operating system, the data base management system, an application program, or a data base. This is accomplished by making a back-up copy of the data bases and recording to a journal every significant event that occurs. When a catastrophe occurs, the back-up copy and the journal are used to restore the data base to the state that existed immediately before the failure. Catastrophies such as application program failures, operating system failures, data base management system failures, and data base failures are corrected with these tools. If the user or the application program generate incorrect data, this approach fails, since it cannot duplicate the decision-making capability that caused the data to be updated originally.

Users of an on-line data base management system depend upon short response time to perform their work productively. While response times of 30 seconds may seem very short, the overall loss of productivity is significant when multiplied by the large number of requests encountered. Response times of one to five seconds are typical in an on-line environment.

Since the on-line environment is so complex, additional tools are provided to computer operators to allow them to answer the questions of users when extraordinary events occur. Most of the data needed already exists in the data dictionary. The data dictionary can be extended with operating information about the on-line environment. The computer operator uses the data dictionary to determine the interaction between application programs, data bases, remote terminals, and users. Once this information is obtained, the operator contacts the data base administrator or the application programmer so they may take corrective action.

REVIEW QUESTIONS

9.1 Why is additional security needed in an on-line environment?

9.2 What is the most common form of security in an on-line environment?

9.3 Why is a password not displayed when entered by a user?

9.4 How is data secured to prevent unauthorized viewing when transmitted across communication lines?

9.5 What data base management system facility is used for security?

9.6 What additional form of terminal security can be used?

9.7 In an on-line environment, which major program owns the data bases?

9.8 In an uncontrolled environment, if two programs simultaneously update the same record, one change will be lost. Why?

9.9 In an uncontrolled environment, what problems may occur if other programs read a data base while one program updates the data base?

9.10 What is lock-out? Why is it used?

9.11 What problem can be caused by lock-out?

9.12 What is the purpose of a data base back-up?

9.13 What is a journal? How is it used?

9.14 If a user erroneously enters incorrect data, how is this corrected?

9.15 How is data integrity maintained when an application program abnormally terminates?

9.16 What action is required if the operating system or data base management system abnormally terminates?

9.17 If the secondary storage media is damaged, how is the data base repaired?

9.18 What are the two categories of individuals involved with the on-line operation of a data base management system?

9.19 Why is short response time important to the enterprise?

9.20 What tool can be employed by the computer operator as an aid in problem resolution?

9.21 What are two types of operations performed on data bases on a regular basis? Why are they performed?

DATA BASE IN THE WORKPLACE

Acme Widgets' Successful On-line Environment

Acme Widgets has a moderately active data base management system which processes about a million transactions a month. It is a continuous operation running 24 hours a day, 365 days a year. Both on-line and batch transactions are processed concurrently, with on-line transactions accounting for 85 percent of the volume. The number of transactions has increased by 15 percent monthly.

The types of transactions processed by Acme range from inquiries and updates of a personnel record-keeping system, to control of an assembly line. Many of the functions performed are critical to successful operation at Acme. For instance, if access to the Order Entry System is not available or not responsive, lost orders could result. Similarly, if transactions which control the assembly line cannot be executed or are not responsive, the assembly line is shut down, resulting in the idling of hundreds of workers and production facilities. The costs of these stoppages are measured in thousands of dollars per minute!

At Acme, three different methods are in place to ensure maximum availability and performance.

First, to minimize failures, Acme maintains two parallel data base management systems. One data base management system, called the test system, is used to test new data base management system software, all new application programs which are being developed, and maintenance to existing programs. When the vendor of the data base management system distributes new software maintenance or enhancements, they are applied and tested on the test system. The same process is followed for all programs written or modified by development teams. The second data base management system is reserved for the execution of production programs. No software is ever executed on the production system without having first been tested on the test system. This allows the vast majority of errors to be caught and corrected on the test system without affecting the users.

Second, a Control Section has been established to isolate failures. Before any program is scheduled for execution on the production system, it is executed under controlled conditions by the data base administrator, who ensures that it meets all installation standards. When a program successfully undergoes this process, the Control Section is notified and given the name of the program, the data bases accessed by the program, the phone number of the programmer responsible for the program, and the users who are authorized to execute the program. Since failures are often associated with changes to software, whenever any failure occurs, the Control Section analyzes the failure to determine whether it was caused by a program which has just been changed. When a failure of a critical program occurs, the programmer responsible is called to fix the problem. The programmer is on call 24 hours a day, 365 days a year.

Third, a Performance Section has been created at Acme to monitor the performance of the system. The Performance Section uses two different types of tools. One type of tool measures the performance of each program executed under the control of the data base management system, and it also measures the performance of the data base management system itself. If an application program performs poorly, the responsible programmer is notified and given the symptoms of the problem. If the data base management system is performing poorly, the systems engineer is notified and corrective action is suggested. The second performance tool updates a data base with performance data about the data base management system and each program which operates under its control. On a daily basis, every performance deviation is noted and investigated. Over a longer term, the Performance Section uses a fourth-generation language to determine performance trends and computer resource utilization. Trending information permits them to correct performance problems before they occur. Trends, coupled with the projected growth rate, permit them to project when new computer hardware is required. This permits Acme to install additional computer capacity immediately before existing capacity is exhausted.

These procedures have permitted Acme to develop a good service record with its users. While they have not eliminated all problems, the problems which occur are minimized and are corrected within a short time. Careful tuning and judicious purchases of computer hardware have permitted Acme to provide this service to its users at a very reasonable cost.

10

DATA BASE ADMINISTRATION

CHAPTER OBJECTIVES

Upon completion of this chapter, you should be able to:

1. Explain the need for a central control function for the data base management system embodied in the data base administrator
2. List the functions performed by the data base administrator
3. Explain the distribution of job responsibilities in organizations with a large data base staff

NEW WORDS AND PHRASES

data base administrator

data administrator

10.1 CHAPTER INTRODUCTION

Prior to the implemention of data base management systems, systems using conventional files were relatively easy to control and manage. A file, such as a payroll file, was physically stored in only one sequence. If the contents of a file needed to be changed, by reviewing the documentation, an analyst could determine the programs which accessed it. If data was needed in a sequence other than the stored sequence, data was sorted into the desired sequence before processing. Files tended to be owned by the department within the organization that paid for the development costs of the system that created the files. The world was much more simple then.

Data base management systems evolved which reduced data redundancy and improved compatibility between systems. The data base management system software which provided these functions became very complex. A technical specialist was needed who understood the complexities of the data base management system. This specialist coordinated the use of data bases and knew the physical storage sequence of the data base as well as the logical relationships which existed. The specialist knew which programs accessed the data base and the functions the programs were allowed to perform. These are the functions we think of when we speak of the data base administrator.

But the job of data base administrator is much larger in scope. Because of his or her central role, the data base administrator performs several additional functions. The data base administrator must provide design assistance to the teams performing new system development, to ensure that the data structures developed will provide adequate performance both at the time they are implemented and in the future. The data base administrator must understand the business enterprise and the data structures needed to support it. The data base administrator must understand the legitimate information needs of each user and must have a mechanism in place to ensure that these needs are satisfied. These functions are in addition to the technical functions normally associated with the data base administrator.

10.2 ORGANIZATIONAL STRUCTURE

Thus far, the data base administrator has been described in such a manner as to appear to be one person. It is more correct to speak of a data base administration function. The number of people performing the data base administration function depends upon the size of the installation and the functions actually performed. In small data processing shops, the data base administration function may be performed by one person as one of many responsibilities. In large installations, the data base administration function may be performed by many people. Some installations may provide a separate job title for each function performed within the data base administration function. Data security may be controlled through a *security officer* or a group called *security administration.* Planning may be performed by a *data base planner.* Data base design may be performed by a *data base analyst.* Schema definitions, subschema definitions, and tuning may be performed by a *data base technician.*

In some installations, a function may be established which is responsible for all of the data within an installation, not just the data stored using a data base management system. These people, responsible for planning and use of all data of the installation, are called *data administrators.* The basic functions performed by a data administrator and a data base administrator are the same, but the data administrator must manage a significantly larger amount of data. Throughout the remainder of the book, we will refer to the data base administrator.

The position of the data base administrator within the structure of an organization varies. In some installations, a person called the data base administrator may exist on each project development team (see Figure 10.1).

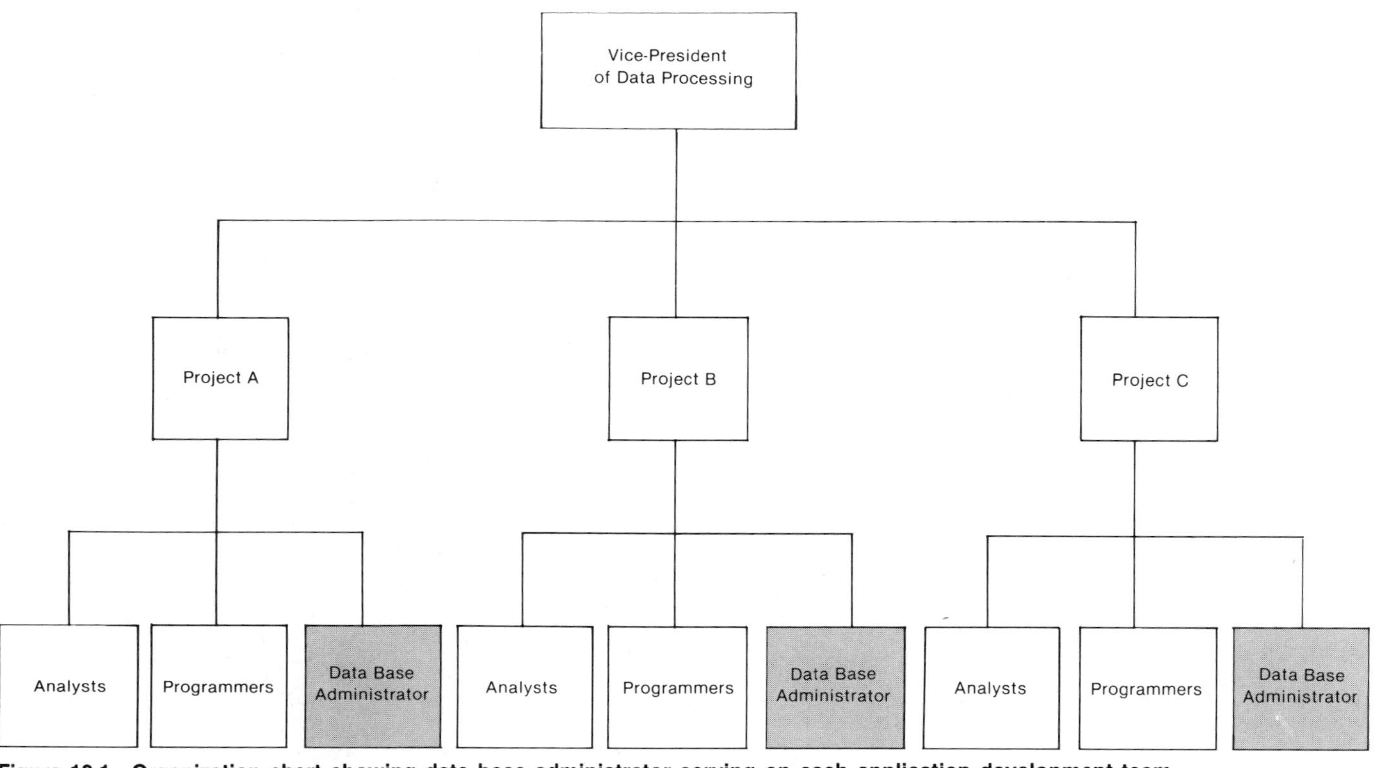

Figure 10.1 Organization chart showing data base administrator serving on each application development team.

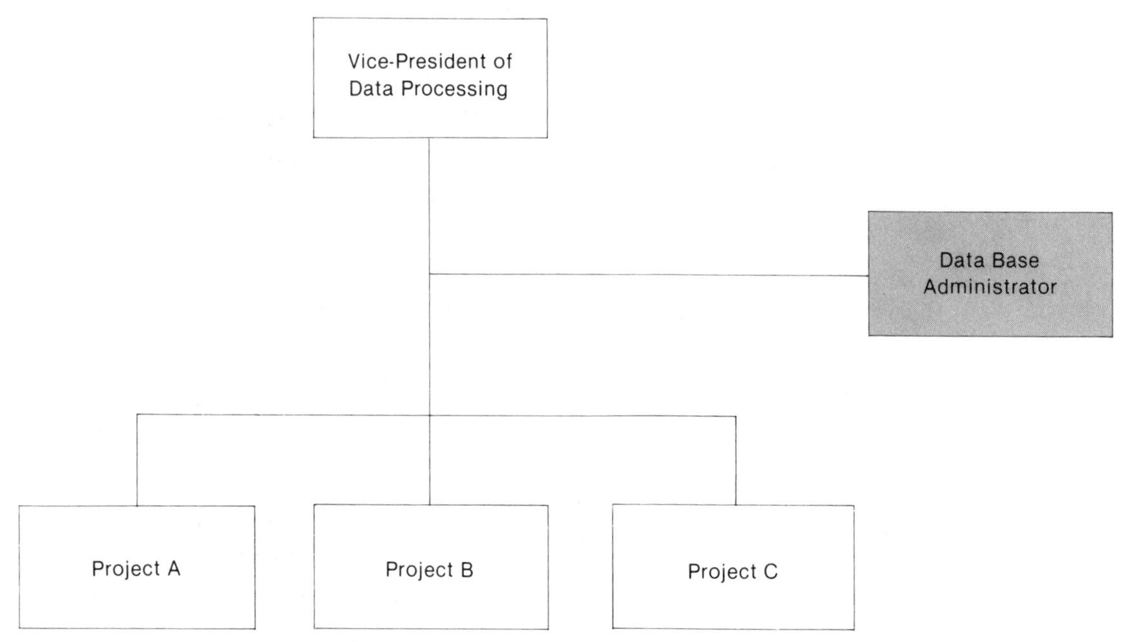

Figure 10.2 Organization chart showing data base administrator serving as a staff position to the Vice-President of Data Processing.

At such a low level of authority, it is very difficult to perform global planning, coordinate groups, and administer effective installation standards. The data base administration function may exist as a staff position to the manager or vice-president of data processing (see Figure 10.2). This is a much more desirable position because it provides a global perspective of the direction of the enterprise. At this level of authority, the data base administrator has the power to enforce standards and administrative decisions. These two positions represent the extremes of the placement of the data base administrator within the organizational structure. Most installations house the data base administration function somewhere between these two positions.

10.3 FUNCTIONS OF THE DATA BASE ADMINISTRATOR

The major functions of the data base administrator are to perform planning as it relates to the data base management system; to establish, publish, update, and enforce standards; to perform data base design; to implement data security procedures; to implement data integrity procedures; to coordinate users of the data base; to implement quality-control procedures; and to perform data base tuning and monitor performance.

Planning

The data base administrator is responsible for planning as it relates to the data resources of the enterprise. Planning includes the implementation of new systems, the modification of existing systems, and the administration necessary to ensure their success. The planning function of the data base administrator combines knowledge of the business of the enterprise with knowledge of the data base management system. The data base administrator must have a sense of the direction of the enterprise. This knowledge comes from creating a Business Systems Plan, a functional analysis, or a similar analysis of data flow within the enterprise, as described in Chapter 8. The data base administrator must also have a sense of the direction of data processing. This comes from reading trade journals and announcements of new hardware and software. By combining knowledge in these two areas, the data base administrator can provide input into management decisions about the sequence in which new applications should be installed to ensure functionality and minimize duplicated effort, and the purchase of software to facilitate work performed by the user and the Data Processing Department.

Example F7 illustrates the type of planning performed by the data base administrator.

Example F7
Planning by the Data Base Administrator at International Gismos

International Gismos is developing an inventory control system. A means is needed to account for gismos entering the inventory. In the diagnostic study, the inventory control project team designed a function to count gismos as they are brought into the warehouse after they leave the production line.

Through an analysis of future projects to be installed, the data base administrator knows that a production reporting system is scheduled to be installed after the inventory control system is completed. Through an analysis of the data flow of the enterprise, the data base administrator knows that a function identified for the production reporting project is to record the production of gismos and their movements to the warehouse (see Figure 10.3). However, the inventory control project has a higher return on investment and is scheduled to be developed first. The data base administrator, knowing the function to be provided by the production reporting system, suggests that one phase of the production reporting system be developed out of the proposed sequence, in order to capture the data needed by the inventory control project.

Although the two courses appear similar, they are not. The second proposal satisfies the needs of two projects: the inventory control project and the production reporting project. The first solution only satisfies the needs of the inventory control project. To ensure that redundant data is not generated, the solution proposed by the inventory control project would either need to be redesigned when the production reporting system was installed or scrapped altogether.

Thus, the knowledge of the data flow exhibited in this instance by the data base administrator has helped the overall productivity of the data processing department by preventing the development of a portion of a system that has a very short life expectancy.

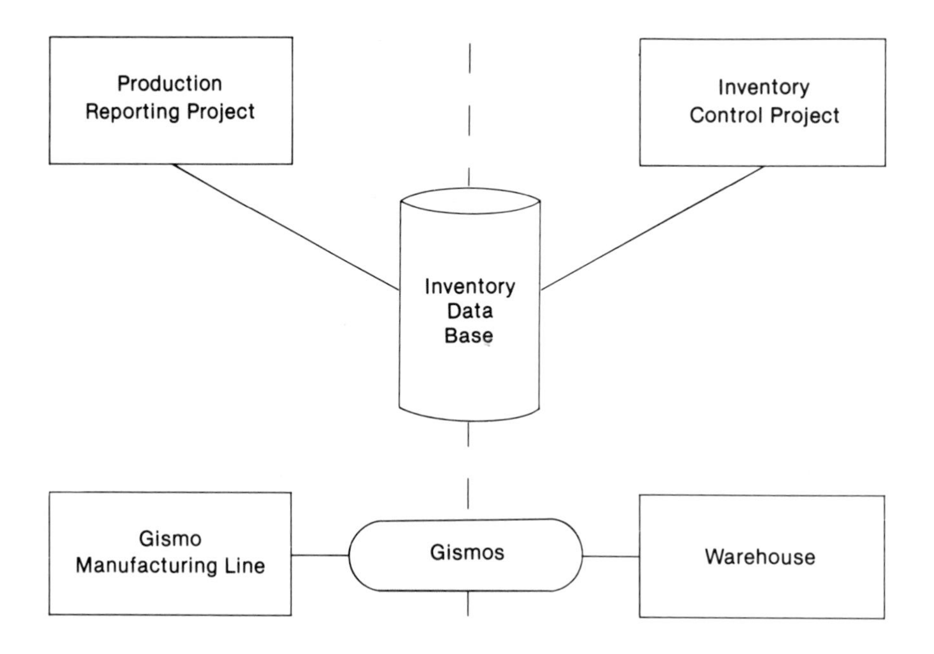

Figure 10.3 Production reporting project providing data for the Inventory Data Base.

By understanding the direction of the data processing industry, the data base administrator can prepare the Data Processing Department for new software products as they become available. Data base management systems are not unchanging. The vendors of data base management systems are constantly increasing the functions available, and other software vendors develop packages which complement data base management systems to provide additional services to the user.

For example, fourth-generation programming languages such as SQL are now in vogue. They allow manipulation of data by specification of what is to be performed, not how it is to be performed. Thus, less intensive training is required to produce results using nonprocedural fourth-generation languages than is required for lower-level languages. Many different fourth-generation languages are available. The data base administrator can select the software packages which are beneficial to the installation and schedule their implementation, allowing the enterprise to use state-of-the-art software to better service its users.

Standards

Since a data base management system is such a complex software package, standards must be established so that each group interfacing with the data base management system understands what is expected of it (see Figure 10.4). The data base administrator, playing a central role in the operation of a data base management system, is in a position to develop standards documenting the responsibilities of each interface group. The application developers must understand the naming conventions to be used, perfor-

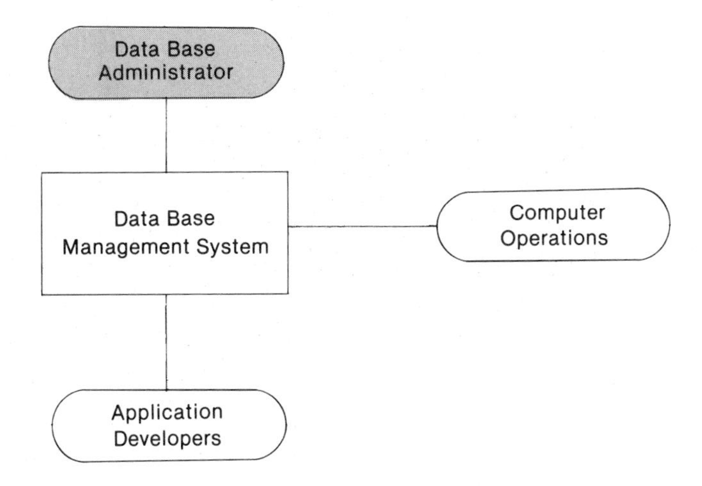

Figure 10.4 Data processing functions interfacing with a data base management system.

mance standards against which their programs will be measured, change control procedures, procedures to be followed during testing, procedures to be followed to install a production system, and procedures for the maintenance of the data dictionary. Computer operators must understand their responsibilities to all other users in both a development and a production environment.

As with any documentation, the standards developed by the data base administrator must be distributed to all involved groups and updated periodically to reflect the changes that occur over time. Documentation is often the least desirable work in data processing, and it is put off as long as possible. The data base administrator must guard against this happening.

Standards for the naming of data items, records, data bases, and programs are important. As we have stated, large-scale organizations operate thousands of programs. Naming conventions are used to ensure that two different objects will not be called by the same name. As you recall, the data dictionary is a repository for the names of all attributes identified within an enterprise throughout the life span of a data base management system. It ensures that everyone understands the name associated with an attribute. The data dictionary can also be used as a training aid when new people interact with the data.

Chapter 11 addresses the need for individuals from all levels of the organization to have access to the data needed to perform their jobs. With naming standards and a data dictionary in place, individuals can access the data dictionary to learn the names of the data items desired and the location where they are stored.

When used in this manner, the data dictionary is somewhat like a translation tool such as an English-to-French, French-to-English dictionary. The user may look up a data name such as MET-GRADE, and the data dictionary entry specifies which data base(s) contain MET-GRADE, the meaning of MET-

GRADE, and how it is derived. If authorized, the user may access the data bases containing MET-GRADE, viewing occurrences of the data and the data items with which it is used. The user may also access the data dictionary to determine the meaning of other data items used with MET-GRADE. This is not intended to be a fishing expedition. Instead, it may, for example, be used by a manager accessing data in a decision-making process.

Performance standards of the installation must be documented so that programmers know the objectives they must satisfy to meet the performance needs of the end user. Seemingly trivial processes such as the sequence in which an application program requests data from the data base management system can have an impact on performance. For instance, the use of locking and the desire for rapid response time are conflicting objectives. Rapid response time requires a program to have immediate access to desired records. Locking, while providing data integrity, prevents one application program from accessing a record currently used by another application program. The data base administrator must document performance standards which specify the maximum number of records that are locked between commit points in an application program. The maximum number of records that can be locked is determined by the number of records from a data base that are maintained by a program in a logical unit of work. The length of time the records can be locked must be defined. The length of time the records are locked is determined by the processing performed in the application program.

The length of time a record is locked may be related to the sequence of steps performed to update a data base record. Since an installation does not convert all conventional files to data bases en masse, an application program may access and lock a record from a data base and then search records in conventional files for additional data needed for processing. Thus, the data base record is locked for a longer time than necessary. The amount of time a data base record is locked can be reduced by searching conventional files to obtain data from which the data base will be updated first, then updating the data base record (see Figure 10.5). Programs should only lock records for the time required to update them. This sounds so logical, one would think an application programmer would always adhere to this rule. In reality, this is not always the case. The data base administrator must set and enforce standards of this nature.

Setting and enforcing program standards for performance reduces the number of occurrences of deadlock and update interference and also reduces the length of time of each occurrence. This, in turn, leads to more consistent performance for all users. Standards affecting locking are just one example of the kinds of performance standards to be documented. Performance standards are dependent upon the needs of the users within each installation and may vary from installation to installation. They may be directly related to the data base management system installed. The data base administrator must quantify the needs in terms of program performance specifications against which each program will be evaluated.

Figure 10.5
Lock data base records for as short a time as possible by requesting them only when you are prepared to update them.

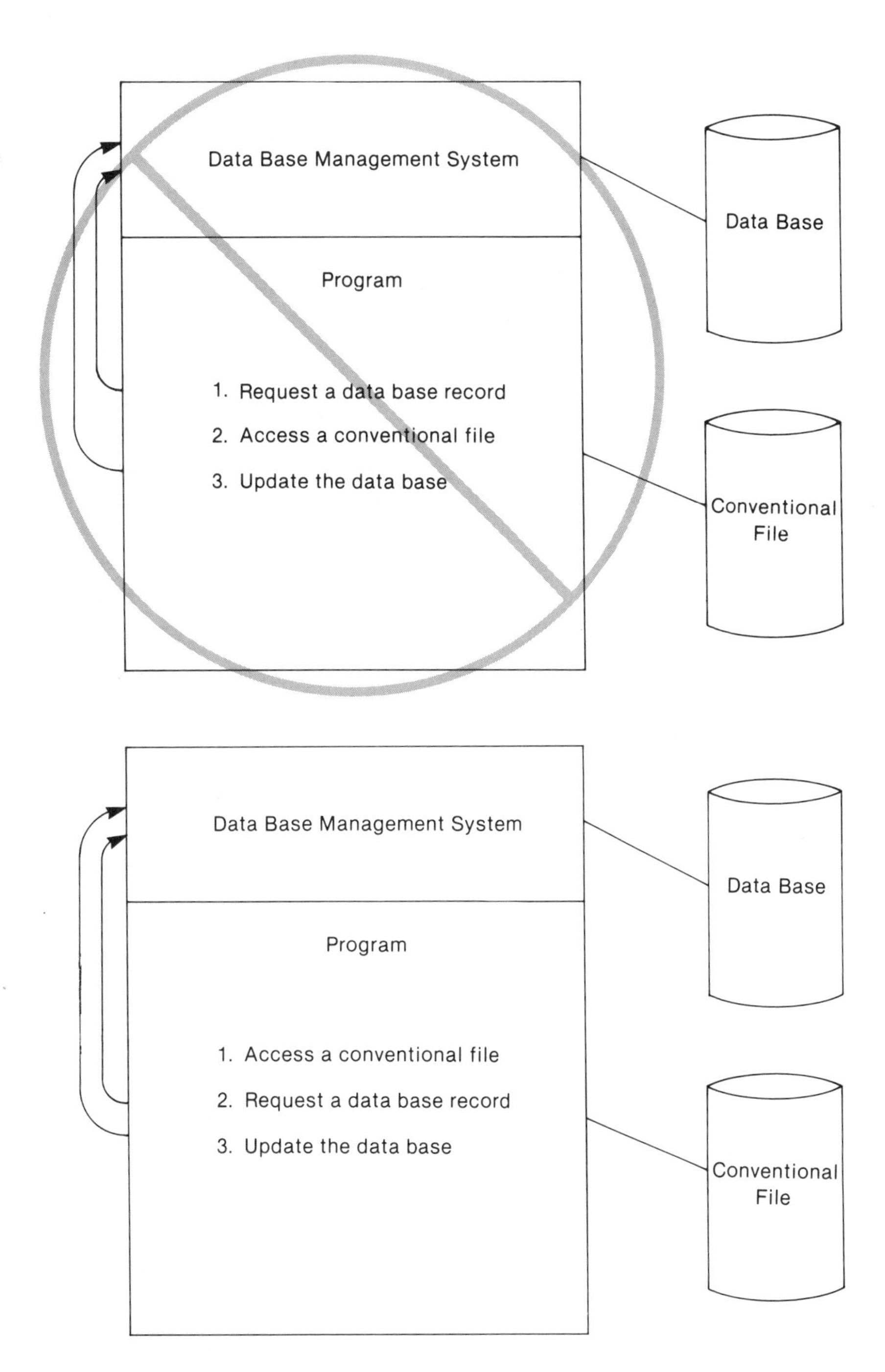

Data Base Design

Design assistance is provided to the application developers to ensure compatibility between existing and new applications and to provide performance which satisfies the needs of the end user.

When an application is developed, systems analysts determine the logical view of the data base necessary to support the application. The data base administrator analyzes the logical view for an application, using the data dictionary to determine what data already exists and in which data base it is located. The data base administrator determines what new data is to be captured, where it is to be placed, and any modifications necessary to existing data bases. As described in Chapter 8, this is an iterative process. When complete, the data base administrator creates new schema definitions and modifies existing definitions as required. Subschema definitions are created to reflect the logical views needed to support the design.

Data Security

Data for each end user to perform his or her function within the enterprise must be made available without providing the user more data than is necessary to perform that function. Using conventional files, each department had a sense of ownership of the data necessary to perform its role within the organization. Since data is shared among many departments when using data base management systems, each department no longer maintains exclusive ownership of the data. Each department, and each individual within a department, has different rights and responsibilities with regard to the data.

Administration of the data security function appears to be a mundane clerical task. This is not necessarily the case. Since data redundancy is minimized, the output from one operation is often input to the next, or the same data may be used by different users for different processes. It is sometimes difficult to determine where one user's responsibility ends and another's begins. Since users may have conflicting needs, an arbitration panel may be needed to resolve differences. The arbitration panel and the rules defining the circumstances under which access is granted must be firmly established. The panel should not have to be formed at the time a dispute occurs.

Example F8 illustrates the conflict over the access of data.

Example F8 Access-of-Data Conflict at International Gismos

At International Gismos, the data for each plant is partitioned because each is a profit center and is responsible for the profit made at that location. The corporate sales manager wishes to have access to the Inventory-Order Data Base to prioritize orders to provide better service to those customers that are served by many locations and have the greatest impact on the profits of the corporation. However, the local plant managers do not want this access to be granted because it will reduce customer service to individual customers served by each plant. If access by the corporate sales manager is granted, increased profits will be generated by the corporation but individual plants may experience a reduction in profitability. To resolve this conflict, the arbitration panel must meet and grant or deny access, basing its decision on rules established before the conflict arose.

The data base administrator must be aware of the needs of each department to ensure that each user has access to data to support its function within the enterprise. Yet, at the same time the data base administrator must deny access or authority to those individuals or departments that cannot demonstrate a need connected to their responsibilities.

Data Integrity

Procedures must be in place to ensure that data is sound—that data integrity exists. This means that when a failure occurs, each data base update process has either completed or has been rolled back to the status of a previous commit point (that is, no data is in a state where a partial update has occurred). Data base management systems, as part of their design specifications, preserve data base integrity. The design specifications generally include the period of time in which the data base management system is in control—during the active operation of an on-line or central version system, for example. Data base management systems cannot maintain data integrity for periods of time or in circumstances that they cannot control—batch operation of the data base management system or a hardware error on a secondary storage device on which a data base resides, for example.

The data base administrator is responsible for designing recovery systems for failures outside the control of the data base management system. This does not mean that the data base administrator writes software to support data base integrity. Rather, the data base administrator's responsibilities include a thorough knowledge of the recovery functions performed by the data base management system and the conditions when they are performed. Armed with this information, the data base administrator can use utility programs supplied by the vendor of the data base management system to perform the necessary data base recovery.

The data base administrator does not wait until a failure occurs to establish recovery procedures. At the time each data base is installed, the data base administrator begins contingency plans for failures:

1. Contingency plans start with a job that invokes the correct set of utilities to handle a worst-case failure.
2. Procedures to be followed by all who are involved in the recovery effort are documented.
3. A list of users affected by the failure is developed. Since users access a data base from their work stations instead of the computer room, they are unaware of specific problems which may occur. A damaged data base may severely affect their functions within the enterprise. Whenever a failure occurs, users of the data base must be notified and given an estimate of the time needed to repair the problem.
4. To ensure thorough and accurate preparation of recovery procedures, a failure is simulated. The recovery procedures are followed to determine whether they will function as designed or contain errors. It is important that the procedures be tested before an actual disaster occurs, for if they are incorrect, they can compound problems caused by the

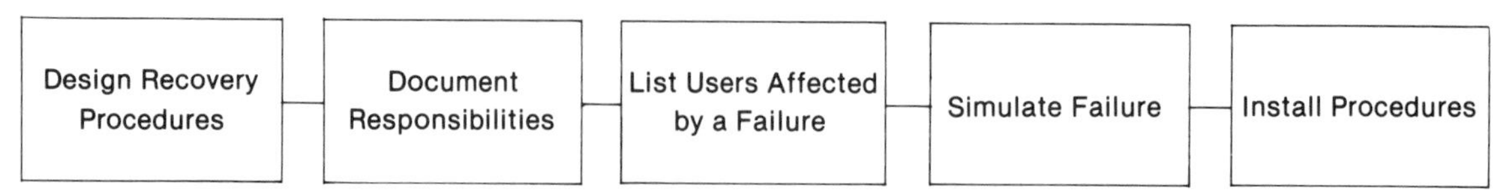

Figure 10.6
Steps taken to install data base recovery procedures.

original failure. Faulty recovery procedures elongate the time needed to recover the data base and in an extreme case may even prevent its recovery.

5. After recovery procedures have been thoroughly tested, they are installed with the hope they will never have to be used (see Figure 10.6).

Coordination

Although it seems natural that all employees would be interested in the survival of the enterprise that provides their jobs, it is not unusual for an employee to be interested only in a small segment of the business of the enterprise. Usually only in the smallest business do employees see the overall needs of the enterprise. More often, employees are segregated into individual departments such as order entry, accounts receivable, accounts payable, etc. Each department has an inflated sense of being, feeling the work it is doing is most important to the survival of the enterprise. It is in this environment that the data base administrator performs a role of coordinator. The data base administrator makes a number of decisions affecting the use of the data base, including the availability of, performance of, and access to a data base.

One of the primary concerns for the data base administrator is the availability of the data base to a user. To reorganize a data base, the data base administrator must ensure that no users are accessing the data base during the reorganization process. Many installations operate their data base management system 24 hours a day, 365 days a year. Each department may need access to a data base during a different time period during the day.

Example F9 illustrates the data base administrator's role as a coordinator.

Example F9
The Data Base Administrator as Coordinator, Part One

International Gismos is an international organization with its home office in Baltimore and sales offices in Honolulu and Lisbon. The home office contains a data base which is used to store messages. An employee may send a message via terminal to any other employee in any other sales office (see Figure 10.7). If the employee at the receiving location is unavailable, the message is stored in the data base at the home office until the recipient "picks up his mail."

With a common data base, there are conflicting requirements of the users. No matter what time of day is chosen for reorganization, some users will not to able to access the data during their prime shift of operation. The data base administrator will be looked upon with disfavor by one group of users. Which group of users should he or she choose?

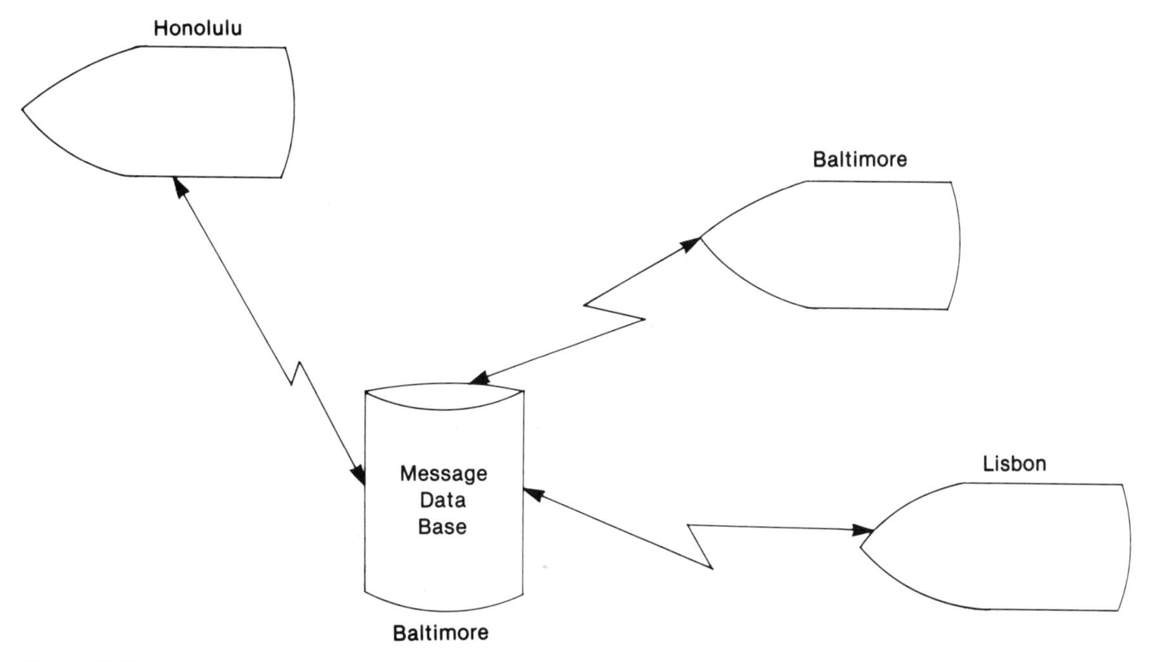

Figure 10.7 International Gismos' electronic mail system.

The role of coordinator extends to the design of the data base, which directly affects performance. Decisions made during the design process may affect one group of users more than another. No one design provides optimum performance to all users. The data base administrator must consider the needs of all users and select the design which benefits the greatest number of users or the most important users.

Example F10 is an illustration of this aspect of the data base administrator's role as a coordinator.

Example F10 The Data Base Administrator as Coordinator, Part Two

At International Gismos, salespeople access the Order Entry Data Base directly. They may enter a new order or correct an existing one. Each operation requires access to a specific order in the data base. The Shipping Department must scan all orders to develop a list of orders to be shipped next week and to generate picking lists for items to be shipped. This process requires a sequential scan of the data base to determine the orders and items to be shipped.

A number of design decisions will affect these users. The choice of a direct access method will speed the response for the user who directly accesses the data base. However, this will degrade performance for the user performing a sequential scan of the data base, since the data base must be accessed by its physical order. The choice of an indexed sequential access method will have the opposite effect: Since instead of using a hashing scheme the user directly accessing the data base must read one or more levels of indexes to determine the location of the record, performance is degraded. Users sequentially accessing the data base will have improved performance due to the proximity of records stored using the indexed sequential access method. A small blocking factor will improve performance for the user who directly accesses a record but degrade performance for the user performing a sequential scan of the data base. High blocking factors have the opposite effect. Creation of a secondary access path improves performance for those users of the path. However, the secondary access path must constantly be maintained, so it degrades performance of all users of the data base when data base maintenance is performed. With the high-density secondary storage devices now available, many data sets can be stored on one volume. Placement of the data sets on a volume has an effect on seek time to access a record in a data set.

Each of these decisions has a favorable effect on one set of users and a deleterious effect on another set of users.

The preceding example was simplified in that only two groups of users of the data were presented. In reality, many users access the same data. Each user does not have a constant data access pattern. The data access pattern can change by the functions performed. Access patterns may also vary by the day of the month, or even by the time of the day. The data base administrator must understand the global access patterns of a data base and make design decisions that have a beneficial effect on the greatest number of users and/or the most important users, while at the same time do not have a severely negative effect on any users of the system.

The data base administrator must understand the access requirements of each user. A security mechanism must be established to grant access to authorized users of data while denying access to those without legitimate reasons. This process was presented earlier in this chapter.

Example F11 shows that the data base administrator not only acts as a coordinator between user departments but also within the Data Processing Department. In data processing departments divided by application, each project team sees only one part of the picture. Each team may request changes to a data base to satisfy individual needs. The data base administrator must collect these requests, determine how they fit into the long-range plan, and determine the best method to effect the change. When two project teams must modify the same data base, the data base administrator coordinates the changes to ensure that they do not conflict with each other and to ensure a minimal disruption to the user community as changes are being made.

Example F11 The Data Base Administrator as Coordinator, Part Three

At International Gismos, the inventory control project team has a request from the Inventory Department to capture additional data about each inventory item. Customers place orders for parts but request that the part not be shipped until some specified time in the future. This means that the Inventory Department has inventory on hand that is committed to be sold. Therefore, the Inventory Department cannot determine the reorder point and amount by

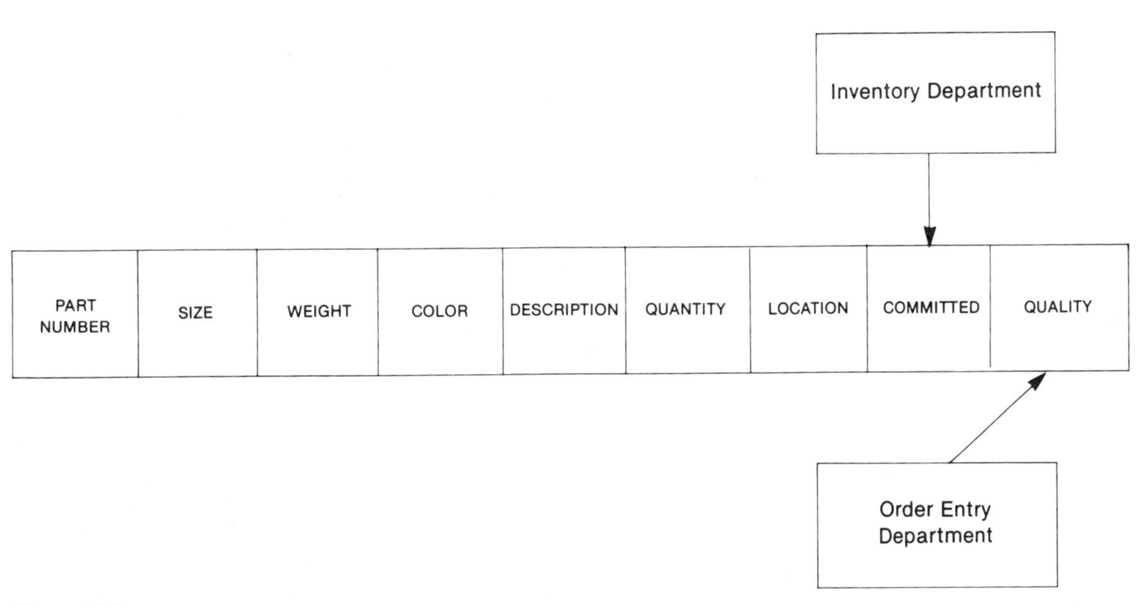

Figure 10.8 Two different application groups modifying the Inventory Data Base.

counting the number of items in stock. The Inventory Department needs to know the quantity in inventory committed to be sold, so they may send orders to the Production Department with sufficient lead time to prevent a stock-out.

Concurrently, the order status project team has a request from the Order Entry Department to determine the quantity of an item in inventory that is not first quality, so that these items can be sold at a lower price (see Figure 10.8).

In this situation, two different project teams need to make changes to the Inventory Data Base. The data base administrator considers the requests from both project teams and arranges the changes to be made at the same time. By coordinating the change, the data base administrator has reduced the interruption of service to the user.

Quality Control

The quality-control function of the data base administrator ensures that individual programs as well as the data bases perform satisfactorily. Since the data base administrator must define the schema and the subschema to the data base management system before a new application can be installed, the data base administrator acts as a funnel for the installation of new applications (see Figure 10.9). This places the data base administrator in a position to act as a quality-control point for all new applications.

When a new application is ready to be installed, the development team responsible for the application notifies the data base administrator. The data base administrator performs a series of inspections. Both valid and invalid data are presented to the application program to ensure that it performs properly under both conditions. Responses to the users are examined to ensure that they are correct and "user friendly." The data dictionary entries relating to the application are examined to ensure that they are correct and complete. Run documentation for the application is reviewed to ensure that

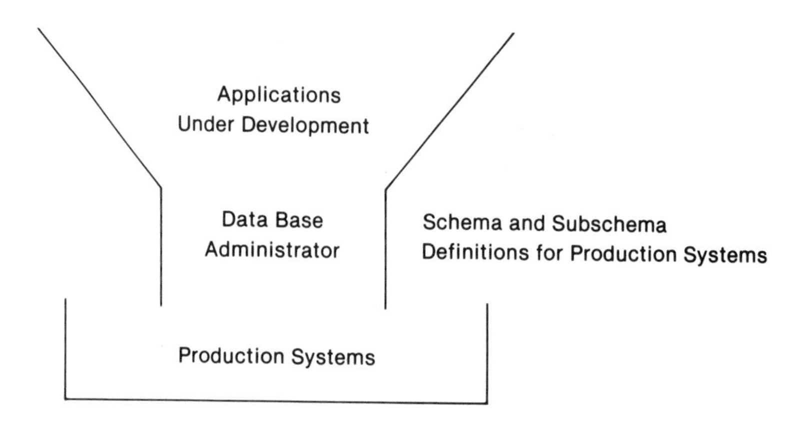

Figure 10.9
The data base administrator acts as a funnel through which all development applications must pass before going into production.

it adheres to standards. Performance measurements are taken during the quality-control inspection to ensure that it is within documented performance standards.

Only after the application passes the quality-control inspection is it placed into production. This ensures that the application is consistent with the minimum standards of quality required by the enterprise.

Tuning and Performance

The data base administrator is responsible for the tuning of the data bases and the identification of performance problems in application program design. Tuning of data bases includes manipulation of the physical structures, without destroying needed data relationships, to ensure maximum performance to the greatest number of users. The manner in which a transaction performs is determined by three major factors: the performance of the data base management system software, the data base design, and the application program design. Systems engineers monitor performance of the data base management system software to ensure that it performs optimally. The data base administrator monitors performance statistics concerning the data base design and the application design. Since rapid response time is important to the effectiveness of the user, the data base administrator must monitor performance statistics not only when a new application is installed, but also throughout the meaningful life of an application.

When a new application is installed, the data base is usually at the smallest size that will exist throughout the life of the application. At this time, the data base is stored using the optimum configuration in secondary storage. As time passes, the data base increases in size and records become dispersed throughout the secondary storage. By monitoring performance statistics generated by the data base management system, the data base administrator can determine when records have become sufficiently dispersed within secondary storage to warrant a reorganization of the data base. With continual monitoring, the data base administrator can predict periodic intervals in which a reorganization of the data base will improve performance. With this knowledge, the data base administrator can schedule data base reorganizations at fixed intervals.

Monitoring of performance statistics also permits the data base administrator to determine whether the global access patterns of the data base are changing. Perhaps, due to business fluctuations, one user of a data base has a lower access rate than originally predicted or lower than historical patterns. By the same token, another user may have a higher access rate. Due to these changes in access patterns, the file organization, block size, or secondary keys need to be altered to improve performance. This is another responsibility of the data base administrator.

As the data base grows over time, or as new applications are added that access a common data base, access strategies that were efficient when an application was installed degrade in performance. By monitoring performance statistics, the data base administrator can determine the applications with degrading performance and take corrective action before the users' activities are affected.

Data base applications, as do all other applications, tend to change over time. Even if change control procedures within an organization are followed, many small changes, made over a long period of time, can significantly affect the performance of an application. Since each change is so small, the global impact of many changes may go unnoticed. The data base administrator is in a key position to monitor performance statistics of an application and compare the statistics with the historical performance of the application. The data base administrator can determine, at any time, whether the application is changing. The data base administrator can then initiate appropriate corrective action.

10.4 SUMMARY

The role of a data base administrator is an important one in the successful operation of a data base management system. Initially, the data base administrator was a technical specialist. However, as data base management systems supported more application systems and more users, the data base administrator's role grew to include administrative functions.

The data base administrator performs those planning functions which are associated with the data base management system, such as giving input to management regarding the sequence in which new applications are developed and the acquisition of supportive software. The data base administrator writes standards affecting the data base management system, including naming standards, performance standards, and standards for the maintenance of the data dictionary. The data base administrator provides data base design assistance for new applications and performs the schema and subschema definitions. The data base administrator is responsible for data base security and must provide access to data for those users who have a legitimate need. The data base administrator is responsible for data base integrity and, as such, must understand the integrity functions built into the data base management system software and develop procedures to handle functions not provided. The data base administrator also must act as a coordinator and establish procedures to satisfy users' needs in a manner that provides the best overall use of the data base management system for the enterprise.

In small data processing installations, one person may perform all data base administrator functions. In large-scale installations, many individuals are required to perform these functions.

REVIEW QUESTIONS

10.1 How many people are required to staff the data base administration function?

10.2 Where does the data base administrator fall on the organizational ladder?

10.3 What is the difference between a data administrator and a data base administrator?

10.4 What is the nature of the planning function performed by the data base administrator?

10.5 Why does the data base administrator perform a planning function?

10.6 What types of standards must the data base administrator establish?

10.7 What is the data base administrator's role with respect to data base design?

10.8 What role does the data base administrator have with respect to data security?

10.9 How does the data base administrator ensure data base integrity?

10.10 Why is it desirable for the data base administrator to act as a quality-control point?

10.11 What are the data base administrator's responsibilities with respect to performance?

DATA BASE IN THE WORKPLACE

The Data Base Administration Function at Acme Widgets

Acme Widgets has made the transition from a predominately batch operation to a predominately on-line operation in less than a decade. When they first ventured into data base management systems, one person performed all of the tasks necessary to support the data base management system, from the systems engineer function to the data base administration function. Now, the systems engineer function has been separated and placed in a different functional area. The data base administration function is currently performed by 13 people.

The staff of 13 is supporting over 120 people in the development of 15 active projects, including 5 large projects, one of which will require 130,000 hours to develop. To support these development teams, the staff has been divided into four functional areas: data base design, data base technical, data dictionary support, and data modeling. These four areas are directed by one individual who has the title data base administrator.

Each development team develops the logical view of data to support each function of the system. They do not provide the physical data base structures. The data base administrator has found that when each team designs its own data base, it encourages data redundancy and discourages the sharing of data between applications. The data designers analyze the data requirements of each function of the system, normalize the data, develop the physical structure to store the data, and superimpose the logical structures on the physical structure. The design of the physical data bases takes into account the access patterns of the data. Functions which have short response time requirements are designed first, to ensure that they are responsive. Functions which have less critical response time requirements are designed last.

The designers review the data elements required by the system and use the data dictionary to determine whether the data currently exists or must be created. If data does not exist, modeling information is used to determine where the data is to be stored.

The design process is aided by having a data architecture in place. Systems which are needed to support the business processes are planned for well in advance. Therefore, as each new system is installed, the designers know how the current system is related to future systems, and redesign efforts are kept to a minimum. A concentrated effort is placed on developing foundation data bases (called subject data by James Martin). On occasion, a user has had specific requirements which have not clearly fit into the foundation data bases. When this has occurred, a data base has been created which contains planned redundant data to satisfy these requirements. The data bases created for special cases have been kept to a minimum in order to satisfy the long-range goals of minimal data redundancy and shared data.

The data base designers ensure that each development team updates the data dictionary to include the definitions for the data elements added by their system, and they also ensure that the definitions adhere to the procedures established by the data dictionary coordinator. Acme has become so large, it is impossible for one individual to know everything about all of the data bases. Maintenance of the data dictionary data base is important so that other designers may share the data.

At one time, individuals performed both data base design and technical functions. However, they became so involved in the technical details, they did not have the time to support the design effort. Therefore, the functions were divided and given to different individuals. Now, the data base technicians are responsible for monitoring and tuning the data bases, aiding those having technical problems, and installing data base software tools which aid the design, recovery, and tuning of the data bases. If a data base is damaged, it is the data base technicians' responsibility to recover the damage in as short a time period as possible to minimize the impact on the user. While the data base designers' responsibility is to implement new data bases, the technicians' responsibility is to make changes to existing data bases to permit new functions to be added to a system or to change the physical structure to improve performance. Since the data base technicians have a higher skill level, they are responsible for aiding programmers in solving data base problems.

Since Acme is developing so many projects at the same time, it has had difficulty obtaining people with the necessary experience. Although there are enough people in the marketplace with third-generation programming language skills, there is a severe shortage of people trained in the DML for Acme's data base management system. To keep pace with development, the data base administrator has taken a novel approach.

The data base administrator has created a new position for a data base technician who has extensive experience in the DML. Acme has also hired four programmers who do not have DML skills. The programmers write all of the program instructions except the DML. The data base technician writes the DML commands for all four programmers, in addition to her regular work. She spends about half of her time writing the DML commands and half performing her normal duties.

This innovation by the data base administrator has enabled Acme to continue development despite a shortage of skilled people. In addition, the new programmers are gaining on-the-job experience with the data base management system, and within a year they will not need the help of the data base technician; they themselves will have the skills that Acme needs.

The data dictionary coordinator is responsible for developing data dictionary procedures and providing data dictionary tools necessary to support the data base designer. This includes implementing the data dictionary, ensuring that users have adequate education to use the dictionary, and establishing the naming conventions used to name the data elements. Standard naming conventions are used to ensure that synonyms and homonyms are eliminated, or at least kept to a minimum. Since each data element has a unique name, the data dictionary is used to generate data names for COBOL programs. This is an automated process which reduces the coding by a programmer; the same data name is used for the same data element in every COBOL program. This facilitates not only new development but also program maintenance.

The data dictionary has been expanded beyond its designed use to store information gathered during data modeling. The data dictionary contains both existing data elements and modeling information which is made available to the data base designers. The data dictionary system is an inventory system for the data resource of the enterprise. It has become even more important with the recent creation of an Information Center (see the Data Base in the Workplace section at the end of Chapter 11) in which users, with fourth-generation programming languages, directly access and analyze data to satisfy their own business needs and develop ad hoc reports.

The person performing data modeling is responsible for working with each phase of the business to determine the data required to support the business processes and to develop a data model. The data model identifies business functions and the data to support each function. The person performing the modeling develops the relationship between data classes. (This terminology is somewhat different from that used in Chapter 8, but the functions are equivalent to the entity-relationship model). This person is also responsible for developing the data architecture, which identifies which data elements must be created before other data can be created. The data model and data architecture are used to prioritize development of applications which are needed to support the business functions.

The data model and data architecture are also used to aid the designers in determining which data should be created out of sequence in order to satisfy the needs of the system. When data is created out of sequence, it may not be in final form, but redesign when that system is finally developed is minimized. The data model and data architecture provide management and the development teams with direction to show them where they are now and where they are going in the future.

Establishing a data model and data architecture in tune with the plans of the business has allowed Acme to concentrate on the systems which support the functions that meet the business's needs. This has permitted Acme to minimize unplanned redundant data while at the same time allowing Acme to develop those areas of the business which have the highest impact on profits.

11

CURRENT TRENDS

CHAPTER OBJECTIVES

Upon completion of this chapter, you should be able to:

1. List the problems which remain after the installation of an integrated data base management system
2. State the type and volume of information used in the decision-making process
3. Explain how the Information Center improves the overall productivity of the enterprise
4. Explain how decision support systems aid management in making decisions to support the business of the enterprise

NEW WORDS AND PHRASES

information pyramid
Information Center
decision support systems

11.1 CHAPTER INTRODUCTION

The installation of a data base management system in and of itself does not provide a solution to all of the information needs of the enterprise. In Chapter 1, we discussed the disadvantages of data base management systems—their large size, complexity, high cost, increased hardware requirements, and high impact of failure. Of particular importance are the short supply and high cost of individuals trained in the operation of data base management systems. This in turn causes long delays between the time a user places a request for information and the time the information is provided.

In the past, systems were installed to automate the operational flow of business processes instead of providing a basis for high-level management decision making. As each operational system is installed, the Data Processing Department must commit more and more resources to the maintenance of programs. Users find increasingly new ways to request data to solve business problems. Each new request from a user adds to the ever-increasing backlog of work for the Data Processing Department. Problems such as these have caused the Data Processing Department to be always searching for new techniques to provide better service to its users.

In Chapter 8, we described how the data base design process starts with conceptual design, using a top-down approach that begins with the management of the enterprise. Once the data is captured in the data base, it is useful to more than just the operational processes of the business. The current direction in the use of data base management systems is to ensure that captured data is immediately available to all authorized employees, at all levels within the enterprise, in a format which addresses their information needs. Once the foundation systems are in place, each user who demonstrates a need can access data from a data base using the facilities of the Information Center and build decision support systems.

In this chapter, we will discuss the current direction of the industry. First, the information pyramid will be used to describe the way information is used within a business. Second, we will present the current information problems. Finally, we will show how data processing departments are meeting the challenge.

11.2 CURRENT DIRECTION

Information Pyramid

The information pyramid is known by a variety of names in data processing literature. It is an example of the single record concept, in which data is placed in machine-readable form once and is used in many different ways afterward. The information pyramid shows the types of decisions made in an organization, the level at which the decision is made, and its relation to the volume of data needed to support the decision (see Figure 11.1).

The lowest-level decision is a functional decision which affects the operation of the enterprise. A second-level decision is a supervisory decision made by someone in a lower management position. A third-level decision is a tactical decision made by middle management. The highest-level decision is a strategic decision made by top management. Each higher level of decision making is supported by a smaller volume of data from within the enterprise and larger volumes of data from outside the enterprise.

Thus far, we have concentrated in this book on operational applications used to accomplish the day-to-day business of an organization. Functional decisions which support the operations of the enterprise are supported by large volumes of information. At a manufacturing business this includes such functional areas as generating picking slips for orders to be shipped, maintaining an accurate inventory of finished goods and raw materials, and so on. But data which is entered to maintain an automated means of tracking

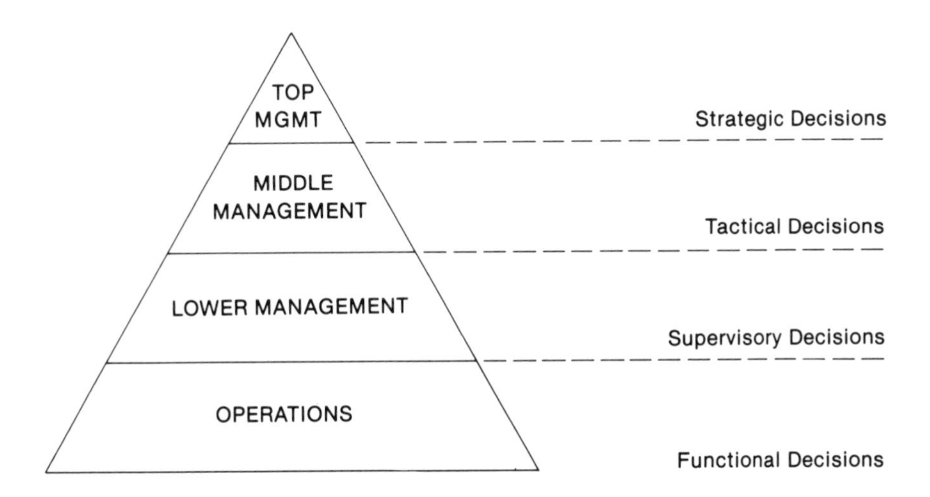

Figure 11.1
Information pyramid.

an order may not only be used for that purpose. It may be used at all levels of the organization to allow managers to make informed decisions. The same data captured to support functional processes, when properly summarized and presented, provides a foundation for supervisory, tactical, and strategic planning to be performed.

Data captured to support business functions provides a basis for making supervisory decisions when properly summarized. Supervisory decisions plan for business operations days to weeks in the future. Even though supervisory data is used to make decisions about the future, the data supporting these decisions specifies events which are known will occur in the future—for example, the number of orders that will be shipped the next week. Large volumes of data may be summarized into a smaller mass to provide information to be used by lower management to perform supervisory functions that are relatively short term, such as scheduling of personnel. For example, a supervisor determines the total number of orders to be shipped next week and determines the number of employees to be scheduled, by day, to meet the shipping requirements. Or, by determining the levels of items in inventory, the schedule of the production line can be altered to manufacture items which have run low unexpectedly. In both of these decisions, data is captured for one purpose (to automate the shipping of orders or to determine adequate levels of inventory), and is used for an additional purpose (to schedule employees or to schedule a production line).

Middle management is responsible for making tactical decisions to support the goals specified by upper management. Tactical planning is aimed at what will occur months to two years in the future. Tactical decisions are based upon a further summarization of the huge volume of data from the operational level (to determine what has occurred in the past), in conjunction with data captured about conditions outside the enterprise. With this data, middle management makes tactical decisions for allocating resources in line with the strategic goals of the enterprise.

Order information may be captured for product lines, such as for 50-centimeter gismos, for 100-centimeter gismos, and so on. Historical data for orders can be examined over a period of time to determine trends which occur. Order data is again summarized for longer periods of time, such as months. For example, if the number of 50-centimeter gismos sold shows a decline for the previous year, and if data captured about the economy shows declining consumer purchasing power, middle management can either discontinue the manufacture of 50-centimeter gismos or make a decision not to invest additional capital to modernize that manufacturing line. The tactical decision is supported by a further summarization of order entry data and data about the state of the economy.

Top management is responsible for making strategic decisions which will affect the business two to five years in the future. Strategic decisions are based upon a still further summarization of operational data and even more data about the forces outside the business. Again, historical data is summarized to show trends. Upper management uses this data as a basis for the strategic plan and sets the long-range goals and objectives of the business—for example, whether to expand or contract, merge, or make acquisitions. Decisions at this level are based on trends.

Order entry data and profitability data may be summarized by product line. For example, the trend can be examined to determine whether gismos or widgets show increasing or decreasing order patterns and the contribution of each to the profits of the enterprise. When coupled with an analysis of the economy and industry trends for a product line, top management decisions can be made. The enterprise may buy additional manufacturing facilities for gismos or may decide to sell all manufacturing facilities for gismos and acquire facilities for a new product line.

Current Information Problems

Today there is a crying need for information at all levels of the organization in order to make informed business decisions. However, enterprises are struggling to install foundations systems—systems which are at the base of the information pyramid.

Most application development is performed using third-generation procedural languages such as COBOL. These languages are very formalized and require a significant expenditure of the application programmer's time to develop nontrivial programs. Within the industry, a programmer in a third-generation language is not considered to have mastered his craft until he has obtained one or two years experience, for a programmer must understand the operation of a data base management system and learn how to use the data manipulation language efficiently, in addition to learning third-generation languages. This requires even more time and is one of the reasons for the shortage of people with the qualifications to develop applications using a data base management system.

The net effect of the current state of the industry is long application backlogs in data processing departments. During development, the user knows his or her own needs but has difficulty communicating them to the developers. Although the Data Processing Department provides report layouts showing the specifications for the report, it is difficult for the user to place the specifications in the context of the business operation. It is not unusual to go through several iterations of the report design to arrive at a format which the user finds acceptable. The Data Processing Department concentrates its effort on the projects which have the highest return on investment and the highest visibility to management. Given the current manpower and development tools, some data processing departments have backlog requests that will take decades to fill! The Data Processing Department is getting farther and farther behind. It cannot satisfy requests which have a smaller return on investment or that will provide additional input into the decision-making process, even if they require minor resources to complete. Maintenance of existing programs and one-time requests by users add to the backlog of work for the Data Processing Department. The backlog has created an extensive latent demand—that is, a demand for service which exists but is not visible because users feel their requests will not be satisfied in a timely manner.

Users are becoming frustrated. They have a function to perform for the enterprise, but the Data Processing Department will not give them the tools they need to perform their jobs. At the same time, users are becoming more sophisticated. They purchase time from time-sharing services and develop their own applications. This satisfies individual users but places valuable data outside the control of the enterprise, where it cannot be shared by other users.

Even though much of the new development is geared toward systems which provide information to operational and supervisory users, systems are not being installed fast enough. When systems are installed, they leave the user wanting more. There is a shortage of information upon which to make decisions at all levels of the enterprise. This is especially true for middle and upper management. The time is right for a change from past practices. The Information Center is one such change.

Information Center

IBM has developed a concept called the **Information Center** to aid the Data Processing Department in reducing the backlog of requests and providing the user the information needed for decision making (and also selling more IBM equipment!). The Information Center allows users to write the programs needed to satisfy their requests, given the appropriate tools by the Data Processing Department.

When a user has a need for information, he or she approaches the Data Processing Department with a request which specifies the data to be manipulated and the end result to be achieved. The Data Processing Department evaluates the request. If the request requires a procedural language, access to high volumes of data over long periods of time, and critical response times, the Data Processing Department processes the request according to traditional procedures. If the request can be accomplished with a nonprocedural language using smaller volumes for data for shorter periods of time without critical response times, the user is scheduled to use the Information Center.

When the user is scheduled to use the Information Center, the Data Processing Department provides several services, including providing the user access to the necessary tools, providing the data from which the results are determined, providing the back-up and recovery of the data, ensuring appropriate levels of security, and providing adequate training to perform the task. Using the tools provided, the end users develop their own applications and have the ability to improve the overall productivity of the enterprise.

Both hardware and software tools are available to the user of the Information Center. The user's application determines the type of hardware needed. The cathode ray tube is the traditional type of terminal used for access to data. This permits the user to interact with data and software stored on a mainframe. Graphic terminals, with or without color, are available if needed for Information Center applications.

If the user requires summarized data transmitted from a large mainframe, a spreadsheet, document handling, or electronic mail, a microcomputer may be used. Due to the decline in the cost of microcomputers and the increase in their capabilities, they are replacing "dumb" terminals. Microcomputers are appearing on the desktops of people from clerks to high-level corporate decision makers. The microcomputers are linked to large-scale computer systems. They have access to the data of the central computers. A decision maker can request selected data from a data base on a central computer and have it transmitted to the microcomputer. If direct interaction with the host is desired, the microcomputer performs much like a CRT. If the communication line between the mainframe and the microcomputer fails, or if the user does not have a need for the facilities of the mainframe, the microcomputer can be operated stand-alone. The microcomputer can then manipulate the data to supply the decision maker with the information on which to base decisions. Even when operating stand-alone, it can be used to do modeling, process data stored in the relational data base management system format, analyze data, and return graphic output.

One of the most popular software packages on the microcomputer is the spreadsheet, which permits the user to analyze data in a tabular format. The derivation of the value for each cell of the matrix is specified by the user. The spreadsheet is an effective way of making a decision when the user has several alternative courses of action but does not know which provides optimum results.

With spreadsheet software, the user has the ability to label columns and rows with meaningful names such as LINE or ENERGY (see Figure 11.2). Each cell of the matrix may contain data entered by the user or data computed by a formula expressing the relationships between cells. For example, in Figure 11.2, the formula for the cost of producing 150-centimeter gismos (cell E1) is:

Figure 11.2
Spreadsheet with initial values in all columns.

	A	B	C	D	E
	Line	*Production*	*Energy*	*Labor*	*Cost*
1	150	1000	19	1.0	179.50
2	200	2500	43	.5	685.00
3	300	1700	23	.70	304.30
4	700	4900	24	1.4	1161.30
5	900	1300	33	.9	323.70
6					2653.80

```
E1=(B1*C1*.0055) + (B1*D1*.075)
```

This formula causes the number of 150-centimeter gismos produced (B1) to be multiplied by the number of units of energy required to produce one unit (C1) and that product to be multiplied by .0055, the per-unit cost of energy. This product is added to the product of the number of 150-centimeter gismos produced (B1) times the number of hours needed to produce a unit (D1) times the labor rate per unit, .075. Each time any number in column B, C, or D changes, the values in column E are recomputed. Since the user knows the shipping requirements of the customer, the amount produced may be varied one customer at a time to determine which pattern will both satisfy the customer and also provide the minimum production cost. In Figure 11.3, the user changed the number of 200-centimeter gismos and the number of 900-centimeter gismos produced. All cost values in column E are recomputed.

The user may make multiple changes, noting the effects of each change. This allows the user to measure the effects of one change versus another.

This is one of the Information Center tools available to the user to make functional and supervisory decisions. Another Information Center tool is software which can be manipulated by users with minimal training. Fourth-generation programming languages are most often used in the Information Center. These languages enable the user to describe what is to be accomplished without describing how it is to be accomplished. Fourth-generation programming languages include facilities for generating reports in a format specified by the user, developing graphic displays to determine trends, and developing spreadsheets which allow the user to manipulate numeric data in a tabular format.

Figure 11.3
Spreadsheet with revised values.

	A	B	C	D	E
	Line	*Production*	*Energy*	*Labor*	*Cost*
1	150	1000	19	1.0	179.50
2	200	1800	43	.5	493.20
3	300	1700	23	.70	304.30
4	700	4900	24	1.4	1161.30
5	900	1400	33	.9	241.34
6					2379.64

A specialist in the Information Center makes the necessary data available to the user. The user may be given access to a production data base or may be given a copy of the data from a production data base. There are many reasons for providing the user with a copy of the data instead of permitting the user access to the production data base. First, it may be dangerous to provide access to a user! Since the user is inexperienced and is learning by doing, an accident could destroy data critical to the operation of the enterprise. Second, the data access patterns of the Information Center user were not considered by the data base administrator when designing the physical data base. Direct access of the production data base may provide poor response time to the Information Center user, or worse, may degrade the response time of production users of the data base. Third, when data is obtained from the production data base, the user is provided the minimum subset of the data which will satisfy the problem at hand. This, again, improves performance by reducing the amount of data manipulated by the user. A subset of the data may also be provided to the user due to security reasons. Fourth, the means in which data is stored may be altered before data is provided to the user. Hierarchical and network data base management systems are used in a production environment due to their high performance characteristics. When data is provided to the user, it may be stored in a relational data base management system to simplify the access for the user. For these reasons, the user is usually provided with a copy of the data needed to support the project. If the user's request is such that the data must be current, the data processing specialist provides a current copy of the production data to the user on a periodic basis.

Since the user's primary background is in the business of the enterprise, he or she may not be acquainted with the necessity to perform periodic back-ups of the data, or may not know how to restore the data from an appropriate back-up copy after a failure occurs. In an attempt to allow the user to work on the solution to a business problem and not worry about the internal functions of the computer, the Data Processing Department makes periodic back-ups of the users' data and will restore data from the proper back-up if necessary.

Even though individual users are accessing data to solve a specific problem, one user may not be authorized to access data obtained by another user. The Data Processing Department must ensure that appropriate levels of security exist whether the user accesses a copy of the production data base or the production data base itself.

The issue of security becomes even more critical with the use of microcomputers, which store significant amounts of data on floppy disks. Since floppy disks are very portable, sensitive data can be copied to a floppy disk and transported inconspicuously if adequate security procedures are not established.

In the Information Center, a data processing specialist who is trained in nonprocedural languages (fourth-generation languages) and in traditional data processing skills teaches the user how to use terminals and the appropriate nonprocedural language. The data processing specialist does not perform the development of the request but instead instructs the user how to use the tools of the Information Center to satisfy his or her own request. Special care is taken by the specialist not to use data processing jargon when instructing the user.

The Information Center permits the user to increase his or her efficiency and provides sufficient data to support the decision-making process. The user does not have to wait years to see results.

An Information Center in Action

Example F12 shows how the Information Center may be used to solve a business problem.

Example F12
The Information Center at International Gismos

International Gismos has experienced an increase in the number of complaints about the quality of the products shipped to their customers. Specifically, customers have been returning gismos that do not meet specified tolerances. Although customers expect some material to be over tolerance, a seller's market has changed to a buyer's market, and the customers are more rigid in their standards for acceptable material.

To improve customer satisfaction, the Sales Department requests the Data Processing Department to provide an analysis of the customer complaints. Since the request will operate on existing data, it does not require large volumes of data over long periods of time, and it does not have critical response time requirements, the Data Processing Department determines that this request can be satisfied by the user in the Information Center. The data base administrator uses the data dictionary to determine where the data for reject material is stored and the attributes which members of the Sales Department are permitted to view. The specialist in the Information Center extracts the data needed for the analysis from a production data base operating under a network data base management system and places it in a relational data base for access by the user. The specialist determines that the request necessitates training the user in a nonprocedural fourth-generation language such as SQL, its reporting capability, and graphics. This is the first time the Sales Department has used the Information Center, so the data processing specialist provides the training necessary to permit the user to develop the desired information.

After many iterations of manipulating the data, the user determines that the problem occurs most frequently with gismos smaller than 60 centimeters. The user issues the following SQL command to obtain data for further analysis:

```
SELECT PARTNO SIZE SHIPPED
       REJECTS
    FROM CLAIMS
    WHERE SIZE < 60
```

This query generates the CLAIMS relation shown in Figure 11.4. Upon examining the data, the user still cannot pinpoint the cause of the problem. The user wishes to put the data in a different format and create a printed report for further analysis. With additional training from the specialist, the user is able to use the data collected

Figure 11.4
CLAIMS relation showing shipments and rejects.

CLAIMS

PART NUMBER	*SIZE*	*SHIPPED*	*REJECTS*
783	40	70,000	900
128	50	13,000	500
778	30	10,000	140
921	20	21,000	10
783	40	15,000	120
783	40	7,000	40
128	50	7,000	400
880	10	38,000	350
880	10	43,000	430
921	20	14,000	120
778	30	30,000	140
128	50	6,000	140
783	40	7,000	44
880	10	76,000	660
880	10	17,000	120
880	10	44,000	525
880	10	28,000	375
921	20	16,000	210
921	20	38,000	105

Figure 11.5
Report generated from CLAIMS relation.

CLAIMS

SIZE	PARTNO	SHIPPED	REJECTS
10	880	38,000	350
		43,000	430
		76,000	660
		17,000	120
		44,000	525
		28,000	375
20	921	21,000	10
		14,000	120
		16,000	210
		38,000	105
30	778	10,000	140
		30,000	140
40	783	70,000	900
		15,000	120
		7,000	40
		7,000	44
50	128	13,000	500
		7,000	400
		6,000	140

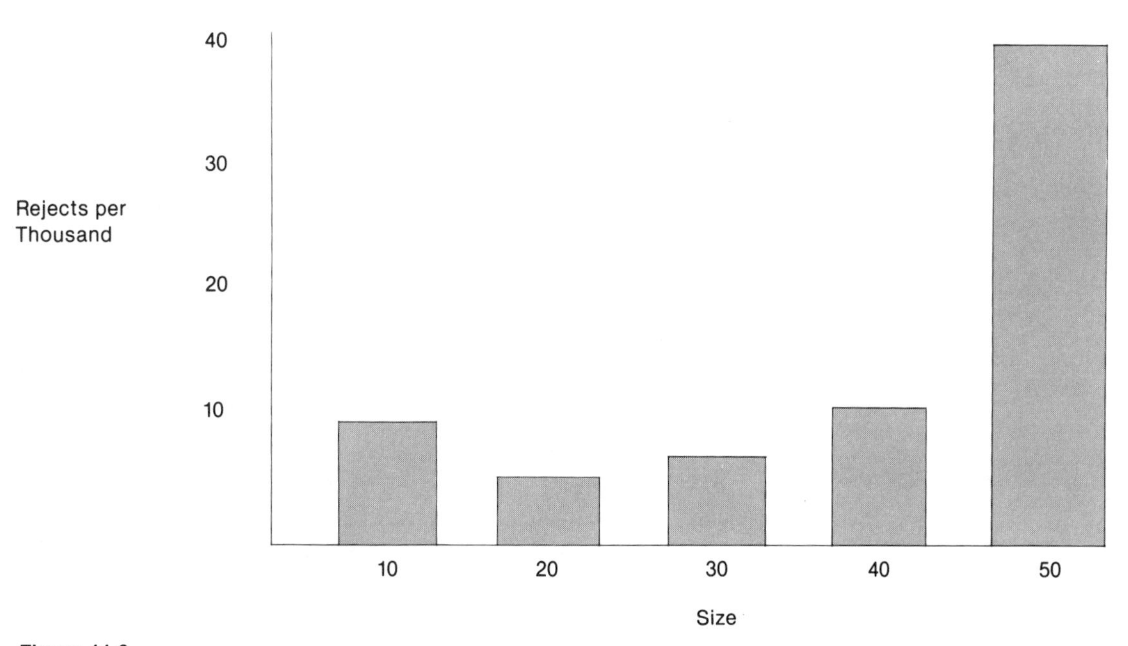

Figure 11.6
Graph generated from CLAIMS relation.

in the query and generate the report in Figure 11.5. The report summarizes the data, but the solution still is not obvious. The user wants to see the number of rejected items per thousand items shipped and wants to graph the results to further clarify them. Again, with more training from the specialist, the user graphs the data as shown in Figure 11.6. The graph clearly shows that the problem is in the shipments with 50-centimeter gismos. Armed with this information, the user goes to the assembly line to determine the point in the manufacturing process which is causing the high reject rate.

This is the type of request best handled through the Information Center. Several key points must be noted. First, the data to satisfy the request already existed in a production data base, the request did not require large volumes of data over an extended period of time, and while response time requirements were important, they were not critical. Second, while this process was very important to the Sales Department, it was the type of request that would have been given a low priority by the Data Processing Department, due to their backlog of work. Third, the data dictionary was used to determine the location of the data and its security requirements. If users encountered data names with which they were not familiar, the data dictionary was searched to find the definition of the name and the means by which the value is derived. Fourth, the user was trained to perform the data manipulation by the specialist in the Information Center. The specialist did not perform the work! If the user had previously used the Information Center, little or no training would be required. Fifth, when the user began the analysis, the direction to be taken to solve the problem was unknown. Several iterations were required before the user began to narrow the scope of the problem.

Sixth, the use of graphics quickly identified the area to be investigated to solve the problem. Finally, the role of the Data Processing Department was that of custodian of the data and educator. The Data Processing Department did not provide the solution, but provided the tools to allow the user to determine the solution.

Example F12 demonstrates multiple uses of the same data: Reject data that was entered to support the Accounts Receivable Department was manipulated and summarized for the decision-making process. Note that this process is concentrated in the bottom half of the information pyramid.

Decision Support Systems

Although systems supporting operational functions are abundant, systems to support the managerial decision-making process have been limited. The preceding examples have concentrated on the bottom half of the information pyramid. In the past, if managers needed certain information to make a business decision, they issued a request to the Data Processing Department. The Data Processing Department searched its documentation to determine where the data was located, then wrote the programs to summarize the data in the manner requested by the executive. The process may take from days to weeks or even months. If the executive was not exact in the specifications, the whole process may have to be repeated. The result, quite often, is that the data is not exactly what the executive desired, or the executive needs additional information, or the Data Processing Department needed such a long time that the response, when received, is too late. These problems robbed management of timely information to make important business decisions.

The current solution to these problems is packaged under the title of **decision support systems.** Decision support systems are systems of hardware and software which permit management to access the data they need directly and manipulate it in a manner to provide support for business decisions. Since decision support systems are relatively new to the industry, people have different interpretations of how they should be implemented. At one extreme is the software package marketed by vendors; at the other extreme is a totally integrated information system in which the information needs of management are included in the design specification. Decision support systems usually include the following four features.

First, decision support systems have integrated data bases as their foundation. No longer does the manager have to wait extended periods of time while data is extracted from multiple files and data bases and placed in the desired format. Managers have access to the current data of the enterprise.

Second, decision support systems provide a simple method of communication between the manager and the system. Fourth-generation programming languages are one of the communication tools. Commands are structured to permit the manager to specify what is desired. Some terminals used in decision support systems reflect the push-button society in which additional keys are included on the CRT to accomplish specific results. (This has an additional advantage in that it does not give the appearance that the executive is performing clerical work, which could be a threat to the prestige of the executive!)

Third, decision support systems permit iterative requests for information with timely responses that may be expressed in many forms. Queries can be formulated in a short period of time and returned in time to take corrective action to solve a business problem. Decision support systems allow the executive to issue multiple requests. This is important if the response to one inquiry does not provide conclusive information to make a decision. Several iterations of an inquiry may be issued until the executive has sufficient information to make a decision. The response to an inquiry may be in the form of a report, but more often is in the form of charts or graphs.

Fourth, one or more modeling software packages may be included in a decision support system. Modeling software permits the executive to ask "What if?" questions such as, "What effect will a rise of 1 percent in interest rates have on sales during the next four quarters?" In response to this query, modeling software analyzes the sales data from the enterprise data base and data collected about the external environment and uses mathematical formulas to project sales. The models may provide for goal-seeking inquiries that allow the decision maker to specify the desired goal, and the modeling software will specify the value of the named variable which must be achieved to obtain the goal. An example of a goal-seeking query is, "What value of net sales will be needed to produce an annual pre-tax profit of $1,525,000?" Based on previous historical data and the math model of the enterprise, the decision support system can return the value of net sales to produce the desired profit. Through iterative inquiries, the user identifies alternative solutions to a problem. The use of the model permits the user to determine "What's best?" With this type of inquiry, the alternatives are specified and the model determines which combination of alternatives provides an optimum solution.

To summarize, decision support systems provide tools to middle and top management to make tactical and strategic decisions. Decision support systems, the Information Center, and operational systems based on integrated data bases support the information needs of all levels of the information pyramid.

11.3 SUMMARY

Integrated data base management systems do not provide all of the information needs of the enterprise. Because of the education required to develop systems using data base management systems, there is a shortage of qualified personnel. The users continually find new ways to use data, causing an ever-increasing backlog in the work requested from the Data Processing Department. The Information Center is a means to reduce the backlog of work and to permit users to develop certain applications themselves. The Data Processing Department provides tools such as fourth-generation programming languages, the appropriate hardware, and training for the user. The user develops the application with assistance from the Data Processing

Department; the Data Processing Department does not perform the work.

The preceding tools concentrate on the bottom half of the information pyramid. Decisions made at the top half are based more on trends and uncertainty instead of historical data. Decision support systems are used by middle and upper management to make tactical and strategic decisions for the enterprise. Decision support systems facilitate communication between the decision maker and the system. They permit the user to use modeling to answer "What if?" and "What's best?" questions.

REVIEW QUESTIONS

11.1 What types of data are used to make functional and supervisory decisions?

11.2 How is the data used in the decision-making process in the top half of the information pyramid different from that used in the bottom half?

11.3 What factors lead to the creation of the Information Center concept?

11.4 How does the data dictionary support the Information Center?

11.5 What is the value of graphics in the Information Center?

11.6 Give three reasons for not providing an Information Center user access to a production data base.

11.7 What is the primary role of the Information Center specialist?

11.8 Why are models provided in decision support systems?

11.9 What is the purpose of goal seeking in decision support systems?

DATA BASE IN THE WORKPLACE

Contributions of an Information Center at Acme Widgets

Acme Widgets' Information Center has been open for about six months. In this short time, it has had an impact not only on the users, which was expected, but also on the Data Processing Department, but not without some growing pains along the way.

The data base administrator has concentrated on gathering data dictionary information for data bases; no data was collected for conventional files. This was especially true for historical data retained on magnetic tape, which is a significant part of Acme's tape library. The manager of the Information Center undertook an effort to develop a users' data dictionary which contained data not captured by the data base administrator. Now the user has a complete inventory on all machine-readable data available for analysis.

One of the major projects being tackled in the Information Center is Acme's problem with the quality of its products. The cost of quality in material rejected by both customers and Acme's quality-control inspectors costs Acme over $10 million a year. No one knows how all the operations on the assembly line affect quality of the final product. In the past, eäch department could only analyze its own data. Now they can examine data for the entire assembly line. Using Information Center tools, they are analyzing hundreds of thousands of records. This could not be done with previous tools. New data is available to users which was never before available. This is important because the farther a widget goes in the production process, the more expensive it is to reject it. A complete widget containing a defective part costs more to repair than if the defective part were found before it was placed in the assembly line. Also, small, acceptable defects in two different areas may become a major defect in the final product.

Using the Information Center, engineers are attempting to model specific components of the assembly line using historical data captured from operational systems. Each month, as new data is created it is processed to validate the model. Adjustments are made in the model as new factors are identified. When the model is complete, it will be used to monitor the production process to determine what factors give maximum production and quality. The model will also allow Acme to examine hypotheses about techniques to improve the production process before the technique is implemented on the assembly line. Each 1 percent decrease in defective goods will save Acme $100,000 annually.

Not only are users performing modeling, but they are also developing additional functions for existing systems. Users generally use the Information Center to satisfy a one-time request. Sometimes, the same request occurs repetitively. When this happens, the users document the job according to the Data Processing Department's standards, and the jobs are then executed by the Data Processing Department.

As users gain experience, they are given more responsibility. At first, users' jobs were segregated from those written by data processing professionals, and users were restricted in the functions they were permitted to perform. Now, their jobs are intermixed and they are performing functions once performed only by data processing professionals.

Since Acme opened the Information Center, its method of project development has changed. With traditional development, the user requested the same data in multiple sequences in many different reports. Designers tried to design for every need the user would ever have. This was an impossible task, since the business was constantly changing. Even with all of the reports provided, the user still did not have all of the data needed. Often the user had to leaf through hundreds of pages of paper, manually calculating results, to find the solution to a specific problem. If the data was not available in an existing report, the user generated a maintenance request to modify an existing program to generate the report, or to write a new program to generate the report.

Current projects generate certain base reports generic to a given area as part of the development of a system. For instance, in an order status system, the user must have the ability to access all open orders. However, instead of generating many different reports in many sequences, part of the development of the system is to create a flat file containing the raw data generated by the system. The user goes to the Information Center and using tools available, can develop the solution to ad hoc requests in a matter of minutes instead of the hours or days required using traditional techniques. The users are much better off, since they do not have to wait in line for the Data Processing Department to write programs to find the solutions to their queries.

The manager of the Information Center says the biggest advantage has been the change in the attitude of the users. Previously, analysis of data was labor-intensive and was done only in small quantities. The only way to analyze data was by working overtime. Since this was expensive, users were only permitted to do it in selective cases where a positive result was guaranteed. They have never had the opportunity to deal with the volumes of data currently available. They are controlling areas now that they never had control of before. They have a positive attitude. They feel that they are making a real contribution to the company, and this gives them job satisfaction.

ANSWERS TO EVEN-NUMBERED REVIEW QUESTIONS

CHAPTER 1

1.2. Five advantages of data base management systems are:

a. Data independence—The data base may be expanded without changing current programs unless they access the new data.

b. Nonredundant data—With the proper design, there is no unplanned redundant data. Data is stored once.

c. Data security—Data security is part of data base management systems' designs. The systems restrict the access and functions of programs that access a data base.

d. Data integrity—Data is consistent. It is not represented two different ways in two separate files. The data base management system updates all related data within the data base.

e. Economy of scale—Since data base management systems are large, they provide economies of scale.

1.4. Data security—The process of ensuring that each individual can access and update only the data necessary to perform his or her function within the enterprise. This prevents users from intentionally or inadvertently abusing or destroying data.

1.6. Four different categories of personnel are:

a. Systems engineers, who install, maintain, debug, and tune the software.

b. Data base administrators, who develop standards, provide design assistance, do long-range planning, and provide quality control.

c. Application programmers, who write programs to access the data base for the end users.

d. End users, who use the data base management system to perform the business of the enterprise.

CHAPTER 2

2.2 a. Seek time is the time required to move the read/write head from the current cylinder to the cylinder that contains the record to be read or written.

b. Head switching is the electronic activation of the read/write head that floats above the surface containing a record to be read or written.

c. Rotational delay is the time spent waiting for the desired record to rotate under the read/write head.

d. Data transfer rate is the rate at which data is transferred from secondary storage to primary storage or vice versa. It is a function of the density at which data is recorded and the speed at which the disk rotates.

2.4. Records may be blocked to reduce the number of count and key areas and the gaps between them on secondary storage. This allows data, instead of administrative information, to be stored on a track. High blocking factors improve performance when data is being retrieved sequentially, because several records can be brought into storage with one I/O operation. High blocking factors degrade performance when data is being retrieved randomly, because records within a block that are unnecessary to satisfy the request are brought into storage.

2.6. Sequential access obtains all records within a file and is beneficial when most records in the file are processed. Direct access of files is typical of on-line systems when one, or at most a few, records are processed to satisfy a user request.

2.8. Direct addressing uses a numeric key to map directly to a location in secondary storage. Indirect addressing uses either a numeric or alphabetic key which is operated upon by a hashing technique to determine an address in secondary storage where the record is to be stored.

2.10. Each synonym requires an additional search to be made to locate the desired record. Each search prolongs the time needed to obtain the desired record.

2.12. 10,000. The calculation is:

$$.75x = 7500$$
$$x = 7500/.75$$
$$x = 10{,}000$$

2.14. The sequential file organization requires the least space to store a given file. No space need be reserved for future additions such as overflow areas in the indexed sequential file organization or for less than 100 percent packing density as in the direct file organization.

CHAPTER 3

3.2. Three advantages of using linked lists instead of physically ordered lists are:

a. By following links, multiple logical views of the data can be obtained without the extra effort that would be necessary to physically resequence the file for every logical view the user desired.

b. When an addition is made to the list, the record can be placed in the next available physical location. The links can be updated to place the record in the correct logical sequence. If a physically ordered file were used, the entire file would have to be rewritten to add a record.

c. When a record is deleted from the file, the links can be modified so no link points to the deleted record. The space from the deleted record can be made available for immediate re-use. If a physically ordered file were used, the entire file would have to be rewritten to delete a record.

3.4.

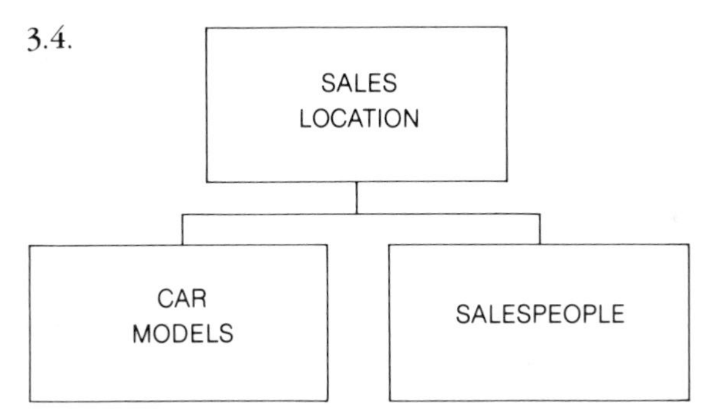

Child and twin pointers are used. Since two distinct types of data are represented—salespeople and model, both will not be required in a single pass of the data base. This will enable access of only the data required in each pass.

3.6. When a parent has several different type children, child pointers allow direct access of the desired child type without processing all other child types.

3.8. In a simple network, a child is the object of a one-to-many relationship with more than one parent. In a complex network, the child has a many-to-many relationship with one parent.

3.10. In a linked list with both backward and forward pointers, the forward linked list is followed until the damaged area is reached. Then, the backward pointers are followed until the damaged area is reached. All records, except those in the damaged area, are retrieved.

3.12. Inverted files are supplemental files used to improve random retrieval of a primary file using a key other than the storage key.

CHAPTER 4

4.2. Two components of the DDL are the schema and the subschema. The schema describes the overall logical view of the data base. The subschema describes the view of the data base as seen by the application program.

4.4. To add a field to a record using conventional files: (1) documentation is analyzed to determine which programs access the file; (2) all of the source programs are changed, compiled, and tested; (3) the change is synchronized in the production schedule; and (4) finally, the change is installed. Using a data base management system: (1) documentation is analyzed using an automated tool called a data dictionary; (2) programs *that use the data* are changed, compiled, and tested; (3) the new field is defined in the DDL; and (4) the change is installed.

4.6. Data base management systems provide increased data security through the subschema. Its two techniques are (1) restricting the type of records within a data base a program may access, and (2) limiting the functions performed, such as READ, REPLACE, INSERT or DELETE.

4.8. The data manipulation language (DML) is a set of commands available to the application programmer to direct the data base management system to store and retrieve data.

4.10. The data base management system does not make pointers available to the application program. If the application program was provided, and used, pointers to the data, data independence would be lost. If a change was made to the data structure, corresponding changes would have to be made to the application program.

4.12. Without standardization, the enterprise is locked in to one vendor's software and the hardware. Standardization provides machine independence.

CHAPTER 5

5.2

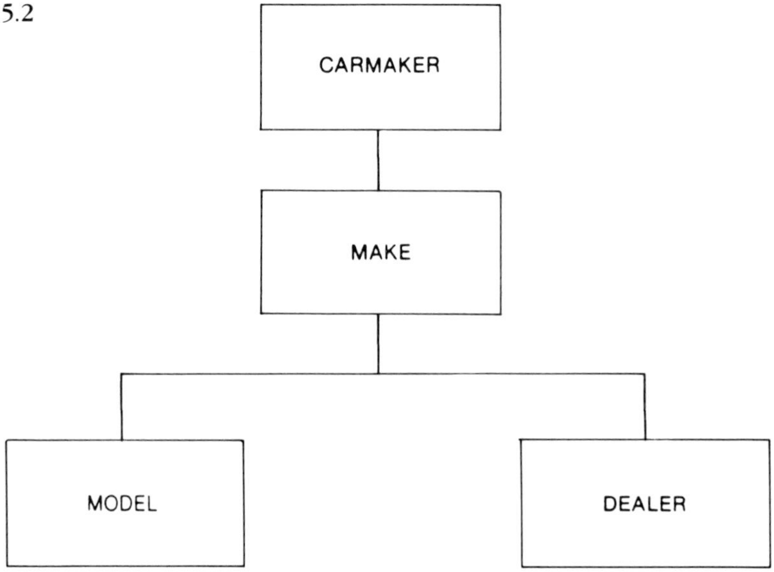

5.4. The PROCOPT statement specifies the processing options a program is permitted to perform. The options allowed are GET, INSERT, REPLACE, and DELETE. A program may be authorized for any one option, any combination of the options, or all options. PROCOPT limits the authority of the program to manipulate a segment.

5.6. A new logical structure was created through a logical DBDGEN. The logical DBDGEN defined new data relationships to be created from existing data bases. Only programs needing the new data relationships were changed. Existing programs, not sensitive to the COURSE segment, needed no modifications. DL/I eliminates the redundant data using logical pointers.

5.8. Intersection data is stored in a logical child segment. It depends upon both its physical and logical parents to give it meaning. The grade a student obtains for a course is stored in the logical child segment for COURSE in the Student-Course Data Base. The grade depends upon the segment for the student who obtained the grade (physical parent) and the course in which the grade was earned (logical parent).

5.10. GU or the hold form of the command GHU.

5.12. The GN command retrieves every SPORT segment for every student in the data base. The GNP command retrieves only the SPORT segment for the student segment just retrieved.

5.14. The "U" specifies that this field is unique. DL/I will not permit two parent segments which have the same value in this field to be stored in the data base if this is specified at the root level. If this is specified at a dependent segment level, DL/I will not permit two dependent segments of the same parent having the same value in this field to be stored in the data base.

MODULE A

A.2. HISAM permits sequential access to all segments in the data base. The root segment can be directly obtained using the index.

A.4. HIDAM provides rapid direct access to all segments in the data base, in addition to providing sequential access capability.

A.6. HDAM performance is improved by a randomizing algorithm that generates a minimum of synonyms. HSAM performance is improved with anticipatory buffering. Reorganization of the data base improves HISAM performance after many additions or deletions have occurred. HIDAM performance is improved by reorganization of the index data base if many root segments are added or deleted. (There are other answers possible.)

A.8. HSAM most closely resembles conventional sequential file processing.

A.10. A secondary index on zip code can be used. A secondary index is used to provide alternate data sequences.

CHAPTER 6

6.2.

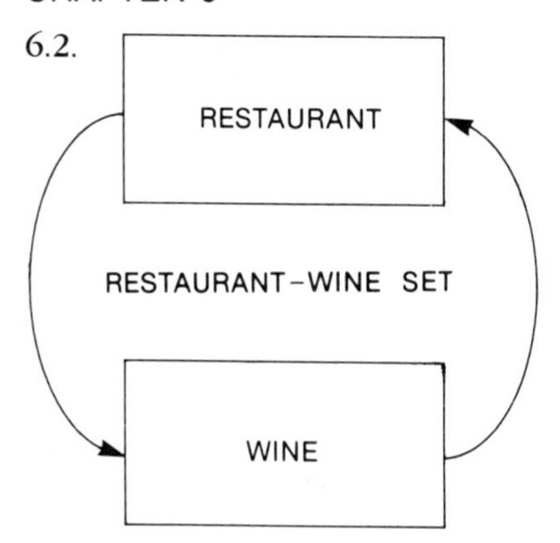

6.4. Simple networks are represented directly in the DBTG model.

6.6. The ORDER clause is used to provide a logical sequence for the member records in an occurrence of a set.

6.8. The RETENTION clause determines the conditions under which a member may be removed from an occurrence of a set.

6.10. The INSERTION status is MANUAL. The application program has the responsibility for connecting the member record into the correct occurrence of the set at the time the member record logically satisfies the qualifications for set membership.

6.12. One indicator is used for each record type and each set defined in the subschema, plus one indicator for current of run.

6.14. The DISCONNECT command cannot be used for a member record type having a retention status of FIXED.

6.16. The FIND command locates a record but does not make it available to the application program.

6.18. The Data Base Task Group was a committee formed by the Programming Language Committee of CODASYL.

6.20. A record is the unit of data transferred from the data base management system to the application program.

6.22. With a MANDATORY retention status, a member record can move from one occurrence of a set to another. With a FIXED retention status, a member record belongs to one occurrence of a set; it cannot move to another occurrence without being deleted from the original occurrence.

6.24. The DBTG subschema allows for the definition of alternate names (aliases) for names used in the schema. DL/I does not provide for renaming.

6.26. Standardization of data base management systems allows an enterprise to switch from one data base management system to another or to a different brand of computer hardware without losing any functions and without a massive conversion effort.

MODULE B

B.2. A page is divided into four distinct parts: a header, a footer, line indexes, and the data. The header identifies the specific page within an area through a page number stored in the header. The header also contains a space-available count field which indicates the number of bytes of space available within the page. The footer marks the end of the page and contains a field which indicates the amount of space used for line indexes.

B.4. The DIRECT location mode allows the application program to specify the target page to store a record. For critical applications with a known and constant access pattern, proper use of the DIRECT location mode allows an application program to access records more efficiently than can be done with other location modes. However, if the access pattern changes, or if the data relationship changes, the application program may require changes. Due to its low degree of data independence, the DIRECT location mode is not often used.

B.6. NEXT pointers are used by themselves when performance would not be improved by the addition of PRIOR and OWNER pointers.

B.8. OWNER pointers are normally used when an owner record is accessed from a member record and many member records exist between the current member record and the owner. OWNER pointers reduce the number of I/Os required to obtain an owner record.

B.10. Space management pages identify data pages which are less than 70 percent full. When IDMS must determine where available space exists to add a new record, it reduces the number of I/Os needed to find this information by consulting the space management page instead of accessing each page in storage. The space management page is updated only when a data page crosses the threshold of 70 percent full, which reduces the number of I/O operations to the space management pages.

CHAPTER 7

7.2. DEALER (<u>D-NAME</u>)
CAR (<u>D-NAME, SERIAL</u>)

7.4. FARMER (<u>NAME</u>)
CROP (<u>CROP</u>)
FARM-CROP (<u>NAME, CROP</u>)

7.6. The elimination of path and sequence dependencies allows new systems to modify existing data bases without the need to change existing application programs due to the modifications.

7.8. The relational model eliminates path dependencies by using data values instead of pointers as the link between related tables. It eliminates sequence dependencies through the basic rules of relations—columns and rows may be presented in any sequence.

7.10. The duplication of the key of the parent record in the table containing the data of the child record allows hierarchical and network structures to be represented in the relational model. A table containing intersection data and the primary key of each of the parent record types is used to represent complex networks.

7.12. Selection only presents the rows of a table to the user that meet specified criteria.

7.14. SELECT DESCRIPTION
FROM COURSE

7.16. DELETE FROM STUDENT
WHERE S-ID = '111111111'

7.18. GRANT INSERT, DELETE ON STUDENT TO REGISTRAR

7.20. The CREATE INDEX creates a physical path between values in the specified column. Indexes are used to improve retrieval performance in SQL.

CHAPTER 8

8.2. When data is stored in the first normal form, anomalies occur because functional dependencies occur which are not based on the full key of the relation.

8.4. In a central data base, all data about a subject is stored in one location. In a replicated data base, all data about a subject is stored in multiple locations. When an update is made to one copy of a replicated data base, the update must be made to all copies of the data base.

8.6. The conceptual schema is the view of the data relationships needed to perform the business of the enterprise independent of any data base management system. Logical data base design is the mapping of the conceptual schema into a framework of a specific data base management system.

8.8. The major advantage of top-down design is the planning for future integration of data.

8.10. The major advantage of bottom-up development is the relatively short period of time needed to implement an application.

8.12. Intuitively, functional dependency is the ability to determine the value of attribute *Y* when the value of attribute *X* is known.

8.14. A data dictionary is an automated tool for storing data about data.

8.16. Partitioning improves performance during physical data base design by segregating records whose characteristics are different from other records in the data base.

8.18. Proper selection of pointer options improves retrieval of records but causes additional overhead when records are added or deleted.

8.20. The factors to be considered when determining the period of reorganization are the loading factor, the number of record insertions across the data base, the degradation in response time permitted by the user, and the data base unavailability permitted by the user.

CHAPTER 9

9.2. The most common form of security in an on-line environment is a sign-on function. The first interaction between the user and the host computer is a request from the host computer to the user to identify himself or herself. The user enters a user identification number and a password for unique identification.

9.4. Data is encrypted to prevent unauthorized users from viewing the data.

9.6. Each request can be restricted to a specific terminal. Each request is analyzed to determine if the terminal issuing the request is authorized to receive the requested information. (There are other answers possible.)

9.8. In an uncontrolled environment, each program can access the same record concurrently. Each program's copy of the record is identical. The first program to complete requests the data base management system to write its changed copy of the record. The second program to complete requests the data base management system to write its changed record. The record written at the request of the second program does not include the updates made by the first program. Therefore, the changes made by the first program are lost.

9.10. Lock-out provides exclusive ownership of a record during the update process. Ownership is maintained until the owning program commits to its change. Lock-out ensures that only one program has access to an updated record until the update is complete.

9.12. A data base back-up is used as a starting point to recover a damaged data base.

9.14. Erroneous data entered by a user must be corrected by the user. A data base management system does not have the facilities to correct the data. Correction of erroneous data is complicated by the frequency of requests processed by the data base management system: Other users may view the erroneous data before it is corrected and make business decisions based on the incorrect data.

9.16. The operating system or data base management system must be made operable after a failure. Then, the data base management system uses the journal to determine what programs were active at the time of failure. The changes made by the active programs are rolled back, and the programs begin execution as if the failure never occurred.

9.18. Users and computer operators are the two categories of individuals involved in an on-line operation.

9.20. The data dictionary can be extended to provide the computer operator with information to be used for problem resolution.

CHAPTER 10

10.2. Each enterprise may have a different position in the organizational structure for the data base administrator. The position may range from a member of each application development team, to a staff position under the vice-president of data processing.

10.4. To properly perform the planning function, the data base administrator must have a knowledge of both the business of the enterprise and the data base management system. By combining the knowledge of these two areas, the data base administrator provides input to management as to the sequence in which projects are to be developed and the data created and accessed by each application.

10.6. The data base administrator must establish standards for program performance, naming conventions, change control procedures, maintenance of the data dictionary, and day-to-day operational interfaces with the data base management system.

10.8. The data base administrator must provide access to data for all users who have legitimate needs associated with their functions within the enterprise, while preventing access by those without such a need.

10.10. Since the data base administrator must perform the schema and subschema definitions to the data base management system before an application is permitted to interact with the system, all new development must funnel through the data base administrator.

CHAPTER 11

11.2. Data used for high-level decision making is summarized and examined in a search for trends; in addition, data from outside the enterprise is used to make tactical and strategic decisions. For the bottom half of the pyramid, larger volumes of data about the enterprise are needed for supervisory and functional decisions.

11.4. The data base administrator uses the data dictionary to determine the location of the data to satisfy the users needs and associated security requirements. Users examine the data dictionary to determine the meanings and derivations of data names with which they are not familiar.

11.6. Users may not be given a copy of production data (a) to ensure that they do not accidently destroy production data; (b) to prevent the degradation of response time to production system users; and (c) to allow data to be transferred from a network or hierarchical structure to a relational structure.

11.8. Models permit the decision maker to obtain responses to "what if?" questions.

BIBLIOGRAPHY

Ashany, R., and Adamowicz, M. "Data Base Systems." In *IBM Systems Journal,* Vol. 15, No. 3, 1976.

Blasgen, M. W., and Eswaran, K. P. "Storage and Access in Relational Data Bases." In *IBM Systems Journal,* Vol. 16, No. 4, 1977.

Blasgen, M. W., et al. "System R: An Architectural Overview." In *IBM Systems Journal,* Vol. 20, No. 1, 1981.

CODASYL Systems Committee. *Feature Analysis of Generalized Database Management Systems.* New York: Association for Computing Machinery, 1971.

Codd, E. F. "A Relational Model of Data for Large Shared Databanks." In *Communications of the ACM,* Vol. 13, No. 6, June 1970.

Codd, E. F. "Further Normalization of the Relational Data Base Model." In *Courant Computer Science Symposium,* Vol. 6, 1972.

Codd, E. F. "Relational Database: A Practical Foundation for Productivity." In *Communications of the ACM,* Vol. 25, No. 2, February 1982.

Curtice, Robert M. "Data Independence in Database Systems." In *Datamation,* Vol. 21, No. 4, April 1975.

Date, C. J. *An Introduction to Database Systems.* 2nd ed. Cambridge, Mass.: Addison-Wesley, 1977.

Elson, Mark. *Data Structures.* Chicago: Science Research Associates, 1975.

Engles, R. W. "An Analysis of the April 1971 Data Base Task Group Report." *ACM-SIGFIDET Workshop on Data Description, Access, and Control,* Nov. 1971.

Fagin, Ronald. "A Normal Form for Relational Databases That Is Based on Domains and Keys." In *Transactions on Database Systems,* Vol. 6, No. 3, September 1981.

IDMS Database Design and Definition Guide. Westwood, Mass.: Cullinane Database Systems, 1983.

IDMS System Overview. Westwood, Mass.: Cullinane Database Systems, 1981.

IDMS Programmer's Reference Guide—COBOL. Westwood, Mass.: Cullinane Database Systems, 1983.

IBM DATABASE 2 SQL Usage Guide—GG24-1583-00. Santa Teresa, Ca.: IBM, 1983.

IBM DATABASE 2 Concepts and Facilities Guide—GG24-1582-00. Santa Teresa, Ca.: IBM, 1983.

IMS/VS Version 1—Data Base Administration Guide SH20-9025. White Plains, N.Y.: IBM, 1981.

IMS/VS Version 1—System Administration Guide SH20-9178. White Plains, N.Y. IBM, 1981.

IMS/VS Version 1—Application Programming: Design and Coding SH20-9026. White Plains, N.Y.: IBM, 1981.

IMS/VS Version 1—System Programming Reference Manual SH20-0927. White Plains, N.Y.: IBM, 1981.

Kapp, Dan, and Leben, Joseph F. *IMS Programming Techniques*, New York: Van Nostrand-Reinhold Company, 1978.

Kroenke, David. *Database Processing Fundamentals, Modeling, Applications*. Chicago: Science Research Associates, 1977.

Martin, James. *Application Development without Programmers*. Englewood Cliffs, N.J.: Prentice-Hall, 1982.

Martin, James. *Computer Data-Base Organization*. 2nd ed. Englewood Cliffs, N.J.: Prentice-Hall, 1977.

Martin, James. *Strategic Data-Planning Methodologies*. Englewood Cliffs, N.J.: Prentice-Hall, 1982.

Teorey, Toby J., and Fry, James P. *Design of Database Structures*. Englewood Cliffs, N.J.: Prentice-Hall, 1982.

Thierauf, Robert J. *Decision Support Systems for Effective Planning and Control, a Case Study Approach*. Englewood Cliffs, N.J.: Prentice-Hall, 1982.

Weiderhold, G. *Database Design*. New York: McGraw-Hill, 1977.

GLOSSARY / INDEX

Access method. A series of programs in the operating system that provides the instructions to transfer data between primary and secondary storage for several file organizations.
  with conventional files, 9, 31, 38, 88, 90
  DL/I, 121–139
    HDAM, 129–133, 258–259
    HIDAM, 133–137, 258
    HISAM, 125–129, 133, 137, 258
    HSAM, 122–125, 258
  selection of, 258–259

Access time. The time required to move the read/write head from the cylinder where it is currently positioned to the desired cylinder. *See also Seek time*

Addressing. Methods of mapping the key field of a record to a specific location on a direct-address storage device that uses direct organization.

Addressing, direct, 44–45. An addressing technique in which the key maps directly to a secondary storage location. One location in secondary storage exists for every possible key field value.

Addressing, indirect, 45–50. An addressing technique in which the key is manipulated to determine the secondary storage location. Due to the manipulation, two different keys may be directed to the same secondary storage location.

Affinity matrix, 248–249

Aggregation, 237. In the development of the conceptual schema, the use of a higher-level element to identify the association between two lower-level elements.

ANSI, 144

Anticipatory buffering, 38–39, 50, 125. Using sequential processing, the access method anticipates the next physical record needed, retrieves it, and places it in a temporary primary storage area called a *buffer*.

Area, 178–180, 257. In CODASYL, a physical subdivision of a data base that allows the data base administrator to segregate data to improve performance.

Association, degree of, 234–239

Attribute, 197, 200, 225, 233, 247–254. (1) In the relational model, the mathematical term meaning one column of a table. (2) In data processing terminology, a field.

Back-up, data base. *See* Data base back-up

Binary search, 63–64. A method of searching a table or a file in which the population is stored in ascending or descending sequence and is successively divided in half with each probe until the desired segment is found or is determined not to exist.

Binding, 84, 87. The process of connecting or applying the description of the data to the data itself.

Bit map, 133–134. In DL/I direct-access methods, a separate block in secondary storage that identifies the data blocks that contain free space. In the bit map, a 0 representing a block indicates that the block does not have sufficient room to store the longest segment in the data base; a 1 indicates that the block has sufficient room to store the longest segment.

Block descriptor word (BDW), 34–45. The first field in a physical record containing variable-length logical records; contains the total number of bytes in a physical record.

Blocking, 31, 37–38, 50, 129, 256, 258, 260–261, 264. Placing two or more logical records in a physical record to save space on secondary storage and improve performance when accessing the logical records within one physical record.

Buffering, anticipatory. *See* Anticipatory Buffering

CALC. In CODASYL, a location mode for obtaining data directly by hashing a key to determine the target page to store or retrieve a record.

Candidate key, 200, 225. In the relational model, an attribute or a combination of nonsuperfluous attributes that uniquely identifies a row of a table.

Central data base, 243–244. A single location for storage of all data for an enterprise.

Child, 65–72
  logical, 105, 112
  physical, 105

Clustering, 256–257

CODASYL, 144. An acronym for COnference on DAta SYstem Languages. A voluntary and informal group that established the specifications for COBOL, which was accepted as a national standard by the American National Standards Institute.

Codd, E. F., 196, 200, 249–250

Computer operators, 285–287

Conceptual schema, 232–240, 263–264. A global, high-level design that is independent of any data base model and describes the data and data relationships needed to support the business of the enterprise.

Concurrent processing, 273–277

Count-data, 28

Count-key-data, 28–30

Cross-reference list, 45

Currency indicators, 163–170. In the DBTG model, fields reserved to mark current navigation points within a data base. One currency indicator exists for each record and each set defined in the subschema, in addition to one for the run unit.

Cycle, 74–76. A special implementation of the network (DBTG) structure in which a dependent segment is an antecedent of its parent.

Cylinder, 23. An imaginary geometric figure created by all of the recording surfaces that can be read